HEY AMERICA!

A NOTE ON THE AUTHOR

Stuart Cosgrove, originally from Perth, was a fanzine writer on the northern soul scene before he joined the black music paper *Echoes* as a staff writer. He became media editor with the *NME*, a feature writer for a range of newspapers and magazines, and a television programme executive at Channel 4, for which he won numerous awards. Stuart is a prominent radio broadcaster in Scotland and is the author of several critically acclaimed books on music, most notably his trilogy of books on soul music and social change.

PRAISE FOR STUART COSGROVE

CASSIUS X

'A delightful ride in a cherry-red Cadillac, with soul music on the radio and a steady hand at the wheel. A thoroughly enjoyable journey'
Jonathan Eig, author of *Ali: A Life*

'Crisply written, fast-paced and original, this book surges with the kind of effervescence we have long associated with a young Cassius Clay. Even the most informed Muhammad Ali fan will learn something new from this book . . . Filled with colourful details, with a learned eye toward the music of the era, *Cassius X* hits all the right notes'
Michael Ezra, author of *Muhammad Ali: The Making of an Icon*

'An exciting trip through the urban worlds of boxing, soul music, and crime, as Cassius Clay joins the Nation of Islam, becomes Muhammad Ali, and ascends the ranks of boxing to become World Heavyweight Champion during the early 1960s'
Lewis Erenberg, author of *The Rumble in the Jungle*

'There are many books about Muhammad Ali, but none like Stuart Cosgrove's *Cassius X*. Focusing on the athlete's transformation from Cassius Clay to Muhammad Ali, Cosgrove provides the reader with an extraordinary view of the radical psychological and spiritual changes that Ali experienced during the early part of his career. He does this while expertly weaving in the social upheaval during the Civil Rights era and how those events shaped the boxer's personal evolution . . . a model of how biographies of African Americans should be written'
Ray Winbush, author of *Belinda's Petition: A Concise History of Reparations for the Transatlantic Slave Trade*

'A fresh hook on the Muhammad Ali story'
The Times

'An engrossing and revelatory read . . . and a great playlist. You do not have to be a fan of boxing or soul music to love this book'
Val McDermid

HARLEM 69: THE FUTURE OF SOUL

'Cosgrove's impressive, dogged groundwork is matched by a deep devotion to the music that is the backbone of the narrative . . . An essential read for anyone interested in the politics and culture of the late 60s, when soul music reflected the momentum of a tumultuous era that resonates still'
Sean O'Hagan, *The Observer*

'An impressively granular month-by-month deep dive into Harlem's fertile musical response to a time of social and political upheaval'
Financial Times, Best Books of 2018

'Not only a gripping socio-cultural history, it feels truly novelistic. Harlem throbs thrillingly . . . and Cosgrove captures it vividly: heroin, civic decay, gravediggers' strikes, gender-fluid gangsters, Vietnam vets, Puerto Rican boxers and all . . . *Harlem 69* makes startling connections across time and place'
Graeme Thomson, *Uncut*

'The best music writing this year is about black music. Cosgrove's deep dive into the year's events is an epic feat of archival research that has been expertly marshalled into a narrative that joins the dots between Donny Hathaway, Jimi Hendrix, the Black Panthers, police corruption and the Vietnam war'
Teddy Jamieson, *The Herald*, Best Music Books of 2018

'Cosgrove's series can be read separately, but to read them as a trilogy gives a real sense of black music and social movements . . . paints a vivid, detailed picture of the intensity of social deprivation and resistance, and also the way that's reflected in, but also affected by, the music of those cities. Reading *Harlem 69* made me want to do two things – dig out and play some of the records mentioned, and fight the powers that be'
Socialist Review

MEMPHIS 68: THE TRAGEDY OF SOUTHERN SOUL

Winner of the Penderyn Music Book Prize, 2018
Mojo – Books of the Year #4, 2017
Rough Trade – Music Book of the Year, 2018
Shindig – Book of the Year, 2017

'Offers us a map of Memphis in that most revolutionary of years, 1968. Music writing as both crime reporting and political commentary'
The Herald

'Cosgrove's selection of his subjects is unerring, and clearly rooted in personal passion . . . an authorial voice which is as easily, blissfully evocative as a classic soul seven-inch'
David Pollock, *The List*

'Highly recommended! Astounding body of learning. Future classic. Go!'
SoulSource.co.uk

'As ever, Cosgrove's lucid, entertaining prose is laden with detail, but never at the expense of the wider narrative. Hinging on that Memphis destination, he traces the savage dichotomy at the city's heart: it was the site of multi-racial soul imprint Stax but also the place where Martin Luther King was killed. A heartbreaking but essential read, and one that feels remarkably timely'
Clash Magazine, Best Books of 2017

'Stuart Cosgrove's whole life has been shaped by soul – first as a music journalist and now as a chronicler of black American music's social context'
Sunday Herald

DETROIT 67: THE YEAR THAT CHANGED SOUL

'The story is unbelievably rich. Motown, the radical hippie underground, a trigger-happy police force, Vietnam, a disaffected young black community, inclement weather, The Supremes, the army, strikes, fiscal austerity, murders – all these elements coalesced, as Cosgrove noted, to create a remarkable year. In fact, as the book gathers pace, one can't help think how the hell did this city survive it all? . . . it contains some of the best ever writing and insight about Motown. Ever'
Paolo Hewitt, *Caught by the River*

'The subhead for Stuart Cosgrove's *Detroit 67* is "the year that changed soul". But this thing contains multitudes, and digs in deep, well beyond just the city's music industry in that fateful year . . . All of this is written about with precision, empathy, and a great, deep love for the city of Detroit'
Detroit Metro Times

'Big daddy of soul books . . . weaves a thoroughly researched, epic tale of musical intrigues and escalating social violence'
TeamRock

'Cosgrove weaves a compelling web of circumstance that maps a city struggling with the loss of its youth to the Vietnam War, the hard edge of the civil rights movement and ferocious inner-city rioting . . . a whole-hearted evocation of people and places filled with the confidence that it is telling a tale set at a fulcrum of American social and cultural history'
The Independent

'Leading black music label Motown is at the heart of the story, and 1967 is one of Motown's more turbulent years, but it's set against the backdrop of growing opposition to the war in Vietnam, police brutality, a disaffected black population, rioting, strikes in the Big Three car plants and what seemed like the imminent breakdown of society . . . You finish the book with a real sense of a city in crisis and of how some artists reflected events'
Socialist Review

FIGHT THE POWER

BERNIE SANDERS + PUBLIC ENEMY RADIO

MARCH 1, 2020 ★ LOS ANGELES CONVENTION CENTER

Fight the Power: Presidential candidate Bernie Sanders shares the stage with hip-hop activist Chuck D of Public Enemy Radio in 2020. Band co-founder Flavor Flav, not a Sanders fan, had been fired hours before they took to the stage.

Let us realize the arc of the moral universe is long,
but it bends toward justice.
—Dr Martin Luther King Jr

I was always a politician from the day the civil rights
people chose me as their protest singer.
—Nina Simone

Life is a wheel of fortune and it's my turn to spin it.
—Tupac Shakur

HEY AMERICA!

The Epic Story of Black Music and the White House

STUART COSGROVE

First published in Great Britain in 2022 by Polygon.
an imprint of Birlinn Ltd.

Birlinn Ltd
West Newington House
10 Newington Road
Edinburgh
EH9 1QS

www.polygonbooks.co.uk

1

ISBN 978 1 84697 584 4
eBook ISBN 978 1 78885 519 8

British Library Cataloguing-in-Publication Data
A catalogue record for this book is available on request
from the British Library.

Typeset by 3btype.com

CONTENTS

FOREWORD

It has been an immense privilege to have had the opportunity to write extensively about African American music. It was a journey that began at the Letham Community Centre Soul Club in Perth, Scotland, where I grew up and first heard the great sixties soul singers of Motown and Stax. I had the privilege to win a Major Scottish Studentship, funded by the Scottish Education Authority in the years before we had our own Parliament. It was a scholarship that supported my studies at Hull University and took me variously to Howard University in Washington D.C. and George Mason University, North Virginia. But the greatest training came not within formal education but on the northern soul scene – an unrivalled academy of underground and independent soul. It was through the soul fanzine movement that I came to write for *Black Echoes*, the *NME* and *The Face* before a career in television at Channel 4.

The roots of this book were sown in the Soul Trilogy. My three books spanning the latter years of the 1960s across three remarkable cities – *Detroit 67*, *Memphis 68* and *Harlem 69* have all been published by Polygon, an independent imprint in Edinburgh, who also published my most recent book *Cassius X*.

My thanks to everyone who has helped me on the way, not least my close friends and family but special thanks go to my editor Alison Rae, who has guided me through the tunnel.

Stuart Cosgrove
2022

Prince, audacious superstar of the Minneapolis Sound, died in 2016 while Barack Obama was on a presidential tour of Europe and the Middle East.

1

THE AUDACITY OF SOUL

Listen Up: 'Lean On Me' by Mary J. Blige,
live from the Lincoln Memorial at Barack Obama's
Inaugural Celebration

At 9.43 a.m. on 21 April 2016, an unidentified male phoned the Sheriff's
Office in Carver County, Minnesota. 'We have someone who is
unconscious,' he mumbled. The caller had no idea what address he was
calling from so the emergency responder, Emily Colestack, a 45-year-
old mother of two teenage kids, deployed geolocational software. She
identified the address as a private dwelling at 7801 Audubon Road in
Chanhassen, southwest of Minneapolis. The emergency response team
arrived to find a body, alone and unresponsive, in a lift. They performed
emergency CPR, but the man had been dead for at least several hours
and the team sent word to the Sheriff's Office to prepare for the
aftermath. The body was that of a 57-year-old African American male
from Minneapolis, whose registered birth name was Prince Rogers

Nelson but who was known globally by the stage name Prince – and briefly, during a spat with Warners, by the rebellious 'love symbol' that translated as the Artist Formerly Known as Prince.

According to a press release issued by the Midwest Medical Examiner's Office, the star had died of an accidental overdose of the opioid fentanyl, which is used both as a legitimate painkiller and as a recreational drug when mixed with heroin and cocaine. It emerged that after his last-ever show in Atlanta, six days before his death, Prince's private jet had been forced to land in Moline, Illinois, where doctors gave him a 'save shot' of naloxone, an emergency procedure used in cases of opiate overdose. There were rumours that Prince had been suffering from pneumonia in recent weeks, that he had been due to meet with an addiction specialist the following day, and the musician's brother-in-law claimed that Prince had worked '154 hours straight' the week before.

President Barack Obama was several thousand feet above Saudi Arabia on *Air Force One*, the presidential plane, when he heard of Prince's death. He had just left a frosty meeting with the Saudi king, Salman bin Abdulaziz, about the war in Yemen and a congressional report implying that Saudi Arabia may have played a role in the attacks on the Twin Towers and the Pentagon on 9/11.

Even Obama's effortless charm had not thawed the atmosphere and their conversation had been stilted, burdened by interpreters and the contested events in a turbulent Middle East. There were large sections of Saudi society who did not trust Obama, whose visit came five years after the country's most infamous citizen, Osama bin Laden, was killed in Abbottabad, Pakistan. The aftermath of the operation, which was led by US Navy Seals, was a triumphalist moment for America. Obama, together with Vice President Joe Biden and Secretary of State Hillary Clinton, had watched the early-morning raid from the White House Situation Room, and the scene had engendered a fury in al-Qaeda, who resented the US's military presence and any display of American supremacism.

Obama had been relieved to leave the region, and by the time *Air Force One* landed in the UK on the next leg of the President's trip, Prince's body was under the care of the Midwest Medical Examiner's Office, in a brownstone building off Veterans Drive in Ramsey, Minneapolis.

The autopsy report confirmed the singer had died of poisoning by self-administered opiates. Obama scribbled a personal note, which was soon circulating via social media.

> Today, the world lost a creative icon. Michelle and I join millions of fans from around the world in mourning the sudden death of Prince. Few artists have influenced the sound and trajectory of popular music more distinctly or touched quite so many people with their talent. As one of the most gifted and prolific musicians of our time, Prince did it all. Funk. R&B. Rock and roll. He was a virtuoso instrumentalist, a brilliant bandleader, and an electrifying performer. A strong spirit transcends rules, and nobody's spirit was stronger, bolder, or more creative. Our thoughts and prayers are with his family, his band and all who loved him.

Obama's requiem to Prince went viral and for the first time ever the word 'funk' entered the formal lexicon of the White House. It was a moment that said much about fame and celebrity but even more about the journey of African American music across the twentieth century. The Obamas were attracted to Prince not simply because of his fame but because of the way he had broken the rules around race and representation and created a space where two of the major genres of the twentieth century, rock and soul, could merge. A year earlier, Prince had performed at an informal private party at the White House, joining Stevie Wonder on stage. Despite his outrageous stage presence, Obama found Prince to be quiet, self-deprecating and seemingly overawed by the event.

Obama was in the UK to meet Prime Minister David Cameron, on a mission to persuade wavering British voters not to ditch membership of the European Union in a forthcoming referendum. Following in the footsteps of previous presidents, Obama stayed at Winfield House in Regent's Park, the official residence of the US ambassador, Matthew Barzun. Barzun was a major 'bundler' and one-time Obama fundraiser who had raised over $1 million in grassroots campaigns during the presidential elections. He was also a music fan who, on leaving his post, bowed out to a song by the Trinidad and Tobagian calypso singer Lord Kitchener: 'London Is The Place For Me'. It was the era of vinyl revivalism and Barzun had bought a vintage turntable for the sumptuous

Gold Room at Winfield House. It was here, on the morning of the bilateral talks, that the two men, one the first black president and the other a white ambassador, paid their respects to Prince. Barzun dug out Prince's signature song, 'Purple Rain', and together they listened as the needle gently found its groove. For all its extraordinary and life-affirming moments over the decades, this was the point when soul music finally triumphed – not in its ghetto heartlands of Detroit or Chicago, nor on the stage of the Harlem Apollo nor in the studios of Muscle Shoals, but here amidst the antique furniture, porcelain and glass chandeliers of a palatial townhouse in London. By every measure of political decorum and protocol it was bold. Here was the first black president, interrupting the business of state and delaying a meeting with the British to listen to 'Purple Rain' on an old turntable.

In Obama's eyes, Prince had merged the two great railway tracks of twentieth-century music – rock and soul – and in that respect he was a pioneer rather than just a pop star. At a press conference in central London later that day, Obama again picked up the theme of requiem in a speech broadcast around the world. 'I love Prince because he put out great music and he was a great performer,' he said. 'I didn't know him well; he came to perform at the White House last year and he was extraordinary, and creative, and original, and full of energy.' In fact, for all the outward respect, Prince had not even voted for Obama. 'I'm one of the Jehovah's Witnesses,' he told talk show host Tavis Smiley. 'And we've never voted. That's not to say I don't think . . . President Obama is a very smart individual, and he seems like he means well. Prophecy is what we all have to go by now.'

At their meeting, Cameron gave Obama an assurance that the referendum would reconfirm Britain's commitment to the European project and that the 'special relationship' that dated back to the Second World War would continue untroubled. He was wrong. The UK voted by a narrow margin to leave the European Union, and Cameron resigned. For months ahead of their meeting the media had portrayed the relationship as a 'bromance' and like a 'buddy movie' – the two men even attended a collegiate basketball game together in Dayton, Ohio. They were superficially friendly, but it was just another day in a carefully massaged media circus where Obama excelled as the charismatic ringmaster. There was no great bond between them, and there never had been. According to one of Cameron's closest aides, political strategist Steve Hilton, Cameron thought Obama was 'one of the most narcissistic, self-absorbed people he'd ever dealt with'. For his part, Obama never dignified the remarks, suspecting that most Americans couldn't identify Cameron in a police line-up.

Soul music was nearly fifty years old when the first black president came to power. Among Barack Obama's many attributes was the eloquent way he crafted an inspiring story of social change. Music played a substantial part in his narrative, energising his presidential campaign, providing the soundtrack to his years in the White House, and acting as a harbinger of hope for a different kind of America. More than that, he reached out to new and younger forms of urban music which in the main had been demonised by past presidents. His years in power were the culmination of decades of political upheaval during which soul music shifted from the margins to the mainstream of American life, through the setbacks and victories of civil rights. It was music that spoke mostly of love and devotion but often gave voice to the interminable fight against discrimination. As it transformed across the years, fragmenting into many different urban genres, Obama's presidency signalled the final triumph of black music, a radiant brilliance that can only be described as the audacity of soul.

One of Obama's most potent techniques was in using music as a mode of communication, as a touchstone and as an emotional signpost. For Obama, embracing soul was not simply about being the first black president: it reflected a deeply held sense of history. He understood that the music had emerged from the great journey from slavery to emancipation, from the rural South to the urban North and from segregation to civil rights. He also knew instinctively that respect had to be shown to every station on the track, from spirituals to gospel, from blues to soul and from disco to hip-hop, that the music had echoed the hopes and dreams of his people and the inevitability of change.

In its simplest sense, the audacity of soul is the story of civil rights, but it is much bigger than that: it is a story of immaculate voices, of vile exploitation, of deprived inner-city upbringings, of unrivalled glamour, of racy over-consumption and, eventually, global success. But for most occupants of the White House, if soul music registered at all it was synonymous only with civil rights, and even then, only for a few epic songs like Sam Cooke's 'A Change Is Gonna Come' and Aretha Franklin's 'Respect'. Beneath that historic canopy lies a more complex story, one in which black music became the messenger, communicating injustices and challenging the authority of the presidency, sometimes in ways that were opaque and sometimes by giving voice to full-blown anger and fiery social protest. There was Johnny Copeland's 'Sufferin City' (Atlantic, 1969), a hyped-up blues song that captured the pressures of urban life; Mary Love's 'Lay This Burden Down' (Modern, 1967), a sixties soul release still carrying the burden of slavery; and James Carr's 'Freedom Train' (Goldwax, 1968), a Memphis classic which looked back to the underground railroad and indentured slaves' escape north to freedom.

In the decades before Obama's presidency, the black musicians who were invited to perform in the White House were those who had the highest status and most trusted reputation. The embossed invitations sent out by previous presidents to the aristocracy of black music conferred a coded racial acceptance. The great gospel legend Mahalia Jackson performed for President Eisenhower in the White House and sang at the inauguration of John F. Kennedy in 1969; Duke Ellington was presented with the nation's highest civilian honour, the Presidential Medal of Freedom, by President Nixon; and, in 1976, jazz singer Ella Fitzgerald performed for President Ford and his guests at a diplomatic reception. All three were universally established, critically acclaimed and uncontroversial enough to be performers at the East Room – but they were the exceptions.

The great classical singer Marian Anderson (born in 1897), hailed by Arturo Toscanini as 'a voice in a million', was one of the earliest trailblazers. The daughter of an ice and coal vendor at Philadelphia and Reading Railroad's Terminal Station first performed at the White House in 1936 at a party in honour of Circuit Court of Appeals Judge William Denman and his wife Leslie Van Ness. Three years later, she was to headline an Easter concert to raise funds for the black college, Howard University. There was enormous public interest, so the university searched for a venue that could accommodate a large crowd. The organisers approached Constitution Hall, then owned by the Daughters of the American Revolution. Like many other concert halls, restaurants and businesses of the time, the hall imposed rules of segregation on artists and audiences, and only permitted white artists to perform. (Albert Einstein provided Anderson with lodgings when she toured, as she was unable to stay in hotels due to the Jim Crow legislation.) The First Lady, Eleanor Roosevelt, a committed supporter of theatre and the performing arts, and champion of racial tolerance, was disgusted by the decision to refuse permission for Constitution Hall to be used and resigned from the organisation in protest. The President intervened and arranged for the Lincoln Memorial to be used for Anderson's benefit concert. Over 75,000 people attended, and it was broadcast live on radio, securing Marian Anderson's status as one of the most famous black singers of the era and resulting in a life-long friendship with the First Lady. It was not until Michelle Obama took up residency that a First Lady would repeat history and go out of her way to welcome black artists into the house that slaves had built.

The one genre of black music that had protected status in the ceremonies of state was gospel, or what for a time was known as 'negro spirituals'. In his 1903 collection of essays, *The Souls of Black Folk*, the socialist intellectual and historian W. E. B. Du Bois wrote that 'despite caricature and defilement', the music of the black church 'remains the most original and beautiful expression of human life and longing yet born on American soil'. Songs like 'Amazing Grace', 'Precious Lord, Take My Hand' and the black national anthem 'Lift Every Voice And Sing' are still sung at funerals, ceremonial openings and presidential inaugurations. As Mahalia Jackson commented: 'Blues are the songs of despair, but gospel songs are the songs of hope.' They also had another abiding strength because they fulsomely praised the Lord and were unlikely to offend even the most upright citizen.

The pervasive power of gospel music is that it delivers ritual and ceremony and casts an imperious gaze over congregations from the rural Baptist churches of the Deep South to the grand cathedrals of the major northern cities and to highly choreographed state occasions like funerals and inaugurations. For all its factionalism, Christianity exerts a pervasive power over America whether it is the fundamentalism of white segregationists or the raucous marches for civil rights. The unifying symbolism of gospel is immense. Mahalia Jackson sang at President Kennedy's inauguration in 1961, the African American mezzo-soprano Denyce Graves sang 'The Lord's Prayer' at the funeral of Ronald Reagan, and, most recently, as a statement of towering modernity, the Queen of Soul, Aretha Franklin, sang 'My Country, 'Tis Of Thee' at Barack Obama's inauguration.

In July 2020, in the middle of the COVID-19 pandemic, a ceremony for the late congressman and civil rights leader John Lewis was held in the Capitol rotunda. US lawmakers, masked and dressed in black, wept when Wintley Phipps delivered his melodramatic rendition of 'Amazing Grace'. He had performed for a long line of American presidents including Jimmy Carter, Ronald Reagan, Bill Clinton, George W. Bush and Barack Obama.

The story of black music and the White House is one of gradual change and, eventually, one of accommodating even the excommunicated. The journey from spiritual song to secular soul music took decades to complete, and as soul evolved into funk and new forms of urban dance, the doors were rarely open. As the twentieth century unfolded, soul left the church to embrace sexuality, psychedelia, street politics, afro-futurism and the hedonism of underground disco. Then it came under the influence of different regional expressions such as New York hip-hop, Washington go-go, Chicago house and Detroit techno, and once again was out on a limb. Many of the most innovative practitioners were far removed from conventional electoral politics and thus considered too unruly, too militant and too sexual to be invited into the mainstream. Obama changed that.

Hip-hop, the most successful and disruptive prodigy of black music, tested the White House to the limit. For many years during the Republican administrations of the eighties, hip-hop was perceived as the enemy within, a metaphor for some of society's problems such as poverty, gang violence, crack cocaine and criminality. Although previous presidents and their political fixers were comfortable with gospel and the spiritual celebration of life and death, contemporary black music was anathema to most of them – too black and too strong. Rappers would have to wait for the arrival of the Obamas before they could enter the White House, and even then, the unwritten rules of engagement were tightly monitored.

Chicago looms large in the story of soul music and politics, and it was poetic justice that, on 4 November 2008, president-elect Barack Obama gave his now-historic victory speech in the city where his wife had been born and he had built his career. Obama looked out on a cold dark night to an estimated audience of a quarter of a million people packed into and around Grant Park. Conscious of the life-expectancy of presidents across the years, Obama was protected by bullet-proof glass to deflect any shots from the skyscrapers overlooking the park. Security was tight throughout, but the queues waiting to be frisked and the heavy police presence did not dampen the excitement of a crowd that had come to witness history: the first speech from the first black president.

So much hope was invested in Obama that night, that it is difficult to imagine any subsequent president engaging with the people so directly. The African American writer Ta-Nehisi Coates, former Howard University student and national correspondent for *The Atlantic*, wrote powerfully of the feelings that Obama's victory had unlocked. 'It now seemed possible,' he wrote, 'that white supremacy, the scourge of American history, might well be banished in my lifetime. In those days I imagined racism as a tumour that could be isolated and removed from the body of America, not as a pervasive system both native and essential to that body.' From that perspective, it seemed possible that the success of one man really could change history. The expectation was unprecedented and ultimately flawed.

It was clear from the outset that Obama was soul music's president. He took to the stage with his family to the song that had almost become his imprimatur, Stevie Wonder's 'Signed, Sealed, Delivered (I'm Yours)' (Tamla, 1970), a buoyant Motown love song co-written by Lee Garrett who, like Wonder, is blind. The song was played nightly at rallies across America and exemplified the upbeat momentum of Obama's campaign. During the primaries, Stevie Wonder had toured with him to Indiana to perform at a promotional concert. As Obama's bid for the presidency gathered pace, it changed from a love song into a statement of intent, of national engagement and, finally, of elected office. The song was so embedded within the campaign that David Axelrod, Obama's political strategist, had it as the ringtone on his phone.

'It's been a long time coming,' Obama told the Grant Park crowd, channelling a line from the iconic civil rights song 'A Change Is Gonna Come', by one of Chicago's most famous singers, Sam Cooke. 'But tonight, because of what we did on this date in this election at this defining moment, change has come to America.'

On the morning after the election result, an Obama supporter in Harlem joyfully holds up the front page of the *Daily News*. The headline channels the title of Sam Cooke's civil rights anthem of 1964.

'A Change Is Gonna Come' was released as an album track in 1964, the year the Civil Rights Act ended segregation in public places and banned employment discrimination based on race, colour, religion, sex or national origin. Sam Cooke's younger brother, the one-time gospel singer L. C. Cooke, was watching the event on television at home when Obama quoted the line. He told the *Chicago Tribune* of the surge of pride he felt that his family had played such a part in Obama's election. Sam and L. C. were toddlers when their mother took them on a Greyhound bus from Mississippi to their new home in Chicago in the early thirties. They were part of the Great Migration, which brought more than six million African Americans north from the segregated rural South. Half a million of the hopeful migrants settled in Chicago, mostly in the teeming South Side, a few miles south of where Obama now stood. Sam Cooke's father was a minister: four of his six children sang in a group called the Singing Children, and the teenage brothers sang together in the famous gospel group, the Highway Q.C.'s. Now, Obama was in their neighbourhood, quoting from their songs.

'A Change Is Gonna Come' was written after an incident in which Cooke and his entourage were turned away when they arrived at a whites-only Holiday Inn in Shreveport, Louisiana, despite having made reservations. Cooke protested and was arrested for disturbing the peace. For Obama, the song served as a powerful shorthand: 'Change will not come if we wait for some other person or some other time,' he told his audience. 'We are the ones we've been waiting for. We are the change that we seek.'

A gathering of local politicians and councilmen from Cook County sat in a shielded area off to the side of the stage. Among them was the legendary soul singer Jerry Butler, the former lead singer of the Impressions. He had co-written 'I've Been Loving You Too Long' with Otis Redding when the two were holed up in a hotel in Buffalo, New York, during a break in a concert tour. When Butler's recording career waned in the early eighties, he began to pursue an interest in local politics. His sister Mattie was a leading community activist in Chicago and had been involved in the 'arson for profit' scandals, in which crooked entrepreneurs bought up insurance on old buildings in the Woodlawn neighbourhood only to burn them down and sell the vacant land at a profit. One night in October 1980, a series of fires broke out in Woodlawn, one of which claimed the lives of thirteen children two doors away from Mattie's home. Having seen his sister at work and been inspired by Harold Washington's election as Chicago's first black mayor in 1983, Jerry Butler stood for election himself. By the time Obama staged his victory rally, Butler was the longest-serving member of the Cook County Board, serving as chair of the Health and Hospitals Committee. The two men had met when Obama first arrived in Chicago and was working for the Developing Communities Project, driving voter registration campaigns in the city's Altgeld Gardens housing projects.

In Grant Park, by now jam-packed, the crowds cascading over the South Loop erupted. The opening bars of Jackie Wilson's '(Your Love Keeps Lifting Me) Higher And Higher' soared into the night air. Butler smiled at the euphoria that greeted the song. Both the soul anthems that Obama had chosen to energise the crowd owed their origins to the streets of Chicago's South Side and a remarkable square mile of music history that lay only five minutes away on Record Row, where a cluster of independent record labels had lined the blocks just south of Michigan Avenue. On the 2100 block, one of the most famous record labels in the story of African American music once had their offices. Chess Records was the label that connected the blues of John Lee Hooker, Howlin' Wolf and Muddy Waters to the sixties soul of the Dells and the Radiants. Nearby were the offices of the Cincinnati indie label, King Records, who had James Brown on their roster, and further south were three venues that occupied a starring role in the story of sixties soul: the Regal Theater, the Peyton Place Club and Billy Taylor's High Chaparral. It was in these few square miles that some of the most galvanising civil rights anthems were written and recorded, including 'Move On Up' by Curtis Mayfield, and 'People Get Ready' and 'We're A Winner' by the Impressions.

The backing track for Jackie Wilson's global hit '(Your Love Keeps Lifting Me) Higher And Higher' was recorded on 6 July 1967 at Columbia's studios in Chicago, the product of a corridor of creativity that stretched from there to the other major city of soul: Detroit. The song was produced by Carl Davis and the recording session, arranged by Sonny Sanders, featured the legendary Motown backing band the Funk Brothers, including bassist James Jamerson, drummer Richard 'Pistol' Allen, guitarist Robert White and keyboardist Johnny Griffith.

The Motown house band often moonlighted on sessions in Chicago to augment the low wages they were paid back in Detroit.

Jackie Wilson had grown up in Detroit's Highland Park neighbourhood where he was a teenage recruit to the Detroit Shakers street gang. His alcoholic father was unemployed and persistently absent from home, and his parents separated when he was nine. Wilson dropped out of high school at the age of 15 and was twice sentenced to detention for fighting and knife crimes. His delinquent days were lived out at a time of deep-seated poverty and youth crime. Wilson's teenage life had been described by John F. Kennedy's Assistant Secretary of Labor, Daniel Patrick Moynihan, in the controversial 'Moynihan Report: The Negro Family, the Case for National Action' in 1965. It described a 'destructive vein in ghetto culture', a kind of urban youthquake that undermined inner-city life. Between 1960 and 1976, the number of juveniles apprehended increased by 416 per cent, and in Michigan, juveniles under the age of 17 accounted for 33 per cent of the state's crime reports – and that was before the impact of the 'War on Drugs' legislation introduced by Presidents Nixon and Reagan. When Wilson returned to the streets after his second stint in detention, he got married and began to sing at the Sensation Club in Detroit, joining local supergroup the Falcons, his first real step on the ladder to success. He came to personify the slicker elements of sixties soul with his dynamic dance moves, virtuoso singing and impeccable dress sense. Wilson was a womaniser and was arrested on 'moral charges' in South Carolina in March 1967 after he and his drummer Jimmy Smith were discovered in a motel room in South Carolina with two 24-year-old white women. (At that time, interracial sex was such an emotive subject that, after pressure from his overbearing father, President Kennedy banned Sammy Davis Jr from appearing at his inaugural concert – Davis had recently married a white Swedish woman, May Britt.)

Michelle Obama's upbringing was in stark contrast to the horrors sketched out in the Moynihan Report and the chaotic lifestyle experienced by Jackie Wilson. When Chicago soul came of age in the sixties, she was an infant, the daughter of Fraser and Marian Robinson who lived on the upper floor of 7436 South Euclid Avenue on the South Side. Fraser was a pump operator for the Chicago Water Department, and despite being diagnosed with multiple sclerosis at a young age, he rarely missed a day of work. Marian was a homeworker who raised Michelle and her older brother Craig in a hugely supportive family environment, with piano lessons, dedicated hours for school homework and encouragement to go to university. Michelle attended Whitney Young High School at the same time as her friend Santita Jackson, the oldest daughter of civil rights leader and two-time presidential candidate, Jesse Jackson, and later a backing singer for Roberta Flack. Santita was the Maid of Honour at Michelle's marriage to Barack Obama and sang the national anthem at Bill Clinton's second presidential inauguration.

Although there were exceptions – notably James Brown – the vast majority of sixties soul singers who recorded in the northern cities of Chicago and Detroit tilted towards the Democrats, and in the case of Motown, there was an unwritten rule that staff should support the Democrats during elections, on the campaign trail and at fundraisers. Jesse Jackson's family and the Obamas led close and interconnected lives. The first time Obama ran for national office, he made sure he was not stepping on the ambitions of Jesse L. Jackson Jr, the son who later became a co-chairman of his 2008 presidential campaign. Although he was not from Chicago, Obama learned to love the city after his move there in the eighties: it became his home, his 'hood and his political turf. He worked his way through college with scholarships and student loans, and became involved with a group of churches to help rebuild community spirit in areas devastated by deindustrialisation before attending law school, becoming the first African American president of the *Harvard Law Review*. After graduation, he returned to Chicago to lead voter registration drives and work as an intern. Michelle Robinson – 'the woman who put the "O" in Obama' – met him in the summer of 1989 at the law firm Sidley & Austin, where she was already an associate. On their first date, they saw the Spike Lee film *Do the Right Thing* at the cinema and then went for ice cream at a Baskin-Robbins in Hyde Park – pure rom-com material. A plaque was put up in the spot where they first kissed, and it has since become a gathering place for young lovers.

Neither Barack nor Michelle had much money, and Michelle remembers driving around the South Side in a car that was 'so rusted out, I could actually see the pavement going by through a hole in the passenger-side door'. The couple married in 1992 at the United Church of Christ in Chicago. Michelle's brother Craig walked her down the aisle, and Barack's brother Malik was best man. Their first dance was to one of soul music's most majestic love songs, Stevie Wonder's prophetic 'You And I (We Can Conquer The World)', from his 1972 album *Talking Book*. Their honeymoon was a road trip round California, taking in places like Big Sur, Napa and San Francisco.

Although he had the support of the Democratic Party, Obama had precious few corporate donors to draw upon and he had maxed-out his credit cards to attend conventions. So, he set about building a broad grassroots movement from his Chicago base, raising money through micro-donations, crowdfunding and social media. There would be glamorous nights to come, but only a few months out from the 2008 election he was still leaning on the support of Chicago's lower-profile soul music community. On a Friday in July, only months before election day, his core local support crowded into the Park West concert venue on West Armitage to see R&B veteran Otis Clay, who had last grazed success ten years before, when his single 'The Only Way Is Up' was covered by Yaz and the Plastic People. By comparison with the big presidential fundraisers, the $100 ticket price on the night was paltry, but from the moment Obama clinched the Democratic nomination, black musicians were increasingly warming to him. Rappers Young Jeezy and Nas recorded 'My President', paying tribute to a blue Lamborghini and the future president with the slogan 'My president is black, my Lambo's blue'. 'My President' joined '(Your Love Keeps Lifting Me) Higher And Higher' and 'Signed, Sealed, Delivered (I'm Yours)' as a campaign song and, although it was never officially endorsed because of its flagrant use of the word 'nigga', it was often nodded into playlists as the campaign gathered momentum.

Obama fought off a compulsive tendency in his campaigning days, sticking wherever possible to familiar routines and rituals. In 2008, as his campaign intensified, he maintained a laser-like focus by playing Miles Davis's 'Freddie Freeloader' repeatedly while writing speeches and pacing backstage. Obama reached the White House with 52.9 per cent of the vote, buoyed by a tantalising sense of hope, an innovative use of social media and a targeted system of statistical analysis that dug beneath the surface to uncover the nuances of what people were really thinking. He had built a partnership with his running mate, Senator Joe Biden of Delaware, as a safe bet, to counteract any perception of riskiness with the electorate. The most memorable poster of his presidential campaign was designed by the street artist Frank Shepard Fairey, skateboarder and founder of the Obey clothing brand. It depicted a stencilled image of Obama with the word 'Hope' in block capitals. What began as street art was quickly picked up by Obama's savvy campaign team and turned into an electoral icon.

By the time of his re-election, he finally shook off his dependence on the Miles Davis track and moved on to a new compulsion, hitting replay on Jay-Z's 'My 1st Song'. The song, which featured the voice of Biggie Smalls, had a 'keep your eyes on the prize' message and gave Obama an inner resolve for the increasingly disruptive events to come.

Among his proudest presidential achievements – the one that resonated most powerfully with his home base in Chicago – was what is dubbed the Till Bill. In December 2016, Obama sat at his desk in the Oval office and signed the Emmett Till Unsolved Civil Rights Re-authorization Crime Act, an Act of Congress introduced by the late John Lewis in 2007 that allowed cold cases of suspected violent crimes committed against African Americans before 1970 to be reopened. For Obama, signing the bill into law was honouring a promise he had made to many residents of Chicago as he worked his way to the White House.

Emmet Till, a high-spirited teenager, was a member of a gospel group from Summit-Argo, Illinois, who frequently appeared on stage in amateur contests against Jerry Butler and Curtis Mayfield in Chicago's Cabrini-Green. Till was murdered in the Delta town of Money, Mississippi, in 1955 during a summer vacation spent visiting relatives. It was claimed that he had flirted with a white woman at a local grocery store. Several nights later, the woman's relatives abducted the teenager and subjected him to torture before dumping his body in the Tallahatchie River.

Simeon Booker, the Washington bureau chief of *Jet* and *Ebony* magazines, was in Chicago when he heard of the boy's disappearance. He earned the trust of Emmett's mother, Mamie, and accompanied her to the funeral home, where she insisted on seeing her son's body as it was removed from a rubber bag. At Mamie's request, *Jet* carried a series of photographs of her son's disfigured face, turning his death into a cause célèbre for civil rights.

Historian David Halberstam has since described the photographs, published at the height of the trial of Emmett's killers, as 'the first great media event of the civil rights movement'; in Chicago, the Reverend Jesse Jackson called it the movement's 'Big Bang', an issue of savage social injustice that all reasonable people could rally around; and John Lewis later said, 'Emmett Till was my George Floyd.' Crammed in between features on the top musical acts of the time – Duke Ellington, Louis Armstrong, Nat King Cole and Bo Diddley – were some of the most disturbing documentary photographs ever committed to print. 'Mutilated is the word most often used to describe the face of Emmett Till after his body was hauled out of the Tallahatchie River in Mississippi,' reported *The New York Times*. 'Inhuman is more like it: melted, bloated, missing an eye, swollen so large that its patch of wiry hair looks like that of a balding old man, not a handsome, brazen 14-year-old boy.'

At A. A. Raynor's morgue on Roosevelt Road, tens of thousands of people filed past the open casket to pay their respects. It was a gruesome awakening that brought rage to the streets of Chicago and ignited the civil rights movement. An all-white jury acquitted the killers, but in a magazine feature in January 1956, the pair confessed. Almost every conversation about civil rights and racist violence in Chicago returned to Emmet Till, and, although the atrocity took place six years before Obama was born in Honolulu, he heard the story repeated hundreds of times and grew to understand its potency and significance to the people of Chicago.

One of the people who spoke to him frequently about the murder was a dynamo by the name of Willie Barrow, a mentor to the future president and an influence on his attitudes towards minority communities. Known as 'the Little Warrior', Barrow was a tiny woman with a long and unimpeachable pedigree in the civil rights movement. She was only 12 years old when she led her first demonstration to demand the right to travel on a school bus in her home of Burton, Texas, during the Great Depression. After high school she worked as a welder at the Kaiser Shipyards in Swan Island, Washington, much like the mythical Rosie the Riveter, and also became ordained as a minister. She moved to Chicago after the war. Barrow journeyed to the March on Washington in 1963 and south to the famous march from Selma to Montgomery, Alabama, in 1965, where marchers were beaten back by law enforcers at the Edmund Pettus Bridge. Like the Reverend Jesse Jackson, she was part of the Chicago branch of Martin Luther King's movement, helping to set up his northern offices there. Together with Jackson, she also co-founded Operation PUSH, the community organisation, and managed the itinerary of the Operation Breadbasket Orchestra and Choir, a remarkable coalition of musicians who toured America raising funds for civil rights campaigns. The orchestra was led by the great Memphis saxophonist Ben Branch, the last person to speak to Martin Luther King in the minutes before he was assassinated at the Lorraine Motel in Memphis, in 1968.

Barrow effectively 'adopted' Obama when he moved to Chicago and considered him her godson. On her death in 2015, Obama spoke lovingly of her inspiring personality: 'Reverend Willie T. Barrow was a Civil Rights icon and a Chicago institution, a 'Little Warrior' in pursuit of justice for all God's children . . . To Michelle and me, she was a constant inspiration, a lifelong mentor, and a very dear friend. I was proud to count myself among the more than 100 men and women she called her 'Godchildren,' and worked hard to live up to her example. I still do.'

What Obama did not mention was the event that changed Willie Barrow's life and how it would come to affect his own political prospects. Willie Barrow had one child, a boy called Keith, who was born in 1954. As a teenager, he followed in the footsteps of the great Chicago gospel stars who were breaking away from the church to embrace secular soul. Like Sam Cooke (of the Soul Stirrers), Jerry Butler and Curtis Mayfield (of the Northern Jubilee Gospel Singers) and Major Lance (of the Five Gospel Harmonaires), Barrow was a chorister who went solo. He began singing at Vernon Park Church of God on East 77th Street where his mother was a pastor, but soon set up a secular group, the Soul Shakers. After recording a solo gospel album for Jewel Records, with sleeve notes by the Reverend Jesse Jackson, he signed a solo deal with Columbia/ CBS. To progress his career, Keith Barrow moved to New York, where he became a well-known figure in the city's underground dance clubs including David Mancuso's the Loft, the Paradise Garage, the Saint and the Gallery. He immersed himself in the burgeoning disco scene and enjoyed some success with the Top 50 R&B hit 'Teach Me (It's Something About Love)' (Columbia, 1977) and the elegant dance record 'Turn Me Up' (Columbia, 1978).

While touring Europe, Barrow fell ill in Paris and rang his mother in

Chicago, worried that he was too unfit to go on stage. He was admitted to hospital in France, the tour was cancelled, and Barrow was flown back to Chicago where he was cared for by his mother before his death from AIDS in October 1983. He is buried in Oak Woods Cemetery near the family home in Chicago's South Side.

Driven by her son's death, Willie Barrow had a shift of conscience. She reorientated the PUSH movement towards what eventually became known as intersectionality – the understanding that people are often disadvantaged by multiple sources of oppression: race, class, gender identity, sexual orientation and religion. The famous civil rights organisation was eventually rebranded as Rainbow/PUSH, focusing on minorities across the spectrum. It was one of a network of organisations that supported Obama and extended his appeal beyond the mainstream movement.

From Willie Barrow, Obama learned the need to reach out beyond the African American community in which his wife had grown up and that he had adopted as his own. Arguably, Obama's greatest gift is that he is a conceptual thinker who sees the world as one of ever-changing complexity. Unlike many other presidents, Obama rarely gave in to superficiality. 'Issues are never simple,' he once said. 'One thing I'm proud of is that very rarely will you hear me simplify the issues.'

The critic Ta-Nehisi Coates saw something else in Obama's approach to the presidency that went beyond political crowd-pleasing. He described a set of cultural cues, sometimes predicated on soul music, which became an important part of his popular appeal: 'Obama doesn't merely evince blackness; he uses his blackness to court African Americans, semaphoring in a cultural dialect of our creation – crooning Al Green at the Apollo, name-checking Young Jeezy, regularly appearing on the cover of black magazines, weighing the merits of Jay-Z versus Kanye West, being photographed in the White House with a little black boy touching his hair.' Although Coates acknowledges that some of these gestures tip into mawkish populism, he argues that they allowed Obama to reach out to people, to close the gap that often separates a president from ordinary citizens and create an immensely powerful bond. That self-confidence, which allowed him to clown around in the Oval Office and fist-bump janitors in the corridors of the White House, was endearing to those who liked him, although could irk those who didn't.

As his presidency unfolded, Obama increasingly used music as a tool of emotional and ideological communication. *Rolling Stone* writer Ryan Bort saw it as an extension of his relaxed personality:

> One of the charms of Obama's time in office was his appreciation of popular music, especially anything with soul. During a 2012 campaign fundraiser at the Apollo Theater in Harlem, he famously sang a few bars of Al Green's 'Let's Get Together' . . . From 2009, when he sang Dionne Warwick's 'Walk On By' during a Democratic rally in New Jersey, to 2016, when he chimed in – and then ultimately led – a performance of 'What'd I Say' during a White House tribute to Ray Charles, Obama was never shy about expressing himself through song.

Perhaps the most powerful occasion came in a deeper moment of reflection during the funeral of pastor and state senator Clementa C. Pinckney of South Carolina, who was assassinated by Dylann Roof in June 2015 when he opened fire in the Emanuel AME church in Charleston, killing nine of the congregation. Roof was a disenchanted white supremacist who harboured a bitter hatred of black people and hoped to spark a race war. He ranted on his arrest that he had no choice. He couldn't 'go into the ghetto and fight. I chose Charleston because it is the most historic city in my state, and at one time had the highest ratio of blacks to whites in the country. We have no skinheads, no real KKK, no one doing anything but talking on the internet.' He awaits execution in Terre Haute, Indiana. At Pinckney's funeral, after giving the eulogy, President Obama paused, bowed his head and seemed to call on an inner strength, then began to sing 'Amazing Grace'. The voices of the mourners swelled up and supported him. It was an astonishing performance, heartfelt yet conscious of the watching millions.

Obama's ability to engage effortlessly with people riled Republicans. Some of them called his Chicago connections into question, pointing out that he had not been born there but in a middle-class household in Hawaii. The implication was that there was something fraudulent about the man, an idea that was whipped into a national obsession – birtherism – that implied Obama wasn't even American and should not therefore be president. Even after his presidency was over, the right wing of the Republican Party and the bitterly oppositional President Donald Trump railed against his identity. Fox News host Tucker

Carlson accused Obama of giving 'a divisive and deeply dishonest campaign speech' in his eulogy at the funeral of John Lewis, then, in an old Republican trope, dismissed Obama's 'fake accent' and called him 'Mr Hawaii Guy'.

Barack Obama had moved to Chicago in June 1985 to become a community organiser and stayed for the best part of twenty-five years. He met his wife there, was married there and was elected to the Illinois State Senate in 1996. Until he became president, his entire political life was anchored in Chicago; it was politically dishonest to deny him the right to sing a Sam Cooke song or joke with young boys from the South Side. He might not have been born there, but he adopted the city with genuine passion.

Obama deployed elements like his love of soul music and his smooth oratorial style to gently nudge the American mainstream into accepting black people in positions of power and influence. Obama knew his history. He knew all about music's journey from the dusty backroads of the blues to commercially successful contemporary R&B. More importantly, he understood that soul had always been the music of change. For rock critic Charlie Gillett, soul was 'the sound of the city' and for Motown it was 'the sound of young America', and then, as it evolved and diversified, for Ben E. King it became a music of extra dimensions – a 'supernatural thing'. Soul music broke the rules of segregation, tore down the barriers to chart success and eventually came to dominate the mainstream. As recently as 1985, Prince had been a Beltway outcast, described as a peddler of filth and sexual promiscuity, and identified as a member of the notorious 'Filthy Fifteen', the list of artists that the Parents' Music Resource Center (PMRC), founded by Vice President Al Gore's wife Tipper, had identified as being unsuitable for American teenagers. By the time Prince died, the PMRC had folded, Al Gore was on the lecture circuit talking about global warming, and Prince was a global icon. Obama had opened the door of the White House to edgier talent. He understood hip-hop as a vibrant art form, articulate, popular in the streets and capable of a much broader range of emotions than hatred, misogyny and rage.

Obama's presidency coincided with substantial technological change as streaming came to displace physical sales of compact discs and retro vinyl. It was Obama who metaphorically opened the doors of the White

House to urban artists but that was, in part, enabled by his family. The First Lady had grown up enraptured by the great R&B female singers who had been born in Bronzeville and Hyde Park in her hometown, and, as her daughters Sasha and Malia grew into teenagers, they influenced their mother's taste in music, which took in hip-hop, house and urban soul.

Black music in all its transgressive forms was knocking on the White House door, although in fairness to the outgoing president, George W. Bush, he had not been as tone deaf as many of his predecessors. Bush had proclaimed June 2001 'Black Music Month', encouraging 'all Americans to learn more about the contributions of black artists to America's musical heritage and to celebrate their remarkable role in shaping our history and culture'. However, there was nothing new or disruptive about the performers invited to attend the launch; they were drawn largely from a 'safe' musical heritage – Lionel Hampton, Shirley Caesar, the Blind Boys of Alabama and the Harlem Jazz Museum Artists among them. Then, in October 2003, less than three years into Bush's presidency, Beyoncé featuring Sean Paul topped the *Billboard* charts with 'Baby Boy'. It was a significant moment: all the top selling singles that month were by African American artists. While Obama's presidency seemed to directly reflect these seismic changes in the recording industry, they neither began nor ended with the first black president. By 2017 and the first year of the Trump presidency, the change had become even more measurable: hip-hop accounted for 20.9 per cent of all songs consumed by listeners, and that number jumped to an unprecedented 24.7 per cent in 2018. Nearly a quarter of all tracks listened to in the US came from the once outlawed and reviled genre of rap music, while mainstream rock, once the heartbeat of middle America, was waning. This was not just a shift in music tastes alone; it paralleled the changing dynamics and demographics of American society.

As part of his mission to signal change, Obama built up a close working relationship with Aretha Franklin, a woman whose life seemed to echo the developments that black America had experienced. A child of civil rights and a personification of a new kind of patriotism, Franklin brought a mature glamour to Obama's inauguration, where she sported an ostentatious silver-bowed hat while singing the anthem, 'My Country, 'Tis Of Thee'. This was a statement of Democratic continuity, in that Franklin had sung a medley of Duke Ellington hits for Jimmy Carter back in 1977 and performed at a pre-inauguration festival for Bill Clinton with Stevie Wonder and Diana Ross at the Lincoln Memorial in 1993.

Given her family's long-standing support for the Democrats – Franklin was a staunch Hillary Clinton fan – it was no great surprise that she turned down the chance to perform at the inauguration of President Donald Trump in 2017. (Musicians Adele, Elton John, Steve Tyler, Neil Young, Pharrell Williams and R.E.M. also released statements denying the use of their music during Trump rallies, and Eddy Grant issued a cease-and-desist letter regarding the use of his hit 'Electric Avenue' in an ad campaign that attacked Joe Biden. Grant sued Trump and, in September 2021, won.)

As Obama wrote in a letter to the editor of *The New Yorker*, David Remnick:

> Nobody embodies more fully the connection between the African American spiritual, the blues, R&B, rock and roll – the way that hardship and sorrow were transformed into something full of beauty and vitality and hope. American history wells up when Aretha sings. That's why, when she sits down at a piano and sings 'A Natural Woman', she can move me to tears – the same way that Ray Charles's version of 'America The Beautiful' will always be in my view the most patriotic piece of music ever performed – because it captures the fullness of the American experience, the view from the bottom as well as the top, the good and the bad, and the possibility of synthesis, reconciliation, transcendence.

American history wells up when Aretha sings. Obama's words were brilliantly chosen but they hid as much as they revealed. Aretha Franklin's story was neither one of rural poverty nor overwhelming barriers to success. She did have an emotionally troubled life, however, and the Franklin family home in Detroit concealed many secrets. Her father, the Reverend C. L. Franklin, was a flamboyant character who dressed in flash suits, sported ostentatious jewellery and often shocked the staider members of his congregation by preaching the gospel in the conk hairstyle associated with Detroit's pimps and gangsters. When Franklin's New Bethel Baptist Church had to relocate to Linwood in 1961 to accommodate the Chrysler freeway, ever the showman, he led a convoy of parishioners from the site of the old church to the new one in a noisy congregation of Buicks and Cadillacs.

Mary Wilson of The Supremes, one of the congregation's most enthusiastic singers, was a childhood friend of another of Franklin's daughters, Carolyn. The two girls were bussed to Alger Elementary School in what was then a predominantly white neighbourhood, as part of the city's policy of racial integration. Wilson once described the reverend as a 'sexual' preacher. 'Women loved him,' she said. 'He was a lady's man! My mother adored him.' Franklin preached fire and brimstone but lived like a star. After his divorce from his wife Barbara, he brought up their four children himself, but he was rarely, if ever, alone. A string of housekeepers, many recruited from the Bethel congregation, helped out and the reverend had several 'unofficial' wives, among them the brilliant gospel singer Clara Ward with whom he had a long affair and who assumed the role of surrogate mother to Aretha. Like her friend and hero Sam Cooke, Aretha made the move from gospel to pop, crossing the Rubicon that many in the Christian community saw as a betrayal of their core values. As a teenager at Columbia Records in 1962, she released one of her most precocious records, a rocking R&B song called 'Rough Lover', in which she shocked the gospel circuit by demanding a 'mean sweet daddy who the devil wouldn't cross'. The lyrics had the traditionalists reeling, and they heaped criticism on Aretha's young head.

By the time Aretha sang at President Obama's inauguration, she had become one of the most venerable singers on the planet. The 73-year-old took to the stage in a floor-length fur coat, sat at the piano and brought President Obama to tears. Her performance of '(You Make Me Feel Like) A Natural Woman' was so powerful it provoked a standing ovation a full minute before the song was finished. Yet, Aretha's outstanding voice, always an intriguing, rich blend of religious devotion and secular pain, hid a personality burdened by self-doubt and sadness. She had given birth to her first child at the age of 12, and her second when she was 15. She'd always insisted that the father's identity be kept secret. After her death, the father was revealed to be Edward Jordan, a fast-living playboy whose reputation Aretha savaged in a series of angry wills found in her home when she died. Jerry Wexler, her producer at

Atlantic Records, christened her 'Our Lady of Mysterious Sorrows': 'Her eyes are incredible, luminous eyes covering inexplicable pain. Her depressions could be as deep as the dark sea. I don't pretend to know the sources of her anguish, but anguish surrounds Aretha as surely as the glory of her musical aura.' Linda McCartney, an aspiring young photographer when she first met Aretha, also sensed a darkness, later recalling: 'We met at the Hilton Hotel in Los Angeles, and she was in tears. She was . . . drinking vodka, and she was just a mess, so depressed. I took pictures of her . . . and the sadness was amazing.'

Aretha Franklin fought a lifelong battle with agoraphobia, which made her anxious about crowds and major public events. She cancelled numerous concert tours as a result and seemed often to be unwell. For all her troubles, Aretha was a slave to political duty. Her father had instilled in her a respect for the cause of civil rights and a sense of historic calling – that she should become the voice of change. On 9 April 1968, in Atlanta, Georgia, she performed at the funeral of Martin Luther King. She paid tribute to her father's fallen friend with a raw and tender rendition of 'Precious Lord'. It was a moment of national recognition, which the singer Peabo Bryson highlighted with understated profundity: 'There was a time in American history when almost every white person knew who Aretha Franklin was.'

Later that year, in August, she was invited to sing the national anthem at the opening of the Democratic National Convention in Chicago. At 26 years old she was the top-selling solo female artist in music history. Among her nine Top Ten hits were her anthem to womanhood '(You Make Me Feel Like) A Natural Woman' (Atlantic, 1967) and her reinterpretation of Otis Redding's 'Respect' (Atlantic, 1967). When she sang the closing line of the national anthem – 'O say, does that star-spangled banner yet wave/O'er the land of the free and the home of the brave?' – she used the cadence of her voice to emphasise the question mark at the end rather than asserting a fact. It was a subtle signifier: democracy itself was on trial, and within hours of Aretha's performance, armies of protesters against the war in Vietnam besieged Grant Park in and around the area where Obama would give his victory address. Chaos reigned as the Yippies swarmed over the Statue of Christopher Columbus, paying mock homage to their preferred presidential candidate, a 145-pound pig called Pigasus.

Grant Park is a story in its own right. It was where the young Emmet Till had performed at amateur gospel shows in the hot summers of the early fifties, and then by the late sixties, it was besieged by notoriety during the Democratic Convention. Then, in July 1971, the area where Obama's stage would be erected was used to accommodate a free concert by Sly and the Family Stone, the most outrageous purveyors of psychedelic soul. The band were late on stage and the impatient crowd started rioting. Over a hundred people were injured, including several police officers, and the reason given to the press was that the band had refused to perform. It became one of pop and rock's great mysteries when the band released their 1971 album *There's A Riot Going On* with a cryptic track of the same name with no sound, no music – just silence.

By 2008, the year of the presidential elections, Aretha Franklin had settled into a graceful semi-retirement, although she turned up to support Obama throughout his presidential campaign as she had done for numerous Democrats before him. For years, she had only come out of her family home in Detroit for special occasions or to record lucrative duets with global stars. She recorded 'Sisters Are Doin' It For Themselves' with Eurythmics in 1985, 'Jumpin' Jack Flash' with Keith Richards in 1986, 'I Knew You Were Waiting (For Me)' with George Michael in 1987, 'Through The Storm' with Elton John in 1989 and 'What Now My Love' with Frank Sinatra in 1995. None came close to her towering solo performances, but they solidified her status as the world's greatest female singer, the one the biggest stars wanted to rub shoulders with. Her empowerment duet with Annie Lennox of Eurythmics also paved the way for similar anthems, not least Beyoncé's 'Run The World (Girls)' and Alicia Keys' 'Girl On Fire'.

Although never her most famous song, Aretha received her eighteenth Grammy Award for 'Never Gonna Break My Faith' (2006), a collaboration with Mary J. Blige and the Boys Choir of Harlem, which featured in *Bobby*, a film about the last hours before the assassination of Bobby Kennedy. She released a solo version to commemorate June-teenth, the day celebrated annually to mark the end of slavery. 'Never Gonna Break My Faith' acted as a baton passed to a new generation, symbolising the journey from slavery to civil rights, from assassination to democracy, and from spirituals to self-confident R&B. The woman Aretha handed the baton to was Mary J. Blige.

Mary J. Blige sings Bill Withers' 'Lean On Me' during President Obama's
We Are One: Inaugural Celebration at the Lincoln Memorial
in Washington D.C., 18 January 2009.

Mary J. Blige has appeared at more presidential functions than any singer in history, many of them during Obama's presidency. Thanks to her urban credibility, her modern vibe and the influence of the two young girls then resident in the White House, Blige was perfect for the Obama White House. Like the President, she recognised that the passage of musical influence across the generations was a powerful tool of communication. 'As a child I always wanted to be a singer,' she said about her upbringing. 'The music my mother played in the house moved me – Aretha Franklin, Chaka Khan, Mahalia Jackson. It was truly spiritual. It made you understand what God was. We are all spirits. We get depressed. But music makes you want to live. I know my music has saved my life.' She was perfect for the times, offering both a continuity back to civil rights and sixties soul and a break – a shock of the new – that embraced hip-hop and electronic R&B.

Mary J. Blige came to the attention of Obama's inner political circle during his first presidential election campaign when she appeared at a series of get-out-the-vote rallies with hip-hop moguls Sean 'Puff Daddy' Combs and Jay-Z, and urban singer Beyoncé. The first of these was the Last Chance for Change rally at Florida Memorial University, followed by a street party in Philadelphia. Crowds spilled out into the surrounding area, stopping traffic and evoking memories of the rent parties of twenties Harlem. The race against Republican war veteran John McCain and his running mate Sarah Palin was tightening and Sean Combs wore a T-shirt emblazoned with the words 'Vote or Die' in a plea to African American voters to come out and support Obama. 'We have a responsibility to ourselves, our children and our country and our new leader, but we have to go out and vote to make the difference,' Blige said at the height of the rally.

In the first months of Obama's presidency, she became one of black America's new superstars, selling 80 million records worldwide and joining the super-league of modern R&B artists. Her story carried a powerful weight of its own. She was born in the Bronx, just as hip-hop began to surface in the schoolyards and public parks of Morrisania. Her mother Cora was an alcoholic, but, as a nurse, it was her wages that subsidised the family. Her father Thomas, an unpredictable Vietnam veteran turned low-paid jazz musician, left the family home when Mary was only nine. As a child, she moved in with her grandparents in

Richmond Hill, Georgia, where she was sexually molested by a family friend. But she also absorbed a different way of life there, joining her grandfather's Pentecostal church choir and, like so many African American singers before her, including Aretha Franklin, Gladys Knight and Whitney Houston, she shone as a gospel prodigy. In her early teens, Blige returned to live with her mother in the William A. Schlobohm Housing projects, in Yonkers. Already flirting with the music industry, she didn't graduate from high school.

She was working as a telephone directory services assistant on what was known as the '4-1-1 beat' when one of her demo tapes was picked up by the Uptown Records label. She joined their studio as a backing singer. A solo album was not far off, and its title, *What's the 411?* (Uptown, 1992), was borrowed from the argot of her day job. In something of a musical realignment, Blige brought the gospel and soul traditions together with urban hip-hop.

'Growing up in New York was all about learning how to survive,' she told National Public Radio. 'Learning how to live through tough times. Learning how to be quiet when you're supposed to be quiet. Learning how to speak when you're supposed to speak. That's what New York taught me. It taught me the more rigid side of life.' She has described how 'New York made us really street smart and tough, but the musical influence came from both the North and the South and from my grandparents'. It was this confluence of North and South, of the Church and the Projects, that led to Mary J. Blige inheriting a repurposed title from Aretha: the Queen of Hip-Hop Soul.

On 18 January 2009, at We Are One, Obama's inaugural celebration, the President set the tone for a new kind of leadership. He was by now suffused in the story of black music but smart enough to understand the symbolism of rock and pop, so he put together a concert that touched almost every base in America. Bruce Springsteen, the wordsmith of blue-collar patriotism, headed a bill that included Irish rock gods U2, heartland-rock singer John Cougar Mellencamp, country-rock singer Garth Brooks, jazz musician Herbie Hancock, Latin diva Shakira, singer-songwriter Sheryl Crow and a battalion of R&B performers, among them Beyoncé, will.i.am, John Legend and Usher.

It was Mary J. Blige who stole the show.

Dressed all in white on a bitterly cold day, she stood on the steps of the Lincoln Memorial, the site of Martin Luther King's 1963 'I Have a Dream' speech, and sang with an awareness of the symbolism of King's implied presence. Her set was carefully curated to refer backwards to the civil rights movement and forwards to the legacy on which her own generation drew. The song that stood out was her version of Bill Withers' 1972 hit 'Lean On Me'. For a moment, the cameras cut to Michelle Obama in the front row, mouthing the lyrics as if this was the most important song ever sung – and for a few triumphant moments it was. This was a song that had been inspired by the socialism and community spirit of Slab Fork, West Virginia, the small mining town where Withers grew up in abject poverty. It was a perfect anthem for Obama, for the Rust Belt towns that had voted for him and for the caring America he hoped to forge, with affordable healthcare and revitalised communities. Obama's vision was a society where there was always, metaphorically at least, a shoulder to lean on.

On the evening of Obama's formal inauguration on 20 January, Michelle and Barack greeted the crowds at the Washington Convention Center for the Neighbourhood Inaugural Ball, described by the press as 'an egalitarian festival where his ordinary supporters hogged the lime-light from the great, the good and the glamorous'. Mary J. Blige sang a version of 'Just Fine' (Geffen, 2007), which she introduced with a few heady, aspirational words: 'Today is the beginning of no more separa-tion.' She was only upstaged by the arrival of the President himself, in white bow tie and tuxedo. The stars and stripes fluttered behind him as he uttered the words 'Hey, America', in a nod to one of James Brown's most famous songs. 'This is an inauguration for all Americans,' he continued. 'I wanted to make sure that we had an event that would be open to our new neighbourhood here in Washington D.C., and also neighbourhoods across the country.' It was a raucous and largely local crowd, encouraged by free tickets and affordable seats, and it became the first official inaugural ball of its kind, a show built around a neighbourhood rather than an elite. The event was made possible by Obama's high-profile donors: George Soros, Steven Spielberg, Halle Berry and Berry Gordy, the founder of Motown Records, which had remained faithful to the Democratic Party since its foundation in 1958. The celebrations featured an unprecedented ten official balls, bringing together Washington powerbrokers, Hollywood celebrities, the swaggering stars of hip-hop and, carefully arranged centre-stage, the people who helped elect the first black president. Nas, one of the greatest rappers and wordsmiths of all time, captured the sense of history when he said, 'I never stood for any president in my life, never voted, before Barack Obama. It changed my life to vote. It starts there with me. I never cared for politics before Barack Obama. I never thought it mattered to people like me.'

The ball concluded with the couple's first presidential dance, to Beyoncé singing 'At Last'. The song, which was synonymous with R&B singer Etta James, linked romance and emancipation, the dream that Martin Luther King spoke of and the dream of love itself – a 'dream to press your cheek to'. Michelle Obama, as she would do in the years to come, took the lead, guiding her husband around the stage. Obama attended all ten balls in different venues in Washington, returning home to the White House after midnight, exhausted and ready for bed. Instead, the couple joined a late-night private party in the East Wing, featuring the Wynton Marsalis Quintet.

Later that year, Mary J. Blige supported the Obamas at the traditional Christmas in Washington celebration at the National Building Museum, an annual event since the Kennedy era. She returned to Washington in 2012 to sing at the Democratic Convention, between short sets by James Taylor and Foo Fighters. Wearing a fitted silver and gold gown, Blige kicked off with an emotional rendering of U2's song 'One' as delegates clapped along, followed by her own song, 'Family Affair', a sexually loaded party song. 'Get it crunk for President Obama!' she told the packed arena, using an urban word for partying to the max that might have sent a shiver of bafflement through Obama's people. They worked hard to maintain his respectability across mainstream America and were keen to prevent any ghetto talk straying into profanity or causing political outrage. For example, Obama never invited the rap outlaws Public Enemy to the White House, perhaps recognising the potential controversy inherent in songs such as the street anthem 'Fight The Power', which raged against American icons Elvis and John Wayne – although both Michelle and Barack have included the rappers' songs on personal playlists over the years.

For all his openness to new music, Obama was, at heart, a conciliator and did his best not to offend anyone. When the rapper Common was invited to appear at the White House in 2011, the right-wing press tried to throw up a dust storm, claiming that Common's rap 'A Son For Assata' glorified the former Black Liberation Army activist, Joanne Chesimard (born JoAnne Byron and now known as Assata Shakur). Shakur was convicted of the murder of a New Jersey State Trooper, Werner Foerster, in 1973 but escaped to Cuba, where she was granted political asylum in 1984. She remains on the FBI's Most Wanted Terrorists list to this day. It was a flash-in-the-pan controversy, stoked by Sarah Palin and Karl Rove, a former adviser to George Bush. Nonetheless, it was a reminder to Obama that hip-hop was a genre that might never gain universal acceptance within Beltway politics and that for much of the presidencies of George H. W. Bush and Bill Clinton it was a genre widely demonised by the mainstream media.

In his collection of essays, 'We Were Eight Years in Power', Ta-Nehisi Coates, suggested that Obama was held back by his anxieties about the complexities of race: 'Despite his sloganeering for change and progress, Obama is a conservative revolutionary, and nowhere is his conservative character revealed more than in the very sphere where he holds singular gravity – race.' Obama loved the idea of hip-hop rocking the White House, but he was wise enough to its history to know that it was divisive music, employing an urban language that was often replete with sexism and unvarnished language, that had glamourised the gun and was not as tolerant as the music of the civil rights movement. Obama and his people handpicked the artists and the material they engaged, careful to avoid controversy or hand an opportunity to his many critics.

In October 2020, talking to the BBC, Chuck D of Public Enemy described how he'd hoped that Obama being in the White House would have balanced out some of the distorted representation of black people that had built up 'animosity and hate' over the years, but he concluded that dislike of the President was plain 'old school racism' and that these prejudices worked in favour of Donald Trump.

The tension between hip-hop and what was perceived as public acceptability had been tested in previous presidential disputes. In March 1992, President George H. W. Bush had fought a very public battle against Ice-T and Body Count's metal rap track, 'Cop Killer', and in June 1992, presidential candidate Bill Clinton repudiated the MC and activist Sister Souljah for what he saw as intemperate remarks about racial violence. Obama and his campaign team ensured that there were no catastrophic blunders on the way to success. The exit polls showed that Obama had won the largest share of white support of any Democrat in a two-man race since 1976 and that a remarkable 54 per cent of young white voters supported him, compared with 44 per cent who voted for Republican John McCain. Although 96 per cent of black voters supported Obama, it was his success in white working-class communities that had taken him over the line.

Back on the campaign trail to re-elect Obama in November 2012, Blige and actress Julianne Moore appeared in a commercial supporting Planned Parenthood, an organisation that provides sex education and reproductive health care. Dressed in bright pink 'Yes We Plan' T-shirts, the pair urged voters to protect women's health choices by turning out for Obama. Blige told *Rolling Stone*: 'He's our generation. He knows it. He gets us, and he gets all of pop culture. That's a great president. That means he's not dealing with just one generation – he's dealing with all generations, and children are enlightening him on things. He's very real, down to earth. He's not missing out on the real world.'

Blige was back at the White House in February 2014 to perform at a state dinner on the South Lawn of the White House for French President François Hollande. It was an auspicious event and an achievement for Blige, who had now surpassed Ray Charles, Mahalia Jackson and Aretha Franklin to make the most appearances on behalf of a president. Soulful signature tunes had become a familiar part of campaigning, pioneered by Obama himself. An example was Kendrick Lamar's 'Alright', which seemed to signal a highly personal kind of hope. The black music website okayplayer described the song as a whisper of perseverance, 'like warm soup, nourishing the soul during the coldest day of winter'. In November 2020, Kamala Harris walked on stage at the Chase Center in Wilmington, Delaware, to deliver her first speech as vice-president-elect to the strains of another signature tune, Blige's 'Work That'. Harris had deployed the song many times since the Democratic primaries: Blige had become the unofficial queen of the Democratic movement. Wearing white in homage to the suffragettes and echoing the lyrics of 'Work That', Harris was cheered as she said, 'While I may be the first woman in this office,

I will not be the last. Every little girl that's watching tonight sees that this is a country of possibilities.'

Blige, like Obama, had become a personification of change, her performances a sign that black music was no longer solely the music of spiritual devotion or civil rights – it was the music of the modern family. It was no longer the music of the outsider or the disadvantaged, it was the audacious music of modern popular America. It felt entirely natural that she would appear yet again at an inauguration, this time sharing the bill with the father of Democratic rock, Bruce Springsteen, to champion Joe Biden's swearing-in as president and bid a relieved farewell to Donald Trump.

In June 2016, Biden and Obama had travelled together to Orlando, Florida, a year after the church killings in Charleston, to console the survivors, relatives and staff in the aftermath of the Pulse nightclub shootings, where forty-nine people were killed and fifty-three wounded by gunman Omar Mateen. Pulse was a popular bar and nightclub that attracted a predominately male clientele. Mateen's homicidal rampage still baffles investigators, and theories abounded that he was an ISIS-trained terrorist, a vengeful homophobe or a gay man who had turned brutally on a nightclub he knew well. The 29-year-old was born in New York to Afghan parents and had had a chequered career in law enforcement and security. He posted several messages on Facebook about seeking revenge for US airstrikes in the hours before the mass shooting, the second worst in the country's history.

Along with Vice-President Joe Biden, Obama placed forty-nine white roses at a memorial for the victims at a performing arts centre near Orlando's city hall. The touching ceremony came just a few days before gun control legislation failed to find a majority in the Senate. Obama told the grieving families in Orlando:

> For so many people here who are lesbian, gay, bisexual, transgender, the Pulse Nightclub has always been a safe haven, a place to sing and dance, and most importantly, to be who you truly are – including for so many people whose families are originally from Puerto Rico. Sunday morning, that sanctuary was violated in the worst way imaginable. So, whatever the motivations of the killer, whatever influences led him down the path of violence and terror, whatever propaganda he was

consuming from ISIL and al Qaeda, this was an act of terrorism, but it was also an act of hate. This was an attack on the LGBT community. Americans were targeted because we're a country that has learned to welcome everyone, no matter who you are or who you love. And hatred towards people because of sexual orientation, regardless of where it comes from, is a betrayal of what's best in us.

One of Pulse's anthems, played regularly in similar clubs throughout Florida, was 'Dance (Louie Vega Latin Soul Version)' featuring gospel giants the Clark Sisters and the Winans. It is an immersive history of modern America, a propulsive dance track overseen by a Puerto Rican club genius from the Bronx, who conducted soaring Christian voices over a spiralling and hypnotic mix. Obama seemed increasingly attuned to the changing beat of America and, unfailingly, he found words to describe the tragedy of mass shootings. Speaking of the dancers on the floor at Pulse, he said, 'We often say people were in the wrong place at the wrong time, but they were in the right place, a place they loved and felt safe.'

As soul music's numerous ancestors continued to dominate popular music, the Queen of Soul abdicated her throne. Aretha announced that 2018 would be the last year she would tour. A month later, she cancelled a string of performances, citing health concerns. She never sang for Obama or the Democratic Party again. Franklin died of cancer at the age of 76 on the morning of 16 August 2018, at her home in Detroit, surrounded by friends and family. Her publicist Gwendolyn Quinn, who had worked closely with the singer since her days at Arista Records, said: 'In one of the darkest moments of our lives, we are not able to find the appropriate words to express the pain in our heart. We have lost the matriarch and rock of our family. The love she had for her children, grandchildren, nieces, nephews, and cousins knew no bounds.' Aretha lay in state at the Charles H. Wright Museum of African American History in Detroit, where there had recently been an award-winning exhibition of the 1967 Detroit Rebellion. Thousands queued round the building to pay their respects.

Obama's friend and one-time presidential rival, the Republican senator and Vietnam war veteran John McCain, had also died. His was a funeral bristling with personal hurt. McCain's daughter Meghan directed her anguish at the uninvited Donald Trump, a man she had grown to loathe. She told the 2,500 guests: 'We gather to mourn the passing of American greatness, the real thing, not cheap rhetoric from men who'll never come near the sacrifice he gave so willingly nor the opportunistic appropriation of those who lived lives of comfort and privilege while he suffered and served.'

Other commitments prevented Obama from attending Aretha Franklin's funeral at Detroit's Greater Grace Temple, so the Democratic Party was represented by Bill and Hillary Clinton. Obama did, however, write a letter, which the Reverend Al Sharpton read at the funeral.

> Michelle and I extend our heartfelt sympathies to all those who have gathered in Detroit, and we join you in remembering and celebrating the life of the Queen of Soul. From a young age, Aretha Franklin rocked the world of anyone who had the pleasure of hearing her voice. Whether bringing people together through a thrilling intersection of genres or advancing important causes through the power of song, Aretha's work reflected the very best of our American story – in all of its hope and heart, its boldness and its unmistakable beauty.
>
> In the example she set, both as an artist and a citizen, Aretha embodied those most revered virtues of forgiveness and reconciliation, while the music she made captured some of our deepest human desires: namely affection and respect. And through her own voice, Aretha lifted those of millions, empowering and inspiring the vulnerable, the downtrodden, and everyone who may have just needed a little love.
>
> Aretha truly was one of a kind. And as you pay tribute, know we'll be saying a little prayer for you. And we'll be thinking of all of Aretha's loved ones in the days and weeks to come.

With great strength of character, Jennifer Hudson sang the anthemic 'Amazing Grace' in front of the gold-plated Promethean casket in which Franklin rested before being entombed with her father in Detroit's famed Woodlawn Cemetery. She was posthumously awarded the Pulitzer Prize for her 'indelible contribution to American music and culture for more than five decades'. When Obama talked about her in public, which he did often, he didn't talk about her Grammy Awards or national achievements, choosing instead to describe the night he hosted a celebration of gospel music at the White House, headlined by Franklin and the Morgan State University Choir. The air-conditioning system had malfunctioned and an unforgiving heat had gripped the congregation, inspiring Aretha to even greater emotional intensity. Afterwards, Obama took to the stage for the official round of thanks. 'We've been to church tonight,' he said. 'It feels like old-time religion here. Air conditioner broke. Women all fanning themselves.' It was classic Obama, emotionally rich, kindling memories of the Deep South and speaking out to older Christians who might otherwise have felt excluded by his enthusiasm for secular soul and urban music.

In the final days of the Obama presidency, the cable network Black Entertainment Television (BET), commissioned a spectacular entitled *Love and Happiness: An Obama Celebration* to mark the family's departure from the White House. More than 300 guests assembled for the two-hour concert, among them supermodel Naomi Campbell, comedian Dave Chappelle and actor Bradley Cooper. Everyone was required to surrender their phones – a common practice when the Obamas wanted to relax – to prevent any inappropriate photos leaking onto social media. The crowd gathered on the South Lawn, where, just days before, the Obamas had hosted the Italian prime minister Matteo Renzi and his wife, Agnese Landini, for a final 'bittersweet' state dinner. In his opening welcome, President Obama joked, 'Much to your sadness and regret I will not be singing Al Green this evening.' He continued: 'While much of the music that you will hear this evening – gospel, R&B, rap – is rooted in the African American experience, it's not just black music. This is an essential part of the American experience. It's a mirror to who we are, and a reminder of who we can be.'

Obama's last event was a star-studded evening featuring speeches by Jesse Williams, Samuel L. Jackson, Bradley Cooper and Angela Bassett and performances from Usher, Common, De La Soul, Michelle Williams, Janelle Monáe, Yolanda Adams and Jill Scott. Also performing were Bell Biv Devoe, who were former members of the teen group New Edition and pioneers of the briefly fashionable soul genre new jack swing.

Jill Scott, a singer, poet and actor from North Philadelphia who had starred in the James Brown biopic *Get on Up* would soon appear in an entirely new kind of soul media phenomenon, Verzuz TV, a webcast created by rappers Timbaland and Swizz Beatz, which aired on Instagram Live and Facebook.

Verzuz, a virtual DJ battle featuring rival singers or MCs, emerged during the COVID-19 pandemic, when many people were stuck at home and in need of entertainment. During the vitriolic campaign to unseat Donald Trump in 2020, Verzuz became one of the main mechanisms for ensuring voter registration among African Americans. Michelle Obama was a massive fan and often appeared in short political infomercials along with Kamala Harris.

The music within the White House had changed beyond all recognition, transformed by the Obama family's taste and by the immediacy of social media and new platforms of communication. Soon, presidents and their advisers would rush to Twitter as a new era of instant reaction gripped politics. The BET extravaganza at the White House was not just a swansong for the Obama era; it was a glorious farewell to the kind of all-star television spectacular that dated back to the early days of television in the time of Dwight D. Eisenhower.

In his pitch-perfect introduction, Obama joked, 'There will also be no twerking tonight – at least not by me. I don't know about Usher.' A highlight of the night came when Angela Bassett, Queen Romanda in *Black Panther*, delivered an epic tribute to Michelle Obama.

> To be married to a man who's dedicated his life to something bigger than himself, who's committed to making the world a better place, is to live a life that looks beyond your own love for each other and to imagine a future beyond your own lives together – Mrs Obama, you have been a beacon of light these past eight years. You have been a paragon of dignity in the face of the worst kinds of politics. In the face of attacks and obstruction, you have been a steady reminder that the high road is the only road.

Bassett's remarks echoed the funeral oration of John McCain's daughter; both were barely concealed references to the incoming president Donald J. Trump, who not only despised Obama but was already planning to dismantle his legacy and destroy his reputation. He would eventually attack the Affordable Care Act, disrupt America's partnerships with countries throughout the world by withdrawing from the Paris Climate Agreement and rip up membership of the World Health Organisation in an extraordinary act of defiance that would ignore scientific and epidemiological advice during the COVID-19 pandemic.

In his 2020 memoir, *A Promised Land*, Obama described Trump's election as a triumph for 'the dark spirits that had long been lurking on the edges of the modern Republican party – xenophobia, anti-intellectualism, paranoid conspiracy theories, an antipathy toward black and brown folks'. Trump's presidency of division brought parts of America to insurrection and near civil war, but black music in all its urban forms was by then the most commercially successful music in the world. Inevitably, it did not recoil or stay silent. It rediscovered an angry voice that would reverberate around urban America and out onto the tense streets of Washington D.C. where a battle for the soul of America was looming yet again.

An American GI sports a peace sign during a combat operation outside Da Nang in South Vietnam, 1972.

2

HEY, HEY, LBJ! HOW MANY KIDS DID YOU KILL TODAY?

Listen Up: 'Sam Stone' by Swamp Dogg (1972)

Frankie Boyce was one of the unlucky ones. In what *TIME* magazine described as 'the jungled peaks and malarial valleys of the central Highlands', on 18 January 1969, his unit came under heavy enemy grenade, rocket and small-arms fire, and just over a year after his arrival in Vietnam, he was dead. Dak To was an area where the enemy had all the advantages: local knowledge, a vantage point from the hillsides and determined fighters living in and around the tribal villages that surrounded the town of Kontum. Boyce had dashed over open terrain to warn his comrades of infiltrating enemy forces, and in the ensuing battle, he was wounded and rushed to a field hospital, where he died two days later.

Back home, the heavy losses at Dak To were being spun like honeycomb. The Vietnam News Agency conservatively reported that 2,800 US soldiers and 700 from the Army of the Republic of Vietnam had perished in the intense battle, but despite being completely out-manoeuvred, the US military claimed the battle as a victory and proof of progress in the war. In reports on US television, much was made of the benign presence of the American forces; the CIA had launched the Village Defence Program, building dams, roads and bridges, and providing rudimentary health care for the Montagnard or 'people of the mountains', the indigenous people who had been corralled into supporting the American war effort as a modern military war surged through their communities.

Neil Sheehan, a war reporter for *The New York Times*, claimed at the time that a Special Forces colonel tried to prevent the carnage at Dak To, reportedly telling Boyce's commander Major General William R. Peers: 'For God's sake, General, don't send our people in there . . . That's what the bastards want us to do. They'll butcher our people.' And that is precisely what happened.

Boyce's body was flown home with his guitar and the handwritten lyrics of an unrecorded song, 'Soul Soldier'. He was buried with full military honours at Franklin Memorial Park, North Brunswick, New Jersey – a life cut short.

Boyce had been an aspiring soul musician, and until his tour of duty in Vietnam began in September 1968, he was a member of the New Jersey family group Jo Jo and the Admirers, which also featured three of his brothers. When he left for Vietnam, he was deputising as a guitarist with the soul harmony group the Parliaments, led by the charismatic eccentric, George Clinton. Clinton ran a barber's shop in Plainfield where Boyce had hung out, and was fostering a generation of musicians who were about to revolutionise the sound of black America. The Parliaments were enjoying some national success with their song 'I Wanna Testify' on Detroit's Revilot label when Boyce left, and they were now transforming into one of the most influential funk bands ever, the Parliament-Funkadelic collective, better known as P-Funk. Few could rival Clinton's visionary leadership as he waged war on sixties soul and shifted his band away from the well-established Motown sound to an afro-funk futurist style. Funkadelic's early trilogy of albums –

Funkadelic (1970), *Free Your Mind . . . And Your Ass Will Follow* (1970) and *Maggot Brain* (1971) – was soul music's shock of the new. Clinton defied classification and heralded a new decade, a new sound and substantial new talent. 'Yeah, free association and the first black group to do it,' he told local journalist William Leikam. 'There were a lot of groups doing rock 'n' roll: Sly and the Family Stone, the Chambers Brothers, but we were like all of it all at once. We were like Motown, Jimi Hendrix, James Brown, Eric Clapton, The Beatles. We were all of them at once.' According to the rock critic Robert Christgau, Funkadelic's challenging music 'scared the bejesus out of fans of upful blackness on both sides of America's widening racial divide'.

Vietnam was more than a war or a noble cause: it was what brought America to the harsh reality that it was no longer the greatest force for good in the world. Throughout the sixties, soul music had uncannily paralleled public attitudes to the war. The music evolved from naive patriotism to darkening doubt and then to full-scale rage and repudiation. It was a playlist that President Lyndon B. Johnson certainly never listened to, but soul music's shifting commentary on war would have dragged him deeper into the trough of despair that marred his later years in office. Speaking at a White House press conference on 28 July 1965, he had described the war as a matter of global obligation that portrayed the USA as the good cop in a world of evil. 'We do not seek the destruction of any government nor do we covet a foot of territory . . . but we insist, and we will always insist, that the people of South Vietnam shall have the right or the choice to shape their own destiny . . . and they shall not have any government imposed upon them by force and terror as long as we can prevent it . . . we did not choose to be guardians at the gate, but there is nobody else.'

From the military to Motown, almost everyone in America believed that the war would be a demonstration of exceptionalism which would reinforce their role as caretakers of the world. In the early, hopeful days, the small number of soul records that strayed from love affairs and dance crazes to address the war in Vietnam were either dutifully patriotic or conveyed a mood of romantic melancholy as, typically, a soldier left his lover at home for the battlefield overseas. The title of one of the first, 'Greetings (This Is Uncle Sam)' (Miracle, 1961) by the Valadiers, presented the war as a gallant adventure and the departing soldier as a liberator doing his duty. It was recorded soon after President John F. Kennedy sent detachments of Green Berets to South Vietnam in May 1961, and was an early commentary on America's involvement in a war that passed most people by. Produced in Detroit when the Motown Corporation was still in its infancy, it was one of Berry Gordy's few ventures into white pop, a recording by one of a myriad of white garage bands that were emerging across the small towns and suburbs of Michigan. Sentiments had not greatly changed by the time Marvin Gaye sang 'A Soldier's Plea' (Tamla, 1962), which opened with a call-to-action drum roll and portrayed the war as a 'fight for freedom'.

Four years later, 'Christmas In Vietnam' (Rojac, 1966) by the precocious young soul singer Private Charles Bowens and his group, the Gentleman from Tigerland, sang a brutally honest dispatch, as if from the heart of the battlefield. It was recorded in Harlem and featured a group assembled in Bowen's regimental base in Fort Polk, Louisiana. By that time, Vietnam had moved from the distant edges of foreign affairs to the heart of American life. Yet, despite the draft cards that were dropping into mailboxes across the land, most Americans had no great knowledge of Vietnam nor that they were being embroiled in a savage imperial war against people with much to fight for. Ho Chi Minh, the revolutionary president, had already warned the American military of the determination of his people: 'Our resistance will be long and painful,' he stated, 'but whatever the sacrifices, however long the struggle, we shall fight to the end, until Vietnam is fully independent and reunified.'

A key moment in changing public attitudes came with the historic speech – 'A Time to Break Silence' – delivered by Martin Luther King at the Riverside Church in New York City, on 4 April 1967. The speech was explosive, and it alienated King from the presidency and instilled vengeance in the offices of the FBI.

> There is at the outset a very obvious and almost facile connection between the war in Vietnam and the struggle I, and others, have been waging in America. A few years ago there was a shining moment in that struggle. It seemed as if there was a real promise of hope for the poor – both black and white – through the poverty program.

There were experiments, hopes, new beginnings. Then came the buildup in Vietnam and I watched the program broken and eviscerated as if it were some idle political plaything of a society gone mad on war, and I knew that America would never invest the necessary funds or energies in rehabilitation of its poor so long as adventures like Vietnam continued to draw men and skills and money like some demonic destructive suction tube. So I was increasingly compelled to see the war as an enemy of the poor and to attack it as such.

By connecting the struggle of civil rights and the war on poverty to the battlefield abroad, King was challenging mainstream thinking about the conflict. And twenty-four days later, another heavyweight champion was about to do the same.

Muhammad Ali had become an unlikely symbol of resistance to the war. His own brushes with the military dated back to 1960, when the teenage 'Cassius Clay' registered for the draft with Selective Service Local Board No. 47 in his native Louisville. Nearly four years later, a month before he fought Sonny Liston for the heavyweight championship of the world, the boxer was ordered to attend a military aptitude test at an Armed Forces Induction Centre in Florida. He had not been singled out. Like many young men of his generation, he was part of the military's general trawl of likely recruits, a victim of random bureaucracy rather than racism or collusion. Despite the fast-talking style that had earned him the nickname the 'Louisville Lip', he had a low IQ and poor literacy skills. He failed the military test and was officially classified as 1-Y – unqualified for military service. 'I said I was the greatest, not the smartest,' Ali joked years later, but the failure to meet even the most basic levels of literacy haunted him and led to years of over-compensation. Recruitment officers regularly toured inner-city ghettos as part of what was known as Project 100,000, an initiative devised by Defence Secretary Robert McNamara to recruit those individuals who had previously been rejected for failing to meet the army's most basic physical and mental-aptitude requirements. Many poorly educated African Americans found themselves drafted after military recruitment centres sprung up in ghettos across the land, in cities like Detroit, Memphis, Cleveland and Philadelphia. In a 1995 article, the *Washington*

Monthly described what would become known as 'McNamara's Folly': 'the program offered a one-way ticket to Vietnam, where these men fought and died in disproportionate numbers . . . the men of the "Moron Corps" provided the necessary cannon fodder to help evade the political horror of dropping student deferments or calling up the reserves, which were sanctuaries for the lily-white.' Forty-one per cent of those recruits were black compared with only twelve per cent in the armed forces. It was a scheme with a built-in social bias and one that some Black Power radicals called 'state-sponsored genocide'.

Ali's popularity in the Projects was in marked contrast to the cooler regard of the boxing cognoscenti. The fight authorities had yet to embrace the vociferous, excitable young champ, and his conversion to Islam had rattled the conservative world of boxing to its core. Columnist Jimmy Cannon of the *New York Post* could not bring himself to endorse Ali and berated him as a coward and a draft-dodger. He regarded Ali's draft evasion as symptomatic of the sixties and refused to call him by his Muslim name.

Events were crowding in on the President and on Muhammad Ali. With Project 10,000's reclassification of the criteria for military service, Ali was now 1-A: 'fit for military service'. His previous failures to meet the required level of mental aptitude were consigned to the past. He was instructed to report for induction in his hometown of Louisville, but lawyers managed to delay the date and shift the venue to Houston, Texas, to allow Ali to prepare for his fight with Zora Folley. As the date for his induction approached, Ali grew increasingly critical of the draft and the integrity of the war itself, and his high-profile resistance found favour among Detroit's black militants, who had, dating back to 1965, launched a campaign to urge '50,000 angry blacks to appear at the Fort Wayne Induction Center to destroy the draft'.

Ali's argument that he was a conscientious objector, not a coward, fell on deaf military ears. He had run out of road. On 28 April 1967, he was instructed to report to the Armed Forces Examining and Entrance Station in Houston. It was non-negotiable. Like many young men of his generation, Ali was staring Vietnam in the face and the clock was ticking on his heavyweight career. The Houston station processed 440 inductees a month, all of them bound for Vietnam. On the pavement, a small posse of protesters gathered in support of Ali. One smartass carried a placard saying, 'DRAFT BEER – NOT ALI', and another young black demonstrator, risking immediate arrest, set fire to his draft card and held it aloft to the cheering crowd. Inside, names were called out in alphabetical order, and inevitably 'Cassius Marcellus Clay' was announced. Ali stood rigid, and when it became clear he would neither acknowledge the name nor step forward and accept the draft, a Navy lieutenant escorted him down the hall and informed him that he had committed a felony by breaching the Universal Military Training and Service Act. Ali acknowledged the charge but again refused to acknowledge his name whereupon he was invited to agree to a statement: 'I refuse to be inducted into the armed forces of the United States because I claim to be exempt as a Minister of the religion of Islam.'

Behind the scene, months earlier, he had been more loquacious with the press:

Why should they ask me to put on a uniform and go 10,000 miles from home and drop bombs and bullets on brown people in Vietnam while so-called Negro people in Louisville are treated like dogs and denied simple human rights? No, I am not going 10,000 miles from home to help murder and burn another poor nation simply to continue the domination of white slave masters of the darker people the world over. This is the day when such evils must come to an end. I have been warned that to take such a stand would put my prestige in jeopardy and could cause me to lose millions of dollars which should accrue to me as the champion. But I have said it once and I will say it again. The real enemy of my people is right here. I will not disgrace my religion, my people or myself by becoming a tool to enslave those who are fighting for their own justice, freedom, and equality . . . If I thought the war was going to bring freedom and equality to 22 million of my people they wouldn't have to draft me, I'd join tomorrow. But I either have to obey the laws of the land or the laws of Allah. I have nothing to lose by standing up for my beliefs. So I'll go to jail. We've been in jail for 400 years.

Contrasting Ali's career with the harsh reality of war was often used in the press to portray him as arrogant and cowardly. In his defence, Ali appealed to the core principles of American justice.

*

I strongly object to the fact that so many newspapers have given the American public and the world the impression that I have only two alternatives in taking this stand: either I go to jail or go to the Army. There is another alternative and that alternative is justice. If justice prevails, if my Constitutional rights are upheld, I will be forced to go neither to the Army nor jail. In the end I am confident that justice will come my way for the truth must eventually prevail.

By now, the FBI was monitoring Ali around the clock as he toured campuses and spoke out ever more virulently against the war. His movements were tracked, his phones tapped, and his hectic travel schedule involved a relay of FBI field-office staff. In Atlanta, agent R. R. Nichols, who oversaw the local wire-tap unit, intercepted a series of phone calls between Ali and Martin Luther King, in which they discussed the boxer's legal predicament, his conversion to Islam and their shared opposition to the war. King recommended that Ali contact his close associate, Chauncey Eskridge, the Chicago-based lawyer who acted as legal counsel for King's Southern Christian Leadership Conference. Ali took the advice and met Eskridge a few days later; they struck up an agreement that took them on a long journey to the US Supreme Court where, in 1971, Ali's status as a conscientious objector was finally acknowledged.

With Chauncey Eskridge leading his defence, Ali won his battle with the US military but only on a legal technicality. Case law determined that to qualify as a conscientious objector three basic tenets had to be met: 'He must show that he is conscientiously opposed to war in any form'; 'He must show that this opposition is based upon religious training and belief'; and 'He must show this objection was sincere.' Paradoxically, it was the first tenet that caught the Nation of Islam and Muhammad in a bind. Ali was opposed to the Vietnam War but, according to the government's legal team, was not opposed to war 'in any form'. His religion, and the teachings of the Koran, required him to wage war against the unbelievers and to embrace the concept of Holy War. Ali's appeal nearly collapsed on the interpretation of a single word: jihad. It was an unfamiliar term, a word whose time had yet to come. Finally, a legal technicality came to Ali's rescue. The law had not been specific enough about which of the three tenets they were finding against.

It was a victory narrower than anything he had achieved in the ring but, however arduously won, it allowed Ali to return to professional boxing.

Heroism could not disguise the undercurrent of anger and unrest. The war was beginning to lay bare uncomfortable demographic truths on the home front. By 1965, when the war had yet to peak, African Americans already accounted for at least twenty-three per cent of the enlisted soldiers killed in action. Only eight per cent of personnel who served within the borders of South Vietnam were classified as 'black' but over twelve per cent, or 5,711, of casualties were African American. Although statistics are open to interpretation and can tell many stories, there was an increasing – and legitimate – perception that African American men were now disproportionately victims in Vietnam and that young, often uneducated black youths were being used as cannon fodder. In his enduring article 'War Within a War', journalist James Maycock described a country riddled with institutional racism.

> In 1967, there were no black Americans on the boards in Alabama, Arkansas, Mississippi and Louisiana. In fact, Jack Helms, a member of the Louisiana draft board, was a Grand Wizard in the Ku Klux Klan. In one fatuous outburst, he described the NAACP (National Association for the Advancement of Colored People), the highly respected and conservative black civil rights group, as 'a communist-inspired, anti-Christ, sex-perverted group of tennis-short beatniks'. Although a poll in 1966 established that three out of four black Americans supported the draft, by 1969 56% of the black American population opposed the Vietnam war.

The war was affecting music too and edging closer to Black America's most famous musical label, Motown. G. C. Cameron, soon to become the lead singer of the Spinners, was serving in the Marines. Mary Wilson and Diana Ross of The Supremes both had brothers on active service in Vietnam. Ross described her brother, Earl Fred Ross Jr, as a man racked by self-doubt.

> Many of his friends were dying of drug addiction either in Vietnam or when they came back, and he had lost faith in nearly everybody. It was sad to see what had happened to him. We used to send him letters and packages with little things we knew he missed like mustard . . .

He wrote us about how scared he was and how his friends kept dying over there. He was afraid of people he wasn't supposed to be afraid of, other Americans, especially some of the officers. He felt he couldn't trust them.

By the late sixties, those letters and packages from home had become the biggest songwriting metaphor for distant love. Numerous soul songs were crafted around letters, among them Emanuel Lasky's 'A Letter From Vietnam' (Westbound, 1968), Gloria Edwards' 'Something You Couldn't Write About' (Jetstream, 1968) and, as the numbers of war amputees rocketed, the darkly poignant 'I Can't Write Left-Handed' by Bill Withers (Sussex, 1973).

In combat zones, the United Service Organizations (USO) provided recreation and live entertainment to military personnel in a bid to boost morale. It went to great effort to secure the support of popular mainstream entertainers such as Bob Hope. His material was usually the familiar schtick about golf, baseball and the girls back home but periodically he threw in jokes that were edgier and aimed squarely at President Johnson. In 1967, in Vietnam, he joked: 'President Johnson couldn't be here tonight. He's busy. He's placing a wreath on the tomb of the "unknown foreign policy".' It played well among disgruntled troops but not in the increasingly sensitive Oval Office. Johnson had to grin and bear being the butt of such jibes, and during his 1964 presidential campaign against Senator Barry Goldwater, he wrote to Hope asking if he could use some of his jokes in his speeches. Bob Hope obliged.

As part of the USO programme, in the summer of 1966, The Supremes touched down in Okinawa on the first stop of their Asian tour. Little more than a promotional kitsch fest, the band members dressed as geishas, were photographed in a bonsai garden, rode rickshaws through the streets of Taipei and donned washerwomen outfits in a local village. It was only when they boarded the USS *Coral Sea* at Yokasuka navy base that the atmosphere changed. The ship was a support vessel for Operation Rolling Thunder, the systematic bombing of military targets in North Vietnam. On board, they were asked to sing for the wounded, and Diana Ross later recalled feeling 'dizzy' when she met a double amputee recently shipped in from Vietnam. They sang 'Baby Love' to the crippled soldier, backed by a small tape recorder, and Mary Wilson later recorded the trip in print.

> We made a special stop at a military hospital that had a large burns unit, where many of the badly hurt soldiers were sent for treatment. Against the advice of our military escort we visited the burn victims. It was one of the most emotional experiences of my life; I had never imagined that human beings could be so brutally injured and live with so much pain. It was all we could do to keep from crying in front of them.

On 3 June 1967, as complaints about racism within the armed services escalated, the USO announced a new initiative: 'James Brown – and a show of 25 – will sock it to 'em on a USO tour of military bases in the Pacific.' The sixteen-day tour was destined for Japan, Korea, Okinawa and then Vietnam. Behind the scenes, a campaign was afoot to boycott USO concerts overseas, arguing that they propped up the war effort and so discriminated against black personnel. Brown retaliated, telling journalists, 'I'm as much opposed to the war in Vietnam as anyone who loves peace. But I can't turn my back on my own black brothers in Vietnam when they call upon me to entertain them. We're going to Vietnam despite the criticism and despite the risks. We are not afraid of right. We are afraid of wrong.' Brown's itinerary took him to the Tan Son Nhut air base near Saigon, where 2,000 packed into a makeshift stage off the runways, and then Phan Rang, home to the 336th Tactical Fighter Squadron and, later, a base for the controversial spreading of Agent Orange. The herbicide was used to destroy the jungle, undergrowth and natural canopies which camouflaged the guerrilla armies of the National Liberation Front. Remembering his descent into Phan Rang, James Brown famously said, 'We went back there where the *Apocalypse Now* stuff was going on.' The final concert was at the old French military airfield at Camp Bearcat, temporary home to the 9th Infantry Division, where the audience stood on upturned braziers and makeshift bleachers.

The US Army's official newspaper *Stars and Stripes* gave the show a rave review. 'The sweat ran off James Brown's face,' the excited reporter wrote at the time. 'He sang and went through a routine of dazzling footwork that is one of his trademarks and the audience was clapping in time with the beat. "Soul Brother Number One" had been on stage about two minutes. He stepped up to the mike and spoke briefly with the more than 1,000 servicemen and women packed into Saigon's Tan Son Nhut AB's water-soaked main theater. It was the second show of the night. Both were standing-room-only audiences with hundreds more turned away at the doors.'

Martha and the Vandellas' catchy single 'Jimmy Mack' had been recorded in 1964 and rejected by Motown's quality control system, but by late 1966, it was back on the Motown schedule. In the summer of 1967, the effervescent song was on the playlist of every urban radio station and touching the nerves of young women who had brothers, fathers, boyfriends and husbands in Vietnam. The hookline – 'Jimmy Mack, when are you coming back?' – had taken on an unintended meaning and the song sold spectacularly well. A year later, another Vandellas song – 'Forget Me Not', the B-side of 'I Promise To Wait My Love' – had an explicit Vietnam theme. The writer, Motown staffer Sylvia Moy, who had grown up with Martha Reeves in North East Detroit, became the first woman to win a producer's credit at the label when she dedicated the song to her departing brother, Melvin, who had joined the Navy and was bound for Vietnam.

Motown was a Democratic Party corporation to the core, but throughout the sixties it was unfailingly patriotic. Berry Gordy was a veteran of the Korean War and supported the military effort in Vietnam, but many of his artists were becoming increasingly sceptical. In mid June 1967, The Supremes flew to the West Coast to honour a long-standing contract to perform a residency at the Cocoanut Grove in Los Angeles. Motown had also agreed a side contract with White House aides that, on the final night, the girls would be rushed through the late-night traffic to perform for LBJ at a $500-a-plate President's Club Dinner at the Century Plaza Hotel. A coalition of students and pacifists were preparing for up to 50,000 demonstrators and local radicals were predicting 'the biggest anti-war demonstration in history'. Fearing for the President's safety, his aides abandoned the traditional police motorcade and put in place secret plans to fly him into the rear of the hotel via helicopter. Protesters gathered at the nearby Cheviot Hills Recreation Center to hear Muhammad Ali and the prominent peace campaigner and paediatrician Benjamin Spock give emotional speeches, and then, as dusk fell, they began the mile-long march to the President's hotel.

According to reports in the *L.A. Times*, 'a coalition of 80 anti-war groups staged a march to the Century Plaza Hotel where President Lyndon B. Johnson was being honoured'. LAPD field commander John A. McAllister expected 1,000 or 2,000 protesters. 'When the mass of humanity came up Avenue of the Stars and over the hill, I was astounded,' he recalled. 'Where did all those people come from? I asked myself.' Although the protesters had a legal permit to demonstrate, a Santa Monica Superior Court judge issued a last-minute injunction forbidding them to halt outside the hotel entrance. As the streets surrounding the Century Plaza became jammed, the sheer volume of marchers made that an impossible condition to meet, and 1,300 police, one of the largest security forces ever gathered in California, tore into the crowd. A bloody riot erupted. As the violence flared, *Air Force One* descended into Los Angeles International Airport at 7.30 p.m. On board were the President, his wife Lady Bird, nine leading congressmen, a small, hand-picked group of staff and an even smaller press corps. Agent Thomas 'Lem' Johns of the Secret Service stayed close to Johnson throughout. He had been in Dealey Plaza in Dallas when President Kennedy was assassinated and now had the role of shielding Johnson. Having received requests from Defence Secretary Robert McNamara and General William C. Westmoreland for further investment in troop numbers, the President was putting the final touches to what would be a difficult announcement. At this point, 500 American soldiers were dying every month.

To this day, there is no unanimity as to whether the events on the ground were spontaneous or the outcome of a deliberate strategy by the LAPD. According to *L.A. Times* staff writer Kenneth Reich, 'The original idea was to stage a march from Rancho Park, up Pico Boulevard and past the hotel on Avenue of the Stars, then turn onto Santa Monica Boulevard and go home. But as the marchers reached the hotel, a vanguard of radicals ignored the terms of the police permit and sat down in the street. Police to this day say the decision of perhaps 100 demonstrators to sit down on Avenue of the Stars forced their hand.' With hostility rising and the number of marchers swelling, police claimed that they thought the demonstrators might storm the hotel.

Subsequent reports suggest that the dark arts of police surveillance were already at work. There were claims that the police were being fed information by a private security firm, which was hired by the hotel and employed four undercover agents who worked closely with the LAPD. Police claim that they issued a dispersal order several times over a powerful loudspeaker, but many demonstrators said that it was inaudible above the noisy chanting. Then, according to Reich's report, 'hundreds of officers moved in, their nightsticks held in front of them, pushing the demonstrators away. Some of the people fought back. Some photographs show police swinging their nightsticks at marchers who were not resisting.' A particularly brutal clash took place under the Olympic Boulevard bridge where demonstrators were bundled into a vacant lot and beaten viciously.

By now, the USA had 470,000 active service personnel in Vietnam and the President was about to announce a further 45,000; these extra troops threatened to take the fiscal budget soaring beyond $8.5 billion. President Johnson faced the perfect storm: an increasingly unpopular war, the prospect of increased taxation to fund its expansion and a $29 billion budget deficit, the biggest since 1945 – according to the President, 'hard and inescapable facts'. The portents were dire. A three-page advert in the dinner's commemorative menu had been bought by opponents of the war. It must have made uncomfortable reading for the President – 'As of this date, we 8,000 Democrats of Southern California are dis-associating ourselves from you because of your conduct of the war in Vietnam' – and soured the taste of the expensive French cuisine, which was described in grandiose terms: Le Salade Johann Strauss, Le Filet de Boeuf Forestiére, Pointes d'Asperges Fraiches and Rochers de Glace Assortis followed by Petits Fours.

At 10 p.m., as the comedian Jack Benny stood up to host the dinner, protests were still raging outside. According to the President's press secretary, George Reedy, they could hear the noise above the PA system in the hotel. 'It bothered the hell out of him to see the students chanting, "Hey, hey, LBJ, how many kids did you kill today?"' At 10.30 p.m., less than twenty minutes after they had finished their Cocoanut Grove show, The Supremes took to the hotel stage and sang classic Motown hits and show tunes. Diana Ross thanked the President, and as she blew him her trademark kiss, FBI agents and the Secret Service were preparing for his hurried and ignominious departure via the backstairs and a waiting helicopter. The President asked for autographs for his daughter Lynda, and by 11.45 p.m. he was back at the airport. It had been a fiasco.

The anti-war protest smouldered into the night. The Supremes returned to their suites high above the damage outside the Century Plaza, unclear about the war, what they believed or what they had come to represent in the eyes of many black people. They appeared to live in a bubble of fame, increasingly out of touch with the new militancy in the black community and the rising fury of their hometown. Many years afterwards, Mary Wilson explained their support for the President as a choice they made for positive political reasons. 'Though we had never met him,' she wrote, 'we were impressed by his social policies, especially in the area of civil rights, so we were happy to help him.' It was a dubious rationalisation: the forces of liberal protest, including many of black America's civil rights activists, were outside the hotel protesting while The Supremes were inside, seemingly backing the war and adding more weight to the view that they were a compromised mainstream act entirely controlled by the Motown machine.

President Johnson rarely campaigned in public again after the events in Los Angeles, and when he did, it was in safe places like military bases. Within nine months, opposition to the war was so insurmountable that he abandoned his re-election campaign and effectively conceded the presidency.

A conversation in the White House between self-proclaimed sex kitten Eartha Kitt and Lady Bird Johnson is hard to imagine, but in January 1968 the woman Orson Welles once described as 'the most exciting woman in the world' found herself doing just that and, in the process, exposing how deeply divided America was.

Born Eartha Mae Keith on a cotton plantation in South Carolina, in 1927, she survived abuse, poverty and discrimination, and came to prominence with the famous song-and-dance troupe, the Katherine Dunham Company. More of a crooner than a soul singer, her husky, purring voice and charisma cast her as a personality not unlike the legendary Josephine Baker. Kitt had played Catwoman to great effect in the *Batman* television series and was best known for her Christmas novelty record 'Santa Baby' (RCA, 1957). Memorably describing her life as one of 'cotton and caviar', she adored playing the vamp. She draped herself in mink furs and leopard skin, knowingly playing with sexual fantasies to cast a spell over audiences that lasted well into her old age.

Initially, she declined the invitation to the Women Doers' luncheon at the White House, saying in her autobiography, 'I thought it would be a lot of nonsense – flowers, champagne, a chance to show off . . . I felt a con coming on.' After a series of coaxing phone calls, she relented, packed an overnight suitcase, and flew to Washington from her home in Los Angeles. The White House made a reservation for her at the Shoreham Hotel, where in years to come President Bill Clinton would famously channel his inner Junior Walker and play the sax at his inaugural ball. The next morning, a limousine was waiting to take her to the White House. *The Washington Post* covered what happened next.

> At the time, protests against the Vietnam War were raging across the country. Almost 500,000 Americans were fighting in Southeast Asia – a number that was still climbing. And 1968 would prove the deadliest year of the war, with 16,900 Americans killed in Vietnam. Kitt was ushered upstairs to the private family dining room where the women in attendance were served a menu of crab meat bisque and chicken breasts. There was a brief discuss of the challenges facing America's juveniles, the President spoke briefly to the gathering and then handed to the First Lady. In a tense question-and-answer session, Eartha hijacked the meeting and shifted its focus to Vietnam. 'You send the best of this country off to be shot and maimed. They rebel in the street. They will take pot . . . and they will get high. They don't want to go to school because they're going to be snatched off from their mothers to be shot in Vietnam,' she said dramatically.

Lady Bird's face grew pale and her voice trembled as she replied to Kitt: 'Because there is a war on and I pray that there will be a just and honest peace – that still doesn't give us a free ticket not to try to work for better things such as against crime in the streets, for better education and better health for our people.' The guests froze with embarrassment. 'Just because there is a war going on,' she added, 'I see no reason to be uncivilised.'

There was no limousine waiting to take Kitt back to the hotel when she made her way outside so she flagged down a taxi. When she arrived back in Los Angeles she explained to the press that she'd had to say what was in her heart and there was nothing rude about telling the truth. 'All those very nice people kept saying very nice things about putting flowers in Harlem and making bigger street lights to keep the cities safe. I thought they were avoiding talking about the reasons we have problems with crime and problems with our children.'

The reaction to Kitt's exchange with the First Lady was hostile, and the outcry in the press damaging. Major bookings were cancelled, and she struggled to get new engagements for many years to come. These were bleak times for Kitt, and her earnings plummeted to such an extent that she considered work outside the entertainment industry. 'After that White House thing, the government just pulled the gate on me,' she told *The Washington Post* years later. 'Dates simply started getting cancelled. I knew that some government investigators had come around checking. I didn't know what it was for, then. One club owner told me he was sorry, but, "You're a problem."' For several years, Kitt worked mostly in Europe. Then, in 1974, *New York Times* reporter Seymour Hersh, who had famously broken the story of the My Lai Massacre, called Kitt and told her he was about to publish a story about her CIA record, revealing that they had produced 'an extensive report containing second-hand gossip . . . but no evidence of any foreign intelligence connections'. The report was sent to the Secret Service, Hersh wrote, 'a week after Miss Kitt criticized the Vietnam War at a White House luncheon during the Johnson Administration'.

Eartha Kitt, understandably, let rip.

> Because I am black, I had to be taught a lesson, and put back into my place as a singing, dancing, mindless automaton who saw no evil, did no evil, and most important, publicly spoke no evil.
>
> In my case, the CIA apparently didn't even have accurate information. For example, the news stories said the agency had learned I did 'not associate with other black persons'. That's nonsense. I have always taken an interest in the black community, even before it became fashionable to do so. I taught dancing at the Harlem YWCA as early as 1952, and have been teaching a dance class in Watts for almost 10 years.

I don't regret anything that I've said or done. I have suffered a lot financially, but I have survived. I only have pity and sympathy for those who tucked their moral tails in between their legs and cuddled up to the Johnson and Nixon administrations' immoral and unjust policies.

In 1978, after the CIA dossier was revealed and the war was in the rear-view mirror, Kitt made a triumphant return to Broadway in the hit musical *Timbuktu!* Her entrance on the stage as Princess Sahleem-la-Lume was epic. Playing to her sultry reputation, she was carried on stage in the palms of a gigantic man in a loincloth and lowered to the floor. Her opening line was then delivered with her trademark huskiness – 'I am here' – and there was an outburst of spontaneous applause.

She returned to the White House in 1978 after an invitation from President Jimmy Carter and, in 2006, when she lit the Christmas tree with George W. Bush.

As casualties returned home injured, amputated and shell-shocked, opposition to the war intensified and the tone of soul music hardened. A sense of doubt and foreboding crept into new releases. In 1966, Mike Williams' 'Lonely Soldier' (Atlantic, 1966) talked of the stark loneliness of being far from home; Joe Tex's 'I Believe I'm Gonna Make It' (Dial, 1966) tells the story of a distant lover trapped in a foxhole in Vietnam and convinced he's the lucky one who will make it home; and Jimmy Holiday's 'I'm Gonna Help Hurry My Brothers Back Home' (Minit, 1967) reflects on the life of a widow whose husband is not coming back. A far cry from the early mood of patriotic adventure, these songs were redolent of doubt, high risk and looming death.

The love letter was one of pop music's most familiar story-telling tropes, but with Vietnam, letters home began to speak of emotional anxiety. In the great Detroit singer Emanuel Laskey's 'A Letter From Vietnam' (Westbound, 1968) a soldier yearns to be home and admits for the first time that he fears death after seeing his comrades fall in battle. It's a love letter stripped of saccharine and brutally honest about the death toll in Vietnam. Mel and Tim's 'Mail Call Time' (Bamboo, 1970) places a US Marine in the cold, wet muddy battlefields as he waits for his name to be called and prays his girl has dropped him a line, but as the song progresses there is an impending sense that a letter will not bring good news. Gloria Edwards' 'Something You Couldn't Write About' (Jetstream, 1975) is a record seething with pain, which tells the story of a troubled women imagining her lover has not been truthful in his letters home. It would fail modern standards as she imagines her lover has been unfaithful with a 'slant-eyed' woman overseas. But what they all share is a truth about war, that it has the power to overwhelm love and shatter the emotions.

It was a series of letters home from Vietnam that inspired soul music's most iconic album – Marvin Gaye's era-defining, state-of-the-nation masterpiece *What's Going On* (Tamla, 1971). Marvin's brother Frankie was a radio operator in Vietnam and when he returned home, he recounted his experiences in combat. The brothers had exchanged letters between Detroit and Vietnam over the course of three years of Frankie's military service, and it was his first-hand account that found its way into the lyrics of the album.

> I saw all the things I never wanted to see. I was in places I never wanted to be . . . You couldn't stand up: you had to crawl through the mud over things that moved when you touched them. It rained so much that everything on the ground rotted and smelled like week-old garbage, from the heat, rain, and humidity . . . Once you see people dying, cut up or being tortured, day after day of that you get desensitised, then paranoid . . . Still, you want to believe there's a reason.

They played on the mind of Gaye, whose attitude to the war had turned full circle, and he devoted almost two years of his life to recording the album, a landmark critique of war, police violence and a failed economy.

For him, the fallout from the Vietnam War was an emotional battlefield. His cousin Marvin, nicknamed 'Bay-Bay', a 21-year-old Marine Corps regular from Lexington, Kentucky, had been killed in Quang Nam Province, South Vietnam, in November 1968, and he waited anxiously for letters from Frankie. If there was a postal delay, he repeatedly told others that he was concerned he might lose his brother too. Exacerbated by cocaine abuse and a toxic relationship with his father, Gaye's life drifted into darkness and depression.

What's Going On took as its starting point a series of incidents far removed from Detroit and thousands of miles from the jungles of

Southeast Asia. By sheer chance, the bass singer of the Four Tops, Renaldo 'Obie' Benson had been travelling between venues on the West Coast when he witnessed police charging a group of students who were occupying the People's Park in Berkeley, California, in May 1969. Officers in helmets, shields and gas masks laid waste to over 6,000 demonstrators and a hard core reputedly obscured their badges as National Guardsmen. With fixed bayonets, they attacked the crowd. The incident appeared to be pre-planned and became known in countercultural circles as 'Bloody Thursday'. The park had long been a contested issue between residents and the University of California which had plans to develop the area as part of the expansion of the Berkeley campus. It had become a meeting place for student radicals and local bohemians, and had provoked the conservative Governor of California Ronald Reagan to describe it as 'a haven for communist sympathizers, protesters, and sex deviants'.

When an otherwise uneventful student rally about the Arab–Israeli conflict spread to the park, Governor Reagan seized the opportunity to honour his election pledge to curtail student unrest at Berkeley. One hundred and fifty-eight students were injured, some with gunshot wounds. As the battle raged, the Four Tops tour bus was trying to navigate Dwight Way on the fringe of the park and the band members witnessed the worst of the violence through the windows.

On his return to Detroit, Benson recounted the story to his friend, the songwriter Al Cleveland, and together they fashioned a sketchy idea for a song. It was overlooked at first, but then, with Gaye's introspective reworking, it became the opening track of his album. Affected by his private conversations with his brother and the decaying world around him in inner-city Detroit, Gaye broke with unwritten Motown policy and his own career to date and embarked on a candidly political album. Although he had once imagined himself as a crooner – and back in 1964 he had even released a sentimental studio album called *Hello Broadway* – by the late sixties he was in a different emotional place. He increasingly talked about the scarred inner city, the brutality of the Detroit police, the public failure to provide welfare for children, the trauma of veterans returning from Vietnam and the personal anxiety he felt about the role of God and formal religion in his life. Determined to make an impact, Gaye stole studio time and persuaded friends to join him in improvised jam sessions, often recording late into the night in Motown's Studio B complex, a red-brick industrial warehouse building on West Davison Street. When he finally emerged, he had produced a savage, mournful elegy to a failed America.

The final studio sessions that produced *What's Going On* overlapped with the Winter Soldier Investigation, an event sponsored by the Vietnam Veterans Against The War (VVAW). It was a 'truth commission' of sorts, intended to publicise war crimes and atrocities by US Armed Forces in Vietnam. The three-day gathering in Detroit, in January–February 1971, brought together discharged servicemen from each branch of the military service, as well as civilian contractors, medical personnel and academics.

It was here that the first evidence of war crimes trickled out into public awareness. The investigation was conceived in the dying days of 1967, when local Catholics and pacifists tracked down returning veterans and began to record their testimony. As part of a quiet and dignified process of 'bearing witness' the initial recordings were designed to document military atrocities in Vietnam. A total of 125 witnesses agreed to give public testimony, most of them honourably discharged soldiers, retired civilian contractors or medical personnel. With no great financial resource to fund the tribunals, the interviews took time and ended up being conducted in the ignominious surroundings of a windowless room in a Howard Johnson motel in downtown Detroit. The operational centre was a family home on the industrial East Side. A film of the events was sponsored by celebrity radicals, including film stars Donald Sutherland and Jane Fonda, but distribution was problematic, and the participants who testified to war crimes were undermined by senior military personnel who rejected their 'falsified statements'. The national press largely ignored the proceedings.

However, whatever political reasons there had been for America's involvement in Vietnam were disintegrating. War was clearly not the answer.

Stax Records of Memphis had a significantly more complex relationship with the Vietnam War than their Motown rivals in Detroit – one that extended from doubt to outright resistance. Stax singer-songwriter William Bell and songwriter Raymond Jackson were both swept up in the conscription drive of 1966. Bell was recruited to the 14th Infantry's mortar platoon and did his basic training at Fort Polk, Louisiana, where he befriended one of the titans of the New Orleans soul scene, the super-producer Allen Toussaint. He was then airlifted to Pleiku in the Central Highlands, where he saw active service for nearly two years. Before he was flown out, Bell was allowed two weeks' vacation back in Memphis, and he gravitated to his old haunts on East McLemore. He had first entered the Stax studios as an ambitious singer with local Memphis group the Del Rios and provided backing vocals for Carla Thomas on her first major single 'Gee Whiz'. As Vietnam loomed, Bell recorded two songs – 'Marching Off To War' (Stax, 1966) and 'Soldier's Good-Bye' (Stax, 1966) – both delivered with the bittersweet authenticity of a recent conscript headed for a foreign land.

Vietnam soul songs were flooding the market, tapping into a new demographic of the girlfriends, parents and family members left behind and speaking of divided attitudes to the lottery of the draft and the risk of war; these included the Mighty Hannibal's 'Hymn #5' (Shurfine, 1966), Archie Bell & the Drells' 'A Soldier's Prayer 1967' (Ovide, 1967) and the O'Jays' 'There's Someone (Waiting Back Home)' (Neptune, 1969). Others clung to the old narratives of lost or departed love: J. W. Alexander's 'Keep A Light In The Window Until I Come Back' (Mirwood, 1966), Eddie Giles' pleading 'While I'm Away Baby (Keep The Faith)' (Murco, 1967) and the towering 'Don't Cry My Soldier Boy' by Thelma Houston (Capitol, 1967).

Two other musicians from the Stax stable, John Gary Williams and William Brown of the Mad Lads, also came home to draft letters on their doorstep as an army recruitment drive swept through the Memphis Projects like a gale-force wind. Within a matter of weeks, as Williams and Brown were conscripted, new local singers were hurriedly recruited to fulfil live shows and the original nucleus of the group was despatched to basic training en route to the battlefields of Vietnam. Williams served with the 4th Infantry Division and was sent on Long Range Reconnaissance Patrol (LRRP) missions along the Cambodian border. More than 500 GIs died in February 1968 alone. A disproportionate number of the casualties were black conscripts from inner-city neighbourhoods in Detroit, Chicago and Memphis, or dirt-poor farming communities.

Williams returned with eye-witness evidence of the chaos in Vietnam. Gary O'Neal, an LRRP contemporary of Williams, recalled:

These guys were hardcore. This wasn't run anything like the regular army. There was basically only one rule, do whatever you had to do to survive. Most of the time there was nobody looking over our shoulders, nobody telling us what to do or how to do it, no one giving us any bullshit about uniforms or military procedure. We lived for the mission, and . . . the more time any of us spent in the field, the farther away we got from any type of normal behaviour. To survive out there in the jungle, fighting an enemy who understood the environment, we went native.

Williams made it home to Memphis, but he was a changed man. As was his hometown. Memphis had an estimated 90,000 black teenagers: fifty-two per cent of the city's high-school population, they were the core market for Stax, but they faced challenging times in the local job market, where their most common options were the military, manual labour or unemployment. After his discharge, Brown was told by the current members of the Mad Lads that they no longer wanted him in the group. It was a body blow to the returning veteran, and as a compromise Stax hired him to pursue his interest in electronics. He became the first black recording engineer in the Memphis studio system. Williams was reinstated in the group but was now less smitten by their origins in romantic harmony soul. He had been radicalised in Vietnam and now saw his city in a vastly different light. He wanted to drive them in a different direction. Williams befriended other veterans, among them John Burl Smith, a Black Power activist with links to the Socialist Workers Party, who, in 1967, had formed the Black Organising Project (BOP), an influential street-level political party loosely associated with the Black Panthers. These savvy new radicals became known in the city as the Memphis Invaders.

Like Williams, Smith had been shocked at the indifference he faced when he came home from Vietnam. 'When I returned, I really wasn't into Black Power. I was an American who had just served my country, and I was expecting my country to be appreciative.' But he struggled to find work and could only find lodgings in a decrepit apartment complex in Riverside.

The Memphis police were regular and unwanted visitors at the Invaders' headquarters on 1310 Florida Street, which sat among wrecked low-rise buildings near the Illinois Central Railroad, and suspicion grew that the group had been infiltrated by either the FBI or the police department's Red Squad, an elite unit that had emerged during the era of McCarthyism, when American law and order was fixated with communism. Early in the afternoon of 24 August 1968, the police came in force and arrested a leading figure in the Black Power movement, John Henry Ferguson, a Memphis teenager who had joined the police's Most Wanted list after he had threatened officers at a sanitation workers' strike meeting. He was alleged to have waved a wooden toy gun at a passing car. News of Ferguson's arrest spread like wildfire, and the Invaders and their supporters confronted and resisted the police wherever they could.

A series of incidents erupted deep in ghetto neighbourhoods. Teenage gangs took to intersections and jeered at passing police cars, and firebombs were thrown at commercial buildings deemed to be unsupportive of local black communities. Laundry outlets owned by the family of the despised mayor, Henry Loeb, were targeted. Those Invaders who had access to guns were told that the time had come to arm themselves and be public about their rights under the Second Amendment of the Constitution (i.e. to bear arms). By the morning of 6 September, resentment among the Invaders had grown to fever pitch after their offices were burned to the ground in an overnight attack by what were likely rogue agents in the pay of the MPD.

It has never been entirely clear what pulled John Gary Williams into this maelstrom of political radicalism and why he was arrested as part of a plot to attack police officers. Always a bright and well-read young man, who remained steadfast in his religious beliefs, he began to feel that the movement for peaceful change was too slow, and the assassination of Martin Luther King convinced him that America was not yet ready for the change he sought.

The trial of the Memphis Invaders fell short of being a political show trial, but when it came to court it unfolded with all the intrigue and drama of a television special. John Gary Williams' presence in the dock – he had been charged with ambushing a police car – added a dimension that the local press found hard to resist. Stax was by some distance the most famous record label in Memphis, and to have one of their recording artists accused of being a member of the city's most notorious Black Power organisation added spice to an already compelling trial.

The facts had been coloured by dramatic reporting. No one died in the incident, but shots were fired and police were targeted, including one patrol car carrying the city's police chief. A patrolman was injured after a bullet pierced the side of his car and he was only able to hobble into court with the aid of walking sticks.

Williams became a local celebrity. On one occasion, he frustrated the court by arriving late, having travelled to Washington to promote a new single, 'Love Is Here Today And Gone Tomorrow' (written by the talented singer-songwriter writer Bettye Crutcher). His girlfriend, a trendy afro-sporting teenager by the name of Gloria Fay Goodman, corroborated his story that he was only at the scene to try to discourage his young cousin from taking part in the shooting, but the car that the Invaders had used in the attack implicated him more deeply. It was a green Chevrolet Camaro with the initials 'JGW' emblazoned on the side, the car he had bought with the proceeds of royalties from Stax Records. Despite the evidence stacked against him, Williams was given the minimum possible sentence and charges of attempted murder were dropped. He was found guilty of assault with intent to commit voluntary manslaughter. It was clear that the jury did not wholly believe the story that he had tried to thwart the sniper attack, but it was apparent that he was the most honest and penitent of the three accused. Williams told the court: 'I would like to say that what I said on the witness stand, I learned a lesson from it.' He made one request: rather than go to the tough Shelby County Jail, could he see out his sentence in a more useful way at the Shelby Penal Farm? There, he could work outdoors tending vegetables and growing food for the prison population. During his incarceration, Williams read voraciously, continued to write songs and began to imagine a solo career. He stayed in touch with Stax, and they stood by him. On his release, he returned to the studios on East McLemore, where he discovered that the city, the studio and the times had changed dramatically.

In the aftermath of the assassination of Martin Luther King, there was a more intractable political mood in Memphis. Stax were mining a tiny seam of creative gold, deconstructing pop classics. Isaac Hayes had dismantled and rebuilt 'Walk On By' and 'By The Time I Get To Phoenix', and Williams brought out a haunting version of George Harrison's 'My Sweet Lord' and a strident reworking of the Four Tops' 'Ask The Lonely'. But it was one of William's self-penned singles that stood out. In 1973, he recorded one of Stax's greatest ever songs, 'The Whole Damn World Is Going Crazy'. Heavily influenced by the politicised soul of the late sixties, especially Marvin Gaye's 'What's Going On' and the Temptations' 'Ball Of Confusion', Williams' song, written from the depths of an incarcerated mind, described a world of discrimination, gun crime and a city engulfed in hate. It was a song that spoke of the dark and confused forces that engulfed Memphis at the time, and it remains one of soul music's unsung classics – a sign-of-the-times message that few have bettered. The album from which the single was taken makes vivid the change Williams had undergone. On one side, he is pictured in a purple stage suit adorned with bow tie, sitting by a dressing-room mirror about to go on stage. It is the kind of picture that many great singers such as David Ruffin or Teddy Pendergrass might have posed for. But the image on the reverse side sees him staring into another mirror, in full afro, bare-chested in a distressed denim jacket sawn off at the shoulders, in the street style of the Memphis Invaders. It is a powerful image of the soul singer: first as romantic and then as street revolutionary.

While Gary John Williams and the Memphis Invaders were confined to the penal farm, in Harlem, a local chapter of the Black Panthers had been rounded up in a dawn raid and were standing trial on trumped-up charges. In December 1969, Fred Hampton of the Chicago branch of the Black Panthers had been shot and killed during a raid at his apartment by a tactical unit of the Cook County State's Attorney's Office in conjunction with the Chicago Police Department and the FBI. During the raid, Panther Mark Clark was also killed, and several others were seriously injured. It became a widespread presumption among Black Power radicals, the Nation of Islam and anti-war activists that the FBI were conspiring with police forces across the country to destabilise their activities. Although President Johnson had pioneered civil rights legislation, he harboured deep suspicions about those political groups and community organisations that shouted loudest about racism and he was often acquiescent to the FBI's unlawful activities.

On the night of 8 March 1971, the proof that many suspected was out there finally came to light.

In a roadside motel due west of Medea, Pennsylvania, a group of campus activists called the Citizens' Commission to Investigate the FBI assembled with the intent to break in to a nearby FBI storage facility. While guards were distracted by the big Ali–Frazier fight, the burglars broke the locks and found their way into filing cabinets that hid a treasure trove of documents exposing COINTELPRO, the FBI's top-secret mission aimed at 'surveilling, infiltrating, discrediting, and disrupting domestic American political organizations'. It was this break-in that unravelled decades of illegal FBI activity, much of it aimed at demonising Black Power groups. By 1971, when the files were discovered in the Medea burglary, Richard Nixon was ensconced in the White House and the American presence in Vietnam had soured even further with incursions into neighbouring Cambodia.

More and more songs were challenging US war policy. Prominent among them was 'Bring The Boys Home' (Invictus, 1971) by the Detroit-born actress and singer Freda Payne, who in 1970 had an international hit with 'Band Of Gold' (Invictus, 1970). The song was banned by US Command from the American Forces Network for fear that it would 'give aid and comfort to the enemy', and many domestic radio stations fell into line, but the song's popularity among anti-war activists and the pacifist elements within the Christian Church meant it became a gold-selling record despite censorship. It was a song sung from the perspective of a grieving Mother America demanding the return of her boys, the dead bodies and those missing in action. Freda Payne came close to being charged with 'disloyal speech', the catch-all term for published denunciation of the war effort. Around the same time, the Marines had court-martialled Lance Corporal William Harvey and Private George Daniels, two African American Marines, for holding a meeting in which they argued that Vietnam was a white man's war. Similarly, apprentice seaman Roger Priest was court-martialled for publishing an anti-Vietnam war newspaper while working in the Navy's Office of Information in the Pentagon. Increasingly, African American soldiers and civilians were seeing the war as a distraction from civil rights and the war on poverty in inner cities at home.

The nightly news shows on network television made painful viewing for patriots. The media guru Marshall McLuhan famously said, 'Television brought the brutality of war into the comfort of the living room. Vietnam was lost in the living rooms of America – not on the battlefields of Vietnam.' The socialist novelist and screenwriter Dalton Trumbo, who had written about the impact of the First World War on the home front in his 1938 book *Johnny Got His Gun*, argued that relentless daily news coverage was desensitising Americans: 'Numbers have dehumanized us. Over breakfast coffee we read of 40,000 American dead in Vietnam. Instead of vomiting, we reach for the toast.'

With such intense news media coverage, it was inevitable that the trickle of anti-war songs became a flood. One record that stood out was 'War' (Gordy, 1970), a song by the Detroit-based singer Charles Edwin Hatcher (better known by his stage-name Edwin Starr), especially its unforgettable good-for-absolutely-nothing anti-war hookline. The song had first appeared as an album track on the Temptations' *Psychedelic Shack*, a revolutionary album that jettisoned the traditional Motown sound in favour of psychedelic soul, the subgenre that ushered in the production style of Smokey Robinson and the rock guitar, synthesizers and out-there lyrics of Sly Stone to the mainstream of black music. Motown was inundated by requests from the anti-war movement to release the track as a single, but the group was imploding, so producers Norman Whitfield and Barrett Strong decided to bring Edwin Starr into the studios to record the single and an album, *War And Peace* (Motown, 1970). 'War' has been covered numerous times, most famously by Bruce Springsteen and the E Street Band, who intended the song to be a protest against the Reagan administration's aggressive foreign policy in Central America, but it became more relevant to events in the Middle East as it climbed to number one in the charts against the backdrop of Operation El Dorado Canyon, the US bombing of Libya in 1989.

Now mainstream within the once-conservative Motown Corporation, psychedelic soul also dominated the West Coast sound where fusions of the counterculture, psychedelia and R&B were now commonplace. It also found a rich expression among the Plainfield, New Jersey, scene as George Clinton's group the Parliaments buried their cool-suited harmonies and replaced them with a surreal, madcap mixture of rock and afro-futurism called P-Funk. Clinton's inspired eccentricity flourished with a string of innovative albums that rewrote the rules of commercial black music, including *Osmium* (Invictus 1970) and *America Eats Its Young* (Westbound, 1972).

One of the most eccentric and talented singers of the era was Jerry 'Swamp Dogg' Williams. He once said, 'I became Swamp Dogg in 1970 in order to have an alter-ego and someone to occupy the body while the search party was out looking for Jerry Williams, who was mentally missing in action due to certain pressures, maltreatments and failure to get paid royalties on over fifty single records. I was tired of being a jukebox, singing all of the hits by Chuck Jackson, Ben E. King, etc., and being an R'n'B second banana. I couldn't dance as good as Joe Tex, wasn't pretty like Tommy Hunt, couldn't compare vocally to Jackie Wilson and I didn't have the sex appeal of Daffy Duck.'

In the early seventies Swamp Dogg reached out to new audiences, releasing a string of offbeat albums including *Total Destruction To Your Mind* (Canyon, 1970), *Cuffed, Collared & Tagged* (Cream, 1972) and *Gag A Maggot* (Stone Dogg, 1973). It was the opening track on *Cuffed, Collared & Tagged* that shifted the dial yet again on Vietnam War songs. His powerful rendition of 'Sam Stone', written by the late, great lyricist John Prine, stands out as a milestone in early seventies music. It tells the story of a disabled Vietnam veteran strung-out on heroin and dependent on handouts for his family. The vocal adds a deeply emotional dimension to a song that was about to become a folk-country standard.

The more injured and disillusioned veterans who returned home, the more damaged Johnson's presidency grew. None of his seismic achievements in civil rights legislation could deaden the perpetual noise of war and his standing with the public fell into terminal decline. In 'Character Above All', a set of essays analysing the character flaws of ten presidents from Roosevelt to Bush, the historian Robert Dallek saw Johnson's fall as an indicator of unresolving divisions within America itself. He wrote: 'Johnson was much loved and greatly hated – not just liked and disliked but adored by some and despised by others. Some people remember him as kind, generous, compassionate, considerate, decent, and devoted to advancing the well-being of the least advantaged among us. Others describe him as cruel, dictatorial, grandiose, and even vicious.'

In March 1968, exhausted by the burdens of the Vietnam War,

Johnson announced to a deeply divided nation that he would not seek re-election that November. His self-doubt had overwhelmed him. He had rashly told the media that June 1967 was the month that the war would end, a projection founded on wishful thinking. American forces in Vietnam had by then reached 385,000, an additional 60,000 sailors were stationed offshore, and more than 6,000 Americans had been killed in the previous twelve months.

On 20 January 1969, Frankie Boyce's death was confirmed by two military liaison officers who visited the family home in Plainfield. Marvin Gaye's 'I Heard It Through The Grapevine' was America's top-selling R&B single and, in a dark irony, it was the day of President Richard Nixon's inauguration. The battle-weary Lyndon Baines Johnson finally passed the baton of responsibility for the war in Vietnam to the incoming president. In better days, Johnson had said, 'Guns and bombs, rockets and warships, are all symbols of human failure.' It was a comment that would haunt him for the rest of his days.

Before he left for Vietnam, Frankie Boyce had talked about picking up his music when he returned home. The options that awaited him in Plainfield were remarkable in both their range and artistic diversity. He had grown up in a musical community that stretched from the ghettos of Newark to the creaking boardwalks of Asbury Park at a time of great musical transformation. By 1969, it was the settled belief that Detroit and Memphis, the cities that had launched Motown and Stax, were the epicentres of popular black music, but another story was hidden away in the small towns of Boyce's adolescence. The highways and turnpikes of the East Coast hosted a network of live venues, independent labels and start-up recording studios. Boyce was due to be discharged from military service in 1972 and had already weighed up three options: first, to return to his family group Jo Jo and the Admirers, which at the time of his death had rebranded as the Admirations and signed to the vintage New York label Hull Records; second, he could reconnect with the Parliaments who had already grown too big for George Clinton's local barbershop and morphed into Parliament; or, third, he could take up an open offer from a local soul maven, a vocalist called Sammy Campbell, who, when Boyce left for Vietnam, was the leader of the New Jersey soul group the Del Larks.

When Boyce's casket was lowered into the ground at Franklin

Memorial Park in North Brunswick, Sammy Campbell was among the throng of mourners. Campbell had known Boyce and his brothers since childhood, and when Frankie was conscripted, Campbell was on the verge of folding the Del Larks and kissing goodbye to the old soul of the sixties. He had plans to form an entirely new group, something more in touch with the shifting mood of the time. His final record in the frantic Motown style was called 'Job Opening – For An Experienced Heart Mender' (Queen City, 1967); it is now one of the most feted underground soul records of all time. In 1970, Campbell signed a deal with the Philadelphia label, Phil-LA of Soul, which had enjoyed dance-craze success with Cliff Nobles and the Fantastic Johnnie C. Determined to stay in touch with the emergent funk sound and the more socially conscious fashions of African American music, the label owners set Sammy Campbell the task of coming up with a new name and a new group. He chose the pseudonym Tyrone Ashley and the Funky Music Machine and went about recruiting an entirely new band. The nucleus was drawn from the ranks of the Parliaments, but one of the new recruits was a towering teenage saxophonist called Clarence Clemons. By day, Clemons worked as an educational auxiliary at the New Jersey Reform School in Jamesburg, one of the most antiquated youth prisons in America. His music classes bulged with young inmates drawn from the Newark Projects and towns like Elizabeth, Kearney, Plainfield and Perth Amboy. By night, Clemons played with a local band, Lloyd Sims and the Untouchables, at a go-go bar called Leon's Turf Club near the shore in Asbury Park. Each night, it was a race to get from the penitentiary to Springwood Avenue, the thoroughfare where the club was based. Clemons was restless, always keen to move on. One night, when his car broke down near Ocean Township, he went into a rock bar called the John Barleycorn to use a phone and was blown away by the sound of the house band, Norman Seldin and the Joyful Noyze.

Stormin' Norman Seldin was the son of parents who owned a New Jersey jewellery store. Aged 13, he became the youngest member of the American Federation of Musicians but strayed from the family path (both his parents had been classically trained in music) by amassing a formidable collection of R&B records, which he carted up to Harlem during his student days at the Manhattan School of Music. There, he befriended acclaimed R&B musician Bernard 'Pretty' Purdie, who was then the drummer for King Curtis and the Kingpins and destined to become Aretha Franklin's musical director.

Clemons hung around in the bar and introduced himself to Norman Seldin – a conversation that led to his crossing the divide between R&B and rock with nightly work in the network of white bars and clubs along the Jersey Shore.

New Jersey had an unusually pioneering musical outlook in terms of mixed-race bands, and by the early seventies the checklist of disruptors was long and honourable. The Stax house band Booker T. and the M.G.'s had been trailblazers, and with the global success of funk-rock bands like Sly and the Family Stone and the Jimi Hendrix Experience, a new generation was coming to the fore, among them two of Chicago's most progressive groups – Rufus featuring Chaka Khan and the trailblazing psychedelic soul collective Rotary Connection featuring Minnie Riperton. Although the bands themselves were pushing racial barriers, most venues were stuck in a subtle form of audience segregation, with white bar-owners still nervous about hiring black musicians. The presence of Clemons lost Seldin's band several engagements. 'You know what it was like at the Shore in those days – there was a black side and you never crossed the tracks,' Clemons once told a reporter. 'You didn't mix the two together.' He flitted between the two sides of town, often playing with soul group The Chosen Few and backing R&B groups like Billy Brown and the Broadways, vocalist Leon Trent and Ronnie Coleman.

It was during a residence with Norman Seldin and the Joyful Noyze at the Wonder Bar in Asbury Park that Clemons famously met Bruce Springsteen. The lead singer of the Joyful Noyze was Springsteen's former girlfriend Karen Cassidy. On a date believed to be 4 September 1971, during a break in the Joyful Noyze's residency, Cassidy and Clemons walked through a howling gale to another local bar, the Student Prince, where Springsteen was playing. The two men forged a lifelong partnership that is now enshrined in rock mythology. The Boss and the Big Man, as they became known, rejected the bitter prejudice of the past and anchored Springsteen's rock with a baritone sax sound that might have come from the studios of Detroit. Together, they painted the bleak humanity of the New Jersey boardwalks with its one-dog towns and highways lined with broken heroes.

In his song 'Tenth Avenue Freeze-Out' where he mentions the Big

Man joining the band, Springsteen captured their bond in lyrics. 'I will never, ever forget the feeling I got when we hit that first note,' Clemons told author Peter Carlin. 'It was so urgent, so real, so exciting to me. It was like I'd been searching for so long, and now, thank God, I am finally, finally, where I'm supposed to be.'

And in return, Springsteen said:

Standing next to Clarence was like standing next to the baddest ass on the planet. You were proud, you were strong, you were excited and laughing with what might happen, with what together you might be able to do. You felt like no matter what the day or the night brought, nothing was going to touch you . . . We were united, we were strong, we were righteous, we were unmovable, we were funny, we were corny as hell and as serious as death itself. And we were coming to your town to shake you and to wake you up.

The war in Vietnam was in its final, depressing days, Frankie Boyce was dead, Springsteen had met his saxophonist, and George Clinton was wearing hot-pink afro extensions . . . Something strange was happening in America and soul music would never be the same again. Bruce Springsteen was in his early twenties when Mary J. Blige was born in Fordham Hospital in the Bronx. They were never close, but the eddies of the American presidency were swirling in unpredictable ways. Born into very different communities, but nonetheless born in the USA, within forty years they would become the two artists with the greatest presence in the White House, carrying with them the positive ideals of the Democratic Party.

For ten days in June 1968 the hardest-working man in show business,
James Brown, played three shows a day for American troops in Vietnam.
'It was harder than any tour I've ever done,' he confessed. 'We'd ride from place
to place in a Chinook, a big helicopter . . . the GIs treated me like God.'

3

JAMES BROWN – NIXON'S CLOWN

Listen Up: 'Impeach The President' by The Honey Drippers (1973)

James Brown had suffered many indignities in life. He grew up in poverty in Elko, South Carolina, and spent much of his infancy in his aunt's brothel. 'I was stillborn,' Brown said. 'The midwives laid me aside, thought I was really gone. I laid there about an hour, and they picked me back up and tried again, 'cause my body was still warm. The Good Lord brought me back.' Thus, a force of nature kicked into life and James Brown came into the world shrieking like the wild wind.

As a child, he earned a pittance begging by a canal bridge near Camp Gordon, a military installation southwest of Augusta, Georgia, and by the age of 16 he had been convicted of robbery and incarcerated for the first time in the Floyd County Juvenile Institute, a former tuberculosis hospital crudely repurposed as a home for delinquents and hidden away beneath the Seven Hills of Rome. In his segregated cell block, Brown learned that the rituals of racism had marked him out as both troublesome and precocious. His perseverance in the face of brutal childhood poverty and jail time built a character that was unafraid of hard work but terrified that the fruits of his labour might be taken away. 'The Hardest-Working Man in Showbiz' was one of the most successful singers in the highly competitive world of sixties soul but also one of the meanest.

Poverty and imprisonment aside, one of James Brown's most humiliating moments came many years later as he tried to navigate a picket line outside the Apollo Theater in Harlem in May 1973. The crowd were protesting his endorsement of President Richard Nixon, accusing him of ingratiating himself with the Republican Party and so undermining the cause of civil rights. One of the most memorable and acerbic banners read: 'James Brown – Nixon's Clown'. The man who had blazed a trail for roughhouse funk music and become synonymous with the sound of the ghetto was, in the eyes of many of his contemporaries, a sellout and a dupe.

When Brown took to the stage at Nixon's inaugural ball dressed in a single-button, bell-bottomed black tuxedo with velvet lapels and red silk lining, he opened his fiery set with 'Say It Loud, I'm Black And I'm Proud'. Although the episode is now seen as a curiosity in the story of a racially divided America, the reality was significantly more complex. Brown did not appear at the inauguration itself; he appeared at an All-American Gala, at the National Guard Armory, two days before the inauguration. Supporting Brown was the Kansas City funk singer Marva Whitney, a woman with a tempestuous voice who was on the verge of quitting the music industry after long and exhausting years working for the mercurial Brown. The remaining cast list was drawn from more conventional musical genres – Tony Bennett, Dinah Shore and Connie Francis among them. The former Supremes singer Florence Ballard sang during inauguration week too, desperately trying to blow life into her stuttering solo career.

One of the leading black newspapers of the day, the *Baltimore Afro-American*, carried the most detailed review.

. . . after coaxing his audience several times, he persuaded many to respond to his familiar and popular song. When he said, 'Say It Loud', many responded faintly by saying, 'I'm Black And I'm Proud.' And with a change of key, he belted out 'Papa's Got A Brand-New Bag' and 'Please, Please, Please'.

When he finished, many of the younger set rushed to the front of his stage to shake his hands and to get autographs. By this time, Mr. Brown had removed his jacket and stood blowing kisses to the audience in his shirt sleeves. He had a neatly trimmed bush haircut. Sparkling gold cuff links, a gold watch and a sparkling ring on the little finger all glowed as he stood with outstretched hands . . . seemingly elated over his reception. Shining as though machine polished, were his black pilgrim type dress shoes. Truly, the James Brown who campaigned for the Democratic ticket and played for the incoming Republican President, was a star performer.

One person who was notably absent from the audience was the President elect himself, Richard Milhous Nixon. He had been giving a speech in New York earlier that day, and after hurried conversations among the core of his thirty-six secret agents they decided to put safety first. A James Brown show just three months earlier in October 1968 at the Armory ended in late-night rioting and smashed windows as a battle-scarred Washington D.C. tried to resurface from the carnage following Martin Luther King's assassination. Caution won the day and 'Search-light', the presidential codename for Nixon, was re-routed back to the White House while the Godfather of Soul took to the stage blinded by the lights and unaware who was among the mostly white audience in ballgowns and tuxedos. Tickets were priced between $10 and $100 and *Jet* magazine reviewed the event with tongue firmly in cheek.

Soul Brother No. 1, James Brown, burst on stage saying it loud. Every time the little dynamo commanded, 'Say It Loud', a little, black cheering section to the left of stage centre in the $100 seats jumped to its feet to answer back, 'I'm black and I'm proud.' And pretty soon, even a few whites in the overwhelmingly white audience found themselves caught up in the unique Brown brand of musical hysteria, and they too, were saying they were black, and they were proud.

Ironically, Soul Brother No. 1, like most high-profile soul musicians had backed Democrat Hubert H. Humphrey during the 1968 presidential campaign but when the victorious Nixon team called to offer him the inauguration gig, he cancelled a Texas show and shipped his twenty-piece band to Washington. 'I accepted because I want to give our new President a chance to bring the people of this nation together in every respect of our national life,' he told *Jet*.

James Brown has made many claims and counterclaims about his relationship with President Nixon and not all are borne out by fact. He tended to exaggerate their closeness and often made claims of status within the politics of the White House that he never really enjoyed. He was also prone to exaggerating his influence on the mutinous teenagers of the ghetto, frequently claiming to have quelled public disturbances without there being any substantial evidence to back up those claims. The music magazine *Rolling Stone* claimed that James Brown's 'words once cooled rioting in Washington D.C., Boston and Augusta, following the assassination of Dr. Martin Luther King Jr'. It was a comforting myth but largely untrue. In the days after King's assassination Washington D.C. suffered four days of intense social disorder during which large sections of the city were destroyed, but James Brown, if he said anything, had no impact on events.

Boston was a different story. Brown was scheduled to perform there on the day after King's murder. When his retinue arrived in the city, it became clear that the authorities feared a night of rioting and social disorder and were being leaned on by the management of the Boston Garden Arena to cancel the show. As American cities ignited, Boston's new mayor, Kevin White, tried to dampen unrest on the streets. He urged Brown to proceed with the show, but with a safety-net plan: he talked the singer into allowing it to be televised live on the local public broadcasting station, WGBH. The hope was that young people would stay at home to watch the live telecast and not congregate in the streets. According to R. J. Smith, one of Brown's biographers, the anxiety in Boston was 'a marker of how segregated the city was, that one of the most famous blacks in America could fill the biggest venue in town and the leading white official, Kevin White, had no reason to know his name'. All he knew was the venue regularly attracted young kids. Instructed by Brown to stare out the politicians and give no ground, his manager and fixer, Charles Bobbit, demanded hard cash to compensate for any loss in takings if the television cameras were permitted to film. In his Pulitzer prize-winning book *Common Ground*, which focuses on racial and class conflicts in two Boston neighbourhoods, the journalist J. Anthony Lukas described the face-off: 'Martin Luther King had just been killed and here were two black guys putting the squeeze on the Mayor.' Brown demanded that the Mayor's office make up for lost ticket sales. Keeping the peace had a price. Bobbit held out for $60,000 or no show, and by inference Boston could burn. After numerous nervous meetings and frantic phone calls, the show went ahead. Only 2,000 people attended the concert in the 14,000-seat Garden, which was built within the city's crumbling North Station complex. Although its life as a mainline station was wheezing its last, North was still a hub of suburban commuter trains and the area was always busy with travellers. At the height of the show, as Brown performed his signature 'cape routine', a group of teenagers invaded the stage. Police pursued them and Brown stopped the show. 'Wait a minute, wait a minute now – WAIT!' he told the kids. 'Step down, now, be a gentleman . . . Now I asked the police to step back, because I think I can get some respect from my own people.' With his intervention, the atmosphere changed and the moment passed. The disturbance was entirely confined to the venue and had no impact on the streets beyond. Brown invited the Mayor onstage for the kind of attention politicians seem to thrive on, and as the show recommenced the teenagers were escorted back to their seats.

According to news coverage at the time, there were minor skirmishes in Boston that night, but nothing approaching the riots that city officials feared. However, a powerful myth was born and James Brown left Boston with a story that he crafted and embellished in the years to come. It was this particular story, and the way that James Brown skilfully narrated it, that brought him to the attention of the White House, and it was his boundless energy in the studio and on the road that made him a perfect foil.

James Brown was a product of the Chitlin' Circuit, the network of clubs, bar and juke-joints that connected the Apollo Theater in New York, the Royal Peacock club in Atlanta, the Harlem Square Club in Miami, and many more in between. His first single as lead singer of The Famous

Flames was 'Please, Please, Please' (Fidelity, 1956), a plaintive ballad bolstered by Brown's trademark screaming. By 1962, he was on the roster of the Cincinnati R&B label King Records and had recorded a version of 'Night Train', an instrumental made popular by Jimmy Forrest in 1951 which became the signature tune of the heavyweight boxing champion Sonny Liston. In 1963, Brown recorded a live version of his annual show at the Apollo and released an album that even the record company believed would crash and burn. It turned out to be one of the most era-defining live albums of all time. *James Brown Live At The Apollo* became a byword for raw, energetic, irrepressible soul. The hits came fast and furious: 'Prisoner Of Love' (King, 1963), 'Papa's Got A Brand-New Bag' (King, 1965), the energetic 'It's A Man's Man's Man's World' (King, 1966) and the uplifting social message song 'Don't Be A Drop-Out (King, 1966), a song that chimed with the Stay in School messaging of Johnson's presidency. By 1967, James Brown was pioneering a new subgenre of soul music – street funk – best illustrated by 'Cold Sweat' (King, 1967), his collaboration with vocalist Vicki Anderson 'You've Got The Power' (King, 1968), 'Say It Loud I'm Black And I'm Proud' (King, 1968) and, ultimately, his great seventies songs, including the masterful 'Sex Machine' (Polydor, 1970).

In its earliest days in the mid sixties, before the advent of synthesizers and the more widespread use of stringed instrumentation in dance music, funk was a deliberately primitive form of dance music. Its roots were in the small nightclub sector and its primary interests were sex, food and ghetto life. Small-circulation vinyl like Little Rock Brotherhood's 'Girl Watching On Broadway' (Ref-O-Ree, 1969), The Granby St. Redevelopment's 'Jelly Roll/Guess Who' (Legrand, 1969), Willie Gresham and the Free Food Ticket's 'I Cried Boo Hoo/Step By Step' (Majesty, 1970) never troubled the charts, but the infectious sound of funk grew in neighbourhoods hidden away from pop consumerism. It was James Brown who brought funk from the dark corners of the ghetto to the outside world.

A summary of Brown's hits does not fairly reflect one of his key strengths: an ability to be a magnet for talent. Throughout his career, his supporting musicians – variously known as The Famous Flames and then the James Brown Revue – were among the most talented and influential musicians in the story of funk. As far back as 1952, during a scratch baseball game in his prison yard at Floyd County Correctional Center, Brown met the bandleader Bobby Byrd who joined The Famous Flames first as drummer then as featured vocalist. As the band changed personnel over more than a decade, it became a showcase for the Collins brothers from Cincinnati, bass guitarist Bootsy and guitarist Catfish, teenage vocalist Tammy Montgomery, who later found fame at Motown as Tammi Terrell, saxophonists Maceo Parker, Pee Wee Ellis and St Clair Pinckney, master trombonist Fred Wesley, drummer Clyde Stubblefield and vocalist Lyn Collins. It would not be too overblown to claim that James Brown and his band were among the greatest live musicians on the planet. When he first auditioned for the band, Fred Wesley, then a gifted jazz instrumentalist, described Brown as a revelation. In his autobiography, *Hit Me, Fred*, Wesley wrote:

> His dancing was unbelievable. He did things that seemed impossible for the human body to do. How he could sing with that much energy and dance at the same time was amazing. His rhythm, soulful attitude and demeanour epitomised what black music was all about. The band was now literally a funk machine. Overpowering and relentless . . . thrilling and mesmerising.

Brown was a stellar performer who worked tirelessly at making his brilliance seem natural but he was a difficult man to warm to. Like President Nixon, he was burdened by a deep personal insecurity which often erupted in cruel outbursts. Wesley saw his contradictions close-up over many years. 'I learned later that most true stars are never sure or confident about their performances. Mr Brown was a glaring example of the insecurity, although he put up a self-confident and cocky, if paper-thin façade.' At his height, according to Wesley, James Brown was making $500,000 a week from live shows, merchandise, radio recordings and record sales. He had set up his own company and ran it like a personal fiefdom, under-paying musicians, hiding his true wealth from the Inland Revenue Services and using strong-arm tactics to intimidate those who owed him money. 'It didn't take me long to realize that I was involved with a man unique among performers and among human beings in general. James Brown was a great performer, probably the greatest to ever live, but I had to be careful – this was a man with the power and the will and, it seemed, the *need* to control not only the career but the whole life of every person who worked for him.' This streak made Brown not only a unique performer but the perfect uncaring capitalist.

Brown had come to the attention of the White House because of the much-publicised Boston show and the support he had given to Vice President Hubert Humphrey during his failed bid for the presidency. He was first wooed by the White House during LBJ's presidency. On 8 May 1968, Brown was invited to a state dinner for Field Marshal Thanom Kittikachorn, Prime Minister of Thailand and a military dictator who supported the USA in the fight against communism in Southeast Asia.

Dressed fastidiously in a dinner suit and black bow tie, with the trademark gangster ring on his left pinkie, Brown sat down among the dignitaries in the state dining room, which had been majestically refurbished during the Kennedy era by the French interior designer Stéphane Boudin. President Johnson, the burden of Vietnam heavy on his mind, thanked the Thai prime minister for his unstinting support. Brown unfolded a small envelope with a place-setting card inside it, which said simply: 'Thanks so much for what you are doing for your country.' It was signed by Lyndon Johnson. According to his own account, a surge of personal achievement rose in Brown.

'The Hardest-Working Man in Show Biz' considered himself a businessman as much as an entertainer, and by the end of the sixties he had built up a sizeable portfolio of interests including a publishing company, investments in radio stations and a management agency. His name, therefore, came up frequently at a time when Richard Nixon and his aides were seeking to craft a story about the virtues of hard work, self-improvement and what they hopefully defined as 'black capitalism'.

Nixon had inherited a raft of problems at home and abroad – not least deep-seated social deprivation in inner cities. Many African American communities were scarred by unemployment, substandard housing, drug abuse and the aftermath of 'white flight' to the suburbs. In a radio broadcast coinciding with his nomination as the Republican candidate for the Presidential elections in April 1968, Nixon argued that black Americans 'do not want more government programs which perpetuate dependency. They don't want to be a colony in a nation.

They want the pride, and the self-respect, and the dignity that can only come if they have an equal chance to own their own homes, to own their own businesses, to be managers and executives as well as workers, to have a piece of the action in the exciting ventures of private enterprise.' Nixon reviled public spending but struggled to find an overarching solution that could wave a magic wand over derelict land and, despite his scepticism about so-called '[colonies] within a nation', he found up to $14 million of loan guarantees to support Soul City, a town for African Americans to be built on 5,000 acres of farmland flanked by an interstate highway and a railway line near Durham, North Carolina. It was dreamed up by the civil rights activist Floyd McKissick, a Nixon supporter who had negotiated the funding in what the author Devin Fergus described as a 'lapsed moment of liberalism'. The dream was to build a community beyond racism and segregation that would serve as a new town miles from the ghetto. Soul City was already a successful record label managed by singer-songwriter Johnny Rivers, which featured The 5th Dimension and vocalist Al Wilson. But after an exchange of legal letters about using the same name, the Soul City housing project began to be built.

Soul City was in most respects a failure. It was by now illegal to build a racially segregated enclave and McKissick was warned that the federal government could not fund such a project as it would violate the Civil Rights Act. Nonetheless its boldness appealed to many – including the scheming Richard Nixon. The term Nixon put forward, and which McKissick and Brown, albeit differently, endorsed, was 'black capitalism' – the idea that the free market could transform the most blighted areas of the major cities, as long as 'negroes could rise to the challenge'.

Law professor Mehrsa Baradaran, author of *The Color of Money: Black Banks and the Racial Wealth Gap*, describes the policy as a 'political diversion', claiming that 'after the Civil Rights Act, black activists and their allies pushed the federal government for race-specific economic redress. The "whites only" signs were gone, but joblessness, dilapidated housing and intractable poverty remained. In 1967, blacks had one-fifth the wealth of white families.' She also concludes that Nixon's support for people like McKissick and Brown 'highlights Nixon's mastery of the political sleight of hand. By promoting black capitalism, he was able to accomplish a great deal with very little: he gained business support, lost none of his political base, and spent virtually nothing. The promise of black capitalism was so loosely conceived, it curbed the demands of black separatists and appealed to white voters across the political spectrum.'

To get the show on the road and reach out to James Brown, Nixon hired a go-between. Robert J. Brown was born on a hog farm in High Point, North Carolina, and was raised by an industrious, loving Christian grandmother. From childhood she exhorted him to 'do the right thing because you can never do wrong doing right'. After college, Brown became a close friend of Martin Luther King, served on his executive committee, and was recruited to work in the civil rights movement, raising funds and helping to get people out of jail. He had worked as a fixer for commercial companies nationwide, advising companies that had problems pushing through desegregation policies. He had also been an adviser to F. W. Woolworth as they struggled to desegregate their food counters in stores across the Deep South. In February 1960, four young black men had sat down at Woolworth's lunch counter in Greensboro, North Carolina, and ordered coffee. As *TIME* magazine reported, 'the white patrons eyed them warily, and the white waitresses ignored their studiously polite requests for service'. The men were all students at the Agricultural and Technical College of North Carolina. Despite being ignored, they refused to leave the five-and-dime store and remained seated until closing time, then returned over the next few days with increasing numbers of students, finally totalling more than a thousand, determined to integrate the whites-only store. Robert Brown gradually convinced the area manager to uphold the law and desegregate. He built up a reputation as a man who could do deals with white-owned corporations and was less threatening to the boardroom than many of the Black Power organisations that were mobilising in the big cities.

Brown had grown up a Democrat. He was recruited by Bobby Kennedy, who made him a director of information for the Young Democrats in New York, but Kennedy died a few months later. Then, Republican friends encouraged him to work with Nixon, who he believed was passionate about civil rights issues.

I thought he was a man who kept his word and who wanted to do the right thing. That's what impressed me about him . . . when he talked and he wanted something done, there was nobody playing.

Later in life, in his autobiography, *You Can't Go Wrong Doing Right*, Brown admitted that turning his back on Hubert Humphrey's presidential campaign to join forces with Nixon was like crossing to the 'dark side'. He described Nixon as an enigma, a man who 'would do whatever was politically expedient'. After an emollient lunch at the Summit Hotel on New York's Lexington Avenue, however, Nixon's aides won Brown over. He agreed terms and duly crossed over to the dark side.

The demographics were stacked against Nixon. In his 1960 presidential campaign against Kennedy, he had attracted just less than 30 per cent of the African American vote, and private polling had suggested that even that was dwindling. Republicans were privately estimating they might get 12 per cent of the black vote. It was against this backdrop of low expectations that Brown was sent on the road to find black musicians who would join Nixon's campaign to transform the ghettos through black capitalism. The most obvious staging post was Detroit, home of the Motown Corporation, the most successful black-owned company in America. Two substantial barriers stood in his way: the city had already developed its own network of self-help groups, and Motown's success was built on values of hard work, social enterprise and lifelong learning. Motown's owner, Berry Gordy Jr, and most of his famous artists – The Supremes, the Four Tops and The Temptations – had grown up either in union homes, in ghetto businesses or as solid Democrat voters. Neither Motown nor the city of Detroit had any great reason to love Richard Nixon.

While raising her eight children, Berry Gordy's mother Bertha carved out her own career. She was an agent for Western Mutual Insurance, studied retail management at the Wayne State University and ran several local initiatives. She set up one of Detroit's first mutual insurance companies aimed at low-income black families and was an activist in the Detroit chapter of the NAACP. For a period in the early sixties, she was a branch member of the Housewives League of Detroit, a group led by the visionary community activist Fannie B. Peck that sought to convince black housewives that they could influence the economy by targeting their household spending in stores owned by African Americans. Under the galvanising motto 'Stabilize the economic status of the Negro through directed spending', the Housewives League turned their purses into a political force. This spirit of solidarity allied with self-help became the Gordy family's core value, and it was in the New Year of 1959 that Berry Gordy applied for a family business loan to set up Motown. The family claims that the women of the house were methodical and demanding about the rules of issuing loans, and were in awe of the pioneering Maggie Lena Walker, the daughter of a slave and the first African American woman to run a US bank. Her motto might have been the founding principles of Motown: 'Let us have a bank that will take the nickels and turn them into dollars.' Motown thrived on the nickels that fed the jukeboxes of the early sixties and the dollars that bought working-class consumers their own 45rpm discs.

There was nothing that the White House could teach the Gordy family about black enterprise and Nixon's emissary Robert Brown was never likely to shake the family from their Democratic Party affiliations. Nonetheless, he travelled to Detroit, determined to secure their support and recruit one of the family's oldest friends, the Detroit beautician Carmen Murphy. Born in 1915, just outside Little Rock, Arkansas, ex-model Murphy was the owner of a cosmetics franchise and a flagship shop called the House of Beauty (HOB) aimed at the African American woman. Diana Ross of The Supremes had been a client and had learned basic make-up and grooming tips from HOB's trained assistants. Like the Gordys, Murphy had an unshakeable belief in black entrepreneurship and had built one of the most successful businesses in the Midwest, offering 'tip to toe' coiffure, pedicure and manicure services to teenagers and housewives. Murphy battled to develop cosmetics for deeper skin tones, approaching every major beauty company including Avon and Revlon for help, but they rejected her idea, one saying that it would 'spoil their image in the white community'. However, in 1950 she succeeded in attracting support and worked with chemists to develop her own competetively priced line, Carmen Cosmetics – 'everyday beauty for every smart woman'. By 1971, the range was being sold in

Woolworth's and some other department stores, but what Murphy described as systemic racism from the banks who refused credit prevented her company developing any further. She retired in 1974.

Her husband once told *Ebony* that his wife had applied assembly-line thinking to the beauty business. 'Leave my wife alone,' he told the magazine, 'and the House of Beauty would be as large as the Ford plant at River Rouge.'

Less known is the fact that Murphy played a key role in the evolution of soul music in the city, hosting a small recording studio in the basement of her beauty parlour on Mack Avenue. She had been one of Gordy's mentors and had supported his music ventures in the early days of Motown, periodically acting as an executive producer and releasing records on her own HOB label. She distributed several local hit records by pre-Motown artists like Herman Griffin and The Rayber Voices, including songs written and produced by Gordy himself. Although she made her money from beauty and style, Murphy stayed close to the church and sold Christian gospel music via a distribution deal with Wand Records in New York. She was a self-taught business guru who persistently reminded Gordy that he was not in the recording business, he was in the *distribution* business. Ultimately, it didn't really matter how great a song was or how pulsating its rhythm, if it wasn't in the shops it wouldn't sell.

Although Gordy had built his Motown empire on an image of youthful exuberance and teenage love, it was a matriarchy of powerful older women who had provided the off-stage support structures. Both Carmen Murphy and his mother Bertha were informal business advisers and his formidable sisters were ubiquitous at Motown, two of them – Loucye and Esther – occupying senior management roles. Esther was a significant barrier to Nixon's advances: she had often flirted with running for public office as a Democrat and was married to George Edwards, a Democratic Party member of the Michigan House of Representatives. They had an open door to President Johnson and his VP Hubert Humphrey, were close to Mayor Jerome Cavanagh and personal friends of Congressman John Conyers, who co-sponsored the Voting Rights Act of 1965, which prohibited discrimination at the ballot box. Conyers had embarked on a fifteen-year struggle to commemorate Martin Luther King. Days after King's assassination in April 1968,

Conyers proposed the first of many bills calling for a federal holiday in his honour. A fierce critic of the Vietnam War, he had the questionable status of being Number 13 on President Nixon's list of enemies, the people he thought were in league to bring him down.

As Nixon's presidency became engulfed in scandal, Conyers was a vocal supporter of impeachment:

> My analysis of the evidence clearly reveals an Administration so trapped by its own war policy and a desire to remain in office that it entered into an almost unending series of plans for spying, burglary and wiretapping, inside this country and against its own citizens, and without precedent in American history.

Gordy's sisters already ran a network of small businesses across the city, from cigarette franchises to record labels. Esther founded the Gordy Printing Company and Loucye became the first black administrator at the Michigan Army Reserve at Fort Wayne, and although they were among Berry Gordy's most trusted allies, there was an underlying sense that they had been put there to protect the family's investment. When the company faced any major problems, it was to his sisters – rather than salaried managers – that Gordy instinctively turned.

For nearly a century, a lack of working capital and development funding had hampered small independent music labels. Records were pressed in boxes of 250, there was scant money for national advertising and distribution deals were slow to pay out. Great music by hugely talented blues, jazz and soul artists simply died at birth, unable to overcome the mountain of challenges it faced to get it into stores. It was common for soul records to be sold from the backs of cars, at Chitlin' Circuit venues or at local liquor stores. Many aspiring black businesses were also blocked by discriminatory banks or by restrictive commercial covenants, although Gordy had the option of applying to his family's own bank, the Ber-Berry Co-op, a family fund established by his mother, who supported mutuality in the family and invested in business plans. The headquarters of this mutual fund was the family dinner table at their home at 5139 St Antoine. After a tense meeting in which his normally loyal sister Esther voiced significant doubts about the music distribution industry, Gordy was loaned $800 to launch

Tamla, the founding label of the Motown recording company. It was to become one of the most spectacularly successful start-up investments in the corporate history of America.

Berry Gordy and one of his most successful producers, Norman Whitfield, were cut from the same ideological cloth. Gordy had absorbed the message of self-help from his father and the network of small businesses the family operated across Detroit. Whitfield had imbibed the principle of 'reaching for the best' from his uncle, pharmacist Sidney Barthwell. At the height of the Great Depression Barthwell had used his savings to buy a failing pharmacy and built a business empire by installing soda fountains in his premises. By 1967, he owned nine drug stores across the Motor City and had risen to become president of the Booker T. Washington Business Association, which counted several members of the Gordy family within its ranks. His nephew had a creative imagination. Norman was a well-built man with a dark goatee beard and trimmed afro, and he embraced innovation with a bear hug. Whitfield was keen to explore new influences far from Motown's pop mainstream, and by late 1967 he had embarked on a plan to transform the image of The Temptations. By doing so, he changed the direction of Motown. Whitfield had watched the great Detroit groups of the sixties with a sharp eye and was struck by how similar they all were: phenomenal harmonisers dressed in matching clothes with immaculate choreographed stage routines. It was the gold-standard imprimatur of sixties soul with a legacy that stretched back to the doo-wop groups of the fifties.

For the next three years Whitfield drove psychedelic soul on, experimenting with extreme guitar play, anti-war sentiment and expanded consciousness, with The Temptations ('Papa Was A Rollin' Stone', 'Cloud Nine' and 'Ball Of Confusion (That's What The World Is Today)' (Gordy, 1970), Edwin Starr ('War', Motown, 1970) and The Undisputed Truth ('Smiling Faces Sometimes', Gordy, 1971). His efforts were assisted by a new Motown recruit, guitarist Dennis Coffey, whose hard-rock innovations included feedback, distortion, Echoplex tape-loop delay and the spectral glide of wah-wah pedals. It was a noise far removed from the bubble-gum soul of 1965. Otis Williams of The Temptations described it as something close to a mission and grounded in the politics of the day: 'Musically speaking,

Norman set a mood that was worlds apart: dark, threatening, and even hostile.' It was the antithesis of what Motown had been in its joyous and romantic heyday and reflected the discordance of the Nixon era.

Having had no great success in Detroit, Robert Brown experienced another rebuttal in Memphis, where the newly installed Stax vice president Al Bell Jr, a child of civil rights demonstrations, proved as reluctant as the Gordy family. With no luck at either Motown or Stax, Brown then turned his attention to his namesake, James.

By early 1972, while President Nixon was in Beijing trying to build diplomatic relations with communist China, the singer was on the road promoting his single 'Get On The Good Foot' (Polydor, 1972) when the White House invited him to share his thoughts on how to encourage greater entrepreneurialism within America's ghetto communities. Nixon had hit on a typically canny circumlocution: he seemingly embraced the notion of Black Power at a time when it was gripping inner-city America and claimed it was only truly achievable through increased business transactions or creating greater wealth in deprived communities. Black capitalism was a laudable enough policy, but it was a smoke-and-mirrors concept divorced from sufficient federal funding to allow it to address the deeply ingrained problems of urban poverty. 'Instead of government jobs and government housing and government welfare,' Nixon said in a set-piece speech, 'let government use its tax and credit policies' to power 'the greatest engine of progress ever developed in the history of man: American private enterprise.' Many Black Power advocates viewed black capitalism as the move of the moment – the Nation of Islam had some of the most successful businesses of the era, including property developments, restaurants and launderettes – but many more saw the concept as a sleight of hand, a means of cutting back on inner-city projects.

In May 1970, a 16-year-old called Charles Oatman was found dead in his cell in the county jail, in Augusta, Georgia, having supposedly fallen from a bunk. Oatman had mental health issues and had been placed there in the absence of any available psychiatric hospital after the fatal accidental wounding of his niece. When his body was finally taken to the mortuary, it showed signs of assault. Mortician Carrie Mays said at the time, 'I saw right off somebody had really lit into the boy. He had been beaten something awful, and there were cigarette burns on his hands and feet.' The coroner's report concluded that Oatman had died of 'pulmonary edema, bilateral severe; and subdural haemorrhage, due to numerous severe beatings'. Two fellow inmates, both black, were charged with his murder (although their culpability was questioned), but the anger his death unlocked was ferocious. Several hundred locals demonstrated outside the city county building against the policy of confining people in need of mental health care in a county jail. Tensions escalated rapidly as younger members of the crowd tore down the Georgia state flag and burned it in front of riot police. More than fifty fires were set that afternoon and evening, destroying around eighty businesses. Outbreaks of petty vandalism and noisy chanting continued as the crowd marched throughout the downtown area. A community newspaper described the scenes that followed:

> Six Black men are dead, gunned down by police. Dozens more are wounded. Fifteen hundred troops continue to patrol the streets. A tense calm has fallen over this city of 70,000, 49 percent of whom are Black, following the indiscriminate murders by police Monday night, May 11, and Tuesday morning, May 12. They came in with M-14s, and they came in to shoot to kill.

To this day it remains unclear what sparked the clash between law enforcement and demonstrators. Some accounts cite marchers throwing bricks, bottles and punches while others claim police fired the first shot. The violence spiralled out of control and tear gas was launched into the crowd. Regardless of the catalyst, the outcome was devastating: six men were killed by the police, some of whom were shot in the back as they ran away.

James Brown was in Flint, Michigan, when the troubles in Augusta broke out. He was performing at the Giant Ballroom on North Saginaw Street, a venue that a year previously had hosted the militant Weather Underground's Flint War Council, at which the organisation plotted to use guerrilla warfare to overthrow the government. Brown flew home in his private jet for an emergency summit meeting with the Governor of Georgia, the staunch segregationist Lester Garfield Maddox, who had fled his home after 500 students surrounded the mansion in silent protest after the killings. The meeting took place at offices within the city's R&B station WRDW. Maddox's intention was to secure an agreement with Brown, the station's programme director and a senior news director that the station would neither inflame nor exacerbate the troubles outside.

Maddox had a history and was not without blame. He was a populist Democrat who came to prominence resisting school integration and refused to serve black customers in the Pickrick, his fried chicken restaurant in downtown Atlanta. He once flouted the law by refusing to serve chicken wings to three black students and waved a pistol at them, shouting 'You no good dirty devils! You dirty communists!' Maddox also sold autographed pickaxe handles to white customers to ward off black students, branding them as 'Pickrick Drumsticks'. He campaigned hard for states' rights and maintained a segregationist stance throughout his time in office. On the death of Martin Luther King, Maddox denied the preacher the honour of lying in state in the Georgia state capitol and stationed 160 state troopers around the building after being told by undercover agents in the Atlanta Police Department that mourners were planning to storm the building. In the race for the White House in 1968 Maddox endorsed George Wallace, the pro-segregation American Independent Party candidate. After serving four years as governor, Maddox was precluded by state law from serving another consecutive term and was elected lieutenant governor instead. He was one of the last of the infamous southern demagogues who resisted racial integration. Ironically, Maddox was replaced by Jimmy Carter in what was the next step in the Georgia peanut farmer's ambitions to become President.

By all accounts, the meeting between James Brown and Governor Maddox was tense and prickly. Brown insisted that discrimination had played a part in the disturbances, but Maddox stood his ground and said laws were there to be obeyed. It was an inconclusive conversation, with little shared ground, but the radio station did fashion a clever slogan that was repeated in the days to come: 'Don't save face, save your city.' It was a signal that the black community should not back down but neither should they give in to wanton protest.

When Robert Brown took to the road to press flesh with black business lwaders, he came to James Brown relatively late in the day, turning to a man who in his own remarkable way was redefining soul by creating and commercialising funk – the lawless new form of dance music based on drum and bass, stripped of any old-school romanticism.

James Brown visited the Oval Office on 10 October 1972, accompanied by his father Joseph and Charles Bobbit, the president of his company J.B. Enterprises. Bobbit was also an unlikely visitor to the Oval Office. A former member of the Nation of Islam, he was a rock-hard captain of the Nation's security force, the Fruit of Islam, and described by guitarist Bobby Roach as 'one of Elijah Muhammad's main guards . . . a collecting artist; he collected money for the Nation, and he was good at it. He had a black belt and that's how he came to be one of Muhammad's bodyguards.' Perhaps more than anyone else, Bobbit was close to James Brown; he watched his idiosyncrasies grow into obsessions over the years and described his boss as an unusual man, 'changing mood and temperament on a dime'. Bull-headed and difficult to reason with, Brown was a man who acted on impulse and rationalised later. Over years of explosive performances, Brown's knees became arthritic from dropping to the floor during his songs. 'His knees sometimes would bleed and were scarred and busted up, but he didn't share that with people. He was a very private and proud man,' Bobbit explained. 'Mr. Brown was traditional. He insisted on being called Mr. Brown and he himself called people either "Mr" or "Miss." Mr. Brown's word was law. People got along with him as long as you let him be right. That was the way it was.'

This need to be right would lead James Brown to a thunderstorm of criticism. He used the brief meeting with Nixon to push for a national holiday celebrating Martin Luther King. Distracted and barely keeping eye contact with the singer, Nixon admitted he was 'aware of that', meaning the nascent movement to remember King. Although James Brown was immune to the frosty atmosphere, a ten-minute tape recording from the Oval Office reveals Nixon pushing back against the meeting. He barked off-microphone at his aides, 'No more black stuff. No more blacks from now on. Just don't bring 'em in here.' In his unguarded moments, which were many, Nixon was prone to using insults that were already being confined to history. He frequently used anti-Semitic insults and once said, 'I hate intellectuals. There's something effeminate about them. I'd rather talk to an athlete.' It was a view he shared with James Brown.

Concerned that the meeting might be derailed, Robert Brown calmed the President down and explained that the singer was hugely influential in the black community and was there to endorse black capitalism. Nixon reluctantly conceded to the meeting, which is now known as Conversation 795-008 of the White House Tapes. It is muddled but convivial, punctuated with small bursts of throaty laughter and fake bonhomie as Nixon tries to hurry up proceedings. White House photographer Ollie Atkins snaps the encounter throughout, the noise of his camera shutter often noisier than the conversation and obscuring James Brown's small talk. Nixon then steps back into a set-up behind the desk in the Oval Office, where he shows James Brown the presidential flag and coat of arms. They shake hands warmly, and without any significant discussion of black capitalism the meeting is over.

Compared with the now-iconic meeting between Nixon and Elvis Presley two years earlier, Nixon's meeting with James Brown was a perfunctory affair. When Presley showed up at the White House on 21 December 1970, he was resplendent in a purple velvet suit, gold belt and a Colt.45 pistol. The King was back, basking in the aftermath of his successful 1968 comeback special and selling out shows in Las Vegas.

He bore a hand-written letter for the President which outlined his concerns about social issues: 'I have done an in-depth study of drug abuse and Communist brainwashing techniques and I am right in the middle of the whole thing where I can and will do the most good.' He then offered his services as a special agent who could help fight the war on illegal drugs and requested a Bureau of Narcotics and Dangerous Drugs badge (collecting law enforcement badges was an obsession of his).

One of Nixon's aides, Egil Krogh, who was present during the meeting, took notes of the bizarre exchange.

Presley indicated that he thought the Beatles had been a real force for anti-American spirit. He said that the Beatles came to this country, made their money, and then returned to England where they promoted an anti-American theme. The President nodded in agreement and expressed some surprise. The President then indicated that those who

Elvis Presley poses with President Richard Nixon in the White House, 21 December 1970. The legendary meeting inspired the 2016 comedy drama *Elvis & Nixon* (starring Michael Shannon and Kevin Spacey).

use drugs are also those in the vanguard of anti-American protest. Violence, drug usage, dissent, protest all seem to merge in generally the same group of young people.

Although somewhat taken aback by Presley's words, Nixon agreed. In many respects these were his own views and he felt that Presley might help to retain some of his credibility.

According to *The New York Times*, just weeks before he died in 1977, Elvis called President Carter, 'incoherent' and 'totally stoned' in an attempt to seek a presidential pardon for a sheriff he knew. Carter 'talked to him for a long time' and tried to 'ease Presley out of his paranoid delusions' but explained that he couldn't issue a pardon until after a trial. Elvis couldn't grasp the situation and called the White House many times before his death, trying, unsuccessfully, to reach the President.

*

All the time that James Brown was in the Oval Office, Nixon's Sony TC-800B open-reel recorder was working secretly in the background. It is one of the darkest ironies of presidential power that Nixon installed a sophisticated sound-activated system to record his time in office, to ward off hostile surveillance from his many enemies. Only two men in the inner sanctum of the Oval Office knew that the tape recorder had been installed: Richard Nixon and his Chief of Staff, H. R. Haldeman. Nixon had once said to Haldeman, 'You know, I always wondered about that taping equipment but I'm damn glad we have it, aren't you?' It was operated in an adjoining room by Nixon's ultra-loyal secretary Rose Mary Woods, but none of the President's closest circle could anticipate how the tapes would unspool and incriminate them so dramatically in the months to come.

Paranoia had taken over the White House. Secretary of State Henry Kissinger had also rigged up his office with numerous recording devices and had the tapes transcribed by secretaries. In time, Nixon became entrapped by his own deceit and the White House Tapes would sit at the heart of a national scandal. In June 1972, almost four months before James Brown came to the White House, the ramifications of a break-in at the Democratic National Committee headquarters in the Watergate complex in Washington D.C. led to an investigation that unravelled to reveal multiple abuses of power by the Nixon administration. As suspicions around Nixon's involvement in the break-in deepened and journalists pulled at every loose thread, the Supreme Court ruled that the President must hand over the recordings to government investigators. Nixon was adamant that they were his personal property, that he was protected by executive privilege and national security, and that any attempt to demand their release was no more than political gamesman-ship by the Democrats. It was not a defence that lasted. The transcripts made it clear that Nixon had conspired to cover up activities around the break-in and attempted to use federal officials to deflect the investigation. The Watergate scandal unfolded.

Initially, James Brown attributed the hostility towards him on the soul circuit to the age-old curse of jealousy and to the presumption that he was in receipt of kickbacks from the White House. He told his biographer, Bruce Tucker, that many rivals on the circuit resented his success. 'I knew what people were saying about me endorsing Mr. Nixon. People were saying he was buying endorsements with black capitalism grants and contracts. I tried to deal with it upfront. "I'm not a sell-out artist," I said. "I never received a government grant. I never asked for one and don't want one. I'm not selling out, I'm selling in. Dig?"' Unfortunately for Brown, very few did dig it and boycotts of his concerts continued well into the late seventies. 'Less than a week after I endorsed Mr. Nixon I did a show in Baltimore,' Brown recalled. 'There were pickets outside the arena discouraging people from coming to see my show. Usually, I sold out all thirteen thousand seats there, but that night only about two thousand five hundred people showed up. I was disappointed. People just didn't understand.'

Others suffered a similar fate. After Sammy Davis Jr – temperamentally a Democrat who had endorsed JFK's presidential campaign in 1960 – embraced Nixon on stage at the Republican National Convention in 1972 his reputation in the African American community plummeted. Despite his support for Martin Luther King and generous donations to Operation PUSH, he was considered a sellout and an Uncle Tom, and his tour to South Vietnam, at the height of the war's popularity, made things even worse He was booed off stage in Chicago when he attended the first annual Black Expo, which was held under the auspices of Operation PUSH, the group founded by the Reverend Jesse Jackson, and came under fire from an emotional crowd before being ushered off stage to safety.

The New York Times described these incidents as 'indicative of the bitter political battle for black votes this election year [1972]', reflecting 'deep division and continuing strong dislike of President Nixon in a group that traditionally voted overwhelmingly Democratic'. The 'emotionalism and division' were intense, and stemmed from the belief that Nixon was attempting to buy support from the African American community through his black capitalism programmes.

Even staunch Republicans like Harold E. Neely, a gubernatorial nominee and GOP fixer, told James Brown that he had made a colossal error of judgement. Nixon was so toxic to some within his own party that even former presidents recoiled at his name. Harry S. Truman pulled no punches: 'Richard Nixon is a no-good, lying bastard. He can lie out of both sides of his mouth at the same time, and if he ever caught himself telling the truth, he'd lie just to keep his hand in.'

Yet another suitor who sought an audience with Nixon was the reigning heavyweight boxing champion and later Motown soul singer Joe Frazier, who wanted both to ingratiate himself with Nixon and to seek a favour. 'I went to see President Nixon at the White House. It wasn't difficult to get a meeting because I was heavyweight champion of the world,' he confided in his biography. 'So, I came to Washington and walked around the garden with Nixon, his wife and daughter. I said: I want you to give Ali his licence back. I want to beat him up for you.' The boxing industry was salivating about a title fight between Ali and Frazier, one that would ultimately determine who was the greatest and secure both men life-transforming money.

One of many accusations levelled against James Brown and his relationship with Nixon was that he was seeking to benefit from the so-called Philadelphia Plan, a federal affirmative-action programme established in 1967 to end discriminatory labour practices in the construction industry. How Brown was ever likely to benefit from the plan, which in any case had been abandoned by Nixon after numerous legal challenges in 1970, is unclear. Brown became a victim of rumour outstretching reality, but the image of him as a greedy, self-serving maverick who had ingratiated himself with power hung around for years to come. The Congressional Black Caucus, the most powerful grouping in African American politics, named and shamed him along with other black celebrities who supported Nixon.

Baltimore had been something of a staging post for James Brown. Throughout his career he regularly appeared at the Royal Theater in West Baltimore, one of the most famous venues on the city's Pennsylvania Avenue and a key stop on the Chitlin' Circuit. In 1964, he had recorded his live album *Pure Dynamite!* there as the clock ticked down on its future. By 1968, in the aftermath of the assassination of Martin Luther King, the area around the Royal became engulfed in self-destructive rioting and, unable to find a future for itself, the old warhorse of Baltimore's black music scene, which had once played host to Louis Jordan, Duke Ellington, Etta James, The Temptations and The Supremes, was closed and then demolished.

James Brown signed up to return shows at the Baltimore Civic Center but changing demographics and fear of the inner city's corrosion drastically reduced the huge audiences he was used to. Supporting Nixon was not the only explanation, but it was a final nail in the coffin of his popularity in Baltimore, once measured by crowds of up to twenty thousand as sixties soul hit its triumphant peak. By the mid seventies, despite considerable interest in James Brown's releases, not least the instantly recognisable 'Sex Machine' (Polydor, 1975), his ghetto audiences in Baltimore had fallen from their once-epic height.

Of course, Brown did not take these setbacks lying down. He arranged a retaliatory press conference to justify his support for Nixon. A press release in the form of a personal letter from the President was circulated. According to biographer R. J. Smith, it said: 'The mark of a man was standing firm in the face of recent unjust pressure.' But Brown and his stablemate on the day, the singer Hank Ballard, cut a faintly ridiculous presence. Ballard, writer of 'The Twist' and once an R&B innovator and pioneer of soul, had begun a long, slow decline. Two years later, in 1974, he recorded the novelty funk song 'Let's Go Streaking' (Stang, 1974) while stark naked. *Black Enterprise*, the bible of minority-owned business, gave some comfort to Brown's cause, reporting that the total value of loans to minorities had been $100.7 million, three times higher than any previous year. Nixon had at least had some success in encouraging banks to be more welcoming to smaller African American firms but the feelgood did not last long. For those at the bottom of the social ladder it was meaningless, and as the Watergate scandal gained momentum the President lost interest and focused more on saving his own skin.

A curious side to Brown's personality was his ability to do business with racists. It was neither a deferential nor an obsequious trait but more likely a not uncommon rural idea of plain talking. Although he believed in racial justice, Brown was no great lover of the academic end of the civil rights movement; nor was he comfortable in the company of those such as James Baldwin or Stokely Carmichael, whose intelligence drew on sources and ideas far from Brown's humble origins. It was an anti-intellectual quality he shared with President Nixon.

Later in life, Brown befriended the virulent segregationist Senator Strom Thurmond, whom he described as 'one of his heroes' and 'like a grandfather to me'. Thurmond had stood for president back in 1948 on a third-party ticket for the so-called Dixiecrats, also known as the States'

Rights Democratic Party. 'I wanna tell you, ladies and gentlemen,' Thurmond said in one speech, 'there's not enough troops in the army to force the Southern people to break down segregation and admit the Nigra race into our theaters, into our swimming pools, into our homes, and into our churches.' It was the language of the crude southern racist and while James Brown would have passionately disagreed, he preferred Thurmond's straight-talking country-boy bombast to the slick, smooth-talking politicians of urban America.

James Brown's interventions in the racial politics of his day were mainly well-meaning but they were sometimes naïve and frequently self-serving. His endorsement of Richard Nixon's presidency was motivated by the desire to make inroads and build networks, but his approach undermined his many good points and he never really received credit for his unwavering support for a national holiday in honour of Martin Luther King. The baton for that campaign was handed to a much more formidable champion, the Motown superstar Stevie Wonder, who by the early seventies was blazing his own visionary trail founded on synthesized rhythms and socially conscious lyrics.

As Atlantic Records diversified from its R&B origins, embracing countercultural rock and signing Led Zeppelin, Graham Nash, Stephen Stills and David Crosby, some remarkable funk and soul records faded unloved and under-promoted into history. One that was lost to the commercial world was Eugene McDaniels' eloquent single 'Tell Me, Mr President' (Atlantic, 1971). McDaniels, a crooner from Kansas who transformed his image from supper-club vocalist to political seer, released a surreal and savage attack on the failures of the Nixon presidency on the album *Headless Heroes Of The Apocalypse*. In an increasingly diverse and competitive rock-soul moment, it was not supported by the label and stiffed on its release. McDaniels barely earned enough from the royalties to buy a hamburger and earned a living as an Atlantic studio backing singer with his colleagues Cissy Houston and Jo 'Joshie' Armstead. Today, *Headless Heroes Of The Apocalypse* has found new life as an underground classic sampled by numerous hip-hop artists and is revered in the way it uses jazz, funk, soul and even protest folk styles to criticise ghetto poverty, the war in Vietnam and America's dark culture of political assassination. It stands out as a testament to the gathering resentment towards Nixon and his seeming dismissal of using public funding to help inner-city communities.

As funk ignited another influential moment in African American music, James Brown was hit with a bombshell. His stellar success had brought him substantial new wealth but had also attracted the attention of the Inland Revenue Services, who found serious defaults in his tax affairs. Back in 1968, the IRS had informed Brown that he owed nearly $2 million, mostly because of under-reporting of cash payments for his nightly concerts. He had ignored the estimate and continued to pursue a reckless policy of hiding money, carrying suitcases full of crumpled dollars and storing bags of cash in secret places, including holes in the wall in his Augusta home, which at one time supposedly risked the property's architectural stability. As his reputation soared abroad, and he concealed even more cash payments in foreign currencies, Brown was hit with further demands. The more the IRS probed, the more they found wrong. He was by now earning substantial revenues from concerts, publishing rights, contracts with European record labels and movies, television and radio rights. It was a mess of different income sources compounded by a recent takeover of his record company King Records of Cincinnati. When the founding owner of King, the eccentric Syd Nathan, died in 1968, the accountancy muddle that he left behind was inherited by the Texas label Starday Records and sold on again to LIN Broadcasting. It changed hands twice more, by which time artists' payments were a maze. Rather than deal with the problem or hire lawyers who could, Brown took the decision to slide into denial: he threw away estimates, buried his head in the sand and even set alight final demands. He was an unstoppable cash machine, whose business interests were diversified in radio stations, merchandise, income from movie screenplays and property. He bought a hotel on Franklin and Paca Streets in Baltimore, christened it the James Brown Motor Inn and used it as the base for a briefly successful nightclub called the Windjammer. In the way of many an underground nightclub mystery, it was eventually burnt down, a fate that also befell his other nightclub, the Third World, in Augusta.

Mysterious fires and the resultant insurance claims were raising suspicion. In the absence of credible tax returns, the IRS simply calculated more tax, taking the tab to $4.5 million. Threats to seize property and repossess other physical assets did not lead to an agreement, though; in fact it drove Brown deeper into resentful paranoia. Walter Jowers, a guitarist in the Third World club, described Brown's approach to management as a metaphor for the singer's corroding lifestyle.

> In the front of the building, there was a one-sliding-window takeout restaurant that sold only chicken wings. In the back of the building, there was an expansive parking lot. The lot was not paved. Mr. Brown's club had uniformed doormen, but their shoes and pants were covered with mud. There were gold-plated faucets in The Third World's dressing rooms, but the drainpipes leaked and smelled . . . As the situation at the club deteriorated, employees' pay checks started bouncing. It was during this spell that a percussionist from New York said to me, 'If my check bounces, I'll burn this place to the ground.' The next day, The Third World burned down.

As Brown's tax problems mounted, he began to concoct a solution. Surely a presidential pardon would get the IRS off his back? In 1978, believing he still had a friend in the White House, Brown wrote lengthy, meandering letters to Jimmy Carter asking him to intervene. Brown claimed to have known Carter from their shared backgrounds in Georgia, but his letters went unanswered, in part because Carter's knowledge of the Georgia music scene ran deep and he was aware of the gathering storm around Brown's life. The stories of his tax affairs, his dictatorial control over band members, his dysfunctional marriage and a growing problem with angel dust made Carter wary. By 1998, his tax bill had topped $9 million, and so he tried again, writing a pleading letter to President Bill Clinton in which he makes the radical suggestion that African Americans be freed from paying tax as a gesture of reparation for slavery. It was a selfish and poorly judged act. The question of reparation and how to address the legacy of slavery was in the air, but not as a means of solving a musician's financial mismanagement.

James Brown died of a heart attack on Christmas Day 2006 at the age of 73. Among the many personal effects put up for auction to clear his debts was a framed photograph of James Brown and George W. Bush inscribed 'Killings Is Out, School's In', a picture that commemorated the aftermath of the Virginia Tech shootings in 2007, in which thirty-two people died.

*

On the worst night of the Augusta uprisings, as James Brown flew home in his private jet, Richard Nixon was in the White House watching the heist caper *Topkapi*. Nixon was an obsessive film buff who had installed screening facilities at Camp David and in his Florida home in Key Biscayne. He regularly watched a film at night to unwind. US National Security Advisor Henry Kissinger once said that 'the essence of Richard Nixon is loneliness'.

Nixon's tastes in cinema were conservative. He rarely strayed far from Hollywood genre fodder and seemed immune to the new independent cinema that was flourishing during his presidency. Coincidentally *Topkapi* was directed by the once blacklisted director Jules Dassin, who had pioneered a new kind of urban cinema about inner-city racial tensions when he directed the film *Uptight*, a twist on the John Ford classic *The Informer*. Set in Cleveland, with a soundtrack by Booker T. and the M.G.'s, *Uptight* had many of the characteristics of what became known as 'blaxploitation': fast-paced crime films that were inextricably linked to ghetto culture and soul music.

Almost inevitably James Brown had been welcoming of this new genre and profited when movie producer Larry Cohen acquired a script which loosely updated the story of the 1931 gangster movie *Little Caesar*, starring Edward G. Robinson. Cohen approached Brown to compose the soundtrack but most of the work passed to his pivotal band member Fred Wesley, who shaped the score and provided the backing tracks to 'The Boss', a song about Brown himself that provides the background music for a scene in which the central character, Tommy Gibbs, is shot while crossing a street corner.

In a deep sociological twist, blaxploitation films were often an amoral rendering of the black capitalism Nixon was advocating. The films were packed with ambition, street enterprise and individual risk, although unlike Nixon's vision the business was sex, crime and drugs. The actor Ossie Davis, who had become a Harlem celebrity after his passionate oratory at the funeral of Malcolm X, told the magazine *Black Enterprise* that the illegal drugs trade evidenced capabilities that many businesses including the film industry were crying out for.

If you would give me the five biggest pimps and pushers in this country, the black ones, and I could persuade them for one year to drop their hustle on the corner . . . if I could say, 'Look, for one year I want you to take that same push, that same organizational ability, and put it in films' – well, at the end of that one year black folks would take over the whole film industry.

There was a kernel of truth in Davis's words: too many young black men with skills and acumen were being diverted to the drugs trade in the absence of meaningful alternatives in the jobs market.

The movie that crystallised all the complexities and contradictions of black capitalism at street level was *Super Fly*, featuring Curtis Mayfield's epic soundtrack. It would not be too big an exaggeration to say that the Chicago musical genius invented a new purpose for soul music, the art of meta-commentary, music that passed critical comment on the scenes it witnessed. By the power and subtlety of his music, Mayfield took a film that was struggling for narrative coherence, with no clear moral core, and gave it a purpose. According to Mayfield's own son, the music 'became the film's conscience'.

Super Fly was a totemic film, shot entirely on location in Harlem at the turn of the decade and had been financed in an unusual way, through an early version of crowdfunding. The producers approached several Harlem businesses, raising small investments from up to eighteen investors. In the film's press release the consortium was described tongue-in-cheek as a group of 'pimps, madams and drug dealers'. There was an element of truth in the assertion, but the investors were drawn from a much a broader funding base. In an article in *Variety* magazine, the director Gordon Parks Jr specifically thanked his father, the famous photographer Gordon Parks Sr, who had invested, and two black dentists, Ed Allen and Cornelius 'Connie' Jenkins, who were also prominent in helping finance the production.

In a ground-shifting essay, academic Dr Eithne Quinn makes several crucial and frequently overlooked points about *Super Fly*. 'The film, as reported by *Variety*, set two racial precedents in mainstream American filmmaking: the first major-distributed film to be financed predominantly by black limited partnerships and the first to have a largely non-white technical crew.' Although it was a distant connection, these were among the outcomes that Nixon's policy of black capitalism had promised. Furthermore, the local black investors enabled unique access for location shooting. The film critic Donald Bogle saw authenticity at the heart of the film: "'Superfly' looks authentic: the Harlem settings, the streets and alleyways, the bars, and the tenements all paint an overriding bleak vision of urban decay', which was 'new terrain for commercial cinema'.

Although the urban cinema genre became burdened with the term 'blaxploitation', it was an unprecedented opportunity for black musicians to work in a new medium. Curtis Mayfield had spent more than a decade in the music industry but never been schooled in cinema soundtracks. It was only when his final album with the Impressions, *The Young Mods' Forgotten Story*, was released in 1969 that his name came into the mind of the filmmakers. Two particular tracks from that album, the R&B chart number one single 'Choice Of Colors', arranged by Johnny Pate and Donny Hathaway, and the racially charged 'Mighty Mighty (Spade And Whitey)' showed Mayfield in a new light, less wistful and more keenly attuned to the racial fault lines of America in the late sixties. His solo career would pursue those ideas even more aggressively.

It was a crucial time in the life of Curtis Mayfield. The Impressions were destined to split. Mayfield had told them that he planned to go solo and was building a 16-track recording studio in his native Chicago. He worked exhaustively on two solo albums, *Curtis* and *Roots*, determined that his solo career would not get off to a false start, and so in a rush of hectic creativity stretching from the summer of 1969 he wrote or recorded the anti-racist ballad 'We The People Who Are Darker Than Blue', the pleading critique of ghetto deprivation 'The Other Side Of Town' and the anti-spiritual '(Don't Worry) If There's A Hell Below, We're All Going To Go'. Soaring above those was one of the great civil rights records of the era, the masterful 'Move On Up', itself a modernised update on the old Impressions classic 'People Get Ready', which had been recorded back in 1965 in the white heat of the civil rights movement.

The producer of *Super Fly*, Sig Shore, and his screenwriter Phil Fenty, hustled their way backstage at one of the final Impressions concerts at Madison Square Garden and handed Mayfield an early draft of the script of an untitled movie. They exaggerated nearly everything: the state of the script, the funding they had in place and the guaranteed date of principal photography. They pleaded with

Mayfield to give their movie a fair hearing while they wrote revisions and scouted for locations.

For his wellbeing alone, he probably should have turned down the then highly speculative *Super Fly* commission, but his deprived upbringing on Chicago's Cabrini-Green Projects had made Mayfield fearful of poverty and paranoid about missing out on money and opportunity.

Mayfield is ostensibly one of the monumental greats of soul music and his character was every bit as complex as his thoughtful music implies. Like James Brown and Marvin Gaye, he was a bundle of tangled contradictions, a gentle man who admitted to spousal abuse, outspoken about drugs but a serial abuser of cocaine, publicly committed to community politics but protective and selfish about his own personal wealth. Mayfield's voice was reed-thin but his determination to win was immense. In a world of bellowing voices and unrestrained egos, he was a man with quiet if selective sincerity. His whispered soulful delivery frequently needed a dedicated microphone to increase the amplification so his voice would carry to the back of a theatre, but his opinions – fortified by the march of civil rights – were strident and unshakable. In a world of often predictable pop emotions, Mayfield's compositions were suffused with a lyrical texture which positioned him distinctively as a poet amidst the throng.

Many have eulogised Curtis Mayfield but few have pointed to the darker shades of his character. Only his son, Todd, in his admirably fair biography *Travelling Soul: The Life of Curtis Mayfield*, has come close. 'You saw good and evil,' he wrote. 'The vile part came out when it was business . . . He becomes something that you don't want to be around. When it came to business, he was about business. If he's making money, he wants all of it.'

In that respect Mayfield and James Brown had similar motivations, probably exaggerated by the era they grew up in and the horrendous practices they saw on the road as they worked the Chitlin' Circuit. The huge barriers of racism and exploitation that were stacked high in the music industry did not help: songs were brazenly stolen, record sales under-reported and revenues slow to arrive, if they ever did. The world of black music is littered with stories of unconscionable misuse in an industry controlled largely by white men. It was an industry that both James Brown and Curtis Mayfield had grown to distrust and which shaped a legacy that they handed down to the next generation of hip-hop artists who, in their own inimitable argot, demanded to be 'Paid In Full'.

Super Fly opened to an almighty storm of criticism which seemed to build with every new headline. A leading Catholic society, who moralised about cinema, gave the film a 'C' or 'condemned' rating, briefing the press that: 'This kind of black liberation serves only to deceive the brothers and play upon the fears of black audiences.' Black Christian leaders saw an opportunity to picket theatres. Demonstrators carried placards denouncing *Super Fly* with messages such as 'Black Shame for White Profits' and 'We Are Not All Pimps and Whores'.

Perhaps predictably, the furore brought even more attention to *Super Fly* and curious audiences flocked to cinemas to see what the fuss was about. The movie edged further upwards and ranked behind *The Godfather* and *Play It Again, Sam* in the list of top-grossing films of 1972. It had grossed $20 million in seven months alone. Success did nothing to calm the storm; in fact, it invited even fiercer attacks. Vernon E. Jordan of the National Urban League said of the film: 'Hollywood is back to its old game of creating stereotypes of Black people for popular consumption.' Tony Brown, the first Dean of Communications at Washington D.C.'s Howard University and the host of a regular PBS talk show *Tony Brown's Black Journal*, dismissed it melodramatically as 'genocide'.

Elsewhere in Washington, a local church singer had seen an opportunity to bring different values to the stereotype of the ghetto pimp. William Devaughn, a local government draughtsman, had saved up $1,000 to fund a demo at Omega Studios in Maryland before a final session at Sigma Sound Studios in Philadelphia. The outcome was 'Be Thankful For What You Got', which soared to number one on the R&B listings in 1974 and reached number four on *Billboard*'s Hot 100. It sold two million copies. 'Be Thankful For What You Got' occupied a different perspective, bringing an ordinary working-class attitude to the pimp as he drives by with a diamond in the back, sunroof top . . . That refrain became one of the most recognisable lyrics of the *Super Fly* era, but the message was in the title of the song – don't be impressed with flash criminality, be grateful for a more ordinary and honest life, you can still stand tall.

Super Fly became a lightning rod for a dispute that had existed within the African American community for decades, at least since the advent of R&B. The argument was that popular culture was spiritually corrosive, and that music and movies were detrimental to young people, especially those who were exposed to social deprivation and vulnerable to a street life of drugs and crime. It was a dispute with no easy solution and would recur over the decades to come as urban movies came to influence the language of hip-hop and the self-injurious extremes of gangsta rap. A great surge of soul music creativity came in the slipstream of blaxploitation cinema, opening opportunities in the film industry that had hitherto been closed to black musicians.

President Nixon had never heard of Roy Charles Hammond nor did he know how well his aspirations reflected the spirit of the President's now abandoned policy of 'black capitalism'. Hammond was passionate about business and had an entrepreneur's nose for opportunities. Like James Brown, he was a product of Georgia's small-town soul-music conveyor belt. Hammond was from Newington in Screven County and moved north to Long Island to become a lead singer with the R&B group The Genies, a doo-wop outfit who enjoyed brief success in the early sixties with a unique variation on the Twist craze, the feverish 'Twistin' Pneumonia' (Warwick, 1960). As the group stalled, Hammond was drafted into the air force and on his return to New York he set up home in Queens, where he co-owned a local label Black Hawk Records and set up a micro-indie called Alaga Records. Burning away in Hammond's mind was a simple but powerful idea, a song that was both catchy and risqué in equal measure. It opened with a salvo of gunshots and then the first few bars of 'Here Comes The Bride' before settling into a nagging but socially aware groove. Roy C's 'Shotgun Wedding' (Black Hawk, 1965) rose high in the US charts before becoming a cult hit among the mods of Europe, reaching number six in the UK pop charts. Hammond's entrepreneurialism was allied to a fund of smart commercial ideas but success evaded him and he stayed under the radar, unable to secure capital investment that might have launched a successful career.

In 1973, as the Watergate scandal increased in its intensity and Nixon drifted to near-suicidal self-pity, Hammond was busy searching for new talent in his local community. He discovered a group of African American high-school students from Jamaica High School who had already decided on a name for their group – The Honey Drippers.

Hammond sold them on an idea designed to attract national attention, a funk-inspired dance record called 'Impeach The President'. He took the demo tapes to Mercury Records, where he had previously recorded solo releases, but they baulked at the potential controversy, already worried about Hammond's political leanings. He had delivered to the label an album of songs peppered with unashamed social comment, including an anti-Vietnam war song called 'Open Letter To The President', another entitled 'I'm Bustin' My Rocks (Working On The Chain Gang)' and two self-reflective slavery songs 'I Wasn't There (But I Can Feel The Pain) and 'Great, Great Grandson Of A Slave'. On the basis of his forthright lyrics, Hammond lost his major label deal and so struggled to pay for his impeachment track. He could only afford to press up a small box-load of records. Although not hugely popular in its day, 'Impeach The President' escaped from the underground club scene into the crates of the early pioneers of hip-hop, DJ Kool Herc, Grandmaster Flash and Afrika Bambaataa, where it became a staple of the rap revolution. In debt to the bank and with little money to draw on, Hammond returned south and opened a pair of businesses in Allendale, South Carolina, one a record store and the other yet another independent label Three Gems. Until the COVID-19 pandemic, he was still performing concerts but in September 2020, while hatching a plan to update and reissue 'Impeach The President', he died of cancer. He had had his sights set on Donald Trump. 'There's a man in the White House, he should be gone,' he sang to a black music journalist in his final interview. 'There's a man in the White House, he should be somewhere else.'

In the summer of 1974 Nixon's moods were swinging between despondency and scheming. One of his closest allies, the White House Chief of Staff General Alexander Haig, was doubtful that Nixon could lead the nation in a crisis and recalled an astonishing scene from the final days. 'In the army, you open the drawer, and you put a pistol in, and you close the drawer, and you leave, and the fellow takes care of himself,' he reported Nixon as saying. 'I'm beginning to think maybe you better put a pistol in my drawer.' White House doctors and aides had already cleared his private quarters of prescription drugs. Nixon was accustomed to taking a cocktail of drugs including the barbiturate Seconal, an amphetamine-based upper and Valium.

His grip on power was becoming weaker by the day and the tape transcripts were damning, full of presidential hesitation, distracted grunts, unfinished sentences and meandering, nonsensical thoughts. But even when his mood was at its lowest ebb, the cunning spirit that had served him so well across his political career was not entirely extinguished. He called in favours, many of them petty and inconsequential, and reached out to old contacts to ensure they were still with him. The *Saturday Evening Post* columnist Joseph Alsop remained faithful until the end. 'Impeachment would be a catastrophe,' he argued. 'It would shake the foundations of a strong presidency. It would be a triumph for the political fringes'. The issue was not Nixon, he stressed, but the survival of American strength and tradition. The prospect of Gerald Ford becoming the next occupant of the White House was viewed as preposterous. 'The absurdity of a man elected from a single Michigan congressional district, totally without experience in foreign affairs and without any concept of executive authority' was a looming disaster for America. Alsop's compliance with power may in part have been driven by his own survival: both the FBI and the KGB had pictures of him having sex in a hotel room with a man who was a Soviet agent. It was the kind of salacious gossip that both Nixon and J. Edgar Hoover were not averse to exploiting when required.

The Honey Drippers' 'Impeach The President' is one of the great political soul songs of all time, not just for its message but for the way it became a cornerstone of the beats and breaks that fed the hip-hop revolution to come. A false opening features an MC, probably Roy C. Hammond, introducing the band to a lively crowd: 'Ladies and gentlemen, we have the Honey Drippers in the house tonight. They just got back from Washington D.C. I think they got something they wanna say ...' Then the song erupts into a salvo of percussive drumbeats. Although it did not find success at the time, 'Impeach The President' led the charge in a culturally resonant spate of funk records. Arlene Brown and Lee 'Shot' Williams, a sometime duo who both hailed from Mississippi, released 'Impeach Me Baby' (Dynamite, 1974) while Florida funk maestro Lou Toby and His Heavies brought out a pulsating instrumental 'Heavy Steppin'', which was the flip side of a comedy track called 'The Impeachment Story' (Peach-Mint, 1974) credited to Steel, Jake and Jeff.

With his complicity in the cover-up made public and his political support eroding by the minute, the clock ticked down on Nixon's resignation from office on 9 August 1974. Nixon was a man who lacked self-awareness and yet in his final moments as he waited to board the helicopter that would take him from the White House, he said, 'You can hate your enemies, but if you do, they win.' By then Watergate had become a byword for presidential deception and a whole slew of commemorative and satirical records emerged from black music communities across America. From Los Angeles, Hank Porter & 4th Coming issued 'Waterloo At Watergate' (Alpha, 1973), Fred Wesley & The J.B.'s brought out 'Rockin' Funky Watergate' (People, 1974) and, to reassure his hardcore fans that his relationship with the President had soured, James Brown took to the studios to produce the most resilient (and memorably titled) record of impeachment funk, Fred Wesley & the J.B.s' release 'You Can Have Watergate Just Gimme Some Bucks And I'll Be Straight' (People, 1973).

Nixon's downfall led to James Brown denouncing the man he had once fulsomely endorsed and to a litany of criticism from those that had never really supported his presidency. Fiercest among them were the voices of New Journalism, most specifically the noisy and attention-seeking Hunter S. Thompson, who wrote: 'By disgracing and degrading the presidency of the United States, by fleeing the White House like a diseased cur, Richard Nixon broke the heart of the American Dream.'

The rash of Watergate records also introduced a new talent to the public, a young man who would become a thorn in the side of presidents yet to come. On 15 October 1973, Gil Scott-Heron and Brian Jackson finished recording their landmark album *Winter In America* (Strata-East, 1974). The final track they recorded was a spoken-word, speaking-truth-to-power masterpiece in which Gil Scott-Heron pretends to dial the White House only to find it inoperative. The track is called 'H^{2}Ogate Blues'.

For those who subscribed to American exceptionalism, Watergate was the third strike: Kennedy had been assassinated, LBJ had presided over a lost war in Vietnam, and now Nixon had sullied the Oval Office with deception, lies and deleted expletives. His resignation made Gerald Rudolph Ford Jr the 38th President of the United States, saying 'our long national nightmare is over'. But it wasn't. Inflation was raging, the economy was darkening, and the pall of Watergate still hung heavy. 1974 was a ball of confusion. For months it felt as if America was just about surviving without a functioning President and yet it was a year of unrivalled creativity for soul music. The blaxploitation cinema soundtracks came thick and fast, sharing the charts with Barry White's growling romanticism, Roberta Flack's classically trained piano and a new era of bands including Kool and the Gang, the Ohio Players and B.T. Express, who smoothed out the rawness of funk and reached out to the disco floor. Motown, the past masters of sixties soul, had adapted to new ways. Stevie Wonder, The Temptations and the label's new family entertainment band from Gary, Indiana, The Jackson Five, were making inroads into the mainstream. Ironically, one of the bestselling new arrivals was a homage-funk group from Scotland called AWB, the Average White Band, the first ever to go to the top of the Hot 100 black American charts with 'Pick Up The Pieces (Atlantic, 1974). Irked, James Brown retaliated with an answer record and yet another new collaboration called A.A.B.B. – the Above Average Black Band.

One of the top-selling albums of 1974 was the O'Jays' profound concept essay *Ship Ahoy* (Philadelphia International, 1973), which traced a narrative from slavery to the dystopian urban ghettos of the present day and represented a new hub of creativity in Philadelphia and a new generation of socially conscious soul music. Although President Ford lacked the voting power in Congress to turn the economy round, he was able to sign Proclamation 4311, which pardoned Richard Nixon for all his crimes, including Watergate. Ford described the scandal as 'a tragedy in which we all have played a part. It could go on and on and on, or someone must write the end to it. I have concluded that only I can do that, and if I can, I must.'

With Americans nonplussed by Nixon's pardon, James Brown saw an opportunity to regain the approval of the African American mainstream, releasing his suppurating 1974 single 'Funky President (People It's Bad)' (Polydor, 1974). Brown claimed at the time it was a song not about the departing Nixon but the incoming Ford. 'Every time he made a speech,' Brown once said, 'it gave people the blues. He was a nice man, but he talked a lot and didn't say anything. He was there as a caretaker after Watergate, and I think he did that. He was a good man, but I never looked at him as a *president*.'

James Brown was an immense musician and an unrivalled showman, but he was not always the most likable human being. Prone to arrogance and control freakery, he remained unpredictable to the end. His estate was mired in intrigue, dispute and a raft of tax problems which he denied liability for until his final breath. To his eternal credit, James Brown left behind some of the most compulsive dance music ever, and if 'Funky President' *was* inspired by President Gerald Ford then it ranks as one of the greatest accomplishments of Ford's administration.

Jesse Jackson leads a civil rights march through the streets of Cairo, Illinois, in June 1969 as part of the Soul Caravan that toured the small towns south of Chicago.

4

I AM SOMEBODY

Listen Up: 'I Am Somebody' by Glenn Jones (1983)

On a stifling hot Sunday in July 1967, police lowered the body of 19-year-old Private Robert Hunt down from the wire-mesh ceiling of the Cairo jailhouse, and unravelled the stained T-shirt tied around the bruised vertebrae of his neck. It was a classic case of jailhouse suicide, except it wasn't. Most of the African American population of Cairo, Illinois, had serious doubts about the circumstances of Hunt's death. He was home on leave from the army and had been driving around town with his friends when police stopped the car, claiming it had a broken tail-light. After an exchange of words, Hunt was arrested, taken to the local jail and charged with being AWOL from military service. By 1.30 a.m. the next day, Hunt was dead. A doctor was called to the jail and his suspicions were raised immediately. Hunt was beaten and bruised around his legs and body, and the chicken wire that had been dragged down from the ceiling was hardly strong enough to bear his weight. The black community believed that local police had murdered Hunt and as rumours of his beating spread, three days of rioting erupted in and around the town. When the dust settled, Cairo became a landmark in the struggle for civil rights and a reminder of the role that racism can play in destroying a community. Within a matter of a few short years, its population declined, and once-respected public buildings were abandoned. Journalist Ron Powers of the *Chicago Sun-Times*, who visited the town in its decline, sensed an ugly and hopeless side to Cairo, calling it 'a violent and sorrowful little town . . . a crushed snake, waiting for the setting sun to still its thrashes'.

Robert Hunt's body was embalmed without an autopsy and when local community leaders disputed the police version of events it proved impossible to ascertain the facts. Hunt's army commander confirmed he was on leave legitimately and that he had a particularly good army record, and so the suggestion that he had absconded from duty was denied. Suspicions grew that a clean-up operation was under way. The jailer who had been on duty the night of Hunt's death disappeared, reputedly paid handsomely to leave town, thus leaving the police as the sole witnesses. Two months later, an inquest conducted by the Alexander County coroner ruled Hunt's death was suicide. It was a pronouncement that could not turn back the hands of time nor did it ever satisfy a minority community trapped in a town with a fierce legacy of racism.

The riots that followed Robert Hunt's death have been lost beneath the debris of what President Lyndon Johnson referred to as 'the long, hot summer of 1967', the 159 race riots and rebellions that erupted across the United States in the summer of that year. On 18 July 1967, in Cairo, protesters firebombed a warehouse, a car and three downtown businesses, including a lumber mill that employed mostly black workers. The foreman's home was also burned. The following day, shots were fired at a police car, and more businesses were firebombed. Sporadic gunfire was also reported. More than 600 members of the majority white community formed a citizens' militia group known as the Committee for Ten Million, or more colloquially the White Hats, who acted as a vigilante group roaming the town to ensure that black citizens obeyed draconian emergency laws that prevented them from gathering in parks or public areas. The White Hats gathered nightly on the perimeter of Cairo's main public housing project, Pyramid Courts, seemingly guarding the town from its own minority citizens. What then transpired left the police's reputation in tatters. Already accused of having been complicit in the death of Private Robert Hunt, they instigated and engaged in acts of open brutality. Many police officers joined the ranks of the White Hats and targeted a community hub, St Columba's church and rectory, where the protesters had gathered. More than forty bullets were fired into the church from the police station directly opposite and the angle of firing seemed to suggest that snipers – either police officers or their proxies – were taking aim from the cupola windows at the top of the building. By 21 July, a protest leader declared that Cairo would become 'Rome burning down, if the white community did not meet black demands for economic equality'. The Illinois governor, Otto Kerner Jr, the son of a Czech immigrant family, called in the National Guard to 'restore peace and order', which effectively meant that black areas of town were cordoned off and an evening curfew punishable by arrest was imposed. Even when they flew home the body of another local boy, 19-year-old Richard Jones, one of sixty-four Americans who died in an ambush in Ong Thanh, segregation marred the funeral service. Only family and friends from the ghetto projects of Pyramid Courts came to pay their respects; the town's white officials stayed away.

For all its modern bleakness, Cairo could have been a contender. It had a history dating back to the Civil War, it appeared in Mark Twain's *Huckleberry Finn* and was a location for escaped and emancipated slaves to travel north using river barges. Cairo also operated as a safehold along the Underground Railroad. Many African Americans who escaped the South and made it into the free state of Illinois were then transported to Chicago. Situated at the confluence of the Mississippi and Ohio rivers, it was a staging post for river transport and might easily have grown to the size of Memphis or even Chicago, but a punishing darkness seemed to bewitch the area. Highways reduced the need for river traffic, frequent flooding weakened Cairo's early economic strengths and the wealthy, including many business owners, packed up and left town. Cairo reached its peak population of 15,203 back in 1920 but then collapsed into decline and abandonment.

By the sixties the streets were empty, storefronts shuttered, and weeds were growing up through the sidewalks like an alien invasion.

The riots eventually receded but racism left a dire legacy. Cairo had the highest rates of poverty in Illinois, with 30 per cent of its population on welfare. Nor had public investment helped much. The town had approximately 130 public employees in the early seventies but only twelve were black and, of those, ten were garbage workers on the city's lowest pay rung. About 96 per cent of the city's payroll and annual expenses went to whites, and only 4 per cent to blacks.

Given Cairo's reputation for poverty and hunger, it was identified by the Reverend Jesse Jackson as the final station on a state-wide hunger march he planned under the joint banner of Operation PUSH (People United to Save Humanity) and the Southern Christian Leadership Conference (SCLC), the civil rights organisation that Martin Luther King had led until his assassination in Memphis. Jackson's plan was to organise a soul caravan based on the old gospel tours of the Deep South, in which a flotilla of cars, trucks and buses carried the entertainers from one town to another. They were met by local congregations and put up in the homes of their followers. The idea was adjusted for political rallies, with a truck carrying placards, leaflets, donation boxes and recruitment pledge materials. A coach carried the musicians, among them the Operation Breadbasket Orchestra and Choir, the Soul Shakers – a gospel group that featured Keith Barrow, the teenage son of Jesse Jackson's collaborator, the Reverend Willie Barrow – and the hard-soul singer Cicero Blake. Local artists swelled their ranks along the way, supported by a PUSH founding member Bernadine C. Washington, who was also a pioneering woman DJ on Radio Station WVON. Her show *On the Scene With Bernadine* profiled fashion tips, local Chicago nightclubs and developments within the civil rights movement.

The Reverend Jesse Jackson had become a respected figure in racial justice circles, using his base in Chicago's South Side as a platform for national prominence and two tilts at the presidency, when he ran as a candidate for the Democratic nomination in 1984 and then again in 1988. Jackson had even been serenaded in song. In 1971, a Chicago group called the Pace-Setters released 'Push On Jesse Jackson' b/w

'Freedom And Justice' (Kent, 1971) on the West Coast blues and soul label that also featured B. B. King and Ike and Tina Turner. It was a double-sider in support of Jackson's organisation PUSH, promoted heavily in Chicago and the North but never as prominent in either the South or on the West Coast. Like Martin Luther King, Jackson's charisma, his compelling voice and his ability to move crowds was immense. Every prominent preacher had a signature sermon which they repurposed for different places and new congregations. For Aretha Franklin's father, the Reverend C. L. Franklin, one of the old-school stars of the gospel caravan circuit, it was a sermon called 'The Eagle Stirreth Her Nest', which was known nationally in Christian communities. For Martin Luther King, it was famously either 'I Have a Dream' or the sermon he gave the night before his assassination, 'I've Been to the Mountaintop'. For Jesse Jackson, it was an electric piece of call-and-response sermonising called 'I Am Somebody', which was a derivation of a poem written by the Reverend William Holmes Borders, a Baptist minister from Atlanta back in the forties. Jackson knew the original poem by heart but used its title as a clarion call for pride and self-worth. As his fame grew, Jackson popularised the term, first at rallies like the Chicago soul caravan to Cairo, then on stage at Wattstax, the historic free concert that Stax Records hosted in Watts, Los Angeles, in 1972, and then again on national television on the popular PBS children's show *Sesame Street*. The speech was sampled into James Brown's 'Same Beat', performed by Fred Wesley and The J.B.'s, and recurred in a follow-up 'Damn Right I'm Somebody', both released in 1974. But it was an outstanding club record by Glenn Jones of the Florida soul group The Modulations that marked the sermon's crossover to disco. Jones's inspirational club hit 'I Am Somebody' (RCA, 1983) reaches a peak in which Jesse Jackson seems to be reciting a sermon alongside Detroit group The Jones Girls, bringing the song to an emotional, gospel-style climax. Glenn Jones's voice harks back to the golden age of sixties soul but also forward beyond disco to the underground of rave and electronic dance music. It was a song that launched a thousand imitations and inspired the innovative club producer and DJ Andrew Weatherall to sample Jackson's Wattstax concert speech as a component of the Primal Scream track 'Come Together' on their 1991 album *Screamadelica*.

When Jesse Jackson campaigned for the presidency in the 1984 election his rallies fused gospel preaching with political rhetoric, culminating in the rallying cry for black pride, 'I Am Somebody'.

Jesse Jackson's Chicago soul caravan campaign mostly focused on Illinois. But it had three wider, largely unheralded outcomes: it highlighted the scourge of hunger and deprivation in the more affluent North; it set the groundwork for Jackson's presidential nomination bids; and it highlighted the campaign to make Martin Luther King's birthday a national holiday. All three outcomes were supported by one of the most remarkable black music organisations of the time, the Operation Breadbasket Orchestra and Choir led by the formidable Memphis-born tenor saxophonist Ben Branch. Branch had recently moved north to Chicago and worked for Chess Records, where he shared freelance saxophone duties with Monk Higgins, adding beef to songs by vocal harmony groups like The Radiants and The Vontastics. Each Saturday morning, he would host rehearsals at the University of Chicago and Theological Seminary Rooms, where in February 1968 he attended a management meeting with Martin Luther King, Jesse Jackson and Willie Barrow. Together they hatched a plan to extend the commitment to civil rights to focus on poverty and to form an official orchestra – a supergroup – capable of playing spirituals, jazz, R&B and soul, which would tour America to raise awareness and funds, and become in effect the musical wing of King's movement. It consisted of Ben Branch's Chicago contacts and members of his hometown band in Memphis. In 1968 they signed a deal with Chess and moved their base more permanently to Chicago. Branch's capacity for hard work and entrepreneurial spirit stayed with him throughout his life. While still committed to the civil rights movement, he set up Doctor Branch Products Inc. in Chicago, the nation's first black-owned soft drink manufacturing company, and in 1986 signed a $355 million agreement with Kemmerer, the makers of 7Up, to distribute their drinks. Branch spent much of his active working life as president of his own drinks company but still faithfully turned up for rehearsals and for music education classes. The move to Chicago also secured Branch a weekly radio show and an outlet that he had not enjoyed at home in Memphis. The radio station WVON – the one-time 'Voice of the Negro' – championed by the irrepressible DJ and civil rights siren E. Rodney Jones, dedicated a weekly hour-long show to Branch and his Operation Breadbasket Orchestra. It was from this pulpit that Branch, with the support of Jesse Jackson and the Detroit Congressman John Conyers, first mooted the idea of a holiday dedicated to Martin Luther King.

Ben Branch had a unique story to tell. The night before King's assassination in April 1968, he had been travelling with his band members and Jesse Jackson on a flight from Chicago to Memphis. When the plane approached Memphis Airport, the city was suddenly struck by an electric storm. This was no ordinary storm. The tornados that had engulfed Memphis, rural Mississippi and Arkansas destroyed farms, livestock and outbuildings, killing six people and injuring more than a hundred. It was a storm that was soon to become part of Memphis mythology, as news spread within the African American community of an uncompromising speech that Martin Luther King had delivered to striking garbage workers and their families at the Mason Temple, at the height of the storm. The journalist and historian Hampton Sides describes an Old Testament atmosphere as King arrived in the hall. Ralph Abernathy introduced him, 'his words echoing through the vast hall as tornado sirens keened outside'. A local churchman, the Reverend Samuel 'Billy' Kyles, later wrote: 'That night rain was pounding on the roof, and the rafters shook with thunder and lightning. I remember: the thunderclaps and the wind set the windows banging. Each time it happened Martin flinched. He was sure someone was lurking and going to shoot him. But when he got to the end of that speech and told us he had looked over and seen the promised land, a great calm came over him. Everyone was transfixed.' It was a speech rich in meaning and foreboding.

King rose to the lectern and settled into his sonorous tones, the electric storm in the background creating a dramatic backdrop for one of his greatest deliveries of 'I've Been to the Mountaintop'. 'I'm delighted to see each of you here tonight in spite of a storm warning,' King began. Then, in a tour de force of public oratory, he imagined the worlds he might have been born into, finally returning to the world he would have chosen above all others, the here and now. 'Something is happening in Memphis,' he continued, 'something is happening in our world . . . And also, in the human rights revolution, if something isn't done, and done in a hurry, to bring the coloured peoples of the world out of their long years of poverty, their long years of hurt and neglect, the whole world is doomed.' Finally, he turned to his own predicament. 'We've got some difficult days ahead. But it really doesn't matter with me now, because I've been to the mountaintop. And I don't mind. Like anybody,

I would like to live a long life. Longevity has its place. But I'm not concerned about that now. I just want to do God's will. And He's allowed me to go up to the mountain. And I've looked over. And I've seen the Promised Land. I may not get there with you. But I want you to know tonight, that we, as a people, will get to the Promised Land! Now, I'm just happy that God has allowed me to live in this period to see what is unfolding. And I'm happy that He's allowed me to be in Memphis.'

As King addressed the strikers and their families, Ben Branch's flight from Chicago had been diverted to Jackson, Mississippi, and then, after another aborted landing, was finally diverted to New Orleans. Branch, Jesse Jackson and their Chicago band were eventually flown back to Memphis when the storms subsided late into the night. Branch had shared many journeys with King. They had grown up in the same segregated post-war South. Branch had taken his saxophone in a battered case to the Montgomery bus boycott and had been there at the famous Selma–Montgomery marches in 1965, in support of voting rights. When Martin Luther King extended his protests against poverty and racial injustice to major northern cities, Jesse Jackson encouraged Branch to leave Memphis for the North, and he eventually settled in Chicago where he formed a new musical initiative, Ben Branch and The Downhomers.

One of the stand-out songs in Branch's repertoire was an old spiritual called 'Precious Lord, Take My Hand', adapted by the great Thomas A. Dorsey, the man who first gave gospel music its name and grew to be one of its most devoted exponents. Dorsey reputedly wrote 'Precious Lord, Take My Hand' as he fought depression after his wife and baby son both died in childbirth. Gospel mythology claims that he locked himself in a room for three soul-searching days, warding off a nervous breakdown by communing directly with the Lord. It was in this painful period of self-realisation that God directed him to write the song.

Ben Branch had a quite different interpretation, claiming that the song was an Alabama slave anthem sung as a spiritual in the cotton fields of the South. Dorsey had embellished it, and with the help of his own publishing company, and the support of Mahalia Jackson, turned the song into a gospel standard. Branch himself had grown up with an old scratchy 78rpm version in his Memphis home and could play the entire song as a virtuoso saxophone solo with only fleeting guest vocals to support him. He played it at every stop on the way as the soul caravan drove through Illinois. Something about its legacy, its mystique and its closeness to despair had made it Martin Luther King's favourite tune. Bombastic and uplifting Christian drama appealed to his style of oratory, and at times King often wove words from the song into his sermons.

On the morning that King was assassinated, Ben Branch was having a haircut in a barber's near Firestone Union Hall in North Memphis. When he left the barbershop he took a cab to the Lorraine Motel, a black-owned lodging on Mulberry Street on the fringes of the Beale Street ghetto and one of the few places in the city where blacks could book a room. He had stayed in the Lorraine numerous times before and even when he returned to his parental home, his band were always checked into the favoured motel for the travelling entourage of the SCLC. Songwriting partners Isaac Hayes and David Porter were a daily fixture there throughout the humid and sweltering summers, preferring to write by the pool or use an air-conditioned room at day rates, rather than bake in the furnace of the Stax studios. As Branch arrived in the car park near the swimming pool and looked up at the mustard-yellow and blue walls, only a housemaid with a trolley was out on the balcony. The motel was unusually quiet. In Branch's mind, the place was synonymous with bustle and noise, late-night jam sessions, visiting bands disgorging their stage suits and their touring equipment from a fleet of airport taxis, or it was the laughter of the Harlem Globetrotters basketball team as they clowned around the swimming pool. It was in the honeymoon suite that Eddie Floyd had written his greatest hit, 'Knock On Wood', and it was where Stax housed all their visiting black artists. Mable John and Judy Clay were regular clients, and over the years the motel had accommodated Count Basie, Ray Charles, Aretha Franklin and Sarah Vaughan.

Strange things began to happen around the motel, many of them hard to fathom. The Memphis police withdrew one of their most senior black detectives, Ed Redditt, from surveillance there. Redditt was disliked by the striking sanitation workers and his eagerness to court success within the police department was seen by many as betraying his race. There had allegedly been threats on Redditt's life from anonymous calls within the African American community and so the police made the decision to withdraw him from tailing King. Meanwhile, and independently, the only two black firemen in the Butler Street Station near the motel were also withdrawn and given new assignments. One of the firemen, Floyd Newsum, was a supporter of the strike and had been at the Mason Temple rally where King had given his mountaintop speech. Newsum had argued against his new assignment but was forced to accede and was moved to a suburban fire station. The outcome – planned or coincidental – was that the only three black officers representing public services in the immediate vicinity of the Lorraine Motel had been withdrawn. Late in the afternoon Andrew Young and the SCLC legal team returned from a local court ecstatic about small victories: the march the next day, which was planned to intensify city-wide support for the striking sanitation workers, could go ahead but only along a prescribed route and with a set of conditions that would allow the police to contain any potential trouble.

King and Abernathy were in Room 306, preparing to go to dinner. King, who had dry and sensitive skin, took an age to shave as everyone else assembled in the car park below. Jesse Jackson was already there, as was King's local driver Solomon Jones, provided to him courtesy of a local funeral home. King splashed Aramis on his face and headed out to the landing, allowing Ralph Abernathy to use the mirror, the sink still peppered with his hairs. King spoke to the throng below from the balcony rail. He chatted buoyantly to Jesse Jackson and Ben Branch, who was due to go to a soundcheck for a fundraising concert later that evening. The driver shouted that it was getting cold and that they should bring overcoats. King agreed and joked about Jesse Jackson's casual hipster outfit. King then looked down to Ben Branch and asked him if he had his saxophone with him. 'I want you to play "Take My Hand, Precious Lord", Ben,' he requested. 'Play it real pretty, sweeter than you've ever played it before.' As he shared these words with the master-saxophonist, a single bullet from a Remington Model 760 Gamesmaster rifle tore through his neck and he collapsed backwards onto the cinder wall of the balcony. James Earl Ray, an escaped convict with a pathological hatred of civil rights, disappeared back into a nearby rooming house and escaped into a shroud of conspiracy. Within an hour King was declared dead at St Joseph's Hospital, Memphis. A local priest, Father Coleman Bergard, who had been called to administer the last rites, closed King's eyelids. There was a long peaceful silence and then the inner cities erupted.

King's death opened old wounds. President Johnson declared a National Day of Mourning to be held on 7 April 1968, but he wisely decided against attending King's funeral, fearing that protests against the war in Vietnam would dominate the day. Vice President Hubert Humphrey attended in his place. The then-governor of Georgia, Lester Maddox, who considered King an 'enemy of the country', refused a state funeral or lying in state and put riot-helmeted state troopers on the steps of the state capitol in Atlanta 'to protect state property'. Maddox, barricaded inside the building, reportedly ordered the troopers to 'shoot them down and stack them up'. But the tragedy and solemnity of the occasion rendered the riot troops an irrelevance. King's coffin was transferred to an open-air service at Morehouse College on an old wooden wagon drawn by two mules, a signifier of the rural caravans against poverty he had led, but the followers were resplendent in their Sunday best: razor-sharp suits, pretty hats and colourful dresses. King's friend Mahalia Jackson sang his favourite hymn, 'Precious Lord, Take My Hand'. The Operation Breadbasket Orchestra travelled en masse from Chicago, Stax Records gave their staff a day's holiday and many of their artists including Isaac Hayes and David Porter drove to Atlanta. Jazz legend Dizzy Gillespie and Aretha Franklin were also prominent among the mourners. When the hotels in Atlanta ran out of space for visitors, colleges, churches and private homes opened their doors. The Motown Corporation was represented by Berry Gordy Jr, Diana Ross and The Supremes, and by Stevie Wonder. Nine months later, on 15 January 1969, Coretta King, the widow of the dead civil rights leader, launched an appeal for an annual commemorative holiday. It was a campaign that took decades to deliver and outlasted four presidents, splitting America ideologically and becoming a touch-stone for race relations.

Beyond the mainstream, King's voice became an instrument of soul, funk and hip-hop, as musicians commemorated his ideals in song and in sampled dedications. One immediate dedication, 'Abraham Martin And John' by the folk-rock singer Dion, was released on Laurie Records soon after King's assassination but it was subsequent cover versions, first by Smokey Robinson and the Miracles, and then mightily by

Marvin Gaye, that gave the song its towering status. Other interpretations of King's death followed. Pat Boone wrote a half-spoken tribute and 'If I Can Dream' was a stand-out performance in Elvis Presley's 1968 comeback show. Another towering tribute came from another gospel prodigy, the soloist Shirley Wahls, whose 'Remember Martin Luther King' (Blue Candle, 1976) disappeared commercially but was saved from obscurity by the crate diggers of the modern soul and funk scene. Many more followed over the coming decades, including U2's 'American Prayer', Neil Diamond's 'Dry Your Eyes' and John Legend and Common's 'Glory', but, as much as those respectful memorials gained attention, they were low-key by comparison with a technological breakthrough in the restless subculture of hip-hop, where it became fashionable to sample King's awesome voice.

Sermons gradually became a pop phenomenon. It was originally a soul music technique that Philly singer Billy Paul used in his reworking of the Wings' song 'Let 'Em In' (Philadelphia International, 1976). The song mixes the speeches of both King and Malcolm X into a relentless seventies disco masterpiece. From soul it gestated to hip-hop. Grandmaster Flash and the Furious Five's 'The King' is a pulsating and hopeful track reinforced by the Martin Luther King refrain, 'Free at last'. What began as innovation became commonplace. Heavy D & The Boyz' 'A Better Land' opens with Martin Luther King at the Mall in Washington reciting 'I Have a Dream' and Cyhi Da Prynce's 'Ring Bellz' starts with King's triumphant 'Let Freedom Ring' speech. With each new generation from old-school hip-hop to gangsta rap and on to trip-hop, the speeches of King, Malcolm X and Jesse Jackson were spliced, reassembled and mixed in. Another landmark release was Keith LeBlanc's 'No Sell Out' (Tommy Boy, 1983), which raided all the available recorded speeches by Malcom X and turned them into a burning dance record that all but rescued Malcolm X's polemics from the grave: 'I'm not a diner until you let me dine – then I become a diner.' 'No Sell Out' was the splintered signpost that directed Derek Murphy, an elementary school teacher from New Rochelle, to form the rap trio Brand Nubian, with whom he inhabited the name Sadat X and recorded 'Return Of The Bang Bang', which sampled snatches from the 'I Have a Dream' speech and became a rallying force for the modern urban dream. The tense legacy of King and Malcom X's deaths permeated hip-hop. The video for Public Enemy's astonishing 'By The Time I Get To Arizona' begins with a press conference in which a right-wing politician refuses to grant a holiday in the name of King, then a paramilitary army played by the group parade across the screen as the story of civil rights is rewound in a new and resistant style.

Four days after King's assassination, John Conyers, the Democrat Congressman from Michigan, introduced a bill to establish a federal holiday to honour the slain civil rights leader. Conyers was a contemporary of Motown's Berry Gordy when, as young men from aspirational families, they were conscripted to the war in Korea. He and Gordy built up overlapping power bases in Detroit, one in music, the other in civil rights. Conyers had recently hired the veteran civil rights icon Rosa Parks, who had moved north to Detroit, as his strategic assistant and together they worked on three projects: securing insurance claims for citizens who lost goods and property in the riots of 1967, the establishment of the Congressional Black Caucus, which became one of the most powerful African American vehicles in mainstream electoral politics, and the campaign for a holiday on King's birthday. Conyers' holiday bill stalled and ran a serious risk of being permanently derailed until petitions endorsing the holiday were backed by six million names and submitted to Congress again. Conyers and Shirley Chisholm, the first African American to run for a major party nomination for the presidency in 1972, resubmitted the legislation in each subsequent session until it was finally passed and the bill commemorating Martin Luther King's birthday as a national holiday was signed in a Rose Garden ceremony by President Ronald Reagan in November 1983. A fifteen-year-long journey.

The Illinois hunger march and soul caravan was launched by King's successor Ralph Abernathy at a fundraising Easter banquet in Chicago in the April of 1969, with the ambitious goal of ending poverty and hunger across the land. Abernathy's relationship with Jesse Jackson could be modestly described as tense: they disliked each other and had had many disagreements along the way. One sore point that never healed between the two men was who was perceived as the natural successor to Martin Luther King. Abernathy was his deputy and now occupied the most senior role within the SCLC, but Jackson was the more charismatic. Since King's assassination the antipathy had edged closer to visceral resentment. Many thought that Jackson was too keen to seek media attention and there was stunned disbelief when he made the questionable claim that he was closest to King when the civil rights leader was shot and that his blood had spilled onto Jackson's shirt as he cradled King's head. Abernathy's resentment grew when most of the SCLC's key staff members travelled from Memphis to Atlanta to attend King's funeral and Jackson, with a bloody shirt, appeared on television.

Although the caravan was to leave from Chicago, to drive to the poorest communities of Illinois, the city itself was not immune from poverty and hunger. An estimated 50,000 families in Cook County lived below the poverty line. Ben Branch pulled together a concert of freedom songs led by the Operation Breadbasket Orchestra and Choir, and vowed at the opening rally at Union Baptist Church that when the caravan returned to Chicago he would bring together one of the greatest orchestras of saxophonists ever assembled, to waken the city's civic leadership to its failings. Jesse Jackson's set-piece speech welcoming supporters challenged the newly inaugurated President Richard Nixon to rise to the challenge of ending hunger, although he expressed doubts that the President would climb a hill never mind go to the mountaintop. 'We, the ministers of Operation Breadbasket, announce that hunger is much too serious a problem to be postponed as a national priority,' Jackson sermonised. 'Hunger is the most critical issue of this nation and of this state. Therefore, we cannot take the President's lead on this matter, for it would divide us into those who can eat and those who must starve or go hungry.'

The anti-hunger drive began with a walking tour of the once-affluent but now depressed Kenwood neighbourhood. Jackson and his followers had invited reporters and photographers to highlight the poverty in Chicago's own backyard. Kenwood was an area that was showing a quite different set of sociopolitical changes. The non-violent gradualism that had characterised King's movement was under strain. In fact, King's death had energised the Black Power movement, who could argue with some conviction that America was resistant to negotiation when it came to racial justice. Black Americans felt ever more distrustful of white institutions and America's political system, and membership of the Black Panther Party and other Black Power groups surged at home and in Vietnam.

One local teenager raised in Hyde Park, near Kenwood, had already chosen sides. Yvette Marie Stevens was a teenager when she joined her father, his second wife and neighbourhood friends on civil rights marches. A hugely gifted soul singer, she changed her name and became one of the most gigantic talents of her generation. By the time the hunger marches arrived on the streets of Kenwood, Yvette Stevens had met and mingled with the Illinois chapter of the Black Panther Party and broadly supported their Ten-Point Program for change in America. She was a friend of Fred Hampton and Mark Clark, the two Panthers who were executed by the Chicago police in a raid on Hampton's apartment on Chicago's West Monroe Street. According to Hampton's lawyers, the police raid had been part of the COINTELPRO programme and the FBI had viewed Hampton as a potential 'messiah', who needed to be 'neutralized'. As a 16-year-old Yvette Stevens dropped out of Kenwood High School to work on the Black Panther Party's free breakfast programme for hungry children across Chicago. Even earlier, around the age of 13, she took on a new Afrocentric name, Chaka Adunne Aduffe Yemoja Hodarhi Karifi, adding Khan when she married Hassan Khan in 1970. Now using her new name, Chaka Khan, she was offered her first record deal as what she later described as the 'alpha-chick' fronting the white funk-rock band Rufus. Her remarkable career stretched out over the next fifty years and among her many achievements one song stands out, her cover version of Prince's 'I Feel For You', which won the Grammy for Best Female R&B Vocal Performance in 1985. The song features Stevie Wonder on chromatic harmonica and samples beats from Stevie's old hit 'Fingertips', but what sets it apart is the presence of rapper Melle Mel, who introduces Chaka and lovingly praises her throughout. It would not be an overstatement to say that the song changed the future of African American music, not only foregrounding creative collaborations but merging hip-hop and vocal soul in an alliance of style that came to dominate urban music. With that one song, Chaka Khan opened the door for the hip-hop soul generation that would follow, including Beyoncé, Mary J. Blige, Erykah Badu and Lauryn Hill – a generation as comfortable with legacy soul as new urban dance music. Hill's album *The Miseducation Of Lauryn Hill* (Ruffhouse Records, 1998) was inspired by the film and autobiographical novel *The Education of Sonny Carson*, and Carter G. Woodson's *The*

Mis-Education of the Negro, a landmark volume from 1933 which blamed the public education system for the cultural indoctrination of young blacks, and marked the rise of politically aware young women.

A week after the anti-hunger campaign left inner-city Chicago it arrived in Springfield, the state capital of Illinois, two hundred miles away. Jesse Jackson and sixty campaign followers met with state legislators to draft a bill declaring hunger a man-made disaster and pronouncing slums illegal. Senator George McGovern, who would be the Democratic Party nominee in the 1972 presidential election, viewed the campaign as an eye-catching idea and told journalists that he had come to Chicago to support 'the young civil rights leader' and to 'underscore the importance of ending hunger in this rich country. We have a twin burden on our back and it's the Vietnam war and hunger ... the U.S. has got to stop killing Asians and start feeding its millions of poor ... it should choose a federal budget of life and not one of death.'

Buoyed by the attention the campaign was generating beyond Chicago, Jackson and Willie Barrow began to envisage a motorcade that would take the caravan up and down Illinois. It began on 12 June 1969, in Rockford, Illinois, with local leaders taking the Breadbasket protesters through the poorest neighbourhoods. One visitor accustomed to poverty in Chicago described the scenes in Rockford as 'unbelievable and inhumane'. That evening, in Rockford's Central High School, a two-building campus joined by an underground tunnel known as 'Rat Alley', a public event was held beneath a huge banner, 'Hunger Is A Hurtin' Thing'. More than eight hundred people, mostly residents, politicians and journalists, listened to stories of poverty from both black and white people. Breadbasket's musicians gave a soothing touch to an emotional session, performing a show composed of civil rights standards and hits from the R&B charts. The term 'a hurtin' thing' was one of numerous expressions the campaign borrowed from everyday life and soul music. It cropped up in a string of records released at the turn of the decade, among them Gorgeous George's 'It's Not A Hurting Thing' (Peachtree, 1967), Gloria Ann Taylor's 'Love Is A Hurtin' Thing' (Selector, 1972) and a great underground independent soul record from inner-city Washington, in the backyards of the White House, 'Make My Love A Hurting Thing' by William Cummings (Bang Bang, 1969).

In his book on the story of the hunger marches, the Chicago historian Martin L. Deppe describes the various stages of the campaign. When the caravan arrived in East St Louis Jesse Jackson and his followers were shocked by 'the maze of broken-down shacks, outhouses, junk piles and train trestles', the 'wide ravines of polluted water, discarded lumber, and refuse' in 'this bleak housing area'.

The next stop was the tense and depressed town of Cairo. It was now almost two years since the jailhouse death of Private Robert Hunt and Cairo was clinging on to normality, an eerie shell of a place barely able to cope with change. Chicago had come to Cairo but local resistance to racism had flourished too. Protesters took to the streets with a homemade banner 'Before I'll Be a Slave I'll Be Buried in My Grave', the applique lettering interspersed with hippie flowers and held aloft by two of the town's homegrown radicals, Wade Walters and Clarence Dossie, who claimed that Cairo was caught in a racial time warp. 'The only work available to people of colour was over the state line in Missouri picking cotton, or cleaning the local hotel,' Dossie said contemptuously of his hometown. Willie Barrow announced Operation Lift for Cairo, declaring, 'Black people are guaranteed to starve in Cairo, Illinois, now that they have been cut off from food and medical services.' She asked for donations of clothing, food and medical supplies to assist the needy, who had been unfairly affected by a boycott of downtown businesses in the wake of Hunt's killing. The contact person for donations to support the needy in Cairo was Alice Tregay, another formidable, selfless woman at the heart of the Breadbasket movement. Tregay rose to prominence in Chicago when she led a high-profile campaign against the so-called 'Willis Wagons', a pejorative name given to makeshift portable class-rooms set up in ghetto neighbourhoods. The wagons were a temporary solution to overcrowding and had coincided with the reign of Benjamin C. Willis as Superintendent of Schools, who was driven from office for his failures to manage school desegregation. Keen to ensure that the protests against slum schooling had support from the white community too, Tregay leafleted Chicago University and encouraged students to join the campaign. (One of the students arrested at a demonstration hotspot at West 73rd Street and South Lowe Avenue was a 21-year-old student named Bernie Sanders. He was arrested, charged with resisting arrest, found guilty and fined $25.) Tregay also ran political education classes that trained thousands of local people to work across the city on grassroots political campaigns which delivered the re-election of Ralph Metcalfe to Congress, the election of Harold Washington as Mayor, and ultimately underpinned Barack Obama's campaign to become the first African American President.

On its next stop, the soul caravan returned to Springfield. Several thousand people rallied outside the capitol as Jesse Jackson taped a copy of the human subsidy bill to the building's doors, declaring to his supporters, 'We are here to challenge the governor and the state legislature to feed its poor.' Meanwhile Ben Branch was planning a spectacular return to Chicago and had been phone-bashing for days trying to reach saxophonists from across Chicago and Detroit with the view to build a 'saxophone orchestra' that would generate publicity for the cause. Branch put out the word to the big names of soul and jazz: Junior Walker, who was on tour in Canada; Mike Terry, the Detroit baritone sax stalwart; Monk Higgins, the respected Chicago session musician; Illinois Jacquet, who had been arrested in Houston, Texas, for challenging segregation in the local Music Hall there; the jazz great Julian 'Cannonball' Adderley; and Gene 'Jug' Ammons, who had just returned to the Chicago jazz scene after serving a seven-year jail term for heroin possession.

Ammons had recently released his album *The Boss Is Back!* During his years behind bars the eminent jazz label Prestige kept his name in the spotlight as best as it could by releasing several albums from the vaults. The label had also secured a deal with the prison authorities to give Ammons a rehearsal room at the prison as a route back to creativity. His homecoming shows at the famous Plugged Nickel Club in Chicago's Old Town demonstrated that he had lost none of his blistering power. Picking up on the cross-current of the time, he quickly became a master of hard jazz-funk, and what Ammons christened the 'Jungle Strut'. Although he toured in Detroit, Baltimore and Philadelphia, his criminal record prevented him from playing in licensed premises in New York and so he continued to base himself in Chicago.

Cannonball Adderley was a loyal supporter too, touring on the soul caravan and appearing at fundraisers on Chicago's South Side. He credited Jesse Jackson and Ben Branch in the spoken introduction to his live album *Country Preacher*, which was recorded at an Operation Breadbasket event in a Chicago church. The blues and soul singer Syl Johnson also lent his support, appearing at another fundraiser to launch his landmark civil rights album *Is It Because I'm Black* (Twinight, 1970). The album carried four tracks which spoke directly to the politics of the Operation Breadbasket movement – 'Walk A Mile In My Shoes', 'I'm Talkin' 'Bout Freedom', 'Right On' and the emotionally worn-out title track, 'Is It Because I'm Black'. Others showed up at Breadbasket events as their itinerary allowed, among them hard-soul artists from the local Brainstorm label including Cicero Blake and Betty Jean Plummer. Chicago-born Oscar Brown Jr, a regular at Washington D.C.'s Cellar Door club, also joined the campaign, performing tracks from his successful *Sin & Soul* album including modernist favourites 'Humdrum Blues' and the ubiquitous 'Watermelon Man'.

After two weeks criss-crossing Illinois, the Breadbasket army returned to Chicago, having raised largely positive responses from state politicians and senate hearings. The caravan had attracted not only enthusiastic crowds but extensive newspaper coverage. Most encouraging of all was the passage of a human subsidy bill in the Illinois House, which addressed some, if not all, of their campaigning objectives. The soul caravan held a celebration party and fundraiser. When Ben Branch's cherished saxophone orchestra took to the stage it comprised music students, local pick-up musicians and a front three of Adderley, Ammons and Branch himself, and joined Adderley's quintet and the Breadbasket Orchestra to create what the *Chicago Defender* described as a 'soul mass' of sound. In a review, the online jazz magazine *Flophouse* described it lovingly as 'all funk, sleaze, slow drag, tough swing, and sparkling Afro-Jazz . . . a wonderful exercise in rhythm, even these speeches by Cannonball move with a smooth, danceable beat . . . *Country Preacher: Live At Operation Breadbasket* is expressive, eloquent soul power.' The band also played a version of the old Lionel Hampton standard 'Red Top', first recorded by Gene Ammons in 1947 when he had only recently graduated from DuSable High School. In thanking the band for what he described as a stirring highlight and a 'Black expression of our thing', Jesse Jackson gave an open invitation to young musicians across Chicago to come and join the fold. It took the neighbourhood's most travelled star

Chaka Khan until 2013 to accept the invitation and appear at one of Jackson's rallies, by which time Ben Branch was long dead, the dynamic Willie Barrow was in a wheelchair and Barack Obama was in the White House.

The Martin Luther King commemorative birthday movement seemed to progress in parallel to the Breadbasket events. The *Alabama Journal* newspaper reported that in July 1972 'demands for Black history, Afro clubs and a Martin Luther King Memorial Day observance led to notable student walkouts' in the Montgomery public school system. School strikes escalated throughout the seventies. Meanwhile John Conyers was persistent in his legislative campaigning, but the first signs of success were at state level when Harold Washington co-sponsored a bill which the Illinois House of Representatives voted 114 to 15 to endorse. The Illinois Senate later voted in favour of it as well, and on 17 September 1973 Governor Dan Walker signed the bill that made Illinois the first state to adopt Martin Luther King's birthday as an official holiday. It was a move that proved instrumental in getting the holiday accepted nationwide but much of the popular campaigning that made it happen was down to a now-historic song, Stevie Wonder's 'Happy Birthday' (Motown, 1980).

Blind since birth and feted as a child prodigy during his infancy at Motown, Stevie Wonder's reputation changed and developed when he took to the stage at the Black Woodstock, a free concert in Mount Morris Park, Harlem, in the summer of 1969. Stevie Wonder's set hinted at the abundance of creativity yet to come. It was a drizzling wet day when he took to the stage, wearing a chocolate-brown regency-style coat and yellow ruff and sporting his trademark dark glasses. Sitting at his electric piano, protected from the impending rain by a stagehand holding an orange and red polka-dot parasol, he launched into renditions of his major 1969 songs, among them 'For Once In My Life', 'Yester-Me, Yester-You, Yesterday' and the French love song he co-wrote with Motown's Sylvia Moy and Henry Cosby, 'My Cherie Amour'. Wonder's set was bulging with new directions, his live version of what became the hit single 'Yester-Me, Yester-You, Yesterday' seemed to signal a new maturity, the first obvious signs that the young prodigy was absorbing the political energies of the summer of '69 and blossoming into a true talent. Sharing a bill with Nina Simone and Sly Stone, Stevie Wonder sensed that something was happening to soul music as it became shaped by electrification, primitive computer technology and the early days of the synthesizer. A generation of young and tech-savvy musicians were pushing to the fore, mostly keyboard players or multi-instrumentalists. Among their ranks were Donny Hathaway, Herbie Hancock and Sly Stone. Etta James claimed that 'Sly didn't need an engineer. He could play all the instruments and damn near sing all the tracks. He internationalized R&B, integrated it, slicked it up, and put it out in a way where the whole world loved it. He was futuristic, so advanced that he could hardly keep up with himself.' She might also have been describing Stevie Wonder. It would be an understatement to say that throughout much of the seventies Stevie Wonder lit up African American popular music with a succession of ground-breaking albums including *Music Of My Mind* (1972), *Talking Book* (1972), *Innervisions* (1973), *Fulfillingness' First Finale* (1974) and *Songs In The Key Of Life* (1976). He had matured from a young harmonica player who was tutored at the Michigan School for the Blind into a musical master-blaster respected for his complex rhythms, global influences and socially aware lyrics about racism, black liberation and unity. At times, his words seemed disarmingly simple, even naïve, but they were frequently underwritten by radicalism. 'Let us come together before we're annihilated,' he once said. Then, almost as if he were quoting from the works of Karl Marx and speaking for the soul proletariat, he said, 'Life has meaning only in the struggle. Triumph or defeat is in the hands of the gods. So, let us celebrate the struggle.' He also had what turned out to be a revelatory communion with TONTO, an acronym for a then-pioneering piece of synthesizer technology called 'The Original New Timbral Orchestra'.

A friend had loaned him a copy of an album called *Zero Time* by the psychedelic rock band Tonto's Expanding Head Band, featuring programmer and producer Malcolm Cecil, who mainly worked within the New York advertising industry. 'I heard a ring at the door and... stuck my head out of the window to see who it was,' Cecil told *Rolling Stone* in 2013. Bounding down three flights of stairs, he encountered 'this black guy in a pistachio jumpsuit who seemed to be holding our album underneath his arm'. It was Stevie Wonder. A collaboration was born that produced one of the most successful sequences of hit records ever imagined, among them 'You Are The Sunshine Of My Life', 'Superstition', 'Living For The City', 'Higher Ground', 'Boogie On Reggae Woman', 'Sir Duke' and 'Isn't She Lovely'. A milestone in the evolution of electronic dance music was reached.

Stevie Wonder was a force of nature, a great collaborator and a fountain of innovation. He was without question the most important black artist of the decade. In the year 1975 alone, the diversity of his workload was staggering. He worked extensively with Minnie Riperton, another talent from Bronzeville in Chicago's South Side, who had been a member of the Windy City's answer to The Supremes, the all-girl soul group The Gems, before becoming the distinctive lead singer of the psych-rock band Rotary Connection. By 1975, Riperton was promoting her stunning solo album *Perfect Angel*, the cover of which has her in bleached farmer's dungarees holding a melting ice cream as if it is a microphone. Riperton was diagnosed with breast cancer and died at thirty-one, having become a face of the American Cancer Society. The year before her death she was presented with a Courage Award at the White House by President Jimmy Carter.

Stevie Wonder's prodigious work schedule never eased. A few years earlier he had worked with the rock guitarist Jeff Beck, and in a conversation at the Electric Lady Studios in New York they supposedly collaborated on a song then titled 'Very Superstitious'. Either Motown overruled the deal or Wonder himself had second thoughts and kept the song now titled 'Superstition' for himself. It became a global hit and a source of some friction between Beck and Wonder. In 1975, to settle the issue and put any misunderstanding to bed, Stevie honoured his commitment to write for Beck, coming up with a tribute song to jazz legend Thelonious Monk, which appeared on Beck's album *Blow By Blow*. Stevie's next collaboration was with traditional pop singer Andy Williams, then he guested in studio sessions with Buddy Miles and played harmonica on Billy Preston's album *It's My Pleasure*. Next up he was a harmonica player again, this time for jazz-funk pioneer Herbie Hancock, and then back to composition, writing tracks for The Pointer Sisters, Roberta Flack, and finally for his wife Syreeta Wright, whom he also produced. It was only a few months later that the song 'Superstition' re-emerged, this time recorded by Quincy Jones on his double album *I Heard That!!*.

In the summer of 1979, Stevie Wonder had called Martin Luther King's widow to tell her about a dream he had that the holiday would happen, guaranteed. At the time, she shrugged it off. Stevie Wonder kept in touch with her and regularly performed at rallies to push for the holiday, and in January of 1979, he had delivered on his promise to appear at a fundraising concert in King's memory. He told a cheering crowd in Atlanta, 'If we cannot celebrate a man who died for love, then how can we say we believe in it? It is up to me and you.' The journalist Marcus Baram claimed in the online magazine *Cuepoint* that it was Stevie Wonder's high profile, the persistence of labour unions and the work of committed civil rights activists that kept the show on the road.

> The dream was kept alive by labour unions, who viewed King as a working-class hero. At a General Motors plant in New York, a small group of auto workers refused to work on King's birthday in 1969, and thousands of hospital workers in New York City went on strike until managers agreed to a paid holiday on the birthday. King's widow, Coretta Scott King, led a birthday rally that year in Atlanta, where she was joined by Conyers and union leaders. By 1973, some of the country's largest unions, including the AFSCME and the United Autoworkers, made the paid holiday a regular demand in their contract negotiations.

Gradually and fortuitously, it was a cause that President Jimmy Carter felt able to support. King supporters had always hoped that Carter would be swayed by his debt to the unions and their members, who had played a major role in his election victory. The President endorsed the bill, but not even a plea from the sanctuary of King's former church moved the congressional needle.

On 14 January 1979, after breakfast and a phone conversation with the French president Giscard d'Estaing, President Carter and his family flew by Marine helicopter from the South Grounds to Andrews Air Force Base, Maryland, then by *Air Force One* to Atlanta, where he was scheduled to attend a ceremony at King's old church, Ebenezer Baptist Church.

For a white politician raised in the tense rural communities of Georgia, Jimmy Carter was surprisingly comfortable in the company of black musicians. His mother Lillian's maiden name was Gordy, and she was the niece of Berry Gordy Snr and therefore related to the Motown boss. Carter enjoyed dropping his credentials if Motown or any of its illustrious Detroit stars were mentioned in conversation. Typical of Carter's own relaxed and informal image, the family took a detour on the way to the church to call in at Gene and Gabe's restaurant, a dining institution in Georgia, and a place the President nostalgically remembered from his days as Governor. Although Carter's unusual rise to the presidency is now seen to parallel the emergence of southern rock, including stars such as Lynyrd Skynyrd, The Marshall Tucker Band and The Allman Brothers Band, who all supported his campaign, the story was more nuanced.

One of the major funders of Carter's presidential campaigns was Capricorn Records, owned by Phil Walden, famously the manager of Otis Redding and an agent who managed southern tours for Stax soul artists and organised concert engagements for Jerry Butler, Al Green, Sam and Dave, and Percy Sledge. Carter had met Walden in Macon, Georgia, having been introduced by Cloyd Hall, Carter's executive assistant and a former high-school football coach who once had both Otis Redding and Phil Walden in his team. It was Phil Walden who instituted the Let's Get to Know Jimmy benefit drives, bringing rock and soul musicians to perform for the unfashionable peanut farmer. Like Carter himself, southern rock was not as racially simplistic as many generalisations presumed. Phil Walden famously told the British music journalist Barney Hoskyns: 'To the young white Southerner, black music always appealed more than white pop music. Certainly, the Beach Boys' surfing stuff never would have hacked it in the South. It was too white, and it just wasn't relevant. The waves weren't too high down here.' Frequently called to assert his opposition to racism, especially in the southern states, Carter and the First Lady Rosalynn linked arms with Martin Luther King's father, his widow Coretta and King's prodigy Andrew Young, whom Carter had appointed to the role of US Ambassador to the United Nations. It was a strategically important appointment, signalling to the civil rights movement that they had a place at the high table of government.

It was Jimmy Carter who called on Congress to vote on the King Holiday Bill but there was dogged resistance led by the conservative

Senator Jesse Helms of North Carolina, who denounced King as a lawbreaker who had been manipulated by communists. Progress stalled yet again. In November 1979, the bill fell short by five votes but the setback triggered a response that proved critical. Following the 1979 congressional defeat, Stevie Wonder released the single 'Happy Birthday', which became the movement's anthem, familiar in almost every home in America and a catalyst for popular change.

For all the machinations of politicians, it was Stevie Wonder who seemed to speak to a wider pop constituency. His original idea, however, was a little bizarre. He wanted to re-enact Marilyn Monroe's birthday tribute to President Kennedy by singing a traditional version of 'Happy Birthday' but inserting King's name into the lyrics. Fortunately, the more he reflected and consulted with the King family, the more it became clear that a new song, with different lyrics, would be the way to go. He made 'Happy Birthday' the centrepiece song of his 1980 album *Hotter Than July*, a collection that also contained the global hit 'Master Blaster (Jammin')'. The record's inner sleeve featured a large photograph of King and urged fans to support the holiday bill. It read: 'We still have a long road to travel until we reach the world that was his dream. We in the United States must not forget either his supreme sacrifice or that dream.'

Wonder used 'Happy Birthday' to popularise the campaign. During a memorable television appearance in August 1980 on ABC's news magazine show *20/20* with host Barbara Walters, he played the song on keyboards and announced a four-month tour with Bob Marley that would lead into a mass rally to push for the holiday. The highpoint of the tour would be a show on the National Mall in Washington D.C., where King had given his famous 'I Have a Dream' speech in 1963. The announcement came only a few short months before the election that would put Ronald Reagan in the White House, and there was concern within the campaign team. Stevie Wonder even voiced his own personal worries about the 'disturbing drift in the country towards war, bigotry, poverty and hatred'.

The radical soul and jazz poet Gil Scott-Heron was watching *20/20* at home and decided he would go to the Mall, only to later receive a phone call from the event's promoter offering him a support slot on the tour itself. He joined in Houston and was on the bill at the

Centroplex in Baton Rouge, Louisiana, when Wonder called him to come to his hotel urgently. With just the two of them in the room, Wonder confided that Bob Marley had been hospitalised in New York's Memorial Sloan Kettering clinic and was dying of cancer. Spooked by the circumstances, Motown and Stevie's management insisted that a higher-profile act be brought in as a substitute, and amongst those canvassed were the Commodores and the Dazz Band, but the campaign believed Gil Scott-Heron with his legacy as a singer of political invective was perfect to take on a bigger role. Wonder also assured doubters that he would invite special guests along the way. Carlos Santana and his band joined the West Coast leg of the tour and at Madison Square Garden the audience were mesmerised by Michael Jackson, the world's biggest-selling pop star, moonwalking on stage. Gil Scott-Heron described it as like watching 'a boneless man ice-skating'.

Two months later nearly 100,000 people assembled in Washington D.C. The conditions were harsh, with about an inch of new snow on the ground. Stevie Wonder took the opportunity to address criticism that King had a reprehensible love life, often betraying his marriage vows, telling the crowd:

(Although) Dr King was a great man, he was no saint. He was a man, a human being. And being no less ourselves, we should accept no less than what Dr King fought for: a commitment from this nation to make available to all its citizens the equality of opportunity to pursue the American dream of life, liberty, and the pursuit of happiness without regard to the shackles of race, creed or colour.

The 'Happy Birthday' tour had been the final push in a campaign that had begun on a more modest and local scale back in Chicago and Detroit in 1968. Fuelled by the new wave of enthusiasm, Stevie Wonder and Coretta King delivered a petition with six million signatures in favour of the holiday to the Speaker of the House, the Irish-American Democrat Tip O'Neill.

The idea was not universally popular, though, and opened old racial wounds that had only superficially healed since the fifties. In October 1983, Jesse Helms embarked on a plan to filibuster the proceedings and obstruct the passage of the bill. Confident in being described by local newspapers as 'the righteous warrior', Helms had been a white supremacist since childhood. He despised Martin Luther King and saw the idea of a national holiday in his name as anathema. His lengthy and vitriolic speech to the Senate began with an exaggerated claim that the holiday would cost $12 billion in lost productivity, but his real venom was reserved for what he described as King's character, drawn from FBI briefings (derived from illegal surveillance) that portrayed King as a communist and brazen womaniser. Journalist Ed Yoder for *The Washington Post*, who had drawn swords with Helms over many years, called his Senate speech 'Vintage Helms' and accused him of relying on 'debating points dredged from the gutter'. Helms was one of those thick-skinned public figures who seemed to relish his notoriety, goading liberal journalists while nodding to the most nakedly racist elements of his own constituency. He argued to his dying breath that King was being lauded for virtues in death that he had not demonstrated in his lifetime.

On Valentine's Day 1985, Stevie Wonder was arrested at an anti-apartheid demonstration at the South African embassy on Massachusetts Avenue. Maintaining a vigil outside the embassy was part of a two-year campaign to force the Reagan administration to exert more pressure on the Pretoria government to change its policies of racial separation. The rituals had by now settled into a familiar pattern. The protesters would gather at the closest point where the pickets were legally allowed to assemble and then an agreed contingent would approach the embassy entrance and ask to see the ambassador. They were then told that the embassy was closed to them and to move back at least five hundred feet. Instead, the protesters would reassemble on the sidewalk, where they sang songs such as 'We Shall Overcome' and The Special AKA's hit 'Free Nelson Mandela' until police led them away. Some were handcuffed and placed in a police cruiser, while others, including members of Washington Area Scholars Against Apartheid, were taken from the embassy in police vans and a bus. It became so commonplace that the media had virtually given up attending until the day Stevie Wonder showed up. Wearing a stunning ankle-length fur coat, he had met the anti-apartheid campaigners off stage during the show at the Mall and assured them that as soon as his itinerary allowed he would return to boost their picket. He had also recorded the anthemic 'It's Wrong

(Apartheid)' and dedicated the awards he won for 'I Just Called To Say I Love You' to the imprisoned Nelson Mandela.

By the time of his arrest, the boy genius had blossomed into a global talent. According to press reports at the time, he was creative even in his response to the arresting officers. '[I'm a] a conscientious criminal for world equality,' he said, with his trademark grin. Throughout years of poverty and racial intolerance, and despite the disability that had marked his own life, Stevie Wonder's sense of humour, gregariousness and passion for practical jokes marked him out as a man of boundless optimism. When his head shook from side to side in that distinctive manner he had developed since playing harmonica as a child, his personality shone like a light. Even under arrest, Stevie Wonder smiled joyfully. It was a smile that could change America.

Glenn Hughes, the impressively mustachioed leatherman in disco group
Village People, on stage at an open-air concert in San Francisco's
Union Square, in the summer of 1980.

5

DISCO INFERNO

Listen Up: 'Love Sensation (Tom Moulton Mix)' by Loleatta Holloway (1980)

Disco is one of the most misunderstood and misrepresented genres in the story of black music. Often connected in the popular imagination with the movie *Saturday Night Fever* (1977), disco had in fact preceded the film by years and was around as a nascent form of soul as early as 1965 when the uptown dance music song '(At The) Discotheque' (Parkway, 1965) was recorded by the twist-craze maestro Chubby Checker. Checker even uses the original French pronunciation of the term 'disco-tay' to rhyme with 'hey, hey hey'. It was a song that connected to at least two different subcultures. In the north of England at Manchester's rare soul all-nighter the Twisted Wheel it became a popular import for the unforgiving mods who inspired what became known as northern soul. Meanwhile, five thousand miles away in Watts in South Central Los Angeles, it had inspired a group of young gender-fluid and cross-dressing teenagers who christened themselves the Disquotays. One of their leaders was Sylvester James Jr, the son of a teenage couple who had left Palestine, Arkansas, and moved to LA as part of the Great Migration.

Sylvester grew up to become one of the superstars of disco and the talent behind the dance anthem 'You Make Me Feel (Mighty Real)' (Fantasy, 1978). When he teamed up with the gigantic gospel singers Martha Wash and Izora Armstead in San Francisco a powerful strand of gay iconography was born. The image of the diva, substantial of both voice and body, became a much-loved characteristic of high-energy disco. When Sylvester's one-time backing singers stepped out of the chorus line and reconfigured their act as The Weather Girls, they gave life to one of the outstanding songs of gay disco – the tongue-in-cheek yet majestic 'It's Raining Men' (Columbia, 1982).

Although he was unaware of it at the time, Sylvester's fascination with cross-dressing had a powerful backstory that stretched back at least a hundred years to an infamous haunt called the Clam House on West 133rd Street, where the blues singer Gladys Bentley held court cross-dressed in a tuxedo and top hat. The gigantic Bentley, similar in stature to Big Maybelle, was a powerful chanteuse with a blaring soulful voice, who hollered above the music urging her audience into paroxysms of delight. Harlem was inventing the polysexual future. The Hamilton Lodge Ball held annually on 155th Street brought thousands to the street corners to watch flamboyant costume displays in which mostly poor working-class young men danced in over-the-top drag. Throughout the sixties, as mainstream soul swept to prominence internationally, Harlem's underground met at the Rockland Palace in competitions to impersonate the kings and queens of sexualised soul, from Little Richard to Diana Ross. This was the forerunner of what became known as 'voguing', the craze that re-emerged in Harlem in the seventies and mutated into one of the major movements of the urban R&B scene, inspiring in turn Madonna, Beyoncé, Rihanna and Ariana Grande. The vogue balls organised around grandiose names such as the House of LaBeija, House of Dupree, House of Xtravaganza, Ninja, Ebony and the House of St Laurent and Chanel, but the drag balls and the precursors of voguing were underground and never universally welcomed in a community steeped in religion. Harlem's Abyssinian Baptist Church, a church-cum-institution with 10,000 members, and the biggest

Protestant congregation in the USA, campaigned against the drag performances, deriding them as 'the parade of the pansies' and 'the dance of the fairies'.

This tension between private sexual lifestyle and religion was to become one of the overwhelming moral issues for gay men in the black music industry and was prevalent for decades. Most successful soul singers from the golden era of the sixties had come from a church background. Many had very deep and immutable spiritual views. While some could live with the contradictions between drugs, promiscuity and the Lord, others were more troubled by the dilemmas thrown up by secular soul. It was a situation exemplified by the chaotic life of Little Richard. Raised by his mother among the pews of Macon's New Hope Baptist Church, he met and performed with the gospel giant Sister Rosetta Tharpe then made his first significant income touting for an eccentric local spiritualist, Doctor Nubillo. Nubillo, who wore a turban and a multi-coloured cape, carried a black stick and performed juju routines with a model of a dried-up body of a baby with bird's-claw feet and horns on its head. From those contradictory beginnings, Little Richard's career and private life catapulted between the Lord and lascivious showmanship. His nascent rock 'n' roll hits 'Tutti Frutti' and 'Long Tall Sally' came not only with the shock of the new but with a sexual energy that propelled him into a life torn between the gospel church and drag queens. The new-wave rock poet Patti Smith once claimed him as her major influence. She told the New Inquiry: 'To me, Little Richard was a person that was able to focus a certain physical, anarchistic, and spiritual energy into a form which we call rock 'n' roll ... When I was a little girl, Santa Claus didn't turn me on. Easter Bunny didn't turn me on. God turned me on. Little Richard turned me on.'

Disco was where soul went to party. By the first days of the seventies, a wave of new independent labels had emerged in New York's boroughs, releasing records that had a distinctive up-tempo beat and deployed strings and studio synthesizer techniques which differentiated them from the rawer and more percussive street-funk. Samar, an indie label based upstate in Rochester, New York, and whose arteries spread down to Harlem, laid down the blueprint for what became disco. Among Samar's featured artists and producers were Jimmy Norman, Bert Keyes,

Johnny Brantley, the Poindexter brothers and the saxophonist Lonnie Youngblood. One of the label's most cherished releases was The Icemen's haunting '(My Girl) She's a Fox' (1966), which features Jimi Hendrix on lead guitar. Samar was short-lived. The company was part-owned by Bob Schwaid, a Brooklyn native who all but abandoned the label to become Van Morrison's manager at the time of his album *Astral Weeks*. By then Schwaid had cut his teeth on many more obscure independent soul releases, including Madeline Wilson's 'Dial "L" For Lonely' and Gloria Parker's 'The Best Thing For You Baby', both joyous teenage love songs cast in the dominant Motown style of the mid sixties. But hidden within the arrangement was a classical sensibility. Schwaid had hired an old school friend from Brooklyn, a jobbing producer-arranger with the grandiloquent name of Norbert de Coteau.

De Coteau was a thick-set young man with heavy horn-rimmed spectacles who looked more like a schoolteacher than a record producer. Steeped in orchestral music, he brought a richness to soul that made it perfect for the mixers, studio producers and DJs who followed. He had recently graduated from the famous New York conservatoire the Juilliard School and had come into the music business with a personal mission to combine the R&B of his ghetto childhood with the lush strings and complex orchestration he had studied. He is just one of the many hidden talents that made disco happen. Working under the name Bert DeCoteaux, his curriculum vitae was a masterclass in metropolitan soul, including Lou Courtney's 'I Watched You Slowly Slip Away' (1965), Patti Austin's 'Take Away The Pain Stain' (1966), The Charts' 'Livin' The Nightlife' (1966) and Christine Cooper's joyful 'Heartaches Away My Boy' (1966). Within a few years, ploughing a furrow for subtly crafted dance music, he offered a sophisticated alternative to street-funk and edgy political soul, becoming one of the most sought-after producers in the New York dance-music under-ground. When disco came to dominate the charts, his name became an imprimatur of success, and he was known throughout the industry by the nickname 'Super Charts'.

Another emerging star of the New York underground was Van McCoy. In 1969, McCoy was taking baby steps towards what was to become a truly historic album – *Soul Improvisations* (1972). Viewed with hindsight, this was the bridge between soul and disco. McCoy's orchestral arrangements, his virtuoso electric keyboard skills and the driving congas of Ralph McDonald created a sound that was not only original but the shape of things to come. McCoy was impatient about the pace of change in African American music. This impatience was shared by several of his contemporaries, including Thom Bell in Philadelphia and Gene Redd Jr, the son of a well-known swing-era artist, and a man who had worked for Motown's New York office. By 1969, Redd was striking out in a similar direction to McCoy and had set up two parallel labels: De-Lite and Redd Coach Productions, progenitors of funk and disco and eventually home to Kool and the Gang, Crown Heights Affair and Everyday People. In 1969, Robert 'Kool' Bell moved from New Jersey to Harlem, where his uncle was a boxing trainer. Living in his uncle's apartment near 125th Street, 'Kool' and his Gang released their eponymous debut single, which initially hit the stores of Harlem on Gene Redd's minimally distributed Red Coach label. Nothing about its first pressing could have anticipated the stellar success the group would enjoy when disco and jazz-funk came to dominate the club charts.

Viewed in retrospect, the roll call of the early pioneers of New York's independent soul labels is a staggering checklist of disco talent: Bert 'Super Charts' DeCoteaux, Van McCoy, Gene Redd Jr, Kool and the Gang, The Fantastic Aleems, Patrick Adams, Luther Vandross and one of the cult superstars of underground club music, Leroy Burgess. For ten years, often out of sight of mainstream media, this young generation of super-skilled studio musicians shaped the New York indie scene, recording on labels like De-Lite, Red Coach, Perception, Today and Salsoul Records.

By the time the blue-collar Brooklyn-set film *Saturday Night Fever* had become a global hit, Van McCoy had been a producer in under-ground dance music for nearly ten years and his signature hit, 'The Hustle' (Avco 1975), was three years old. The disco or nightclub under-ground had been a settled part of African American life for years, hidden away from wider public attention, unperturbed by the celebrity glitz of Studio 54, which in any event was only open for three short and over-promoted years. This disjointed map of clubs and house parties obscured within ghetto communities was infinitely more important to the evolution of the disco sound than the movies or celebrity nightclubs.

Venues like Pepper's Hideout and The High Chaparral in Chicago's South Side, and Harlem World in New York, or more ostentatiously gay clubs such as the summer-party circuit on Fire Island, the Music Box on Jersey Shore and the Second Story in a converted church at 12th and Walnut in Philadelphia, were tucked away from sight and known only to the dance-music cognoscenti. As the axis of popular soul music shifted from New York metropolitan soul to the Philly Sound, yet another club – Catacombs – opened in the basement of the same building as Second Story in Philadelphia. The first record played at the club was a masterpiece, 'The Impossible Dream', a song that had become a cult classic since it appeared in the Broadway show *Man of La Mancha* in 1965, but this time performed by Roberta Flack. The song begins as a ballad, speculates on the fantasy of an impossible dream, and then soars into high-camp soul. All these influences – opera, high classicism, the diva singer, ceremonial pomp, showtunes and fantasy – became part of the DNA of gay disco.

Another huge influence was a New York City audiophile named David Mancuso. In his obituary, *The New York Times* described his loft parties as 'a '60s dream of peace, love and diversity: multiracial, gay and straight, young and old, well-to-do and down-at-heel, singles and couples, all mingling ecstatically in an egalitarian, commerce-free space'. Unable to afford his rent, Mancuso sold tickets for a downtown rent party, hosting his first event on Valentine's Day 1970. It bore the title 'Love Saves the Day', code for LSD. Tim Lawrence, the author of *Love Saves the Day: A History of American Dance Music Culture, 1970–79*, saw Mancuso's loft parties as the big bang that ultimately gave life to underground disco. 'D.J.'s started to gravitate to the Loft, when they were finished with their own parties for the night,' he wrote, 'and it was there that some of the most influential D.J.'s of the future – Larry Levan, Frankie Knuckles, Tony Humphries, François Kevorkian, David Morales and many more – would learn about the sonic and social potential of the party.'

Uptown, the Cellar nightclub was run by Betty Mabry (who became Betty Davis after marrying jazz trumpeter Miles) and a Harlem-based soul singer called Louis Pegues, whose stage name was Lou Courtney. Courtney was the mighty Lorraine Ellison's musical director and had enjoyed some success with a string of dance-craze tracks on Manhattan indie labels Popside and Riverside, including 'Skate Now' (1966) and 'Do The Thing' (1967), 'Me And You Doin' The Boogaloo' and 'Psychedelic Shing-a-Ling' (1967), and a Verve single called 'Do The Horse' (1968). But Courtney's commercial pursuit of fads and dance crazes belied a significant talent for songwriting and discovering singers with outstanding gospel voices. Among his vast catalogue of songs was the future disco star Gloria Gaynor's debut 'She'll Be Sorry' (1965), Patti Austin's uptown soul song 'Take Away The Pain Stain' and an evocative break-up song arranged by Bert DeCoteaux called 'I Watched You Slowly Slip Away', which Courtney himself recorded in 1965 but was surpassed in quality the following year by Howard Guyton, the one-time lead singer of the Harlem-based harmony group The Top Notes. The Cellar was a forerunner of underground disco and Lou Courtney one of a small band of producers who linked dance-craze and gospel: a big idea was emerging.

Club 57, which began its life in the basement of the Holy Cross Polish National Church on St Mark's Place, became the preferred party venue of graffiti artists Keith Haring and Futura 2000. Another club, Crisco Disco, was tucked away in the Meatpacking District of Manhattan at a time when promoters searched for cheap and out-of-the-way venues beyond the reach of New York's rapacious real-estate profiteers. Sanctuary, at 407 West 43rd Street, occupied the shell of an old German Baptist church adorned with a mural of Beelzebub surrounded by a protective flock of near-naked angels. 'The mural was unbelievably pornographic,' according to Sanctuary's pioneering DJ, Francis Grasso. 'And no matter where you stood in the club, the devil was looking at you.' Drinks were served from metal chalices and the old church's stained-glass windows were lit from outside to cast shards of coloured light across the dance floor. When the club first opened (under the name Church), it had attracted a backlash and was forced to close when the Catholic Church gained a temporary injunction against its use as a nightclub. The mural was subsequently toned down and the venue relaunched as Sanctuary.

The unholy alliance that became disco, a soulful kind of blasphemy that fused Christian spiritual voices with the hedonistic beat of dance music, was forged by the voices of women singers from the gospel tradition, including Jo 'Joshie' Armstead, Linda Jones, Loleatta Holloway,

Thelma Houston, Gloria Gaynor and Jocelyn Brown, floating like celestial angels above the beat. The theologian Michael Eric Dyson, when writing about the late Martin Luther King, described the civil rights leader's sexual urges as being like a 'civil-war inside', a clash of values that nags away in the minds of southern men. It was a tension so powerful it had helped shape the rise of R&B music and eaten away at the soul of many of black music's greatest male singers: Sam Cooke, Solomon King, Marvin Gaye and eventually Al Green. For many in this new fallen generation of disco, the club displaced the church as the most relevant institution in their lives and inevitably gave rise to a new generation of licentious spiritual leaders, DJs who attracted congregations in ways unseen before. Francis Grasso was one of the innovators, composing music with two turntables, learning through trial and error to mix, to phase and to slip-cue records to extend their range beyond the three-minute limit of commercial vinyl. These revolutionary techniques, mastered and shared with others, became the basic skills of the DJ and the primitive trick of dance-music production.

In 1976, two Manhattan entrepreneurs, Steve Rubell and Ian Schrager, took ownership of the old Gallo Opera House on 54th Street and began to imagine New York's most ambitious and outrageous disco. Rubell wanted to scatter tons of glitter on the dancefloor and create a club overblown with fantasy at a time when sex and sexuality were on the verge of becoming divisive political terrain. Studio 54 had yet to open when Democratic candidate Jimmy Carter broke with conventional campaign protocol and gave an interview to the adult magazine *Playboy*. During the astonishingly candid interview, Carter admitted to sexual thoughts: 'I've looked on many women with lust. I've committed adultery in my heart many times. God knows I will do this and forgives me.' His remarks were seized upon by a group of Evangelicals, the Christian Freedom Foundation, who distributed 120,000 broadsheets to ministers which included a manual on how to elect 'real Christians' to office.

A new civil war was on the horizon, one that would bring the Christian right into the forefront of political thinking and turn disco music from a passing metropolitan fad into a symbol of a morally corrosive America.

As the days ticked down on his presidency, and disco tipped closer to bloated clichés, Jimmy Carter was enjoying a week-long vacation on board a Mississippi River paddle steamer called the *Delta Queen* when he received a worrying telephone call from the newly appointed Attorney General, Benjamin Civiletti, who regretfully told him that he had instructed the FBI to investigate two of Carter's closest White House aides, chief of staff Hamilton Jordan and press secretary Jody Powell. Jordan had been accused of snorting cocaine during a visit to Studio 54. At the time the story was broken by *TIME* magazine, Rubell and Schrager were entangled in a tax evasion case which had spiralled into obstruction of justice and conspiracy charges. The two were accused of skimming more than $2 million in unreported income from the club's receipts. Rubell had hired the notorious Manhattan lawyer Roy M. Cohn, a man who had been chief counsel for Senator Joseph McCarthy during the anti-communist witch hunt of the Cold War period and later would be Donald Trump's lawyer in the early days of his real-estate investments in New York. Cohn was that most pernicious of characters, a closeted gay man who disguised his sexuality by making virulent homophobic statements in public. He convinced Rubell that there was a prospect of immunity if they could entrap the White House in a cocaine scandal and so identified a low-level dealer who worked the bathrooms in Studio 54 and tape-recorded him admitting that he had sold cocaine to the White House aides. However, the crisis never quite ignited as planned. A special prosecutor was appointed, no charges were filed, and the disco scandal that could have rocked the White House fizzled out.

However, a powerful wave of Christian fundamentalism was sweeping America, leaning to the right and bringing Ronald Reagan to the presidency. To the fundamentalists, disco was a byword for gay promiscuity, drug abuse and racial miscegenation. Club culture in decadent New York was seen by Christian broadcasters as a seedbed of the HIV/AIDS epidemic, a national health crisis all but ignored by the White House for years to come. Set against that story, John Travolta playing the part of a good dancer from Brooklyn in a white suit seems lame indeed.

*

Loleatta Holloway and Keith Barrow had competed against each other as teenagers in the Chicago gospel world before they both moved to New York and competed in the new disco charts. Holloway was a featured singer in her family group, the Holloway Community Singers, but it was in disco that she truly flourished. Back home, Barrow had been the lead singer of the Chicago gospel-soul group the Soul Shakers, which had toured on the Illinois soul caravan, to Cairo and Springfield. With one gospel album to his credit, which carried sleeve notes by the Reverend Jesse Jackson, Barrow took the decision to shift to secular soul music. As a young gay man only recently out of the closet, he saw New York as a beacon of sexual tolerance and a place he could be free.

Keith Barrow had charming falsetto vocals, comparable to Eddie Kendricks of The Temptations and Eugene Record of the Chi-Lites. His (second) eponymous album was released by Columbia Records in 1977, followed by two other albums, *Physical Attraction* (1978) and *Just As I Am* (1980). In the summer of 1979 Barrow was too sick to perform on a promotional tour in Paris and was taken to a local hospital. He was then flown home and later diagnosed with HIV. Initially nursed at home by his mother, in 1983 he died in Chicago's Michael Reese Hospital, one of the first victims of AIDS. According to his producer and songwriter, Ronn Matlock, Barrow's passing was a milestone. 'We didn't know he'd been sick,' he said years later. 'Keith was the first person I knew personally who died of AIDS.'

His first venture into what became known as disco had been a recording of one of his own songs. 'That's Love' (1974), with a studio group, the Hi-Lites. The record didn't trouble the charts, but it was significant in one respect: it was an imprint of the great Detroit trium-virate Holland, Dozier, Holland on their independent Invictus label, underlining the connections that linked disco to classic up-tempo Motown. Meanwhile Loleatta Holloway had signed a deal with the Atlanta soul label Aware, releasing two significant singles. One was 'Mother Of Shame', a searing critique of welfare provision in the dying days of the Nixon administration, and the other an outstanding song titled 'The Show Must Go On', which cast a desperately sad love affair as a down-at-heel theatre show. Both were written by the soul-music genius Sam Dees, who had struck a deal as an artist and creative producer with Atlantic Records. Before moving north from his base in

Birmingham, Alabama, Dees had handed out hope of studio work to singers that he knew could adapt from gospel to soul, and from showtunes to the disco sound. Among the small posse who joined him in New York were Loleatta Holloway and two singers from Huntsville, Alabama: Bill Brandon and Lorraine Johnson. Within a few weeks of arriving in New York they had brought southern gospel to the Manhattan studio system and were the go-to singers for ambitious DJs aspiring to produce their own singles.

As the underlying rules of disco production were written, high-end soulful voices were in demand. Loleatta Holloway became one of the most sampled voices in disco and house music, featuring on four tracks now seen as disco classics: 'Run Away' (Salsoul, 1977), 'Hit And Run' (Gold Mind, 1977), 'Love Sensation' (Gold Mind, 1980) and 'Ride On Time' (Disco Magic, 1989). With Holloway's voice initially sampled by the Italo-disco group Black Box, due to its ubiquity as a feature of both American and European club mixes, 'Ride On Time' became a benchmark for the underground club music emerging in Holloway's native city – Chicago house.

Holloway's 'Hit And Run' was also one of the first generation of 12-inch singles to be made commercially available, sharing status to this day alongside a stand-out track from May 1976, 'Ten Per Cent' by the soul group Double Exposure (Salsoul, 1976). The latter usually attracts the accolade of being the first widely sold 12-inch single and was a signature song within the epic sets of underground DJ Walter Gibbons. By the time Loleatta Holloway was at the height of her success, DJs and club producers had been improvising with 10- and 12-inch studio acetates for many months, allowing them to lengthen songs, splice different songs together, increase volume and have the vinyl space to repeat key sequences and present alternative mixes. A prominent offering was the a capella mix in which a great gospel voice like Loleatta Holloway's would soar joyful and triumphant, only to then be dropped into the instrumental mix of a different track entirely. Gibbons' club, Galaxy 21, was situated near the infamous Chelsea Hotel and was a long tunnel at the bottom of a building which also housed a restaurant, chill-out zone and a movie theatre. Bill Brewster, in *Last Night a DJ Saved My Life*, his history of the disc jockey, describes the club as 'a glamour tunnel . . . a saturnalian attack on the senses' which offered dancers and club-goers an escape from reality.

*

In 1977, less than a decade after the Stonewall uprising had ignited awareness among gay and lesbian activists, gay disco found a dogged opponent from Florida called Anita Bryant, an evangelical pop star and high-profile spokeswoman for Florida orange juice. Bryant mobilised a backlash against new gay rights legislation, first locally and then nationally. She used her fame to draw media attention to gay rights battles and under the banner of the 'Protect America's Children Campaign' she helped to reverse or defeat anti-discrimination laws in Miami, Oregon and Minnesota. Bryant continued to be the face of Florida orange juice until 1980 and was part of the evangelical wave that helped usher Ronald Reagan into the White House.

According to Emily Johnson, writing in *The Washington Post*, Bryant's subsequent decline was as dramatic as her rise. 'Ultimately, it was her personal life that toppled Bryant,' Johnson claims. 'In 1980, her marriage fell apart. She initiated a messy public divorce over the objections of her husband and her pastor. Once a symbol of cheery suburban motherhood, she could no longer fill that role. Televangelists who had once been her allies now disavowed her as "wicked," rebellious and a "disgrace."' Anita Bryant's anti-gay campaigns faded as Ronald Reagan's first term of office got underway. Beneath the radar of mainstream news coverage, AIDS had already ravaged the United States for several years, affecting at least 7,700 people and killing more than 3,500 by the end of 1984.

According to conventional wisdom, HIV originated in 1920 in what is now Kinshasa, Democratic Republic of Congo. It spread to Haiti and the Caribbean before jumping to New York City around 1970 just as the early seeds of underground disco were planted. The delay in identifying the threat proved decisive. Health officials were aware of a mystery virus in the summer of 1981 when young and otherwise healthy gay men began getting sick and dying of illnesses normally associated with people with weakened immune systems. Scientists later identified the cause and the US Centres for Disease Control and Prevention (CDC) mapped the major transmission routes. Ronald Reagan, however, who replaced Jimmy Carter as President in January 1981, remained largely silent and unresponsive to the national health emergency. Even when Reagan's administration did act it was a pathetic and seriously flawed response, excoriated in *The New York Times*. 'While the AIDS epidemic gets its grip on America,' the newspaper reported, 'Mr. Reagan's Administration spouts, postures and neglects effective measures to curb it. AIDS had by then spread to intravenous drug users and from there to the heterosexual community, turning a marginalised, largely hidden condition into a national panic. *The New York Times* raged:

> AIDS is the most serious threat to public health in decades, Historians will look back in astonishment at the Reagan Administration's flaccid response during the first eight years of the epidemic's spread. They will ask how any President could fail to implement the most obvious public health measures, or tardily assign the making of national strategy to a quarrelling commission with no recognizable expertise. They will wonder how his Cabinet members could be torpid spectators of the virus's spread, seeing it only as a pretext for impressing their own morals on others.

Larry Kramer, the playwright, film producer and author of the 1978 novel *Faggots*, emerged as one of the leading gay activists of the eighties. He later said, 'We didn't exist. Ronald Reagan didn't say the word "AIDS" until 1987.' Gay activists seized on Reagan's silence and turned it into a battle cry. ACT UP, one of the most organised pressure groups, used a dramatic poster – Silence = Death – as part of their campaigning. Clubs that were once the home of hedonism became rallying points, ministries of safe sex and places where health education could be promoted. Although he had been briefed about the history of AIDS and the path of the epidemic, it wasn't until September 1985, years after the crisis was first identified, that President Ronald Reagan first acknowledged AIDS in public. His silence, in part influenced by right-wing Christian ideals and fundamentalist readings of the Bible, allowed the White House to simply look the other way.

Against this backdrop, disco's heavyweight fight pitted Sylvester against Donna Summer, the Euro-disco star whose debut single 'Love To Love You Baby', established her collaboration with Giorgio Moroder. Their most outstanding release 'I Feel Love' (Casablanca, 1977) was an edit of an orgasmic near-seventeen-minute-long album track which

Silence=Death. The iconic pink triangle poster was produced by ACT UP (AIDS Coalition To Unleash Power), a group which was founded in 1987 by playwright and activist Larry Kramer who had noticed his friends in Fire Island becoming sick some years earlier. ACT UP became the most vocal critic of President Reagan's lack of response to the AIDS epidemic.

became one of the pinnacles of disco club mixing. 'The only criticism you can make of Giorgio Moroder's motor-disco landmark is that it is too short,' *Guardian* critic Dorian Lynskey said, praising its use of an 'Escher-staircase bassline to create a dizzying 3D labyrinth with shades of dub, jazz and psychedelia, and premonitions of techno. Sixteen minutes that hint at infinity.' When Summer returned to her religious roots and became a born-again Christian, she reputedly made homophobic remarks about AIDS being God's way of punishing the immoral lives of homosexuals. The fanbase that had given her the status of a goddess deserted overnight. In a letter to ACT UP written in 1989, Summer said it was 'a terrible misunderstanding' and that she was 'unknowingly protected by those around me from the bad press and hate letters. If I have caused you pain, forgive me.' The damage was done, however, and some – among them a group of disco singers led by Sylvester – were not in the mood for late apologies. Sylvester, sometimes acting vengefully, never missed an opportunity to goad Summer, and in *The Fabulous Sylvester*, a biography written by Joshua Gamson, he told the author that he planned to make the ultimate gay-sex disco hit, which he hoped would expose the fakery of Donna Summer's orgasmic style. 'I want to have someone fuck on the record,' he said. 'Not moaning and groaning. But the sound of sex, the sounds of touching, the actual sounds of penetration. Nice music and close miking. It's not gonna be a record for sex. It's a record for dancing with sex.' Although the song never materialised, Sylvester talked about it repeatedly, mainly to provoke Donna Summer to react.

Fittingly, the person most suited to find a reconciliation between Christianity and gay disco was the Reverend Carl Bean, a disco singer in his own right who found brief fame covering the gay anthem 'I Was Born This Way'/'Liberation' (Gaiee, 1975), an indie-soul hit originally sung by a young singer Charles Harris, under the stage name Valentino. Harris was from Alabama and escaped the Deep South as a teenager, moving to New York to study ballet. On the night of the Stonewall uprising in 1969 he watched from the sidelines as the famous battle between New York Police and drag queens raged in and around Sheridan Square. Harris gravitated towards musicals, appearing first in a touring version of *Hair* and then much later playing the scarecrow in a revival of *The Wiz*, the disco version of *The Wizard of Oz*. 'I Was Born This Way' was played on heavy rotation by the influential radio DJ

AIDS activist and 'Queen of Disco' Sylvester (1947–1988). He stipulated in his will that all his future royalties were to go to HIV/AIDS charities. 'If there was one artist . . . who truly exemplified disco's new language of ecstasy it was Sylvester,' said critic Peter Shapiro.

Frankie 'Love Man' Crocker on his urban show on WBLS and became a New York hit. The money to fund the record came from a Manhattan beauty-salon owner, Bunny Jones, who set up the label Gaiee more to support the gay men who worked in her salon rather than as a serious attempt to break into the music industry. Jones secured a distribution deal with Motown, who saw an opportunity and recorded the song again, this time with Carl Bean leading the vocals.

Carl Bean was both a victim and a devotee of Christianity. Born and raised in Baltimore, he had been persistently abused as a child within his church community. Ridiculed and ostracised for being gay, Bean attempted suicide and was rushed to hospital where his stomach was pumped. He was then placed in a psychiatric programme that turned his life round. He left home aged 16 to try his luck as a singer in New York. Although he looked to disco as an escape, he never abandoned his faith and eventually developed a progressive theology, ostensibly a form of liberation Protestant theology, that embraced gay African American men who felt confused about how to reconcile their sexuality and religion. Bean became the founding prelate of the Unity Fellowship Church Movement and argued vociferously against right-wing evangelists who saw gay sex as an abomination.

In the autumn of 1982, the CDC described AIDS for the first time. Despite growing case numbers and a new name, media outlets struggled with how or even whether to cover the disease. Though *The New York Times* initially reported on the mysterious beginnings in July 1981, it wasn't until 25 May 1983 that the prestigious paper gave AIDS front-page space. By that time, 558 people had died from it in the United States. Reagan's administration was even more squeamish, leading to an embarrassing and revealing press briefing in October 1982. The conservative journalist and talk show host, Charles Lester Kinsolving, questioned Reagan's acting press secretary, Larry Speakes, about the President's thoughts on AIDS. When Kinsolving mentioned the disease was known as the 'gay plague', the press pool erupted in laughter. It became an inside joke, and on thirteen separate occasions a White House spokesperson referred to AIDS in a comedic or dismissive way. Kinsolving was vitriolic about gay rights, pilloried activists on his radio shows and labelled them 'the sodomy lobby'. The *New Yorker* magazine, which published the transcripts of the briefing, wrote that 'the entire exchange is, in retrospect, dark and utterly nauseating'.

Reagan's reluctance to react not only left public health experts frustrated but preceded largely ideological cutbacks in health funding. One internal memo sent by a staff member of the CDC in 1983 said,

'The time wasted pursuing money from Washington has cast an air of despair over AIDS workers throughout the country.' By the end of that year, the country had 4,700 reported cases of AIDS and more than 2,000 deaths. Funding for health support fell to the gay and lesbian community and to individuals who had contracted HIV. Nightclubs hosted fundraisers, prominent among them Paradise Garage (formerly 84 King Street Garage) in SoHo, a club owned by Michael Brody and funded by his former boyfriend Mel Cheren. Cheren was the owner of West End Records, the dance indie that produced Raw Silk, NYC Peech Boys, Taana Gardner and Philadelphia vocalist Karen Young. Between 1977 and 1987, Paradise Garage was one of the most important and influential clubs in New York City, primarily attracting African American gay men. Significantly, it was a membership club whose model upended the hidden rules that had dominated membership organisations in America for decades, in that its tongue-in-cheek promotion claimed it was open to gays, Jews and blacks but not bigots. The club opened in 1977 with a series of 'construction' parties and myths have since circulated that it was men in construction outfits there who gave rise to the disco super-group Village People, formed in the same year.

Among Paradise Garage's most significant hires was club DJ Lawrence Philpot, from Flatbush in Brooklyn, who worked under the name Larry Levan. Soon after the club opened, Levan's sets, which deployed drum machines and synthesizers, became known as 'Saturday Mass' and Paradise Garage – often pronounced as Gay-Rage – became a cathedral for black gay men. By 1982 it was one of the centres of opposition to Reagan's silence and provided office space to the Gay Men's Health Crisis (GMHC), which held its first fundraiser there, an event cheekily called Showers. The club closed in October 1987, a few months before its founder Michael Brody died of AIDS.

And still the beat went on. Levan's teenage friend was a young textile design student from the Bronx called Francis Nicholls, who had grown up watching hip-hop DJs at the turntables but still preferred the sound of soul and underground disco. Together Levan and Nicholls, who took on the stage name Frankie Knuckles, drove the role of the DJ into new territory, creating seemingly endless loops of music often with majestic a capella gospel vocals. In the late seventies, Frankie Knuckles took up an offer of a permanent residency in a three-storey former factory on

Chicago's South Jefferson Street called The Warehouse, where he laid the groundworks of what became house music. In a weaving story of connections and influences, one of the Warehouse regulars when he returned home from New York was the singer Keith Barrow, whose 'Turn Me Up' was a proto-house record. Released in 1978, it contained the darkly prophetic line 'My fever's burning like a rare disease'.

Deaths in the gay and haemophiliac community increased exponentially but it was the final days in the life of the film star Rock Hudson that were transformative. In July 1985, the Hollywood star flew to France to seek experimental treatment with the drug HPA-23, at the time unavailable in the USA. Hudson had kept his sexuality a secret, but when he reached out to his friends the Reagans for help, he was rebuffed. After collapsing in the Ritz Hotel, local doctors tried to get Hudson admitted to the Percy military hospital in Clamart, in the southern suburbs of Paris. The commanding officer initially refused to admit Hudson because he was not a French citizen and so Hudson's US publicist sent a telegram to the White House pleading for help. 'Only one hospital in the world can offer necessary medical treatment to save life of Rock Hudson or at least alleviate his illness,' it stated. After a delay, a note came back from a White House staffer that said, 'I spoke with Mrs Reagan about the attached telegram. She did not feel this was something the White House should get into and agreed to my suggestion that we refer the writer to the US embassy, Paris.' When the French authorities finally intervened, Hudson was told that the disease had progressed too far and that the so-called wonder drug HPA-23 would be of no great use. Hudson flew back on a chartered Air France Boeing 747, estimated at the time to have cost $250,000, and was taken to the UCLA Medical Center. He died three months later.

President Reagan sent his condolences. 'Nancy and I are saddened by the news of Rock Hudson's death,' a White House statement reported. 'He will always be remembered for his dynamic impact on the film industry, and fans all over the world will certainly mourn his loss. He will be remembered for his humanity, his sympathetic spirit, and well-deserved reputation for kindness. May God rest his soul.'

After the death of Rock Hudson the pursuit of safe sex and health awareness became a prominent feature inside club culture. As the death toll escalated, many more barriers had to be overcome: personal privacy, little-understood medical symptoms and the reputational damage that an AIDS diagnosis could do to a career.

Freddie Mercury, the larger-than-life front man of pomp-rock band Queen, kept quiet about his HIV status until the day before his death from AIDS-related bronchial pneumonia in November 1991. In a final public statement, he said: 'I felt it correct to keep this information private to date to protect the privacy of those around me. However, the time has now come for my friends and fans around the world to know the truth, and I hope that everyone will join with me, my doctors and all those worldwide in the fight against this terrible disease.'

The famed pianist and light-entertainer Liberace denied he was gay throughout his life and sued a British tabloid in defence of his privacy. He was guarded about his relationship with his chauffeur and secretary Scott Thorson, whom Liberace showered with gifts, claiming he had 'more mink coats and diamonds than Elizabeth Taylor'. When their relationship soured, Thorson filed a $113 million lawsuit against Liberace, the first same-sex palimony case filed in US history. Liberace died of AIDS-related illnesses in 1987. Rudolf Nureyev, erotic god of ballet, who defected from the Soviet Union in 1961 and died of AIDS-related complications, also denied having HIV, fearing it might be the end of his career.

Dan Hartman was one of disco's talented classicists, a child prodigy from near Harrisburg, Pennsylvania, who played piano from the age of eight. As a teenager Hartman became a member of the East Coast pop group The Legends and then joined the Edgar Winter Group, the distinctive rock band led by two albino brothers from Beaumont, Texas. Hartman went his own way just as disco was surfacing and wrote and produced 'Relight My Fire', which spent six weeks at the top of the recently conceived US disco chart, and was a follow-up to another major club record, 'Instant Replay'. Hartman later undertook production duties on Loleatta Holloway's classic 'Love Sensation'. At the height of the culture wars between rock and disco, Dan Hartman was perceived as a traitor and often accused of abandoning the authenticity of rock for the supposedly contrived sounds of disco. Hartman retaliated by saying that disco was derived from the classic Motown sound and much harder to replicate than guitar-led rock. He became one of the club scene's most sought-after producers, writing and producing James Brown's 'Living In America' and tracks for Tina Turner, Dusty Springfield, Joe Cocker, Nona Hendryx and his friend Holly Johnson of Frankie Goes to Hollywood. A supremely confident vocalist, Hartman could impersonate almost any singer and often patched up the voices of more famous performers in the studio. He died in 1994 from an AIDS-related brain tumour.

The downtown graffiti artist Keith Haring was one of the stalwarts of the arts-inspired Club 57 and through his friendship with the DJ Larry Levan came to the rescue of Paradise Garage, painting its interior with his streetwise art and warnings about AIDS. He was diagnosed in 1988 and was a very public supporter of AIDS charities, establishing the Keith Haring Foundation in 1989, the year before he died.

When disco dominated the pop charts the economic runes of the approaching Reagan presidency pointed away from public investment in health and alleviating poverty towards a free-market economy. Ronald Reagan's policies called for widespread tax cuts, decreased social spending and increased military spending, and his famous dictum that the most terrifying words in English are 'I'm from the government, and I'm here to help' did not bode well for those who wanted the government to intervene in the AIDS epidemic. Reaganites made the sweeping claim that tax cuts had a magical power to solve social problems by the 'trickle-down' effect, implying that money at the top would eventually find its way to the needy and the unwell. Subsequent economic analyses, most recently a report by the London School of Economics, have disproved the theory. Tax cuts for the rich help the wealthy keep more of their riches, exacerbating income inequality rather than closing the gap. Even Reagan's vice president George H. W. Bush saw the flaw, describing Reagan's theories while running against him for the Republican nomination in 1980 as 'voodoo economics'. The term that came to capture the low-tax values of Reagan's presidency was the portmanteau expression Reaganomics, a word that proved inspiring as a sinister villain across soul and hip-hop.

One sophisticated dismantling of Reaganomics was undertaken by the soul veteran Johnnie Taylor. Taylor was from a strict church upbringing. He had been a child genius on the gospel circuit in his native Arkansas and a member of some of the finest gospel groups – first, The Highway Q.C.'s, who had sung at the Reverend King's Ebenezer Baptist Church in Atlanta, before being handpicked to replace Sam Cooke in The Soul Stirrers at only 23. There were no greater accolades in gospel and no tougher spiritual standards to live up to. Taylor was already on a gilded stairway to heaven, signed to Cooke's indie label SAR Records, where he recorded a charming love song about fortitude and tolerance titled 'Rome (Wasn't Built In A Day)' (1962). It had a simple message and one that was in every sense compatible with Christian teachings. But after Sam Cooke's death – he was shot dead in a late-night dispute in the Hacienda Motel in California – SAR folded and Taylor moved to Memphis to join Stax Records, refashioning his image not through the cadences of gospel but as 'The Philosopher of Soul', a name that reflected his quiet, contemplative personality. By 1982, traditional soul was in retreat, battered by successive waves of both disco and hip-hop, but Beverly Glen Music founded in 1981 in Los Angeles by industry veteran Otis Smith was one of soul music's last redoubts. Smith had reckoned that out there among older music fans, alienated by dance music and the disruptions of hip-hop, there was still a market for high-quality soul. He was right. A few years before, radio station WHUR-FM, the station associated with Washington D.C.'s Howard University, had pioneered a new form of radio listening called Quiet Storm, a term derived from a Smokey Robinson song of the same name. It was an unexpected success and spread out from the campus in D.C. to other regions, where it became shorthand for slower, more romantic and reflective black music. Beverly Glen Music identified a new market and launched their label with one of the proven geniuses of old-style soul, Bobby Womack, whose album *The Poet* (Beverly Glen, 1981) featured the casually conversational and then searingly brilliant 'If You Think You're Lonely Now'. With Womack back to his best, Beverly Glen tracked down Johnnie Taylor and discovered two new acts wholly suited to Quiet Storm: the Detroit vocal group Chapter 8 and a romantic balladeer from Toledo, Ohio, who had been fostered to a family in Detroit. Her name was Anita Baker.

Johnnie Taylor's 'Reaganomics', released as the B-side to 'What About My Love' (Beverly Glen, 1981), was a darkly satirical perspective from the American inner city. A wave of anti-Reagan soul songs was produced in the early eighties, most powerfully a Boston funk record 'Cash (Cash Money)' by Prince Charles and the City Beat Band, (Virgin, 1982) and another was Spontaneous Overthrow's 'All About Money' (New-Ark, 1984), an amazingly inventive piece of cosmic soul which through its electronica and rarity has become a holy grail record for soul collectors. But both of these were trumped by The Valentine Brothers' 'Money's Too Tight (To Mention)' (Bridge, 1982), a colossally successful record which became a cult classic in Europe. It was a song sung from the point of desperation as a man on welfare watches punishing and soul-destroying legislation being forged on Capitol Hill. The Valentine Brothers were a family duo from Columbus, Ohio, brothers John and William 'Billy' Valentine, a one-time member of the Chicago jazz-soul band Young-Holt Unlimited. They were never consistently successful and shunned the idea of making out-and-out disco records so were frequently overlooked. A further indignity awaited them when the song was a major hit in the Manchester club scene, catching the attention of Simply Red's Mick Hucknall. It was their cover version released three years later that became a global pop hit, resuscitating an argument that had been around since the first days of rock 'n' roll that more anodyne white cover versions were more likely to chart. There was one saving grace: The Valentine Brothers had written the song and had protected their copyright and so gained financially from Simply Red's success.

The overwhelming majority of songs by black musicians that referenced Ronald Reagan spoke of his economic policies: only Prince's 'Ronnie, Talk To Russia' on the 1981 album *Controversy* stands out as a song about foreign affairs and decades of aggressive American rhetoric towards the Soviet Union. Reaganomics stayed the course as a much-despised term in funk and rap music years after Ronald Reagan's presidency had ended, and indeed even during his lengthy decline from Alzheimer's and after his death in 2004. Despised by some because of his assault on welfare funding and his perceived lack of interest in African American affairs, eight years after the former president had been laid to rest the rapper Killer Mike sampled a speech by Reagan, and Kendrick Lamar's debut album *Section.80*, a rap concept album following the lives of two teenagers, Tammy and Keisha, contained a track called 'Ronald Reagan Era (His Evils)' which blamed the dead president for ghetto deprivation.

Notwithstanding the global success of the movie *Saturday Night Fever* and its memorable soundtrack, which sold 40 million copies and spawned hit singles for the Bee Gees such as 'Night Fever', 'Stayin' Alive' and 'How Deep Is Your Love', disco divided opinion and became entwined in the story of AIDS. In the minds of some people disco was the music of minority groups, notably gays, blacks and Hispanics, and so to hate disco was a coded way of exercising hate over minorities. Larry Kramer was unshrinking in his analysis: 'Too many people hate the people that AIDS most affects – gay people and people of colour. I do not mean dislike or feel uncomfortable with. I mean hate. Downright hate. Down and dirty hate.'

A notorious night at Chicago's Comiskey Park back in July 1979 witnessed the most public enactment of that down-and-dirty hate. The Disco Demolition Night, which attracted 50,000 people, was the brainchild of shock jock Steve Dahl, who had invited his followers to destroy disco records. Dahl, dressed up like the general of an anti-disco army, hyped the event up on his show with increasing rage. The *Rolling Stone* critic Dave Marsh, one of the few music journalists to attend the demolition, described a malicious atmosphere. 'Your most paranoid fantasy about where the ethnic cleansing of the rock radio could ultimately lead . . . White males, eighteen to thirty-four are the most likely to see Disco as the product of homosexuals, blacks and Latins, and therefore they're the most likely to respond to appeals to wipe out such threats to their security.' The event took place as a promotion adjunct to a Chicago White Sox game which disintegrated into a riot when crazed fans bearing disco records stormed the field. The organisers denied it, but the mass destruction of the records took on the ugly look of a witch hunt, as if disco was something more than just dance music. Nile Rodgers, leader of the soul group Chic, blames the event for a temporary stall in his career. 'It felt to us like Nazi book-burning,' he told *Vice*. 'This is America, the home of jazz and rock and people were now afraid even to say the word "disco". I remember thinking – we're not even a disco group.'

The demolition inevitably had an economic dynamic too. Radio ratings had shown a decline in traditional rock shows and a plateau in sales of adult-oriented rock. Conservative label bosses, unfamiliar with underground nightlife, dismissed disco as a fad, and extensively used the belittling term 'disco sucks', wrongly assuming it made them hip. Groups such as REO Speedwagon in part blamed disco for diverting young people to clubs and away from concert venues, and for dominating the next generation of urban radio. In her uncompromising cultural essay on disco, Alice Echols, a former DJ in the Rubaiyat bar in Ann Arbor, Michigan, and now the Barbra Streisand Chair of Contemporary Gender Studies at the University of Southern California, saw a wider context. 'Even though record labels were making a lot of money off disco, they were holding their nose,' she says. 'They were worried about it crashing, but they wanted it to crash so they could go back to classic rock. There was also a grassroots anti-disco movement, a national effort on the part of people involved with AOR. There were people who thought it threatened their livelihoods, because of its gobbling up of live venues; there were people who just thought it sounded plastic and synthetic and commercial; there were people who were just nakedly racist and homophobic.'

It was sadly predictable that the most extreme critics of underground dance had no understanding of what disco was and where it had emerged from. Many records destroyed on the night of the demolition were bought cheaply at local Chicago five-and-dime stores and included records by long-standing Chicago blues and soul singers such as Otis Clay, Koko Taylor, Buddy Guy, Tyrone Davis and even Curtis Mayfield.

In 1978, the year after the release of *Saturday Night Fever* and months before the Disco Demolition, disco was supposedly at its height. But the music that dominated the R&B charts that year is testimony to another misreading of the term. Black music was enjoying its own moment of blistering creativity, of which disco was only one strand, and new music was escaping from the studios – Funkadelic's 'One Nation Under A Groove' (Warner Brothers, 1978), Parliament's 'Flash Light' (Casablanca, 1978) and 'Bootzilla' by Bootsy's Rubber Band (Warner Brothers, 1978). All three songs were from the collaborative minds of George Clinton and his madcap bass guitarist Bootsy Collins. To classify their popular dance music as disco would be like calling James Joyce's *Ulysses* a book about Irish pubs. Clinton and Collins were the cutting edge of afro-futurism, drawing on comic-book art, cartoon surrealism and an outrageous self-confidence that towered above almost every other musical act at the time. Their alliance of avant-garde funk bands would have been refused entry at the smoothest suburban discos, their imagination alone setting them apart from the likeable pop of the Bee Gees and the plodding romantic narrative of *Saturday Night Fever*. Other top-selling records of 1978 that were hugely popular in clubs, and so in a sense are disco, were Chic's 'Le Freak', A Taste of Honey's 'Boogie Oogie Oogie' and Cleveland Eaton's 'Bama Boogie Woogie' but their titles alone suggested they were as much a part of the legacy of black American swing, jazz and boogie bars as they were metropolitan disco.

One of the perceptions left behind by *Saturday Night Fever* and the celebrity culture of Studio 54 was that disco existed in a fantasy world of glamorous people, hedonistic nights, fancy dress and revolving mirror balls. Singer and model Grace Jones regularly showed up dressed in eccentric costumes, and daring body-art came to typify the club. But in the end, celebrity and hype came to strangle Studio 54. It had been a recurring curse for club music in decades gone by too. In the sixties, Marilyn Monroe, Liberace and Jackie Kennedy were regulars at the Peppermint Lounge, the home of the Twist, and such was Kennedy's fascination with the craze, she erected a temporary version of the Lounge inside the White House. At Motown's popular height Diana Ross took to the dancefloor with Groucho Marx, and later, as Studio 54's reputation grew within the demi monde, Bianca Jagger famously rode a white stallion into the club. She claims she merely sat astride the horse, but the paparazzi captured the moment and so the myth spread faster than the truth. Andy Warhol, a Studio 54 regular, once quipped that the key to the club's success was 'a dictatorship at the door and a democracy on the dance floor'. The association between disco and glamour tended to efface another important strand of the music. Disco had its roots firmly planted in soul music and so inherited a strand of civil rights and protest music that was grounded in the here and now, far from fantasy and celebrity. Many club records, such as Philadelphia International All Stars' 'Let's Clean Up The Ghetto', The Valentine Brothers' 'Money's Too Tight (To Mention)' and The O'Jays' 'For The Love Of Money', 'Message In Our Music' and their brutal critique of the tax system, 'Rich Get Richer', were about socio-economic issues. McFadden and Whitehead's 'Ain't No Stoppin' Us Now' (PIR, 1979) and 'Am I Black Enough For You' by Billy Paul (Philadelphia International Records, 1972) were about the march for racial justice, and some of the most successful songs of the disco era became anthems of women's empowerment, songs such as Gwen Guthrie's 'Ain't Nothin' Goin' On But The Rent', 'I'm Every Woman' by Chaka Khan and Gloria Gaynor's rallying cry, 'I Will Survive'.

One of the greatest club hits of all time was 'Disco Inferno' (Atlantic, 1975) by the Philadelphia band The Trammps. The title and its lyrics harked back to the urban riots of the late sixties and to the street chants of young teenagers as they looted stores. It was not a protest song, nor was it advocating social disturbance, but its metaphors to describe a club with a hot atmosphere were taken from the world beyond fantasy, one that had been prevalent in the streets of inner-city America since the Watts riots of August 1965. The Trammps had another connection that surpassed pure disco: they were part of the Bicentennial generation of musicians who in 1976 turned Philadelphia into the most creative musical city in the world, replicating the success that Motown had enjoyed a decade earlier in Detroit. The nerve centre of the Philly Sound, with its grand orchestral arrangements and powerful soul vocals, was Philadelphia International Records (PIR). Owned by Kenny Gamble, Leon Huff and their partner Thom Bell, it operated from the Philly studios on South Broad Street. Gamble and Huff wrote more than 3,000 songs within thirty-five years, including 'Love Train', 'For The Love Of Money', 'If You Don't Know Me By Now', 'Me And Mrs. Jones' and 'The Love I Lost'. The acts they nurtured and shaped now read like a who's who of the city of Philadelphia's musical heritage – The O'Jays, Harold Melvin & the Blue Notes, Teddy Pendergrass, MFSB, Billy Paul, Patti LaBelle and Lou Rawls. The studio not only enriched club music with powerful and uplifting songs, but took orchestration to a new level, bathing soul music in sweeping strings, horns, violins and cellos, all driven by the studio band, MFSB. Most of the string players played in the Philadelphia Symphony Orchestra.

Tragically, the studios which had been such a vital part of the story of African American music became a literal disco inferno when they were burnt down in 2010. More than a hundred firefighters helped battle a devastating blaze at the PIR headquarters that destroyed equipment, tapes and the record company's memorabilia. Christopher Cimini, a South Philadelphia ironworker, was caught on surveillance footage. He allegedly used a cigarette lighter to look inside the building after a night on the town drinking. He admitted setting fire to the studios and was charged with arson. Prior to the PIR era, the building had been the home of the legendary Cameo-Parkway record label and the studios where Chubby Checker recorded 'The Twist' and Dee Dee Sharp recorded 'Mashed Potato Time'.

Back in New York a period of urban gentrification was changing the city and club culture. From the late sixties onwards, New York was a tense city struggling to cope with an epidemic of crime and a surge in heroin abuse. Crime and violence had been increasing rapidly for years and the number of murders in the city had risen from 681 in 1965 to 1,690 in 1975. Rapes and burglaries had more than tripled, while robberies had gone up an astonishing tenfold. Blocks across Harlem, the South Bronx and Brooklyn were virtual no-go areas, and even sections of Manhattan were perceived to be too dangerous to visit.

There was one underlying positive story: the underground club promoters and disco DJs who had found cheap property in Hell's Kitchen, in Alphabet City and in swathes of old warehouse blocks South of Houston Street (SoHo) had pointed to hopeful regeneration. Artists, often a bellwether for urban change, had also moved from the old Greenwich Village neighbourhoods to cheaper and more remote loft-style buildings. Kevin Baker, a journalist and resident at the time, described New York's fiscal crisis in the mid seventies as one of the weirdest moments in the history of the city. He wrote in the *Guardian*:

> There was a pervasive sense that the social order was breaking down. Most subway trains were filthy, covered in graffiti inside and out. Often only one – and sometimes no – carriage door would open when they pulled into a station, and in summer they were "cooled" only by the methodical sweep of a begrimed metal fan that just pushed the sordid air about. The trains ran late and were always crowded; their denizens included chain-snatchers, raggedy buskers and countless beggars, including at least two legless individuals, manoeuvring with remarkable agility between the cars on their wheeled boards.

New York reached a nadir in 1977 with the Son of Sam killings, a blackout and urban riots. Democrat Mayor Ed Koch took office in January 1978 and convinced the city that it was worth fighting for. Nightclubs, artists' studios and graffiti came to signify the hope for change. A vandalism that scared people and became a visualisation of chaos was in fact a new form of creativity aligned to the hip-hop culture of the South

Bronx and beyond. Once it moved downtown in the hands of Keith Haring, Futura 2000 and Jean-Michel Basquiat, it became a strident new form of art which was ideally suited to dance music and to the interior design of discos.

In a generous obituary on his death, *The New York Times* cited the range of Koch's influence. It was a significant sweep across civic life.

> Experts cite the investment of billions of dollars in rebuilding abandoned housing, which revived desolate areas of the South Bronx, Harlem and central Brooklyn . . . the restoration of the city's fiscal integrity to the point where banks and government watchdogs were ready to let it manage its own finances; the rehabilitation of neglected parks; the genesis of Times Square's transformation from a sleazy, dangerous crossroads to a family-friendly entertainment and office center; the trading in of federal money designated to build a new West Side Highway for money that would buy subway trains and buses; the pressure on the Metropolitan Transportation Authority to virtually eliminate subway graffiti; and the enacting of a campaign finance law in 1988 under which candidates would limit their spending in exchange for receiving public matching funds.

Into this tax-generous context came a now-familiar villain. The real-estate magnate Donald Trump was one of the earliest beneficiaries of the tax breaks for corporations introduced by Koch, even if he had to sue the city to get them. Whole areas of downtown Manhattan gradually became unaffordable to the artists who had used them as their base, and areas like Hell's Kitchen – once a place where the edgiest clubs were hidden – were gentrified into upscale neighbourhoods. Trump in those transformative days was like a cartoon version of a brash New Yorker: a gaudy, deal-making schmoozer who frequented nightclubs as disco died. He was not responsible for the music's decline, but he was in the neighbourhood at the time. The idea that he would become President of the United States was a fantasy for another day.

The Prophets of Rage. Arguably the most politically militant hip-hop act in history, Public Enemy's classic line-up here features hype man Flavor Flav (front left), Chuck D (centre) and the group's Minister of Information, Professor Griff (right). The Security of the First World (S1W) flank Terminator X in the back row.

6

THE CNN OF THE GHETTO

Listen Up: 'The Bottle' by Gil Scott-Heron (1974)

Good evening, ladies and gentlemen. I understand there are a good many Southerners in the room tonight. I know the South very well. I spent twenty years there one night.

Last time I was down South I walked into this restaurant and this white waitress came up to me and said, 'We don't serve coloured people here.' I said, 'That's all right. I don't eat coloured people. Bring me a whole fried chicken.'

Then these three white boys came up to me and said, 'Boy, we're giving you fair warning. Anything you do to that chicken, we're gonna do to you.' So I put down my knife and fork, I picked up that chicken and I kissed its ass. Then I said, 'Line up, boys!'

(Dick Gregory, Roberts Show Club, Chicago 1961)

Dick Gregory was a trailblazer, a stand-up comedian who laced his act with political invective, and a man who came to influence a generation of hip-hop artists who thrived on his punchy and enraged style. *The New York Times* described him as a 'pioneering satirist who transformed cool humour into a barbed force for civil rights'. He was a familiar face on prime-time television, on the schools protests on Chicago's South Side and on the marches for voter-registration rights in Mississippi.

From the early sixties, during John F. Kennedy's presidency, Gregory dedicated himself to social activism body and soul, viewing it as a 'higher calling', more important than satirical comedy. He was arrested numerous times in the Deep South and spent time in jail in Birmingham, Alabama, where he claimed to have endured 'the first really good beating I ever had in my life'. Increasingly, Gregory dropped out of club dates to march or to perform at benefits for civil rights groups and came to be perceived as an unreliable performer by the networks. He released a string of comedy albums that were popular in ghetto homes across America, including *Dick Gregory Talks Turkey* (1962), *Running For President* (1964) and the black-power comedy album *Dick Gregory's Frankenstein* (1969), which lay buried in bargain bins until it was seized on as source material by the first generation of hip-hop DJs. In 1965, he was shot in the leg during the Watts riots in Los Angeles and in 1967 he ran for Mayor of Chicago as part of a civil rights stunt. His campaigns for the presidency, much like schlock-rocker Alice Cooper's, were never wholly serious. In 1968, he attracted more laughs than votes running for president on the Freedom and Peace Party ticket, securing 47,097 votes.

In November 1968, comedian and civil rights activist Dick Gregory produced a fake dollar bill to advertise his presidential bid. The bill included the universal peace sign and the voter-registration slogan 'Your Vote is Legal, Sacred and Private'. The chairman of the Republican Central Committee, Carl Shipley, denounced Gregory's candidacy as 'un-American in concept'.

Hey America!

By 1984, when the ageing President Ronald Reagan was campaigning for his second term, espousing his free-market philosophy, Dick Gregory was a comedy veteran eking out a living on the college and university circuit. One weekend he appeared on stage at a student event at Adelphi University in Long Island, where he berated Reagan, lacerated his policies and mocked his plastic personality. The show peaked with a sketch in which Gregory proposed a complex medical procedure with a janitor's brush, which he claimed would cure the President's colonic polyps. The show was a masterpiece of strident political humour and outrageous imagination which sowed the seeds of an idea in the mind of a young student standing bewitched in the audience. Carlton Douglas Ridenhour, a street-smart boy from Queens, was a graphic design student at Adelphi who had been distracted from his studies by the control room at the university's radio station WBAU 90.3. He had taken on the moniker Chuck D and was in the early days of forming hip-hop giants Public Enemy. 'Baba Dick Gregory came to Adelphi in 1984 and rocked our world,' he said. 'From there I knew what changes in the world I wanted to attempt.'

Chuck D began to circulate a cassette tape called 'Public Enemy #1' as a promotional pitch to campus radio. For nearly ten years, tapes had been the lingua franca of street hip-hop, many roughly recorded at block parties in the South Bronx, at Harlem World on 116th Street, Savoy Manor on East 149th Street or at high-school battles at the Audubon Ballroom where Malcolm X was assassinated. The best tapes found their way by exchange or recommendation up the hip-hop hierarchy. Public Enemy's tape was one of the lucky ones. It found its way into the hands of Jason William Mizell, better known by his stage name Jam Master Jay of Run-DMC, and from there to Dr. Dre of Death Row Records. According to Chuck D, at this point 'the promo catches fire' and the tape is copied and shared further – to the Hollis Crew, the Beastie Boys and eventually to Rick Rubin, the owner of Def Jam Recordings. As the tape's reputation soared, Chuck D held his nerve and finally a deal was struck. By 1988, liberated by Dick Gregory's no-holds-barred attack on mainstream America, Public Enemy became the most exciting new band in the world. Their music – raw, angry and attitudinal – had the noisy posturing of punk, the cartoon stereotypes of agitprop theatre, the cataclysmic doom of disaster movies and the comic-book heroism of Marvel. It was yet another seismic moment in the evolution of black popular music, and had international appeal, quickly finding favour with predominantly white European journalists raised on the outrage of punk and who in the main were desperate for a new disruptive sound.

Public Enemy were also significant in the way their music abandoned the two great loves of African American popular music: the love of God that had driven gospel and the teenage romance that had made Motown 'The Sound of Young America'. Their song titles alone are among the most dramatic in the history of pop: 'Timebomb', 'Public Enemy No. 1' (both 1987), 'Prophets Of Rage', 'Rebel Without A Pause', 'Bring The Noise', 'Terminator X To The Edge Of Panic', 'Louder Than A Bomb', 'Night Of The Living Baseheads' and 'Black Steel In The Hour Of Chaos' (all 1988). Consistent among their earliest albums was a full-frontal assault on traditional media exemplified by their onstage signature tune 'Don't Believe The Hype'. Like the punk bands of a decade earlier, Public Enemy were masters of contrivance, building looks and characters that reflected existing ghetto archetypes. Chuck D played the role of the ghetto DJ, a community messenger comfortable with the politics of the street, while the incorrigible Flavor Flav, sporting a massive medallion made from a clock, was the ghetto pimp and Professor Griff was the personification of the Fruit of Islam, the Nation's security personnel.

Another defining dynamic, more familiar in jazz, became crucial to Public Enemy: the idea that music could be the messenger. In September 1988, *SPIN* magazine published an interview with Chuck D in which he claimed that rap is black America's TV station. Later that year, at a Black Expo event in Indiana, he returned to the idea and described Public Enemy as a media messenger: 'We're almost like headline news. Rap music is the invisible TV station that Black America never had.' That concept soon morphed into 'Rap is our invisible TV network. It's the CNN that black people never had' and finally became the much shorter and snappier 'Rap is the CNN of the ghetto'.

CNN was founded in 1980 by the media entrepreneur Ted Turner and Reese Schonfeld and achieved success as a 24-hour cable TV station, pioneering the idea that the world never sleeps and that, unlike on the established networks, news was a round-the-clock phenomenon. Not everyone agreed with Chuck D and some over-sensitive magazines resented that he had coined a metaphor that further challenged their importance. In one article in the *Atlantic* magazine, Richard Beck is quoted as saying 'hip-hop is a music before it is a sociological lens, an urban newscast, an adolescent fantasy, or anything else, and it should be discussed as such'. All music, irrespective of its merits, is of course musical but there is a powerful argument that black music has always assumed another responsibility to act as a messenger, often in the face of discrimination and barriers to a free music marketplace. This is a tradition encapsulated brilliantly in a famous quote by the writer James Baldwin: 'The victim who is able to articulate the situation of the victim has ceased to be a victim: he or she has become a threat.'

Before television, the nearest equivalent to a service like CNN was Time Inc.'s *The March of Time* newsreels shown in movie theatres from 1935 to 1951 and launched to 500 cinemas across America during Franklin D. Roosevelt's presidency. Historian Raymond Fielding saw these newsreels as a uniquely American phenomenon, wise to world affairs but sometimes reticent to deal with the uglier side of racism at home. 'Implicit in all *March of Time* issues was a kind of uncomplicated American liberalism,' Fielding wrote, 'general good intentions, a healthy journalistic scepticism . . . and substantial pride in American progress and potential.' Because they were both perceived as 'foreign' to America, the warring ideologies of communism and fascism were treated with caution. *The March of Time* reflected a limited range of black music: an upbeat piece on the Library of Congress preserving the recordings of blues legend Huddie 'Lead Belly' Ledbetter and a lively feature on New Orleans swing. But in the main, African American culture and pressing social issues were sidelined, leaving only specialist papers, word of mouth and music to convey stories of social change.

The brutality of lynching was rarely reported in early twentieth-century media and so was left to local folklore and whispered word of mouth. One of the first silent demonstrations against lynching brought a well-heeled group of liberals drawn from racial improvement groups and the women's suffrage movement to march along Pennsylvania Avenue in 1921 when President Warren G. Harding occupied the White House. Then, on 5 January 1934, Democratic senators Edward P. Costigan, formerly of the Colorado Progressive Party, and Robert F. Wagner, a

Democrat from New York, set out a bill, the Costigan–Wagner Bill, that stated: 'To assure to persons within the jurisdiction of every state the equal protection of the crime of lynching.' The bill offered provisions to outlaw all types of lynching but failed on its journey through the legislature. Significantly, many of the major anti-lynching activists of the time were women: the formerly enslaved Ida B. Wells, an investigative journalist who had watched three men from a local Negro store being lynched in Memphis; Mary Burnett Talbert, a leader of the Christian-inspired Anti-Lynching Crusaders; the new black poet Angelina Grimké; and Juanita Jackson Mitchell, National Youth Director of the NAACP. The influence of the NAACP gradually spread across the states from a New York headquarters that had its own unique mode of communication, a black flag that carried the words: 'A Man Was Lynched Yesterday'. The flag flew from offices on Fifth Avenue and was funded by donations in the aftermath of the murder of Jesse Washington, a teenage farmhand who was lynched in Waco, Texas, in 1916. It was taken down after the NAACP's landlord threatened the organisation with eviction.

It was music, delivered through two outstanding songs, that dragged the dark horror of lynching into the full light of day. One was Billie Holiday's 'Strange Fruit', inspired by the murder of Thomas Shipp and Abram Smith in Marion, Indiana, in 1930. The other, the confessional 'Don't Kill My Baby And My Son' by Woody Guthrie, reflects on the murder of Laura Nelson and her son, whose bodies were hung from a bridge over the North Canadian River in Okfuskee County, Oklahoma. What was extraordinary about the latter incident is that Guthrie's own father had been part of the lynch mob that strung mother and son up and then watched them die. These two songs rich in history and myth came from parallel tracks in the music of social commentary, one from the African American legacy of jazz, blues and soul, and the other from the country-folk traditions that drove the protest singers of the sixties – Pete Seeger, Bob Dylan, Joan Baez and Woody Guthrie himself, whose guitar carried the uncompromising message 'This Machine Kills Fascists'.

'Strange Fruit' was inspired by a single image taken by a local studio photographer which found its way through the radical press to a Jewish schoolteacher in New York called Abel Meeropol, who wrote songs under the pseudonym Lewis Allen. By 1938, Meeropol's original version

Hey America!

of 'Strange Fruit' had become familiar at left-wing gatherings and anti-fascist demonstrations, sung initially by his wife and her friends in the form of a women's choir. It even made it to Madison Square Garden via the jazz-blues singer Laura Duncan, who later recorded with Pete Seeger and toured with the Greenwich Village folk group The Weavers. Duncan's version of 'Strange Fruit' attracted the attention of an audience member at one of her shows. Robert Gordon had recently taken on a job directing the headlining show by Billie Holiday at New York's Café Society, a much talked about nightclub in a former speakeasy on Sheridan Square in Greenwich Village.

Café Society set out to reverse and defy all the rules of selective club membership – it was open to all, had no colour bar and liked to attract edgy clientele. It was also a place that brought artists to wider fame, among them Ruth Brown, Lena Horne and Big Joe Turner. It was a fully integrated venue hugely popular with socialists across the city and had as its motto 'The Wrong Place for the Right People'. The club's owner, Barney Josephson, a natural showman, knew there was no point slipping 'Strange Fruit' into the body of the set and pretending it was just another song. According to journalist Dorian Lynskey, 'He drew up some rules: first, Holiday would close all three of her nightly sets with it; second, the waiters would halt all service beforehand; third, the whole room would be in darkness but for a sharp, bright spotlight on Holiday's face; fourth, there would be no encore.' From the outset, the Café Society crowd knew they had a politically charged song in the nightly repertoire. It was not for the faint-hearted. 'People had to remember "Strange Fruit" and get their insides burned by it,' club owner Josephson once explained.

'Strange Fruit' is a landmark protest song, possibly the greatest ever, and it exists as a towering example of how black music communicated messages that were beyond the reach of the dominant media of the day. Bruce Springsteen, a lifelong admirer of the song, said, 'It's just an epic piece of music that was so far ahead of its time. It still strikes a deep, deep, deep nerve in the conversation of today.' *TIME* magazine named it the 'Song of the Century', but only decades after its release, and Nina Simone – one of a long list of artists who have dared to cover the song – once said that 'Strange Fruit' was 'the ugliest song I have heard. Ugly in the sense that it is violent and tears at the guts of what white people have done to my people in this country.'

Despite Billie Holiday's achievement, the musician who was most visible in the anti-lynching movement was Paul Robeson. On 23 September 1946, he led a crusade to Washington and met with President Harry Truman in the White House. As a multi-talented graduate of Rutgers University, where he was an All-America star footballer, and as a student of Swahili and a successful campus actor, Robeson was one of what the great educator W. E. B. Du Bois called the 'talented tenth': the 10 per cent of African Americans who, through their exceptional achievements, could lead and represent their people. Robeson's meeting with Truman cast him in that role. Since the 1920s, he had been a giant among spiritual singers. His recordings, mainly for His Master's Voice, include 'Ol' Man River', one of around ten songs he sang that used the metaphor of the flowing river of change, a religious image that was seized by the civil rights movement and became commonplace in soul music too.

A few days before he met Robeson, Truman had met with more conservative NAACP leaders and, in response to evidence which included the lynching image that had inspired 'Strange Fruit', the President promised to act. Two months later, he announced the creation of the first-ever presidential commission, or task force, on civil rights. His meeting with Robeson, however, was tense and an argument broke out. Enraged by the language being used in the Oval Office, Truman cut the meeting short and ordered Robeson to leave. It was a watershed moment in Robeson's relationship with government agencies. One of the organisations he was close to at the time, the anti-colonial Council on African Affairs (CAA), was placed on the Attorney General's List of Subversive Organizations drawn up in April 1947 and for the next ten years Robeson was a victim of state harassment, including being implicated in the McCarthy witch hunts and stalked by the FBI. For years he tried to earn a living as a professional musician in Harlem and his refusal to recant his beliefs meant he was denied a passport by the State Department, which meant his income from European tours plummeted. One of his greatest regrets was that his alma mater, Rutgers University, airbrushed him from history and deleted his records as one of their most successful athletes.

At the height of the Cold War, public anxiety about Soviet spies, Russian influence and nuclear war was rife, and so too was the pressure to racially desegregate public places. Desegregation was at its most traumatic in the southern states and many advocated states' rights, putting greater trust in state governments and arguing that they were more responsive to sensitive issues, being more understanding of the culture and values of a given state's population.

One of the key challenges to segregation came from music. In October 1955, a jazz tour starring Illinois Jacquet, Dizzy Gillespie and Ella Fitzgerald arrived at Houston Music Hall. At the time, fuelled by the oil industry, Houston was one of the richest cities in America and had clung to segregation with whites-only neighbourhoods and local covenants that prevented African Americans from using shops, cinemas and theatres. The tour's manager, Norman Granz, one of the great impresarios of jazz and the founder of Verve Records, had set off from New York adamant that the Houston show would be fully integrated. He insisted that seats in the house were available to all comers and even refunded cash to those uncomfortable with sharing the auditorium with blacks. Backstage, Houston's vice squad raided dressing rooms looking for drugs but found nothing compromising. When Granz complained about their conduct, guns were drawn and the jazz musicians were arrested. Dressed in a mink stole, an elegant taffeta cocktail dress and cascading diamond earrings, Ella Fitzgerald was ignominiously booked at the local jail and forced to pay an on-the-spot fine. She signed autographs throughout the bizarre events and her arrest encouraged other touring musicians to insist on desegrated venues. Duke Ellington likewise demanded that a no-segregation clause was inserted in his touring contracts and claimed that he was a musician dedicated to 'the fight for first class citizenship'.

It was the 34th President of the USA, Dwight D. Eisenhower, formerly the supreme commander of the Allied invasion of Normandy, who came to face to face with the mission to desegregate American music. Ike was a man out of his time, struggling to comprehend the new challenges that besieged his presidency. A series of hugely dramatic events – the killing of Emmett Till (1955), the Montgomery bus boycott (1955–6) and the desegregation of Little Rock Central High School (1957) – had brought race and racism to the forefront of national politics. Overarching all these events was a 1954 Supreme Court judgment known as *Brown* v. *Board of Education*, which effectively made segregation in public schools illegal. Faced with the hugely divisive realities of desegregating local schools, the Governor of Arkansas, Orval Faubus, ordered the Arkansas National Guard to prevent African American students from attending the previously all-white Central High School. Faubus's political motivation was to gain approval with white supremacists but it created a dramatic stand-off in which children carrying books and dressed in pristine white uniforms had to run a gauntlet of hate and vitriol as armed guards protected the entrance to the school. For his obstructiveness, Faubus was to assume a humiliating place in jazz history. The 'Fables Of Faubus' (1959) was an explicitly political recording by the mercurial Charles Mingus. Columbia Records baulked at the lyrics – he called Governor Faubus ridiculous and rebuked him for not allowing integrated schools – so they were cut from the album, only to resurface in a follow-up recording a year later. Governor Faubus had given President Eisenhower a near-insurmountable problem. The President was obliged to uphold the Constitution and the law of the land, but he was also determined to avoid bloodshed and mass rioting. Resting at the Naval War College in Newport, Rhode Island, Eisenhower tried to negotiate a compromise with Faubus, but it didn't materialise.

Then Satchmo blew his horn.

On the night of 17 September 1957, three days after the negotiations in Newport and two weeks after the Little Rock Nine were first excluded from Central High School, the legendary jazz trumpeter Louis Armstrong was on tour with his All Stars band in Grand Forks, North Dakota, a two-horse town with fewer than 150 black residents. At the time, a student journalist called Larry Lubenow was an intern working for the *Grand Forks Herald* newspaper. He had managed to secure an interview with Satchmo about the fact that he was the first black man ever to stay at what had historically been a segregated hotel. It was supposed to be a gentle personality piece with no great political angle, in part because Satchmo had told journalists over many years, 'I don't get involved in politics, I just blow my horn.' During the interview, Lubenow nervously brought up the Little Rock stand-off and was shocked by the response. 'It's getting almost so bad a coloured man hasn't got any country,' Satchmo told him. He then went on to accuse President Eisenhower of being 'two faced' and having 'no guts'. Satchmo reserved his best lines for Governor Faubus, using what has been euphemistically referred to as a double-barrelled hyphenated expletive utterly unfit for print at the time. But to ensure the message got across, Satchmo revised the term to a 'thick fucking farmer' and they settled on something safer: 'an uneducated plowboy'. It was only the intervention of his vocalist Velma Middleton that steered Satchmo back on script. The events at Little Rock had angered the jazz legend and he returned to his contempt for the President and his Secretary of State John Foster Dulles, who was trying to secure Satchmo's services to go on a goodwill tour of the Soviet Union. Satchmo's words came at a moment of great anxiety about relations with Moscow. 'The way they are treating my people in the South, the government can go to hell,' he said, savaging Dulles with a string of profanities. He left the young journalist with a rhetorical question about Russia: 'When the people over there ask me what's wrong with my country what am I supposed to say?'

The story hit the wires and broke across America. According to the venerable African American newspaper the *Chicago Defender*, 'Mr. Armstrong's words had the explosive effect of an H-bomb. He may not have been grammatical, but he was eloquent.' The controversy may or may not have nudged Eisenhower, but he eventually ordered that the Arkansas National Guard be placed under federal control and sent 1,000 US Army paratroopers from the 101st Airborne Division to assist them in restoring order in Little Rock. The daring tactic worked, and the African American students were able to attend without further intimidation. The law had been upheld, but the solution left Eisenhower vulnerable and criticised from all sides. He was lambasted by those who felt he had not done enough to ensure civil rights for African Americans, while those who saw the Constitution as a way of holding history back accused him of asserting federal power. Like Paul Robeson, Louis Armstrong paid a price for his outspokenness: concerts were cancelled, invitations withdrawn and awards withheld. His records were ritually smashed (the rock 'n' roll equivalent of burning books) and there were calls for boycotts of his back catalogue. At the height of the controversy, the Ford Motor Company threatened to pull out of a Bing Crosby special on which Satchmo was to appear and a duet with classic pianist Van Cliburn was halted. Set against that came the support from other performers, among them Lena Horne, Eartha Kitt and the classical contralto Marian Anderson.

Except for dedicated African American newspapers such as the *Chicago Defender* and the *Pittsburgh Courier*, the traditional press sided with the President or satirised Satchmo's outburst. There was no CNN. Quiz shows dominated the networks and television was still in its infancy. In 1946, only 7,000 TV sets were sold in the whole of the USA. In 1950, 5 million sets were sold but still only 20 per cent of American homes had a TV, and the wealthiest homes at that, with TV rarely reaching into the ghettos of the North let alone the African American homes of Little Rock, Arkansas, or Birmingham, Alabama.

It was the Kennedy presidency that fast-tracked television into people's homes. On Sunday 15 September 1963, as the President celebrated Mass in Newport, Rhode Island, Thomas Blanton, Bobby Frank Cherry and Robert Edward Chambliss, all members of the Ku Klux Klan in Alabama, planted nineteen sticks of dynamite outside the basement of the 16th Street Baptist Church in Birmingham. The subsequent explosion killed four young girls and injured twenty-two others. Since April of 1963, Birmingham had been the focus of a campaign of civil disobedience by Martin Luther King and his followers which included lunch counter sit-ins, a march on Birmingham's city hall and a boycott of downtown merchants who were not honouring civil rights or desegregation. King was arrested after violating local laws permitting further demonstrations and was locked up in solitary confinement. During this time, he wrote 'Letter from Birmingham Jail', a key text of the civil rights movement. The events also inspired one of the most powerful songs of the era, Nina Simone's 'Mississippi Goddam', written after King's arrest and before the church bombing and in part a response to the murder of civil rights activist Medgar Evers in Jackson, Mississippi, in June of 1963. Eight days earlier, on 11 June, President Kennedy, energised by the scenes in Birmingham, had given a televised speech outlining the civil rights legislation he planned to submit to Congress, telling the television audience: 'The fires of frustration and discord are burning in every city, North and South, where legal remedies are not at hand. Redress is sought in the streets, in demonstrations, parades, and protests which create tensions and threaten violence and threaten lives.' For the impatient Nina Simone, the primal emotions of anger, hurt and suspicion flared up into a song of historic proportion, one which she later referred to as her 'first civil rights song'. When it was released by the Dutch company Philips Records a few months after the Birmingham bombing, the suits worried about the song's undiluted stridency and insisted that it be released as 'Mississippi *@!!?*@!.' But if you listen carefully, Simone's song hints at tiredness and fatalism as much as anger, as if the pace of change has been too slow. The singer's voice goes beyond civil rights and social justice and has a pent-up fury that will in time trigger greater militancy and the rise of Black Power.

Nina Simone was an astonishing messenger. The soul magazine *Wax Poetics* described her to near-perfection:

> Nina Simone had no filter. She spoke with candour about civil rights when many in her position didn't dare. She sang about uncomfortable subjects and made sure her audiences understood what those songs were really about. Whether due to the demons that haunted her or the overpowering desire for social justice that burned deep in her heart, Simone always told the goddam truth.

For sixteen pulsating minutes in the blistering afternoon sun of Sunday 17 August 1969, Simone's brilliance was captured on film by Hal Tulchin, an independent producer. The footage remained in Tulchin's basement for decades. In 2017, drummer and Black Music History professor at New York University Questlove (Ahmir Thompson) was presented with 40 hours of footage from the Harlem Cultural Festival. The resulting documentary, *Summer of Soul*, won the 2021 Sundance Documentary Grand Jury Prize and has received rave reviews.

After a meandering piano solo, a half-smile in the direction of her keyboard player and a series of barely audible grunts to her backing band, Simone launched into an inspired version of another song that would come to symbolise the changing face of civil rights: the declamatory soul song 'To Be Young, Gifted And Black'. It was a moment unprecedented in its defiance. Thousands of people stood on the parched grass of Mount Morris Park, others jostled for position on the rusty stairs, many more hung from the branches of leafless trees, and still more spilled onto the roads that surrounded the park. Gradually, they began to learn the chorus of a song that had only recently been released and was in the infancy of its journey to creative fame. Some members of the audience struggled with the words, others lip-synced along, trying to keep up with Simone's darting and erratic voice, and then the soaring finale brought the crowd together in mass incantation: young, gifted and black. The song was the culmination of one of the greatest live shows in the history of sixties soul, a statement of pride, political resistance and sheer enigmatic genius. 'Simone's explosiveness was well known. In concert, she was quick to call out anyone she noticed talking, to stop and glare or hurl a few insults or even leave the stage,' *The New Yorker* wrote. 'Yet her performances, richly improvised, were also confidingly intimate – she needed the connection with her audience – and often riveting.'

The story of 'To Be Young, Gifted And Black' is remarkable. The song had only just been released by RCA Records, and had yet to chart, but within a matter of months it became an international hit, not only for Nina Simone but for a succession of other artists. Aretha Franklin turned it into a gospel torch song, then Donny Hathaway envisaged it as an educational soliloquy and, via Simone's success in the Jamaican charts, local reggae duo Bob Andy and Marcia Griffiths made it a colossal rocksteady pop song. 'To Be Young, Gifted And Black' was saturated in the story of Harlem but the lyrics were crafted in midtown Manhattan under the most curious of circumstances.

Simone's collaborator Weldon Irvine Jr was travelling downtown from Harlem. He had been tasked with finding lyrics to a song that would inspire young black people and thus far had struggled to come up with much. Suddenly, while driving, he had an epiphany. Irvine told the African American publication *Chicken Bones*:

> It was the only time in my life that I wrestled with creating, usually, I just open the door and it comes. On the fourteenth day, it came . . . I was in my Ford Galaxy on my way to the bus station to pick up a girlfriend from down south. I was stopped at a red light at Forty-First Street and Eighth Avenue when all the words came to me at once. I tied up traffic at that red light for fifteen minutes, as I scribbled on three napkins and a matchbook cover. A whole bunch of irate taxi drivers were leaning on their horns. I wrote it, put it in the glove compartment.

Days later Irvine retrieved his scribbled notes and sat down at a piano in Simone's home in Mount Vernon. Together they shaped a masterpiece.

Nina Simone, c. 1969. 'She was not at odds with the times – the times were at odds with her' – Ambassador Shabazz, daughter of Malcolm X.

It was a collaboration that spoke volumes about their special relationship and dug deep into their complex childhoods. Both were virtuoso pianists, Nina Simone a child prodigy who had gone from rural poverty to Carnegie Hall, and Irvine an abandoned child brought up by his academic grandfather in the leafy surrounds of the campus of Hampton University. He had servants, wore antique knickerbockers and was raised to differentiate between different vintages of fine wine. Piano lessons were given by a tutor on a Steinway grand in his grandfather's study. 'It was almost like a Victorian upbringing,' he once said, 'and it instilled in me a sense of history that's very, very rare. Most people, regardless of their ethnicity, don't have the extremes of experience I have.' After graduation Irvine 'escaped' to Harlem in 1965, where he joined the influx of talent desperate to be noticed in the local jazz and R&B scene.

Weldon Irvine Jr was the closest Nina Simone had to a true collaborator, but it would not last. Simone was grieving the loss of her closest female friend, the great Harlem playwright Lorraine Hansberry, who had died tragically in 1965. Hansberry had been a trailblazer. She had broken into the fiercely discriminatory Broadway theatre scene, winning the New York Drama Critics' Circle Award in 1959 for her internationally successful play *A Raisin in the Sun*. Simone said of her friend: 'We never talked about men or clothes. It was always Marx, Lenin and revolution – real girls' talk.' The friendship and Hansberry's political radicalism had brought the two women to the attention of the FBI. Hansberry was even on the Bureau's 'security index' until she died of pancreatic cancer at the age of only thirty-four. At her funeral, her friend Paul Robeson sang the eulogy and a letter of condolence from Martin Luther King was read out. According to reports, Nina Simone was too distraught to sing at the funeral, but she assured Hansberry's husband Robert Nemiroff that she would remember her in song.

The opportunity soon arose. The dead writer's closest friends from the world of politics and theatre pulled a tribute night together that included scenes from her most famous plays, fragments of personal correspondence and rehearsed readings from yet unpublished works. The performance in honour of Lorraine Hansberry was given the title *Young, Gifted and Black*. Simone agreed to compose a song of the same name and discussed the idea with Weldon Irvine Jr. Together they took inspiration from the theatre show and the seeds of a modern soul classic were sown. Sadly, for both, their creative partnership was short-lived and stormy. In six short months in 1969 they worked together on the countercultural anthem 'Revolution Part I Part II', the anti-love song 'Whatever I Am (You Made Me)' and the mournful 'How Long Must I Wander', a highly personal song about the singer's own weariness in the face of success. And then there was the tribute to Lorraine Hansberry, which became one of the most famous songs of the decade.

Nina Simone had already burnt many bridges – even with her own family. She fell out with Irvine as her career lurched from one crisis to another, including tax problems, bankruptcy, domestic violence, divorces, reckless sexual relations, alcoholism and then finally mental breakdown. In Harlem's local newspaper the *Amsterdam News* she was described as 'the stormy petrel of the piano who has walked out on many a concert'. Set against her ferocious temper was a beguiling honesty. The Nobel Prize-winning writer Toni Morrison described her as fundamental to her generation: 'She was indestructible. Incorruptible. She even scared me a little.' Too temperamental and opinionated for any president to confidently rely on during campaigns, it was not until the summer of 2016, secluded for his summer holiday in Martha's Vineyard, that Barack Obama listed his favourite songs and among them was Nina Simone's 'Sinnerman' from her album *At The Village Gate* (Colpix, 1962).

Nina Simone, for all her influence on others, was her own worst enemy. She refused for years to sing or even acknowledge her timeless cocktail-soul song 'My Baby Just Cares For Me', dismissing it as trite and superficial, and held out against the song until it was picked up by Chanel for a European advertising campaign. It delivered her a small fortune that for a time corrected her dire financial situation. In part chased away by Simone's temperament, Weldon Irvine Jr struck out on his own and throughout the seventies was one of the pioneers of jazz-funk and what later became known as 'acid jazz', producing the seminal album *Liberated Brother* and the rare-groove masterpiece 'Jungle Juice'. The singer Jamiroquai once called him 'the greatest fusionist in the business' and the rapper Mos Def, respecting his musical diversity, called him an 'artist without borders'. What was poignant about Irvine's later life was its parallels with Simone's. Although she became that most implausible thing, a recluse who was also a global superstar, he retreated into mental illness. Both struggled with bipolar disorder, and on 9 April 2002, 58-year-old Irvine killed himself with a rifle on the front lawn of an office complex near the Nassau Coliseum in Uniondale, New York. He left no suicide note and his death mystified his closest friends in urban music, from whom he had successfully hidden his condition.

By the mid sixties, the diversity of black music was prevalent in pop charts around the world, led by the effervescent songs of Motown, the bluesier hits of Otis Redding, the gospel-infused songs of Aretha Franklin and the funk assault of James Brown. So it was no great surprise that branches of the federal government began knocking on studio doors, looking for singers to champion social policy.

One of the most important policies was a centrepiece within Lyndon Johnson's agenda: the belief in continuing education. To ward off summer rioting and prevent young African Americans from drifting into unemployment, Johnson supported an initiative called 'Stay in School'. In just under five years in the sixties, President Johnson, a master of forcing bills through the system, had enacted dozens and dozens of pieces of legislation known collectively as the 'Great Society', an unprecedented set of programmes aimed at improving the lives of ordinary Americans. Most of the Great Society's achievements came during the 89th Congress, from January 1965 to January 1967, still considered to be the most productive legislative sessions in American history. According to *The Washington Post*, 'Johnson prodded Congress to churn out nearly 200 new laws launching civil rights protections; Medicare and Medicaid; food stamps; urban renewal; the first broad federal investment in elementary and high school education; Head Start and college aid; an end to what was essentially a whites-only immigration policy; landmark consumer safety and environmental regulations; funding that gave voice to community action groups; and an all-out War on Poverty.'

When Johnson turned to the public school system, he brought not only new laws but enlightened attitudes that had the potential to transform the lives of young African Americans. Johnson supported good public service broadcasting, and also turned to soul music for help. In April 1965, when he signed the Elementary and Secondary

Education Act, the President reflected on his own young life working as a teacher in a Hispanic school in the impoverished town of Cotulla, Texas, before he launched his political career.

> As a son of a tenant farmer, I know that education is the only valid passport from poverty . . . As a former teacher – and, I hope, a future one – I have great expectations of what this law will mean for all of our young people. As President of the United States, I believe deeply no law I have signed or will ever sign means more to the future of America.

The job of rolling out the programmes to inner-city ghettos fell to Vice President Hubert Humphrey and the US Secretary of Labor Willard Wirtz, who took the time to personally introduce himself to Motown, Stax and Ramsey Lewis's Ramsel Records in Chicago.

On 13 May 1967, African American newspapers carried lifestyle features on Otis Redding and Carla Thomas promoting another simultaneous release, the *King & Queen* album, which featured hit singles 'Tramp' (Stax, 1967) and 'Knock On Wood' (Atlantic, 1967). The album carried liner notes attributed to Senator Howard H. Baker of Tennessee, a future ambassador to Japan known in Washington circles as 'the great conciliator'. Stax launched the album at Washington D.C.'s legendary jazz club the Bohemian Caverns, where Carla Thomas presented a gold disc of the *King & Queen* album to Senator Baker and thanked him for his endorsement of Memphis and the Stax cause. A month or so later Stax ran a high-profile album campaign with the slogan 'Stay in School: Don't Be a Drop Out', featuring Otis Redding, William Bell and jazz-soul pianist Ramsey Lewis, in partnership with the *Chicago Defender*. It was a public information tour which took live music into the inner city, addressing fears that the South Side of Chicago was a powder keg and that a summer of social unrest was inevitable. The 'Stay in School' project also led to the release of a compilation album featuring Otis Redding, Carla Thomas, Eddie Floyd, William Bell, Sam and Dave, Booker T. and the M.G.'s and The Mar-Keys. Stax distributed 10,000 promotional copies to major record stores, urban-based soul radio stations and influential figures within African American business. According to government statistics, more than 5,000 radio stations, 700 television stations and the influential Voice of America network received a campaign kit. The album consisted of songs and public service announcements. One track featured a group discussion with Sam and Dave, Booker T. Jones and the Detroit singer-songwriter Mack Rice, who had relocated to Memphis to pursue his career. It took the form of an unscripted 'bull session' in which the Stax performers improvised their reasons why ghetto teenagers should not give up on education. On the rear sleeve of the album was an open letter from Vice President Humphrey which read:

> First, I want to commend the Stax/Volt family of recording artists for their special interest in trying to help yourself.
>
> These artists know the value of a good education and what it will do for you. By singing their songs and talking to you on this album, they are trying to give encouragement and direction to those young people who are struggling against hardship and difficulty. They are trying to make sure that you understand, fully, the difference an education will make in your life.
>
> These artists know that the high school dropout is headed for disappointment and frustration when he tries to get a job. He'll meet disappointment when he tries to get a good-paying job, and then face frustration when the job he finally gets does not last too long. Machines are taking over more and more of the unskilled jobs that the uneducated used to get.
>
> Today's good jobs are going to young people who are educated, who have 'brain power' and skills. The name of the game is this: <u>Those who learn more, earn more</u>. That high school diploma could mean the difference between a real future and a mere existence. As you listen to what the talented Stax/Volt artists sing and say, make up your minds to complete your education. Remember, THOSE WHO LEARN MORE . . . EARN MORE! My young friends, that's where the action is.
>
> Sincerely – Hubert H. Humphrey

As Stax reached out across the USA, Motown took a hyper-local approach. They were once-bitten, twice-shy of 'Stay in School' campaign records. A year earlier Motown had released a one-sided campaign record called 'Play It Cool, Stay In School', penned by local writer-performer Jimmy 'Soul' Clark and sung by Brenda Holloway with backing vocals by The Supremes. It was released only in Detroit, in co-operation with the Women's Ad Club of Detroit, a powerful lobbying group of female advertising executives, but it was not a noticeable success. In 1967, General Motors in Detroit signed up to the government's job creation scheme and struck a deal with Motown that a song by The Temptations, 'Don't Look Back', could be used as a local campaign song. They funded four promising employees including an apprentice toolmaker Albert Green and a secretary from GM's Ypsilanti plant, Marcie Grymes, to tour Detroit high schools to promote the benefits of education. The entourage included Otis Williams and Melvin Franklin of The Temptations who had studied at Northwestern High School but had dropped out to form their first group The Distants. Franklin had been formally expelled from his high school and sat uncomfortably through the proceedings advocating that teenagers put education first and stay in school.

Decades before hip-hop's Public Enemy coined the phrase 'The CNN of the Ghetto' and positioned themselves as the grassroots group of their day, long-forgotten ghetto soul groups resourced their music with the help of public campaigns. One notable example was the Harlem Youth Opportunities Unlimited charity, whose house band – The Har-You Percussion Group – became one of the most popular community soul groups in Harlem. Youth leader Roger 'Montego Joe' Sanders had put together the Latin jazz orchestra from what was in effect a group of delinquent youths. The band's debut album was a frenetic collection of street-funk and Afro-Cuban jazz, featuring musicians Sanders himself described as 'emotionally unstable young men with no inspiration and no place to go'. One community soul record, which stayed buried in obscurity for years only to become an underground soul classic, was Youth Opportunity Program's 'Of Hopes And Dreams And Tombstones' (Columbia Youth Program Records, 1965), endorsed again by Vice President Humphrey and powered by the R&B vocals of Jimmy Fraser. The record was delivered by Columbia staff producer Bob Johnston, who squeezed the project into the schedules while working on Bob Dylan's *Highway 61 Revisited*.

Community soul and spoken word were thriving in every corner of Harlem. Further east, in the Puerto Rican dominated 'Spanish Harlem', in 1969 a group of young singers had formed under the banner of the East Harlem Federation Youth Association. Around twenty in number, featuring singers aged between twelve and twenty-one, they called themselves The Voices of East Harlem. Meanwhile a disillusioned but sharply articulate university dropout with links to the South Bronx and Harlem had written much-admired beat-poetry under the title *Small Talk At 125th And Lenox*. Convinced he could bring his street poetry into song, Gil Scott-Heron shopped around independent jazz labels until he struck lucky with Flying Dutchman Records. The green shoots of a very new kind of black music were springing up on the cracked sidewalks of Harlem. It merged spoken word with gospel, jazz and a sparse propulsive percussion, challenging the orthodoxy of Motown with a new socially conscious kind of music. It was decades away from its ultimate future, but the seeds of hip-hop had been sown.

Atlanta would become the home of CNN and a media hub delivering global news around the clock. But, as black music evolved and new messengers came to the fore, it was another centre with an extraordinary history that stood out. Harlem, the capital city of Black America, had been in the 1920s the home of the poetic and artistic moment known as the Harlem Renaissance. By 1968 a loft building on 125th Street called the East Wind became the home of Public Enemy's radical predecessors, The Last Poets. The block, between Madison and Fifth Avenues, was pock-marked with distressed tenements that housed an arts centre, a makeshift gallery, a rehearsal space for local talent and an illegal nightclub for the militant cognoscenti. East Wind was a magnet for black artists. Poetry sessions were improvised to the background beats of the loft's resident percussionist, creating a beat-centred form of delivery that set the tone of a musical movement yet to come. Or, as the Last Poet Jalaluddin Nuriddin aka Lightnin' Rod put it – 'We're just the speakers, the amplifiers for the people.'

Felipe Luciano, an Afro-Puerto Rican and member of the Last Poets, had just been released from jail when East Wind found its purpose. Many years later, he described his first visit to East Wind to the Dutch author Christine Otten in her imaginative account of the Last Poets' lives.

It was early evening and dusk was closing in. I found the East Wind easily enough. It was in a loft on the second floor halfway down 125th. You had to go up a set of narrow stairs and came out into a big empty space with timeworn wooden floor. There were low couches, pillows on the floor. An old-fashioned dark red and yellow carpet. It looked lived in. At the back was a small stage, a desk next to it, with a green glass lamp that shone onto the mess of papers and books. I remember it exactly. On the walls there were all kinds of posters, performance announcements. Amiri Baraka and the Spirit House Movers. James Brown at the Apollo Theater.

From their base on 125th Street, the Last Poets spread out through Harlem supporting local political causes, drawing crowds to street corners and showing up at community houses dotted throughout the ghetto. This was a breeding ground of political rap and Afrocentric culture. When he was a teenager, the Black Panther Jamal Joseph (formerly Eddie) saw the Poets perform at a rally for the Harlem Tenants Council in the dark heart of the Lincoln Projects, a warren of sixteen-storey dark-brown buildings on Madison Avenue at East 132nd Street. It had become a community under the control of the tenants, virtually a no-go area for New York police units and a potential flashpoint for social disruption. Joseph described the gathering in his autobiography, *Panther Baby*, as 'more than a political rally – it was a cultural event. There were African dancers, a jazz quartet and a concert by the Last Poets, a group said by many to have invented rap. Their lyrics and poems performed over jazz riffs and African drumbeats were both incendiary and highly entertaining.' The language and legends of jazz featured prominently among the many poems and raps performed: both 'Bird's Word' and 'Bird Lives' paid tribute to Charlie 'Yardbird' Parker. Most rap poems were short, sharp and sarcastic but The Last Poets spent six months shaping a magnus opus by the name of 'E Pluribus Unum', the Latin motto of the USA – 'Out of many, one'. The rap is a critique of capitalism and the way it was enshrined in American society since the founding fathers. As their reputation spread, The Last Poets became best known for Jalal Nuriddin's 'On the Subway', set in a sweaty and rattling subway train as it navigates the IND Eighth Avenue Line, and for the heroin addicts' rap 'Jones Comin' Down', which pulsates with the cravings of a man desperate for his next hit. The term insinuated its way from ghetto streets into soul music. In 1969, The Temptations released the ground-breaking album *Puzzle People*, which broke with Motown's bubble-gum soul in the race-conscious tracks

'Message From A Black Man', 'Slave' and the heroin-abuse song 'Don't Let The Joneses Get You Down'.

The Last Poets first got together on Sunday 19 May 1968, at a festival in Mount Morris Park to celebrate Malcolm X's birthday, creating what the writer Todd 'Ty' Williams in *Source* magazine called 'a workshop of the mind'. The following month, a PBS television executive and sometime jazz producer Alan Douglas turned up at East Wind and recorded them. No significant distribution deal was ever struck but the eponymous album that emerged from the session defied logic. Rather than disappear into obscurity, it sold through word of mouth and via the community networks of the inner cities. A staggering 800,000 were allegedly sold in makeshift deals at community shops, political demonstrations and summer festivals, easily enough to take The Last Poets into the *Billboard* charts had the sales ever been quantified. Douglas subsequently negotiated a meeting with Jimi Hendrix and together they recorded the pioneering 'Doriella Du Fontaine' with Lightnin' Rod and a friend of Hendrix's, the drummer Buddy Miles. It was a project rich in cultural collision that again pointed forward. The music critic Gene Santoro described the fiery collaboration as one that 'foreshadows the rap-meets-metal crossover of later artists like Run-DMC'. Lightnin' Rod went on to record the ultimate street album, *Hustler's Convention* (United Artists, 1973), a tour de force set in the mind of a ghetto hustler as he tells the story of a young gun, Spoon, navigating the cold-cash cafés and street joints of Harlem. Like Theodore Dreiser's Chicago and James Joyce's Dublin, *Hustler's Convention* moves across uptown New York with epic scale, unique characters and a sweeping storyline. Three of the funky backing tracks were provided by emergent jazz-funk pioneers Kool and the Gang. *Hustler's Convention* was the missing link, the biological DNA that led to hip-hop.

Three different strands of thought were influencing this new moment in black music – black pride, raised awareness of African history, and community resistance forged by successive years of social rebellion. Even before it was sung at Richard Nixon's inaugural ball, James Brown's 'Say It Loud, I'm Black And I'm Proud' had become a clarion call for ghetto self-awareness. African nationalism had swept through Harlem for decades and now threatened to dislodge the civil rights establishment that had grown up with Martin Luther King's peaceful campaigns of the fifties.

The Last Poets took their name from a poem by South African revolutionary poet Keorapetse Kgositsile, an exiled African anti-apartheid activist and Columbia University post-grad student living in Harlem on a poetry grant. He published his first collection of poetry in 1969 and among his many contentions was the fatalistic thought that he was the 'last poet' and then there would be guns. All three of the Last Poets had assumed African identities and, although the group's membership changed over time, Jalal Mansur Nuriddin, Umar Bin Hassan and Abiodun Oyewole, along with percussionist Nilaja Obabi, are considered the core members. Resplendent in West African dashiki shirts, they were a familiar sight at street corner gatherings, tenants' group protests and at the bandstands in Mount Morris Park. They were regularly hired to headline at rent-strike meetings and at protests shaming absent slum landlords. Block parties were commonplace across Harlem, the most famous coming in September when Jimi Hendrix headlined the United Block Association benefit concert at a block on 139th Street and Lenox. Hendrix's performance underlined that there was much to differentiate the community groups of Harlem in 1969. The Last Poets only sparingly used musical support beyond bare percussion, and when they did it was almost always angular Afro-jazz, until *Hustler's Convention* added the meaty sound of street-funk and the more mainstream rhythms of R&B.

By contrast, community group The Voices of East Harlem drew on more familiar forms of soul music, mostly gospel and group harmony, and as their career developed moved into fully produced studio backing. They were unquestionably from Harlem, not a mythologised Africa, and so dressed in an urban style, sporting matching denim jackets, Converse basketball shoes and trimmed afros. The Voices of East Harlem were formed by youth worker Charles 'Chuck' Griffin and his wife Anna. In one dramatic performance they came to the stage through the audience, acting out the bridled anger of a chain gang, clapping freedom songs and stomping the floor in workers' boots as they took to the stage. Unlike the Last Poets, who performed a capella, The Voices of East Harlem were backed by a funk band and considered themselves to be a soul choir rather than proselytisers.

As their act attracted more and more attention, they strengthened the group with new talent from across Harlem and recruited the accomplished vocalist Bernice Cole from Philadelphia's Angelic Gospel Singers as a musical director. It was virtually impossible not to be moved by The Voices of East Harlem's chaotic joyousness: goodwill, as much as anything, brought them to wider prominence. They played a high-profile fundraiser with Jimi Hendrix, among others, for the Vietnam Moratorium Fund at Madison Square Garden and also appeared at the Museum of Modern Art's jazz garden in part to placate black audiences who were boycotting the Metropolitan Museum after its pitiful all-white *Harlem on My Mind* exhibition. The cover of their first album, *Right On Be Free*, in keeping with the times, had the entire choir carrying a banner and marching as if at a political demonstration. They attracted support from civil rights influencers, sharing a stage with Carlos Santana at the Fillmore East and with Harry Belafonte and Eloise Laws at the Westbury Music Fair. At the 1970 Isle of Wight Festival, a pop concert which outstripped Woodstock and attracted 700,000 people to a small island four miles off the English coast, they shared a bill with The Who, Sly and the Family Stone and Hendrix again. That may have been their biggest audience but their greatest show was with B. B. King and Joan Baez live at Ossining Correctional Facility in upstate New York, the notorious prison that was better known as Sing Sing. The Voices entertained an intimidating audience that included murderers, rapists, bank robbers and members of the Harlem Black Panthers.

Gradually, The Voices of East Harlem moved away from their community origins and professionalised into an assured soul group. This was in part due to the influence of Donny Hathaway, Roberta Flack and their long-time friend Leroy Hutson, all of whom were hugely influential artists at Atlantic Records. Hutson produced the Voices of East Harlem's eponymous third album and then their fourth, *Can You Feel It*. What Hathaway and Hutson gave them was a musicianship that was missing in their early community soul days, leaving them with at least one outstanding single, the remarkable 'Cashing In' (1973), a morality tale about love and economics which became one of the great Harlem soul records of its era. By then the Voices had signed to indie Just Sunshine, set up by Woodstock promoter Michael Lang, although they were by now leaving the festival circuit behind and becoming part of the mainstream soul community.

At a time when prison unrest was at its volcanic height, The Voices of East Harlem were one of numerous groups called upon to raise funds to support prisoners inside the brutal and dehumanising Attica Correctional Facility. On 9 September 1971, the prison dominated the news headlines when a major civil and human rights protest erupted there. *The New York Times* described it as 'an uprising that is barely mentioned in textbooks but nevertheless was one of the most important rebellions in American history'. Television had unprecedented access to events, and over five dramatic days Americans watched the uprising unfold to its savage conclusion. According to a report in *The New York Times*, 'They watched in surprise as inmates elected representatives from each cellblock to negotiate on their behalf. They watched in disbelief as these same inmates protected the guards and civilian employees, they had taken hostage.' During the negotiations the prisoners requested that observers be drawn from across civic society, but as the rebellion wore on the lawn around Attica filled with hundreds of heavily armed state troopers, under the direct command of Governor Nelson A. Rockefeller. Rockefeller refused to grant amnesty to the inmates if they surrendered and the clock ticked down tensely on a massacre. *The New York Times* recorded the gory details.

> On the morning of Sept. 13, 1971, he [Rockefeller] gave the green light for helicopters to rise suddenly over Attica and blanket it with tear gas. As inmates and hostages fell to the ground blinded, choking and incapacitated, more than 500 state troopers burst in, riddling catwalks and exercise yards with thousands of bullets. Within 15 minutes the air was filled with screams, and the prison was littered with the bodies of 39 people – 29 inmates and 10 hostages – who lay dead or dying.

Guitarist and songwriter Willie Feaster, the leader of the New York-based R&B/funk band Willie & The Mighty Magnificents, watched the massacre on television. Feaster led the house band for Sylvia Robinson's group of independent labels, Stang, Turbo and All Platinum, and worked closely with George Kerr, one of Robinson's main producers. Kerr had recently produced the racially assertive 'Message From A

Black Man' as an album track for The Temptations, the song then going on to greater visibility as a single for The Spinners.

George Kerr was a unique character in the story of soul. He was a jobbing producer and a self-taught intellectual who had developed an interest in prison reform. A close friend and mentor of the great vocalist Linda Jones, he worked with her up until her untimely death in March 1972. Jones had encouraged Kerr to join her on family visits to Rahway State Prison, where her brother was incarcerated, and between them they hatched the idea of recording prisoners behind bars. It was an idea that initially fell on deaf ears, but Kerr bombarded the authorities with letters, phone calls and prison reform literature. Two years after Attica, a mobile recording truck pulled up outside Rahway prison. 'I did some research and found out that it cost about $964 to house an inmate,' Kerr later said, 'and that if the authorities let me record them, they could pay for themselves . . . I went before the Superintendent of Prisons in Washington DC and explained that to them. It took a lot of work, but they eventually gave me permission to record . . .' One young Rahway inmate, Reginald Haynes, who was convicted of armed robbery as a teenager, had by this time formed a prison group called The Escorts. They laid down tracks initially using Kerr's mobile studio and launched their career with a redemptive harmony soul song, 'All We Need (Is Another Chance)' (Alithia, 1973).

George Kerr and bandleader Willie Feaster were openly critical of the Attica killings and discussed the prospect of commemorating the massacre in a song. Together they came up with 'Attica Massacre' (Turbo, 1972), written by Kerr, performed by Willie & West and, like many of Turbo's releases, made using recycled backing tracks from previous sessions. Pressed in limited quantities and only really available at prison reform conferences, it had a proudly partisan feel, too uncompromising for most radio stations. The song remained buried for years until it became one of the most in-demand underground soul records ever, preciously rare and perfect for clubs that featured funk, rare soul and hip-hop. Its story was in every respect typical of the challenges facing radical music in the early seventies: radio and television had opened up to black music, but gate-keeping and silent censorship still restricted entry for the most militant message records.

The Attica massacre unlocked an anger within the prison system that took years to subside and the full truth about what happened there only came to light many years later, adding another deep stain to Richard Nixon's presidency. Academics have recently examined conversations between Nixon and Rockefeller contained in the volumes of tapes that include James Brown's meeting in the White House and the materials involved in Watergate. 'The courage you showed and the judgment in not granting amnesty, it was right, and I don't care what the hell the papers or anybody else says,' Nixon told Rockefeller. 'If you would have granted amnesty in this case, it would have meant that you would have had prisons in an uproar all over this country.' He went further and assured the Governor that compliant editors within the media would ensure that the riot was framed as an uprising by black criminals and that the prison and its guards would not be blamed. It was not the story Willie & West's 'Attica Massacre' told: that lay unloved in ghetto shops while news bulletins across the land piled racist inferences on the story.

Out of the street poetry that The Last Poets pioneered and the community soul that The Voices of East Harlem were now known for came the roots of a new kind of music: spoken word enunciated against obscure funky tracks such as Willie & The Mighty Magnificents' 'Funky (8) Corners' (All Platinum, 1969). It had yet to become a fully-fledged subculture, but it was helped on its way by a coincidence at a family birthday party. Sylvia Robinson and her husband went to celebrate their niece's birthday at a club called Harlem World owned by the record producer and heroin dealer Fat Jack Taylor. What struck them about the night was the energy of the entertainers, all young men and woman, rhyming to club classics. They rushed back to their New Jersey studios at Sugar Hill Records and assembled a group that could approximate the style. They named their group the Sugarhill Gang and released 'Rapper's Delight' to cash in on an emergent trend. The hip-hop revolution that eventually gave birth to Public Enemy had been ignited in the projects several summers before but was now beginning to flare to the surface.

Gil Scott-Heron was a profound influence on the rise of rap and his body of work politically stalks American presidents from Nixon to George W. Bush. With his velvet voice, razor-sharp language and deep knowledge of the poetic giants of African American scholarship, he embarked on a mission to take jazz and soul on a voyage of social comment. As a child, Scott-Heron had lived with his maternal grandmother, Lillie Scott, in Jackson, Tennessee, moving to New York at the age of 13 when she died. The first song on his final album is the ironically titled 'On Coming From A Broken Home', an ode to his grandmother. 'Womenfolk raised me,' he said, 'and I was full-grown before I knew I came from a broken home.' Scott-Heron had moved to the Bronx, and with his forceful librarian mother at his back he won a scholarship through his writing to the prestigious Fieldston School, a place where only the most fortunate and gifted ghetto kids studied. Like his collaborator Brian Jackson, he had chosen to attend Lincoln University, Pennsylvania, in part because it was the place that their mutual hero the Harlem poet Langston Hughes had studied. Hanging out in Lincoln, Scott-Heron befriended the brother of one of The Last Poets and connected with the group through him.

In his memoir *The Last Holiday*, he wrote: 'I hung out with the jazz heavies, the ones you didn't hear too often on the radio. We spent a lot of our time supposedly doing our homework, but really in our rooms checking out the jams – Coltrane, Dexter Gordon, Herbie Hancock.'

Rebel, influencer, poet and musician, Gil Scott-Heron raged against successive US presidents and became one of the most original voices of political song.

Hey America!

Once a month the young Lincoln University crew would travel to Harlem, to the East Wind loft, where they joined in the free-form workshops or stood back frozen in youthful awe simply watching who was about: the radicals, the intellectuals, the drug peddlers and a roomful of musicians from old jazz and the new soul. With the loyal Brian Jackson driving the musicianship, Scott-Heron began to pursue the prospect of a new kind of jazz-poetry, all but abandoning formal education and securing a $5,000 advance for his novel *The Nigger Factory*. Jackson was a classically trained keyboard player, and together they hawked an idea for a jazz-poetry LP around New York's indies. The drummer Bernard Purdie suggested they talk to Bob Thiele, a jazz-scene veteran and one-time producer of John Coltrane and Archie Shepp, who was planning an escape from ABC to set up his own jazz-soul label Flying Dutchman Records.

Gil Scott-Heron took a gamble and went uninvited to Thiele's office, convinced that he would be blocked at reception. The opposite happened, and he hustled his way to a deal. Thiele liked the fresh arrogance of the words and the underlying cadences of jazz, and so took a major risk and agreed to put Scott-Heron's streetwise soul on a 'live' album.

To create a gig atmosphere, the record label borrowed some folding chairs and invited fifty people to join them in the studio with a theatre set arranged much like a coffee shop. The outcome was the album colloquially known as *Small Talk* but its full title was *A New Black Poet – Small Talk At 125th And Lenox* (Flying Dutchman, 1970), and among its many surprises was 'The Revolution Will Not Be Televised'. With its razor-sharp language, comedic ad-speak and sloganeering, the track deconstructs commercial television and political chicanery. Unexpectedly it has minimal musical accompaniment, and irrespective of its innovation and the background crackle of a live audience, the song – if it can be called that – attracted radio play in urban stations across America and has since become a landmark moment in the story of radical soul music.

Gil Scott-Heron's career took off and he blazed a trail for the fusion of pop and politics, scything through nearly every major issue. His up-tempo, near-disco song 'The Bottle' (Strata-East, 1974) from the concept album *Winter In America* (Strata-East, 1974) paints an alcohol-charged picture of ghetto street corners while another track, 'H²Ogate Blues', lampoons the fallout of the Watergate scandal. First and foremost,

Scott-Heron was a poet. His evocative 'Home Is Where The Hatred Is' (Flying Dutchman, 1971) is a powerful tale of a heroin addict more comfortable in street-dives than in his own strained family home. Although Scott-Heron wrote and performed the song, he was impressed by Esther Phillips's self-reflective cover version. Her own heroin addiction came perilously close to ruining her career. Sung from the vantage point of a woman and from a singer of real substance, the song takes on an epic quality.

Scott-Heron had an intellectually inquisitive mind and a magpie sensibility when it came to musical form, sometimes borrowing from be-bop and disco, then jazz funk, but he consistently found ways to bring his message music from the corners of the avant garde into the wider spaces of popular culture. His world-renowned anti-apartheid song 'Johannesburg' (Arista, 1975) became a dance-floor hit while other tracks dug deep into the mines of black history to underline the prejudices of the present.

One remarkable piece of social history was 'Tuskeegee #626' from the album *Bridges* (Arista, 1977), a jazz-rap critique of the so-called 'Tuskegee Study of Untreated Syphilis in the Negro Male.' Herbert Hoover was president when the study began in 1932 and Nixon was president when it was shamefully brought to a halt forty years later. The study had been a deceptive and morally compromised piece of biological science which offered free 'bad blood' tests to poor African American families on the promise of free meals, free physicals and free burial insurance. It recruited 600 black men, of whom 399 were diagnosed with syphilis, for what was in fact a secret experiment conducted by the US Public Health Service to study the progression of the deadly venereal disease. In 1972, an Associated News reporter Jean Heller broke the story that rocked the American medical establishment. The federal government, she reported, had deliberately let hundreds of black men in rural Alabama go untreated for syphilis for 40 years for research purposes. Years later, President Bill Clinton apologised to the survivors of the experiment.

> The United States government did something that was wrong – deeply, profoundly, morally wrong. It was an outrage to our commitment to integrity and equality for all our citizens. To the survivors, to the wives

and family members, the children, and the grandchildren, I say what you know: No power on Earth can give you back the lives lost, the pain suffered, the years of internal torment and anguish. What was done cannot be undone. But we can end the silence. We can stop turning our heads away. We can look at you in the eye and finally say on behalf of the American people, what the United States government did was shameful, and I am sorry.

Another track on *Bridges* called 'We Almost Lost Detroit' takes as its focal point the dangers of nuclear power. The song is often said to be based on the incident at Three Mile Island, a partial meltdown and radiation leak at a nuclear generating station near Harrisburg, Pennsylvania, during Jimmy Carter's presidency but the song had been written two years earlier and borrowed its title from a 1975 book by the author John G. Fuller, about a partial nuclear meltdown of Fermi 1, America's first commercial breeder reactor. Fuller's book was eerily subtitled 'This Is Not A Novel' and recounted in detail how the reactor in Monroe County, Michigan, would have wiped Detroit off the map. Gil Scott-Heron's song, and a later jazz cover version by saxophonist Ron Holloway, took the evocative title and widened it out to the dangers of nuclear power. The lyrics also mentioned the chemical technician and anti-nuclear activist Karen Silkwood, who worked making pluto-nium pellets at the Kerr-McGee fuel fabrication site in Oklahoma. At the time only known within progressive circles, her name entered the mainstream with the release of the 1983 movie *Silkwood*, in which she was portrayed by Meryl Streep.

Each new album by Gil Scott-Heron came with the heft of trust and radicalism, as if he was the Walter Cronkite of the ghetto, a precursor of rap journalists yet to come. The stepping stones to Public Enemy were almost all in place: a cache of old funk and soul records stretching back to the early sixties; a new generation of politically wired street-poets including Amiri Baraka, Nikki Giovanni, Gil Scott-Heron and The Last Poets; the cool mysteries of jazz; a network of independent R&B labels accustomed to navigating the barriers of the recording industry; a long litany of fast-talking communicators from R&B radio such as Jack 'The Rapper' Gibson, Georgie Woods ('the guy with the goods') and New York's Frankie 'Love Man' Crocker; and on television nightly, the shameless self-publicists of heavyweight boxing such as Muhammad Ali. All that was missing was the vital spark: a new ghetto youth subculture. Curiously, without him ever knowing it, President Jimmy Carter lent his support.

'The CNN of the Ghetto' had another similarity with media journalism – the special reporter, those creative musicians whose reputation gave them permission to venture beyond the normal mores of pop music to report on current affairs. Prominent among them was Curtis Mayfield. When he came to release his iconic album *There's No Place Like America Today* (Curtom, 1975) he already had a formidable reputation. Many of his most successful songs, such as 'We're A Winner' (Curtom, 1971) and 'Move On Up' (Curtom, 1972), were anthems of the civil rights decade, while 'Choice Of Colors' (Curtom, 1969) – one of his parting songs with the Impressions – and 'Mighty Mighty (Spade and Whitey)' (Curtom, 1971) dared to raise searching questions about race and racism. Mayfield's success nudged more Chicago soul musicians to embrace social commentary and black power, notably the Chi-Lites on their album *(For God's Sake) Give More Power To The People*, also released in 1971.

The photograph on the cover of *There's No Place Like America Today* juxtaposes two contrasting images from the American past: a line of African Americans carrying bags and bundles wait in line for some unspecified charitable relief, and above them, smiling down from a hoarding, is the advertising industry's portrayal of the American dream, a white family driving an Oldsmobile towards wealth and security. It is a profoundly ironic message that stands out for its bravery alone. The artwork is in fact a retouched and colourised version of an original 1937 monochrome photograph by Margaret Bourke-White. She was a *Life* magazine staff photographer who documented racism and the poverty and desperation of America's Dust Bowl states. She became the first US war photographer to gain access to the Soviet Union in the early days of the Cold War. Bourke-White had taken the photograph, titled 'At the Time of the Louisville Flood', as victims queued for food and shelter directly in front of a billboard advertising 'The World's Highest Standard of Living'.

Music critic David Bennun, revisiting the album many years after its release wrote that it was:

a record of its time, which has its own fascination; but it's also an album of timeless intrigue. The world it portrays is very cold indeed, and the comfort it offers is as spare as its measured, melancholy funk. But it's comfort nonetheless, something buried so deep in the music that maybe those of us whose bones have never ached, day in, day out, on hard city streets . . . can't really get to grips with it . . . Mayfield may have felt that he could hardly sound the call to party when so many of his audience were finding it difficult enough to get though the week.

There's No Place Like America Today is in many respects a concept album for Gerald Ford's brief 895-day presidency. Notwithstanding the official end of the war in Vietnam and the Helsinki Accords of 1975, the gloom of recession and the lingering clouds of Watergate still hung heavy over public sentiment. Unemployment rose to 9 per cent, two assassination attempts were made on the President's life and the problems of inner-city ghettos seemed to calcify rather than ease. The British playwright John Osborne, famous for his 1956 play *Look Back in Anger*, described Ford as 'a loser, a bumbler, a misfit President who for some reason or other . . . was prone to slip on airplane ramps, bump his head on helicopter entrances, entangle himself in the leashes of his family dogs, and fall from skis in front of television cameras'.

Mayfield picked up the mood of hopelessness, stripping it of farce and humour, to leave only the despair. His album begins with a song about a prisoner who is let out of jail and finds out about the death of an old friend, 'Billy Jack', killed in a gun fight, but the stand-out track is 'When Seasons Change', a bleak poem about the ingrained hopelessness of the ghetto, with Mayfield's light and mellifluous voice barely lifting it above a requiem for life itself.

Ford's presidency, however, did coincide with a rich vein of music emerging from the city of Philadelphia. Throughout the seventies, Gamble and Huff's Sigma Sound Studios in the Centennial City was a base for music which articulated themes of black pride and self-determination, including the star-studded community empowerment song 'Let's Clean Up The Ghetto' (Philadelphia International, 1977). All profits from the album of the same name went to charity for five years. The corresponding 'Clean Up the Ghetto' project, which attracted young people from impoverished communities to repair damaged and neglected properties and reclaim derelict land, started in Philadelphia and spread to Los Angeles, Atlanta and Chicago.

On 5 October 1977, when 'Let's Clean Up The Ghetto' was already rising up the *Billboard* R&B charts, President Jimmy Carter walked through a derelict area of the South Bronx and drew the world's attention to the abandonment that made the New York borough a symbol of urban decay. Carter was in the city to give an address on strategic arms limitation to the United Nations but made an unannounced trip to the South Bronx. He met with the Mayor of New York, Abraham Beame, and the Secretary of Housing and Urban Development, Patricia Roberts Harris, and they travelled by motorcade to the corner of East 168th Street and Washington Avenue. The party then walked across rubble-strewn wasteland to a block on 167th Street. 'It was a very sobering trip for me to see the devastation that has taken place in the South Bronx in the last five years,' said Carter. As he was photographed, none of the many locals he encountered could recall any president ever having visited an area like theirs. Almost every social problem – homelessness, poverty and narcotics – strangled hope. The area's notoriety worsened when the movie *Fort Apache, The Bronx* (1981) was released, leaving both Hispanic and African American residents fuming about the way

President Jimmy Carter meets residents of Morrisania in the South Bronx, the spiritual home of hip-hop, on 5 October 1977.

Hey America!

their community was demonised on the big screen. The South Bronx had become a crude shorthand for 'no-go' areas and yet the shoots of a new reputation had been growing in the shadows for five years or more.

The impact of the South Bronx on popular music is every bit as dynamic as the birth of rock 'n' roll. In his ground-breaking local history essay, 'From Jimmy Castor to Grandmaster Flash – The Role of Morrisania in Hip-Hop's Evolution', Dr Mark Naison, Professor of African American Studies and History at Fordham University – nicknamed 'The Notorious Ph.D' – excavates fascinating details of hip-hop's birth and traces it to the very blocks that Jimmy Carter visited.

Morrisania's history is intimately connected with the birth of America and the Declaration of Independence. It was once the estate of Lewis Morris, the ancestor of a colonial family from Monmouthshire in Wales, who became a member of the New York Provincial Congress and one of the signatories of the declaration. By the twentieth century the area's picturesque elegance was in retreat. The Third Avenue Elevated aka 'the Bronx El' opened in 1878, eventually providing a rail link from the Bronx to Harlem and Manhattan, then in 1948 the Cross Bronx Expressway became the first highway built through a crowded urban area. But this phenomenal growth was followed by a tsunami of depopulation between 1970 and 1980, when Morrisania lost 53 per cent of its population, while an adjoining neighbourhood, Hunts Point–Crotona Park East, lost a staggering 69 per cent. This rapid decline, followed by a withdrawal of city services and the end of meaningful business investment, took a devastating toll on Morrisania's culture. Live music had thrived in the area throughout the fifties and sixties, gifting the area a network of clubs and bars such as the Tropicana Club, Club 845, the Blue Morocco, the Apollo Bar and the Royal Mansion. The Tropicana's resident jazz man was Dizzy Gillespie, the Blue Morocco's in-house entertainer was jazz-soul singer Nancy Wilson, and Latin-funk innovator Jimmy Castor led the house band. The neighbourhood's biggest venue was the 2,500-seat Hunts Point Palace, on Southern Boulevard and East 163rd Street, where singers Lloyd Price, James Brown and Jackie Wilson all performed. Doo-wop groups crowded the pavements outside the main clubs: The Crickets, The Chimes and The Chords all lived within two miles of 168th Street. Morrisania attracted many musicians priced out of downtown, among them Donald Byrd,

Thelonious Monk, Lou Donaldson and Herbie Hancock, but by 1970 most of the clubs had closed, bereft of patrons or now unable to afford soaring rates of insurance on blocks where arson was rife.

168th Street was briefly infamous after Carter visited, but that reputation was about to be spectacularly displaced by a new one – as the original home of hip-hop. On 11 August 1973, in the West Bronx, an 18-year-old Jamaican-American DJ began to improvise with turntables. Clive 'Hercules' Campbell had lived his formative days in Kingston and had watched bewitched as reggae DJs caressed vinyl discs and dub-plates, mining rhythms that singers and performers could talk and 'toast' over. By the time he was 13 his family had emigrated to the Bronx and he had assumed a moniker based on his nickname: DJ Kool Herc. Campbell lived at 1520 Sedgwick Avenue, a 102-unit working-class apartment block, with his sister Cindy, his parents and gigantic boxes of speakers, wires and electronic paraphernalia. Cindy was a school committee member at Grace Dodge high school, a technical school which accepted young mothers and pregnant girls among its intake. She talked her brother into mounting a 'Back to School' party within their apartment block's community rooms. Hip-hop folklore suggests the entry price was $1 and it was agreed that Cindy would take a slice of the profits as a school fundraiser and to buy herself new clothes for the term ahead. Herc invited his friend Coke La Rock, a teenager who hailed from North Carolina, to help with the event. Studiously avoiding what he still describes as 'his government name', Coke La Rock began the fashion for imaginative street names. He knew Herc from night-school, a high-school system common in the Bronx for children whose parents worked late into the night. At the party Herc, still channelling his Jamaican background, played reggae to no great response, and so improvised something different. Instead of playing funk and soul songs in full, he played only the percussive instrumental sections, or 'breaks' while his friend Coke La Rock hyped up the crowd with a microphone. One of his improvised lines was 'Rock and you don't stop'.

Hip-hop had arrived.

By 1974, Herc was playing outdoors in the Cedar Park playground near his home on hot summer days and in Bronx nightclubs and community venues as winter fell.

Mark Naison says:

Morrisania's schoolyards and abandoned buildings provided the setting for Grandmaster Flash's first neighbourhood parties, while its afterhours clubs offered a venue for groups ranging from the Cold Crush Brothers to the Fantastic Four. Grandwizard Theodore perfected the art of scratching in outdoor jams in Morrisania schoolyards, while Lovebug Starski honed his skills in discos held at a Morrisania Burger King. The great hip hop philosopher KRS 1 was discovered by social worker Scott La Rock at a homeless shelter in a Morrisania Armory on 166th Street and Franklin Avenue, and Fat Joe launched his career while living in Morrisania's Forest Houses.

The role of Joseph Saddler aka Grandmaster Flash cannot be overstated. Another émigré from the Caribbean, he was born in Barbados and moved with his family to the Bronx. As a teenager, he began experimenting with DJ gear in his bedroom while studying electronics at Samuel Gompers vocational high school in East Morrisania. Flash was an equipment nerd who mastered three technical innovations that shaped the sound of hip-hop and are still standard DJing techniques today – quick mixing, where he listened to one track on his headphones while identifying and cueing the same beats on the other deck; clock theory, in which he overdubbed horn riffs over the beats; and most spectacularly of all scratch-mixing, in which he scratched back on the grooves allowing the sound of the scratch itself to be part of the effect. His magnus opus 'The Adventures Of Grandmaster Flash On the Wheels Of Steel' (Sugar Hill, 1981) is a timeless journey through sound, which borrows and 'quotes' from Chic's 'Good Times', Blondie's 'Rapture', Queen's 'Another One Bites The Dust' and mashes them up with children's storytelling and homages to his namesake, the comic-book star Flash Gordon. Using his remarkable dexterity on turntables, Flash created a brazenly innovative track which disrupted the logic of classic song composition and thrust hip-hop into a twenty-year battle about copyright ownership.

Suddenly the old records of the past, sourced in second-hand record stores, thrift shops and old family cupboards at home, took on a quasi-religious status. In his essay 'The Funky Demise of Black Bands' music critic Nelson George describes how recycling the soulful past became like panning for gold.

The deepest musicologist I've encountered were not scholars at universities or nerds like me writing record reviews. The true scholars were the early DJs and producers, the "diggers" of hip-hop culture, who obsessed over breakbeats, breathing in thousands of dust particles in mould filled basements from dusty LP covers. Their sonic erudition is sometimes frightening in its completeness. This global search for new gold in old vinyl put these DJs on par with the connoisseurs of wine who tasted mouthfuls of vino for a living or searched out the rarest teas in Tibet. I admired their dedication and worried about their mental health.

Among the gold that the prospectors of breakbeats discovered were tracks that lay unloved on old B-sides. One of the most cherished was the flip side of The Winstons' 'Color Him Father' (MetroMedia, 1969), a spiritually uplifting song about a stepfather who marries a Vietnam war widow and adopts her children. The Winstons were a mixed-race group from Washington D.C. who had previously played in Otis Redding's touring band and had secured a short-term recording contract with Curtis Mayfield's Chicago-based Curtom Records. When that deal expired they moved to MetroMedia and, in need of a flip side to back 'Color Me Father', they recorded an instrumental jam called 'Amen Brother', a furious reworking of the old gospel classic 'Amen'. In the middle of the track is a short gunfire drum solo by drummer Gregory 'G. C.' Coleman, which has since been repurposed by N.W.A., Salt-N-Pepa, Eric B. & Rakim, Heavy D and Mantronix. It is believed to be the most-sampled breakbeat in history, having been used more than 5,000 times, and now known by its colloquial name – the Amen

Old-school hip-hop flyer promoting turntable wizard Grandmaster Flash. The show took place on the stage of the Audubon Ballroom, Harlem, where Malcolm X was assassinated.

Grandmaster Flash and the Furious Five in Munich during a European tour in 1984. They emerged from their roots in South Bronx to become one of the first crossover acts of hip-hop.

Break. Crossing over to the mainstream, Oasis used it in 'D'You Know What I Mean?', it surfaced at the start of David Bowie's hit song 'Little Wonder', and it appears in tracks by Plan B, Slipknot and The Prodigy.

Unable to secure bookings in the race-conscious circuit, The Winstons – like so many artists of their era – retired unrewarded and by the early seventies were already history. Coleman, the drummer who created the Amen Break, developed a drug addiction and died homeless in Atlanta unaware of the impact of his drum solo. In a cruel irony, he panhandled in and around Centennial Olympic Park next to the CNN Center, the world headquarters of the news operation. The Winstons' lead singer Richard L. Spencer, who retrained as a high school teacher, admitted: 'It felt like plagiarism and I felt ripped off and raped . . . I come from an era where you didn't steal people's ideas.' Spencer was not alone; one of the raw nerves of hip-hop was gradually exposed. For all its big-break innovation, it was a form that wilfully borrowed from the music of the past. Sometimes that 'borrowing' was influence, homage and creative reinterpretation, at other times it was plagiarism and wholesale artistic theft.

Hip-hop remained underground for much of the seventies, spreading initially across the Five Boroughs to Harlem, Bedford-Stuyvesant and eventually Long Island, where the young Chuck D caught the bug. The 22nd of April 1978 is the historically significant date when Grandmaster Flash and his original Three MCs, Cowboy, Melle Mel and The Kidd Creole, took to the stage at the Audubon Ballroom, where Malcolm X had been assassinated twenty-three years before. It was inevitable that hip-hop could not remain a South Bronx secret for long.

Given the impact it has had on popular culture, it is curious that at the time hip-hop was largely dismissed as a passing fad. It did, however, find friends in high places and forged a bond with the arts community downtown, where the cut-up and montage culture of artistic modernism was better understood. Hip-hop had the disruptive love of postmodern 'quoting' that pop art feasted upon. A key figure in the unlikely cross-collaboration was Fred Brathwaite aka Fab Five Freddy, a member of the Brooklyn graffiti group the Fabulous 5 who had turned subway trains into moving art. With another member of the group, street artist Lee Quiñones, he took graffiti to the galleries, exhibiting downtown and in Rome's prestigious Galleria La Medusa. When Fab Five Freddy and turntable wizard Grandmaster Flash were namechecked in Blondie's hit 'Rapture' (Chrysalis, 1981), a moment of crossover had arrived and hip-hop's inexorable journey to the heart of pop culture was underway.

Hip-hop's rise was in marked contrast to Jimmy Carter's presidency. His campaign for re-election in 1980 was one of the most challenging and least successful in history. As historian Rick Perlstein has recorded scrupulously in his monumental book *Reaganland*, the rightward swing of American politics – driven by an (un)holy alliance of free-market economists, fundamentalist preachers, militant attacks on feminism and gay rights, moral fundamentalists challenging abortion legislation and cadres of anonymous pressure groups – delivered the presidency to the ageing film actor Ronald Reagan. 'I don't know how anybody can serve in public office without being an actor,' Reagan once confided to fellow actor Warren Beatty, and at least in that superficial sense he arrived on the White House stage to bring gloss to a tarnished America. His inauguration was based on nostalgia for a different era: his hand rested on the family Bible and his committee had secured the services of

Frank Sinatra and Dean Martin, the grandfathers of the Rat Pack era. During the inaugural luncheon, Reagan shrewdly stole the show by breaking the news that fifty-two American hostages seized from the US embassy in Tehran had been released – shameless credit-grabbing, given that much of the work had been done by diplomats and intermediaries from the outgoing Carter administration. 'With thanks to Almighty God,' Reagan declared, 'I have been given a tag line, the get-off line that everyone wants for the end of a toast or a speech, or anything else. Some 30 minutes ago, the planes bearing our prisoners left Iranian air space and are now free of Iran.' It was preposterous theatre but it ignited a wave of patriotism across America that buoyed his first one hundred days in office. Yellow ribbons tied on trees, town halls festooned with 'Welcome Home' banners and front lawns graced with the star-spangled banner demonstrated America's support for the hostages and perhaps a long-buried need for national pride that no longer felt obliged to apologise for Vietnam or Watergate.

The surge of public patriotism had networks fighting over the rights to broadcast the dawn of Reagan's presidency. On 19 January 1981, ABC broadcast a special called *The All-Star Inaugural Gala*, which was so imbued with showbiz and old-fashioned glamour that MC Johnny Carson was brought in to host. 'This is the first administration to have a premiere,' he quipped, promising the audience at home an evening of entertainment with one foot firmly planted in the nostalgic, family-friendly fifties. Contemporary music was conspicuously absent as the near-septuagenarian President applauded equally old performers: Ethel Merman (73) belting out old show tunes; Jimmy Stewart (72) praising his old Hollywood pal; and Bob Hope (77) telling carefully weighted jokes ('He doesn't know how to lie, exaggerate or cheat – he always had an agent for that.'). Reagan was sworn in as president the next day, with 41.8 million viewers watching at home. Although his second inaugural gala boasted Ray Charles performing 'America The Beautiful' with a booming choir, his first was almost entirely white and lost in time.

Reagan's take on entertainment was culturally conservative. His inaugural shows revealed how oblivious he was to the emergent music of the era he lived in – rock, punk, garage, soul, disco, rap and hip-hop. But much more difficult to obscure with patriotic fervour were the dire circumstances of those at the bottom rung of the American dream, including the now-restless young tribes of the South Bronx. A hip-hop track was about to go global and become the definitive rap record of the Reagan presidency. It was a track that carried its streetwise values proudly in both its title and lyrics. Grandmaster Flash and the Furious Five's 'The Message' (Sugar Hill, 1982), featuring Melle Mel and Duke Bootee, redirected hip-hop into new and strident territory. The original party raps that had in the main been based on fantasy lifestyles of cash-money, sexual prowess and self-aggrandisement were given a rude awakening by a form of political commentary more armipotent than anything CNN would allow on air.

Like all great records, the truth behind its recording is not quite as simple as the credits suggest. It was put together by a ragged assembly of studio musicians, some of whom were around in the New Jersey studio scene when 'Attica Massacre' was recorded a decade before. Executive producer Sylvia Robinson, whose recording career stretched back to Harlem doo-wop in the fifties, had identified a series of popular nightclub records that she felt would enrich a funk backing track, among them Zapp's 'More Bounce To The Ounce' (1979) and Tom Tom Club's 'Genius Of Love' (1981). One of the studio musicians, Doug Wimbish, added tones from Brian Eno and David Byrne's *My Life In The Bush Of Ghosts*. But what really stood out was the lyrical battering ram of social protest told from the perspective of a man and his family trapped in the crack epidemic of the Reagan era. By its own admission it was music close to the edge, packed full of pop-culture references and desperate poverty witnessed by a man on the brink of becoming a vigilante.

The social journalism behind 'The Message' was crafted by Edward Fletcher aka Duke Bootee. The idea emerged one night in the basement of his mother's home in the impoverished city streets of Elizabeth, New Jersey. Fletcher was from a lower-middle-class family, his father Ernest a truancy officer and his mother Helen an elementary school teacher, but what encroached their home was the kind of deprivation that came to define ghetto life under Reagan. Fletcher was smoking a joint with a friend and fellow musician, Clifton 'Jiggs' Chase, when he began to jot down imagery he saw in the streets outside as they surrendered to poverty and a drug epidemic.

Initially this kind of realism baffled Grandmaster Flash and his crew. 'It was just too serious,' Melle Mel told *Uncut* magazine in 2013. 'We were making party tracks, y'know, and wanted to keep in the same lane. Nobody wanted that song.' Melle Mel eventually caved in to studio pressure and hinted threats from Sylvia Robinson. He contributed a final verse to 'The Message' and shared rapping duties with Fletcher, who also played all the instruments except guitar. As a rapper, Fletcher's haunting baritone voice registered an ice-cool impassivity that stood out in a genre mostly associated with bravado and flash. 'The Message' is the record that best captures the interface between two kinds of breakdown: the collapse of urban society and its impact on mental health.

The song was an instant hit. In years to come, it would be sampled nearly 300 times up to and beyond the day when the song's composer left the music industry while still a young man. The money from touring and the income from Fletcher's epic rap was not worth the hassle of travelling and time spent away from his family, so he returned to what he often described as 'the family business': teaching. He secured master's degrees in media studies from the New School and in education from Rutgers University. He briefly worked as a teacher in a juvenile detention centre and then spent the last decade of his career as a lecturer in Critical Thinking & Communication at Savannah State University in Georgia.

Through Fletcher's dystopian vision and his persistence with the Young Turks of the Furious Five, hip-hop went on to take sides throughout much of the eighties, declaring the Reagan administration an enemy of the inner city and working against the improvement of black communities. Melvin Glover aka Melle Mel, the rapper who featured with Fletcher on 'The Message', was among many who tried to reposition the track as the years passed. 'It wasn't necessarily even a hip-hop song,' Mel Melle told the music writer Damien Love. 'People compared it with Bob Dylan, with Stevie Wonder's "Living For The City", with The Temptations' "Masterpiece". Great songs with the same bloodline. It was bigger than Grandmaster Flash & The Furious Five. It was bigger than hip-hop. It was everybody's song.'

It was the ultimate message.

Ice-T poses with local police outside Dunbar High School in Chicago, in November 1988.

7

'COP KILLER' AND THE COLD DEAD HANDS

Listen Up: 'Rebel Of The Underground' by 2Pac (1991)

In July 2020, an auction house based in Baltimore sold a video camera owned by a self-employed plumber named George Holliday. It was a Sony Handycam, which, at the time of its purchase in early 1991, was cutting-edge technology for amateur filmmakers. But what made Holliday's camera special was that he had used it fortuitously to record a Los Angeles police patrol unit savagely beating a man in the street outside his apartment. The events that followed ravaged a city, brought the LAPD into global disrepute, affected the presidential election and dragged hip-hop into a bitter argument about the power of music to influence young people.

The auctioneers considered the camera a piece of American social history. Maybe not as significant as the Bell & Howell 8mm movie camera with which the Dallas hobbyist Abraham Zapruder captured the assassination of John F. Kennedy in Dealey Plaza, but a collectible item nonetheless. The catalogue described the lot item as follows:

> Although the public had seen examples of police violence before, most notably many years prior during the sixties, those images were most often taken, edited and curated by professional news outlets, and at the time of 1991 seemed a distant memory. Nothing so raw as unedited, uncontrolled video taken by a regular citizen had ever before been witnessed by the public all over the world, confirming what many argued was commonplace in their communities. What resulted was a firestorm, with the video taken that night not only leading to the 1992 Los Angeles riots a year later when the officers were acquitted, but also laying the groundwork for the anti-police brutality movements such as Black Lives Matter that are so relevant today.

The bidding opened at $225,000 and the camera was bought for an undisclosed sum by a private collector.

On the fateful night, Holliday was awoken around 1 a.m. by the sound of a helicopter. The police had been chasing Rodney King, a suspected drunk driver, who was in his car with two other men on a Los Angeles freeway, reaching speeds of up to 160kmh. The chase came to a dramatic and brutal end in front of Holliday's apartment. He went out onto his balcony to look, and when he saw police he grabbed the camera and recorded the scene. No one showed much interest until Holliday contacted a local television station, KTLA, which broadcasts across urban Los Angeles. When they showed the raw footage, it ignited a controversy that virtually consumed the LAPD and led to the arrest of four police officers. It was their use of excessive force and acquittal on state criminal charges that poured gasoline on already fragile community relations, prompting riots that lasted six days and resulted in 63 deaths and 2,383 people injured.

The intersection of Normandie and Florence was the epicentre of the uprising. The first reports of violence, cans and bottles being thrown at passing cars, were reported via 911 calls about two hours after the verdict. Dozens of police officers attended the scene but they were quickly outnumbered and ordered to withdraw.

A day into the riots, the *Washington Post* reporter Lou Cannon described an unfolding nightmare: 'The nation's second largest city became a war zone tonight . . . [a] pall of acrid smoke from hundreds of fires hung over the Los Angeles basin, closing all but one runway at Los Angeles International Airport . . . at least 35 fires sent towering plumes of smoke into the air in a scene reminiscent of Kuwait's burning oil fields after the Iraqi invasion.'

As Los Angeles burned, President George H. W. Bush was forced to send in 1,000 federal law officers trained in urban policing and 4,500 military troops from bases in Monterey and Oceanside, California. The presence of armed National Guards ringing shopping centres helped to prevent a recurrence of the looting and arson that characterised the first two days of trouble and residents gradually began sweeping up in ransacked neighbourhoods. Bush said the violence in Los Angeles was 'not about civil rights' or 'the great issues of equality' but 'the brutality of a mob, pure and simple'. Those words were not universally well received but the President also admitted that he understood the anger of those who could not reconcile the not-guilty verdict with the videotape footage.

The Los Angeles riots served as a reminder to modern America that the injustice that had underpinned the urban rebellions of the late sixties and devasted Detroit and Newark had not yet healed.

Subsequently, two officers were convicted on federal civil rights charges and sentenced to prison, and a jury in a civil case awarded Rodney King $3.8 million in damages. Beneath the stark narrative of tension between heavily armed police and alienated youth was another storyline, that of fractured relationships setting one community against another. In Detroit, a gulf of misunderstanding had been allowed to open between young African American teenagers, often the sons and grandsons of the Great Migration, and the Eastern European immigrants who either owned local shops or had come to populate the ranks of an embattled and unsophisticated police force. In Los Angeles, by 1992, amidst a crack cocaine epidemic similar tensions crackled between Hispanic and African American youth and a recalcitrant police force as well as a wave of new Korean immigrants who had set up businesses across the tense South Side. This multi-faceted story would persist in the years to come, as brutally ill-conceived policing led to nearly 1,000 people being killed by law enforcement officers in 2019, two years into Donald Trump's divisive presidency.

Back in the mid eighties, the success of the New York-based hip-hop label Def Jam Recordings brought together two of America's outlaw genres: rap and hard rock. One record came to symbolise the cacophony – Run-DMC's radical reworking of an old Aerosmith song 'Walk This Way'. The song unexpectedly became a massive hit on rock radio networks, on college stations and on urban radio. It was one of a kind, seemingly challenging the strict parameters that had once separated musical styles into racial demographics. The record opened a floodgate. The cable television network MTV had since 1981 been largely a rock and pop station with next to no coverage of emergent black music. Those attitudes were changing, and with the arrival of *Yo! MTV Raps* in 1988 teenagers across America were regularly exposed to urban sounds and to rock-rap crossover. Nor had 'Walk This Way' been a one-off. The archaeology of rap showed that even the first generation of hip-hop DJs had reworked rock riffs, with Grandmaster Flash using Queen's 'Another One Bites The Dust' and Edgar Broughton Band's 'Apache Drop Out' as the backbone of his sets.

East Coast hip-hop culture and the subcultures of African American teenage life came face to face with full-throttle tabloid journalism in what became known as the 'wilding' controversy. On the night of 19 April 1989, a white twenty-eight-year-old investment banker named Trisha Meili was bludgeoned and raped while jogging along the 102nd Street Cross Drive of Central Park. The attack provoked a media frenzy which led to the wrongful arrest of five teenage boys. African American and Latino and from the projects north of the park, they had been running wild or 'wilding' in the northern arteries of Central Park. In many overheated press reports, hip-hop was portrayed as part of the problem and as the frenzy to convict the 'Central Park Five' grew a racially skewed moral panic gripped New York. Four of the boys were sentenced to five-to-ten years in a youth correctional facility and the fifth boy (16-year-old Korey Wise) was sentenced to five-to-fifteen years in an adult prison. It has since transpired that all five were wrongfully charged and that the actual perpetrator, who eventually confessed, was Matias Reyes, a lone rapist who was known to the police and whose DNA was linked directly to the crime. *New York* magazine reported the wider social context: 'Nineteen eighty-nine was near the apex of escalating crime rates (nearly 2,000 people murdered, a record eclipsed the following year), underfunded social services, brazen muggings on graffiti-emblazoned subways, skyrocketing drug use thanks to the infusion of crack cocaine, and a police force that seemed helpless to do much about any of it.'

The popular press seemed determined to cast hip-hop as a cult of criminality, a cue that was not lost on ambitious politicians. As the compass of rap wavered westwards, the city of Compton, lying between south Los Angeles and Long Beach, became another focal point for public outrage. Once a beacon of black success in the fifties, Compton had come to symbolise urban despair, a victim of the lack of inner-city investment at the height of the Vietnam War and then of deeper cuts in public funding under Reaganomics. In early 1987, a local rap group N.W.A. (Niggaz Wit Attitudes) had recorded their first studio album, *Straight Outta Compton*. Overseen by a local street entrepreneur Eric Wright, better known by his rap moniker Eazy-E, the venture was originally forged in his parents' garage and hard-wired to the street, with resonances back to the early provocations of punk band the Sex Pistols. The album was produced by N.W.A members Dr. Dre, DJ Yella and Arabian Prince, with lyrics written by Ice Cube and MC Ren, and brought a new generation of artists to the fore, melding raw ideas with carefully contrived slogans. Two specific tracks – 'Gangsta Gangsta' and 'Fuck Tha Police' – became destined for greater notoriety: the first gave a name to the emerging hardcore rap music and the second provoked a controversy with the authorities that would ignite in the riotous days to come. Much like the South Bronx ten years earlier, hip-hop was still perceived to be in a ghetto far from the riches of modern America.

As Compton became a new epicentre for hip-hop, the riots that engulfed L.A. became, in a perverse way, a form of social marketing that kindled interest in what was now known as gangsta rap. In 1991, a year before the riots, rapper Ice-T was putting down the early tracks on his fourth album, *O.G. Original Gangster*. He had spent his teenage days at Crenshaw High School, a hardcore school that was something of a rap conveyor belt, producing Schoolboy Q, Michael G and Left Brain. It was with former school friends from Crenshaw that he recorded the noisy guitar-rich track 'Body Count'. In rehearsal they forged such a powerful relationship that they decided to form a band and tour local clubs as Body Count.

Guitar rock was not a wholly original idea. New York guitarist Vernon Reid had already formed his rock band Living Colour and, subsequently, the artists' collective Black Rock Coalition; Nona Hendryx of the Philadelphia soul group Patti LaBelle and the Bluebelles had broken decisively with the sound of sixties soul and moved into progressive hard rock; and further north in Minneapolis, virtuoso Prince had completed his Sign o' the Times tour and was poised to become the most revered guitarist in the world. This alliance of styles helped revolutionise hip-hop. Simon Price, writing for the *Guardian*, described the heavily rotated video for Run-DMC's 'Walk This Way' as the moment that brought hip-hop into almost every American household: 'The two bands – the sleazy old rock slags and the box-fresh rap crew – are rehearsing in adjacent rooms and engaged in a loudness war, but join forces when Tyler literally smashes down the wall between the two rooms/races/genres, and the two groups storm a theatre stage to the delight of screaming fans.'

Although Ice-T was saturated in the dominant subculture of rap, there were others within his family and at school who listened to hard-rock radio and had become bewitched by the noise of the big guitar bands such as Led Zeppelin, Black Sabbath and the Edgar Winter Group. It was Winter's third album *They Only Come Out At Night* and the hit single 'Frankenstein' that gave a clue to what was going on. This was the meeting of two renegade youth cultures whom wider society saw as grotesque. In the eyes of parents, and in particular white American parents, the merging of street-level rap and thrash metal was toxic. What was not recognised was that both were drawing on fantasy: slasher movies, horror comics, computer games and a lurid imagination forged by popular fiction and real-crime documentaries.

Although he became one of the key figures of the West Coast rap scene, Ice-T moved as a child to Summit, New Jersey, on the western outskirts of Newark. Born Tracy Lauren Marrow in 1958, he took his new name from Iceberg Slim, an American pimp who became an influential author writing ghetto-based novels of the nightclub underclass. Marrow lost his mother when he was in the third grade and then his father when he was 13, both to sudden heart attacks. He then moved west to live with his aunt in South Central L.A. and grew up in one of the warring ganglands where the Bloods and the Crips pursued a deadly rivalry. By the age of 17 he had left home and earned money selling weed and stolen car stereos before joining the US military. He spent time in a military jail for theft and going AWOL, then worked down his last two years before receiving an honourable discharge in 1979. On his return to the streets of South Central he entered the trade – a life of crime that included pimping, robbing jewellery stores and running illegal dance nights.

Ice-T grew up in an era and in a city where the prison population was growing out of all recognition. Nixon had kick-started the problem, declaring a 'war on drugs' and justifying it with speeches about being 'tough on crime', but it was during Reagan's administration that rates of incarceration grew exponentially, much of it due to increased punishment of low-level drug crime. In 1980, drug offences accounted for 22 per cent of all federal prison admissions. By 1988 the figure had escalated to 39 per cent and by 1992, the year of the Los Angeles riots and the subsequent presidential election, a staggering 58 per cent of all federal prisoners were drug offenders. Reagan was a passionate advocate of the privatisation of government programmes and services, including prisons. During his time in office the prison population essentially doubled, to 627,000, and the rise in incarceration disproportionately hit young Latino and African American men. Incarceration entrapped the generation that, like Ice-T, were most likely to associate with the gangsta-rap subculture. Some of the major names of what was fast becoming a nationally recognised talent base were either in prison or recently released, including Coolio, Warren G and Snoop Dogg. The prison style – no belt, low-hanging jeans, workwear shirts and tattooed torsos – became absorbed into gangsta rap, as did a tendency to overstate criminality. Many of the exponents of the rap scene in South Central L.A., Houston and Miami embellished their past deeds to upgrade their streetwise status, to the extent that there are few who do not claim to have been drug kingpins or pimps. It is not to say that a subculture wildly prone to self-invention was not punctuated by unscrupulous criminals. Marion Hugh 'Suge' Knight was the former owner of the notorious Death Row Records and managed the release of the label's first two albums: Dr. Dre's genre debut *The Chronic* in 1992 and Snoop Dogg's *Doggystyle* in 1993, which sold 800,000 copies in its first week. From the late nineties into the early noughties, Knight spent a few years incarcerated for assault convictions and associated violations of probation and parole. He dragooned gangsters to intimidate rivals and to add threats to his business dealings, and in September 2018, he pleaded no contest to voluntary manslaughter in a hit-and-run three years earlier. Knight was sentenced to twenty-eight years in prison and is not likely to become eligible for parole until July 2037.

Ice-T told the magazine *Metal Hammer*:

> I grew up in the days of Black Sabbath and Dio and all that kind of stuff
> . . . And I liked it. I liked the energy, and I liked the fact that it was
> hardcore: 'This shit is crazy'. They're just trying to scare the shit out of
> people, right? So, we asked the question: what's scarier than a fucking
> gun in your face? The Devil? Fuck that – how about a .357 [Magnum]?
> And that's why in the Body Count album, when you open it up, all of
> sudden someone's pointing a gun at ya. We could have dealt with
> sacrifices and all that shit, but [we said] let's deal with real fear. My
> whole thing was that when Body Count hits the stage, we take you in
> to the hood; we take you into our environment, our fears, our drama.
> And fortunately, a lot of people understood it.

Although Ice-T was already well established on the hip-hop circuit, his band Body Count had to gain their spurs as a live show. The group played at local bars and clubs and then were given a lift-up when they agreed to tour with Kurt Brecht's Houston-based thrash band, the Dirty Rotten Imbeciles. Throughout much of 1991, Ice-T and Body Count joined the inaugural Lollapalooza tour, fronted by Jane's Addiction and featuring Siouxsie and the Banshees, Living Colour, Butthole Surfers, Violent Femmes and Fishbone. With no significant reaction, Ice-T performed one of the main tracks from the *Body Count* album, the fantasy rap track 'Cop Killer'.

The song was a reworking of 'Psycho Killer' by Talking Heads, which dared to go inside the mind of a serial killer. *Kerrang* described the song as not a rap song at all but a revenge-fantasy rock record: 'Over an adrenalised thrashing punk rhythm that picked up where Anthrax and Public Enemy left off on "Bring the Noise", Ice-T delivers a revenge fantasy where someone pushed to the brink by unfettered police brutality decides to take matters into their own hands.' Ice-T later explained the track's genesis to *Kerrang*:

> I was in rehearsals singing 'Psycho Killer,' by Talking Heads, and my drummer Beatmaster V, rest in peace, said we need a cop killer, He's like, 'Cops are out there killing people, doing their bullshit, and getting away with it.' And this is before Rodney King, but it was happening in the hood – we knew it and we felt it. He's like, 'Motherfuckers need to start taking off on the cops.' So, I thought of a character, like, what if somebody snapped and went after them? And that's where the lyrics come from; I just started imagining if somebody went over the edge based on cop killings. You know, better you than me, I'm not gonna let you kill me.

Body Count were blithely unaware of the furore the track would cause and the strange role it would play in the 1992 presidential election, a three-way battle between the incumbent President George H. W. Bush, the Democratic Party candidate Bill Clinton and the Texas billionaire Ross Perot. Bush's ratings nosedived as a result of the riots in Los Angeles, the economic fallout of eleven years of Reaganomics and a failing 'war on drugs'. The administration needed a scapegoat, something that could be blamed and would bring traditional Republican voters back into the fold. The bogeyman that the spin doctors identified as most likely to get Middle America hot and bothered was gangsta rap.

The *Body Count* album came out in March 1992 to no great fanfare or controversy and included songs in which the singer murders his own mother and impregnates the daughter of a Ku Klux Klan Grand Wizard. It was fantastical, a weird mix of thrash, punk and doom-laden metal. Many critics immediately saw it for what it was: a parody of extremes. It was the politics of an election year that gave 'Cop Killer' its salience. Almost overnight it went from being an irrelevance to the most controversial song in presidential history. Many who had not followed the chronology of events accused Ice-T and Body Count of jumping on the bandwagon after the Rodney King verdict and profiteering on anti-police sentiment. However, the release date of the offending album preceded the court ruling by two months and the 'Cop Killer' track had been written as far back as 1990, and performed nightly during a national tour in 1991. 'Cop Killer' was neither unique nor uniquely provocative, but it came at a high point in a national debate about censorship that had gripped popular music for several years.

Tipper Gore, wife of future Vice President Al Gore, had since 1985 been a prominent advocate of the censorship of rock and rap music. She would argue – with some merit – that her campaigning organisation, the Parents Music Resource Centre (PMRC), was pressing for more accurate classification of records, to help parents assess what was appropriate for children to listen to. It was an idea that angered artists within the music industry and led to a dramatic hearing before the Senate Commerce, Science and Transportation Committee, where a panel listened to a debate on what some groups insist is record-album pornography. *The New York Times* reported:

> Hundreds of people waited outside for scarce seats. Inside, hundreds more watched rock videos – hearing four-letter words that were headed into a Congressional hearing transcript for perhaps the first time – and heard a debate that touched on whether the First Amendment gives free-speech rights to partly clad, long-haired rockers who sing about sex, sadomasochism, suicide, murder and other things.

Senator Ernest F. Hollings, a Democrat from South Carolina, told the panel that the music they were adjudicating on was 'outrageous filth and we must do something about it', insisting that 'if I could find some way constitutionally to get rid of it, I would'.

As well as Tipper Gore, the PMRC, often nicknamed the 'Washington Wives', was founded by Susan Baker, the wife of Treasury Secretary James Baker; Sally Nevius, the second wife of the head of Washington D.C.'s City Council, a self-declared Republican WASP, John Nevius; and Pam Howar, the wife of a wealthy real-estate agent in the District. They all lived within the Washington Beltway and all had young teenage children. Although they led a high-profile campaign to get records withdrawn from the market, their most successful proposal was for the music industry to develop labelling in the form of a rating system like the one that already existed within cinema. Among the PMRC's other proposals were printing warnings and lyrics on album covers, forcing record stores to put albums with explicit covers beneath the counter, or wrap them in plain brown wrappers. They pressurised television stations not to broadcast explicit songs or videos, and – most controversially within the music industry – demanded a reassessment of the contracts of musicians who performed violently or sexually in concert.

As a part of their lobbying campaign, the Washington Wives drew up a list of songs they claimed were unacceptable. Known colloquially as the 'Filthy Fifteen', the chart included songs by Judas Priest, Sheena Easton, Madonna and AC/DC. Subject matter ran the full gamut from fellatio at gunpoint to satanic abduction and sexualising a schoolteacher. Much of it, like Ice-T's 'Cop Killer', was exaggerated fiction with barely credible X-rated characters. The chart was topped by Prince's 'Darling Nikki' (1984), a track that Tipper Gore overheard her 11-year-old daughter Karenna listening to at home. A lyric about 'masturbating with a magazine' caught Gore's attention and provoked her into discussing music and sexuality with her friends.

The panel discussing the classification of pop and rock music stands out as one of the truly memorable if bizarre moments in the story of Capitol Hill. The venerable *Washington Post*, more familiar with covering arcane political arguments, reported the hearings with a disbelieving tone:

> A circus atmosphere pervaded the Russell Senate Office Building, with rock fans and foes angling for the few available seats. Hundreds more lined the halls as the recording industry, which recently agreed to voluntarily label records with a generic warning about explicit lyrics, got its wrist slapped for doing too little too late.

Among the rock 'fans' in attendance were country-folk songwriter John Denver, Dee Snyder of Twisted Sister, and the high priest of avant-garde rock Frank Zappa. Zappa began by reading the First Amendment and proceeded to argue that the proposal to rate or label rock records was:

an ill-conceived piece of nonsense which fails to deliver any real benefits to children, infringes on the civil liberties of people who are not children and promises to keep the courts busy for years, dealing with the interpretational and enforcemental problems inherent in the proposal's design. Taken as a whole, the complete list of PMRC demands reads like an instruction manual for some sinister kind of 'toilet training program' to housebreak all composers and performers because of the lyrics of a few. Ladies, how dare you.

He went on to call the PMRC demands 'the equivalent of treating dandruff with decapitation' and then mocked 'trade-restricting legislation whipped up like an instant pudding by the Wives of Big Brother'.

The PMRC enjoyed limited success. By the end of the year, all sides agreed that the Recording Industry Association of America would voluntarily put 'Parental Advisory' labels on albums it determined needed them. The 'Explicit Lyrics' stickers began to appear on new albums, but it was a pyrrhic victory. Bands and their record labels used the warnings as a promotional device, enticing curious fans to buy albums that promised to take musical content way beyond decency.

There was a controlling and paternalistic mood in the air. In January 1990, an anti-obscenity activist named Jack Thompson sent letters to Janet Reno, then a Dade County State Attorney and yet to become the US Attorney General under Bill Clinton, claiming that Miami-based hip-hop group 2 Live Crew's album *As Nasty As They Wanna Be* was illegal and obscene. The album certainly sailed beyond euphemism with songs like 'Me So Horny' and 'The Fuck Shop'. Thompson called for an investigation into whether the album violated obscenity statutes. Following a local judge's ruling that there was 'probable cause to believe' the album was obscene, Thompson pushed his campaign forward and sent lyrics from the album to sheriffs' departments across the state. Members of the group were arrested for performing songs from their album after a performance at Club Futura in Hollywood, Florida, all broadcast on local Miami TV. This triggered support from the organisation which became known as 'Rock the Vote'. Madonna filmed one of its public service announcements, to catalyse voting in that year's mid-term elections, cleverly adapting the rap in her song 'Vogue' into a plea for freedom of speech.

The following January, a jury acquitted 2 Live Crew and, according to the *Miami Herald*, the war against explicit rap had come to an end 'like a freight train finally running out of steam'. Or so it seemed until the presidential election ignited new passion about law and order. The Combined Law Enforcement Associations of Texas launched a campaign against 'Cop Killer', claiming it was incitement to murder and urged a boycott against Time Warner, whose subsidary, Warner Brothers, distributed the album on its Sire label. Other police bodies lent their support. Dennis Martin, the former president of the National Association of Chiefs of Police, without offering too much by way of detail, claimed that the song had encouraged violence against the police. 'The "Cop Killer" song has been implicated in at least two shooting incidents,' he claimed, 'and has inflamed racial tensions across the country . . . It is an affront to the officers – one hundred and forty-four in 1992 alone – who have been killed in the line of duty.' In a polemical essay, Martin described rap as 'the music of murder' and Ice-T as an artist who had flagrantly abused his rights under the First Amendment. Ice-T retaliated, astutely pointing out that the song was written in the style of a fictional character: 'If you believe that I'm a cop killer, you believe David Bowie is an astronaut.' Others jumped to his defence, asking why there had been no such outcry when Eric Clapton sang the Bob Marley song 'I Shot The Sheriff'. Was it because he didn't shoot the deputy?

Over the coming months the protests intensified. Some police departments exerted pressure on local businesses to withdraw the *Body Count* album from sale. In Greensboro, North Carolina, one store stopped stocking it after being told by local police that 911 emergency calls to police and fire would be ignored if they continued to sell the album. In the noise that grew around the record Ice-T had precious few supporters in either politics or law enforcement. Only Ronald Hampton, the executive director of the National Black Police Association, representing 35,000 black officers, refused to participate in the Time Warner boycott. 'This song is not a call for murder,' Hampton said. 'It's a rap of protest. Ice-T isn't just making this stuff up. He's expressing his concerns about police misconduct. He's responding to a very real issue that affects many Americans, especially blacks and Latinos: police brutality.' It was a lone voice drowned out by moral panic.

Still the battle raged. Houston City Council passed a resolution denouncing Time Warner for distributing the record and the Los Angeles City Council responded to a boycott motion introduced by Joan Flores, a Republican candidate in the 36th Congressional District insisting that certain records be hidden from view.

Robert M. Teeter, Chief Political Strategist of George H. W. Bush's presidential campaign, seized the opportunity. He had run an Ann Arbor-based corporate consulting firm and for twenty years had built his reputation as a pollster with the Detroit-based firm Market Opinion Research. He was portrayed in the media as something of a guru, with a finely tuned understanding of public moods, and had taken the role of being the 'thematic orchestrator' of Bush's campaign. One of Teeter's concerns was that Ross Perot was dragging voters away from the Republicans and was acting as what they considered to be a 'spoiler'. It was Teeter who argued that the Bush campaign needed to combat this by swaying further to the right, especially on the tried and tested subject of law and order. The controversy around 'Cop Killer' came ready-formed and landed in the laps of the Bush campaign.

Late in June 1992, already trailing Clinton in the polls, President Bush opened the Drug Enforcement Administration's new Manhattan office and used the opportunity to recite his administration's achievements in the 'war on drugs' and attack Ice-T, calling him 'sick' and castigating Time Warner for profiting from 'Cop Killer'. 'I don't care how noble the name of the company; it is wrong for any company to issue records that approve of killing law enforcement officers,' he said. His words on the campaign trail amplified the controversy and the full weight of judgemental America descended on the shoulders of Ice-T. In his biography, *Ice*, he described being overwhelmed by becoming a target of state-inspired pressure: 'I tell people today that you don't know what heat is until you've had the President of the United States say your name in anger. Because the minute he does – *boom* – the deepest security check of your life immediately goes into action. The FBI, the Secret Service, the IRS, everybody gets into the game.'

Although it never attracted the same level of attention, a counter-argument to the 'Cop Killer' controversy was also growing. *The New York Times* pointed out that one of Bush's top supporters was the actor Arnold Schwarzenegger, whose character in the movies *Terminator* and

© Courtesy of author

Ice-T fanning the flames of the 'Cop Killer' controversy on the cover of *Rolling Stone*.

Terminator 2: Judgment Day kills or maims dozens of policemen. Others pointed to the wide range of pop songs and movies that starred fictional killers, from John Wayne to the sharp-shooting marshal Frame Johnson in the 1953 movie *Law and Order*, played by former president Ronald Reagan. But at the end of the day, notoriety sells records. Like punk rock before it, 'Cop Killer' became a must-have sound. Sales of *Body Count* leaped 370 per cent across the USA, and in Texas, where the protests started, sales more than doubled in Austin, San Antonio and Dallas. Sire Records stoked controversy when they issued a special edition in promotional body bags.

To his credit Ice-T was no shrinking violet. 'I think cops should feel threatened,' he said in June 1992, at a panel event before delivering the keynote address at the New Music Seminar being held at New York's Marriott Marquis Hotel. 'I feel threatened. I grew up threatened. They should know that they can't take a life without retaliation.' But in the barrage of criticism, Ice-T made the decision to withdraw the album and have it repressed without the offending track. He hit on another promotional stunt, releasing 'Cop Killer' as a single to be given out free at concerts. Time Warner backed the record, citing Ice-T's right to freedom of expression, while he calmly pointed out in numerous interviews that the song's target was not the police in general, but racist and corrupt officers who abused their positions. However, following death threats to label employees, Ice-T announced his decision to withdraw 'Cop Killer' from the market.

By mid July 1992, the thermostat soared. At a Time Warner shareholder meeting the veteran actor Charlton Heston stood up and commanded the room, describing himself as a 'private citizen' who felt obliged to speak out about *Body Count*. To describe himself as a private citizen was disingenuous: he was a world-famous name and a prominent supporter of numerous right-wing causes, including Ronald Reagan's presidency. He would go on to become a five-term president of the National Rifle Association (NRA), from 1998 to 2003. Fighting new gun legislation and defending the right to bear arms became the defining crusade of Heston's later life and at the NRA's 129th convention he held up a replica Revolutionary War-era flintlock rifle and announced that if the government wanted to confiscate the gun, they'd have to take it from his 'cold, dead hands'. Heston told the Time Warner meeting that he was not criticising Ice-T, whom he said was 'trying for his fifteen minutes of fame'. But then he turned to Time Warner's assembled board of directors and said, 'I condemn instead the responsible officials in this company.' His venom was principally aimed at company president Gerald Levin, who was chairing the meeting in place of Steven

J. Ross, absent for health reasons. Levin proved to be a robust defender of Ice-T's artistic freedom, saying:

> It is not a call for anti-police violence. If the lyrics aren't lifted out of the context of Ice-T's work, if you listen to the different voice he takes on, the different characters he plays, if you hear the different messages he gives – against drugs, and gang violence, and racism – it's clear that what the artist is doing is depicting the despair and anger that hang in the air of every American inner city.

It was a nuanced argument that fell on deaf ears.

Bush and his campaign team had brought law and order screeching onto the electoral agenda. It is a subject that rightward-leaning politicians feel comfortable talking about and there are few votes to be won tolerating or psychologically excusing cop killers. Unintentionally, Ice-T had also racialised the subject of inner-city policing. Gangsta rap became a kind of 'trigger terminology' frequently used by newspaper editors and talk show hosts as coded shorthand for street criminality and a generation of young African Americans the Republican campaign could characterise as beyond the reach of conventional society. What they also did was to cast hip-hop as a narrow, lawless and emotionally ugly genre, thereby wholly misrepresenting the diverse threads that were now part of the rich tapestry of urban music.

From the outset, hip-hop had a strong comedic element as parody artists like the Fat Boys and even the pioneering Sugarhill Gang often played for feelgood laughs as much as for street credibility. Fly girls like Roxanne Shante and Salt-N-Pepa, a group formed by two trainee community nurses who met at college in Queens, paved the way for a surge of female artists which eventually influenced soul singers such as Mary J. Blige and Beyoncé Knowles. Then there were creatively outstanding groups like De La Soul, who were members of the Native Tongues collective alongside the Jungle Brothers, Queen Latifah and A Tribe Called Quest, and invented a hip-hop tone that the *Guardian* described as 'an Afrocentric, boho bent with a nerdy, recording room exuberance that was all their own'. To this day, their debut album *3 Feet High And Rising* (1989) is a hip-hop masterpiece, far removed from the street nihilism of gangsta rap. Even when De La Soul resorted to guns on the track 'Millie Pulled A Pistol On Santa', it was to tell the story of a girl who takes revenge on her sexually abusive father who is working a seasonal job as Santa at a department store.

Hip-hop was blessed much more by its creative differences than it was marred by violence but that was buried beneath the over-emotional hype. At the height of the 1992 presidential election, when the 'Cop Killer' controversy was front page-news, the biggest-selling hip-hop act was Arrested Development. Formed in Atlanta in as an antidote to gangsta rap, the group's origins were on the campus of University of Wisconsin–Milwaukee in 1988. Their debut album *3 Years, 5 Months and 2 Days in the Life Of...* was profoundly influenced by the politics of peace and reconciliation, but few if any politicians were listening. The stand-out songs on the album, 'Tennessee' and 'Mr. Wendal', were forged by vastly different observations. 'Tennessee' was written by Todd Thomas aka Speech after he reunited with his brother at their grandmother's funeral in Tennessee. A short time later, his brother died suddenly from an asthma attack and themes of grief and childhood memories bind the song together. The powerful promotional video shot in the stark social-realist style of the great FSA photographer Dorothea Lange resonates through the genealogy of a family and its days in the Deep South. In contrast, 'Mr. Wendal' is about homelessness and the invisibility of the song's central character, who is eking out an existence eating discarded food and sleeping in homeless shelters. Again, it has a dignity and generosity that was largely absent from some of the less critically valued raps of the times.

There was of course a deep political paradox at the heart of the arguments against gangsta rap – gun law itself. Like Charlton Heston and the NRA, the political right had always rallied around the contentious Second Amendment of the United States Constitution, which states that 'a well-regulated Militia, being necessary to the security of a free State, the right of the people to keep and bear Arms, shall not be infringed'. What that had surreptitiously become in the minds of many gun owners was the inalienable right of white people to bear arms and the concordant belief that black gun owners were by their very nature criminals.

As the presidential election unfolded, Arkansas Governor Bill Clinton's political advisers determined that the best route to victory was to take 'a position that blended the best of each party's views but transcended them to constitute a third force in the debate'. In the case of rap music, Clinton needed to address the controversy from a position that differed from the traditional right wing. His general appeal was to people who 'work hard and play by the rules' but in trying to find a way to distance him from the gangsta culture of 'Cop Killer' his team came up with what is now referred to as his 'Sister Souljah moment', the decision taken to oppose the presence of the activist, writer and rapper Sister Souljah at a Rainbow Coalition convention organised by Jesse Jackson and PUSH.

Sister Souljah's real name is Lisa Williamson. She was born in the Bronx when the roots of hip-hop were in the air, and then relocated with her family to Englewood, New Jersey, at the age of 10. Williamson attended Dwight Morrow, a high school whose students parallel some of the key trends in popular black music. The Motown family group The Isley Brothers bussed in from the neighbouring town of Teaneck, where they ran an independent label. Ernie Isley was the writer of some of black music's most enduring songs, including 'Harvest For The World', 'That Lady' and the funk hit 'Take Me To The Next Phase'. Another Dwight Morrow student was Bernard Belle, a former guitarist with The Manhattans. He wrote songs for both Michael Jackson and Whitney Houston but is best known as one of the pioneers of what was called new jack swing, a form of fusion dance music that deployed synthesizers, sampled beats and soulful voices. His sister Regina Belle was also a graduate of Dwight Morrow and a hugely talented singer, whose quiet-storm voice gave her great crossover appeal. In June 2001, Regina performed a solo set in the East Room of the White House during a Black Music Month celebration. Her music, soul tinged with jazz and a hint of opera, was miles away from the angrier urban sounds advocated by Sister Souljah.

Irrespective of the power of her street-writing, Sister Souljah's name came to be linked to Bill Clinton's presidential ambitions. In the spring of 1992, commenting on the Los Angeles riots in *The Washington Post*, Sister Souljah said, 'If black people kill black people every day, why not have a week and kill white people?' It was a rhetorical and highly polemical question which was seized on by newspapers and radio talk shows across America. Although she was virtually unknown at the time, her question gave her a notoriety that has clung to her name ever since. Following Clinton's rebuke, Jesse Jackson criticised him for arguing that Sister Souljah's words were openly racist and comparing her to the convicted felon and Ku Klux Klan Grand Wizard, David Duke. Forced onto the defensive, Sister Souljah retaliated by saying, 'If you ask me my view, even if it's not your view, you have to handle that. Don't tell me I hurt your feelings. I'm not your kindergarten teacher.'

According to Clarence Page, a journalist for the *Chicago Tribune*, 'Tracking polls show the incident pretty much marks the upturn in Clinton's popularity that quickly took him from third place behind Ross Perot to first', where he remained until election night. Clinton turned a normally conservative call for law and order into a defining part of the Democrat campaign. 'We cannot take our country back until we take our neighbourhoods back,' he said at a speech in Houston. 'Four years ago, this crime issue was used to divide America. I want to use it to unite America. I want to be tough on crime and good for civil rights. You can't have civil justice without order and safety.' It proved a critical argument. Clinton's team claim that Sister Souljah's name came up repeatedly in the surveys and focus groups, especially those tracking the attitudes of white suburban and blue-collar swing voters. In his auto-biography *My Life*, Bill Clinton claimed it was not naked opportunism but a plea to common decency: 'Two of my most important core concerns were combating youth violence and healing racial divides. After challenging white voters all across America to abandon racism, if I kept silent on Sister Souljah I might look weak or phony.' It proved productive. Clinton was the first presidential candidate since Robert F. Kennedy in the sixties to bring southern whites, northern blue-collar workers and inner-city blacks and Hispanics together under the same political banner in substantial numbers.

Political historians now claim Clinton's victory would have been impossible were it not for his Sister Souljah moment turning round the opinion polls. It was a calculated act that underscored one of Clinton's great political skills: the art of triangulation. John Hammerschmidt, an Arkansas Republican who was one of the few politicians ever to get the better of Clinton in an election, once said, 'He's probably the best politician the world has ever seen. He has positioned himself correctly, moved towards the middle and can be all things to all people.' It was a trait that others came to see as slippery and self-serving. The historian Joseph Sobran asked: 'What does a Clinton really believe in? You might as well ask a chameleon to tell you its favourite colour.' Michael Kelly in *The New York Times* also pointed to Clinton's calculating polity: 'Clinton means what he says when he says it, but tomorrow he will mean what he says when he says the opposite. He is the existential president, living with absolute sincerity in the passing moment.'

Another factor that seemed to have influenced voters was Clinton's veneer of youth and vitality. When he was elected, he was the third-youngest President in American history, and the first baby boomer to enter the White House. One of the landmark moments in winning over younger voters was his performance on *The Arsenio Hall Show*, in which he donned Ray-Bans and played a saxophone to the surprise of millions of viewers. It was a break with the time-honoured traditions of campaigning, whereby traditional news and current affairs shows secured well-choreographed sit-down interviews with candidates. It's no secret that Clinton is a passable but limited saxophonist who laboured his way through versions of 'Heartbreak Hotel' and 'God Bless The Child', the latter written and made famous by Billie Holiday. But what was important was the parody not the perfection. Clinton had the look and the mannerisms of John Belushi and Dan Aykroyd in *The Blues Brothers*. The film had been a stepping stone on the journey of soul revivalism. It yearned for down-home R&B and raucous soul music from the sixties and seemed to want to relive life before rap. Its influence had prompted record companies to reissue their back catalogues and inspired artists to rediscover the value of doing cover versions. *The Blues Brothers* kickstarted the career of thousands of tribute acts and launched a subgenre of soul music that was played at weddings, small-town festivals and in bar rooms across America. It was the music of nostalgia, brief racial harmony and six-packs, sometimes called 'rhythm and booze'.

Bill Clinton had grown up surrounded by pop parody. For many, he embodied the characteristics of the baby boomers, that privileged generation who seemed to influence everything from marketing to elections. They were not always charming characteristics either: he had a rock star's self-centredness, which verged on narcissism, a tendency to blame others and the spoiled child's sense of entitlement. As Governor of Arkansas, Clinton had been a charismatic local politician who, according to gossip in Little Rock, had a 'zipper problem'. It was the fear of what were categorised as 'bimbo eruptions' – the retaliation of women he had screwed then dumped – that led Clinton to drop earlier plans for a presidential run in 1988. When he won in 1992, it was in large part because George H. W. Bush had lost. For all his longevity in office – Bush was a two-term vice president before assuming the top job – the successful military campaign that had pushed Saddam Hussein out of Kuwait was not enough to deflect from escalating unemployment rates and a settled public perception that he was out of touch with average Americans.

Clinton's Sister Souljah moment would not have had such an impact if it had not coincided with the dark theatre of gangsta rap, and in that playhouse Tupac Shakur was Hamlet. A slender, handsome and enigmatic young man, Tupac stood out from the crowd in asking existential questions of his audience and pushing rap to new levels of creativity. He had the words 'Thug Life' tattooed on his torso and once claimed it was an acronym for 'The Hate U Give Little Infants Fucks Everybody'. Tupac emerged at a time when gangsta rap was being widely stigmatised and accused of stoking violence and gang warfare, but he seemed to offer an alternative, the hope that his music would 'spark the brain that will change the world'. Back in the late eighties, N.W.A. had rankled the authorities with their song 'Fuck Tha Police', a powerful denunciation of police brutality in the tense streets of Compton. Tupac took the concept to a more all-embracing nihilistic rage with 'Fuck The World'. Dressing in a knotted bandana, sporting Cartier frames, a neatly trimmed beard and a nose ring, Tupac understood that popular music was about image as much as rhymes.

Tupac Shakur had led a peripatetic life. Born in New York, he lived variously in Baltimore and then San Francisco, where he collaborated with the Oakland rap group Digital Underground, before moving to Los Angeles. It was there that he gravitated towards Suge Knight's Death Row Records, a viper's nest of criminality, disputes and lethal vendettas. His debut album, *2Pacalypse Now* (1991), released for Death Row by Interscope Records, rapped about racism, police brutality, black-on-black crime and teenage pregnancy. Although it hit the streets almost exactly a year before Clinton won the presidential election, it too become embroiled in the politics of cop-killing when then Vice President Dan Quayle associated it with the murder of a Texas state trooper.

Trooper Bill Davidson was shot in the neck with a 9mm handgun after stopping a stolen car near Route 59 and Guadalupe Street in Edna, Texas. The suspect was Ronald Ray Howard, a 19-year-old high-school dropout who, according to the prosecution, was on probation for car theft. He had been driving a stolen Chevrolet Blazer when Davidson stopped the vehicle to issue a ticket for a missing headlight. Howard had been listening to *2Pacalyapse Now* in the run-up to the killing; police recovered a homemade copy of the album from the tape deck of Howard's stolen vehicle. According to a local reporter's interview with the officer's widow Linda Sue, which was syndicated across America, she said: 'There isn't a doubt in my mind that my husband would still be alive if Tupac hadn't written these violent, anti-police songs and the companies involved hadn't published and put them out on the street.' She would later seek millions of dollars in punitive damages and compensation.

The widow's civil suit attracted national media attention. *The Washington Post* wrote about the case and carried a quote from Ron DeLord, president of the Combined Law Enforcement Associations of Texas, the police group that initiated the boycott of Time Warner over Ice-T's 'Cop Killer'. 'In every other industry, companies are held liable for dangerous products they produce,' he said. 'If it's illegal to produce physical pollution, it ought to be illegal to produce mental pollution.'

Such was the coverage around the time of the murder, Vice President Dan Quayle invited Davidson's daughter Kimberly to accompany him during a campaign stop in Houston. Quayle renewed his attack on Hollywood's cultural elite, demanding – as he had two months previously with 'Cop Killer' – that Time Warner, the owners of distributor Interscope, withdraw Tupac's album from the market. 'Corporations have a responsibility to society beyond merely making money,' Quayle told the *Los Angeles Times*. 'Publishing a record condoning cop killing is an irresponsible corporate act.' Quayle's intervention unleashed yet another flurry of articles about cause-and-effect theory, which blames popular culture for the ills of the world. But it was not a one-way argument. Again, the record industry and many musicians spoke out.

'I always looked up to revolutionaries like Fred Hampton and Bobby Hutton from the Black Panthers. They weren't saying or striving for anything much different from what we are saying and striving for today. They died for that. Right in their own beds. They were so young and how could you forget that?' – Tupac Shakur, 1992.

'Imagine what a nightmare it would be if a preposterous suit like this ever succeeded in court,' Jason Berman, president of the Recording Industry Association of America argued. 'What if everyone who committed a crime could offer the defence that a record or a movie or a book influenced his actions? A ruling like that would not only restrict free speech in the future, but it would also turn the concept of what we consider to be artistic freedom completely on its head.'

Blaming rap became such a commonplace that in years to come O'Shea Jackson Sr, better known as Ice Cube, satirised the concept with the first single from his studio album *Raw Footage*. The track was tauntingly entitled 'Gangsta Rap Made Me Do It' and the video showed a dictatorial teacher, flanked by two American flags, preaching to his class and condemning gangsta rap for the vices of society.

In the case of Tupac, the rapper's attorney John Burris responded by saying:

> Tupac is an artist who is acutely aware of the urban problems that confront young black males and police brutality is something he feels very strongly about. Through his music, he seeks to dramatize the plight of people living in the ghetto and to let his audience know they don't have to buy into the scenario that there is no future. He has a free speech right to express himself.

Tupac's free-speech defence further inflamed the case. Oliver North, a former White House aide to Ronald Reagan and a notorious figure from the Iran–Contra arms-dealing scandal, had set up an organisation called the Freedom Alliance to 'defend the sovereignty of the United States and promote a strong national defense', among other things. It was assisting Charlton Heston in his campaign to boycott Time Warner and contacted Davidson's attorney to offer expert testimony. North said:

> This case provides us with a painfully vivid example of why this kind of music is so dangerous. How many dead policemen is it going to take to convince the executives that run Time Warner and these other companies that putting dangerous products like this out on the street is not the right thing to do?

The defence argued that Davidson's shooting had nothing to do with Tupac Shakur's music and pointed instead to a litany of crime and social problems that had haunted Howard from childhood. Stealing cars from the age of 15, he had perpetually failed at every job; he hadn't completed his training as an electrician, a building maintenance worker or a diesel mechanic, and at the time of the shooting was supposedly an anonymous foot soldier on the lowest rung of the Houston drug scene.

Robert Bell, the Texas district attorney, argued that Howard deserved the death penalty, but also stressed the significance of the trial within case-law.

> Frankly, it doesn't matter to me whether Tupac told him to kill somebody or whether Charlie Manson or the Devil told him do it. There isn't any doubt in my mind that this young man is responsible for his conduct. But the big question here is whether he should be put to death or whether he should get life imprisonment for the crime. Can violent music, like drugs or alcohol, be considered a mitigating factor in the shooting? To my knowledge, there has never been a murder trial before where a jury has had to answer that question.

They did answer it, and in October 2005, at the State Penitentiary at Huntsville, Texas, Howard was executed by lethal injection.

Linda Sue Davidson later said, 'I'm sure Tupac has no feeling for me or what happened to my husband. He obviously has a great anger toward law enforcement. All he cares about is singing his songs and making his money, no matter who he hurts.' It was an understandable emotional response but not entirely true. Tupac Shakur cared about many things beyond money, not least the fate that had befallen his own mother, who had been denied work for most of her life because of her involvement in the Black Panther movement. In his melancholic rap 'Dear Mama' Tupac shows rap's opposite face, a sentimental yearning for a better life. His relationship with his mother was not just unique, it is one of the most remarkable legacy stories of hip-hop.

Tupac's mother was Afeni Shakur. She was arrested as part of an undercover police operation which targeted the Harlem branch of the Black Panther Party, accused of planning a bombing campaign and incarcerated under brutal conditions in the New York Women's House of

Detention. Her husband was the de facto leader of the Harlem Black Panthers. It was a marriage bound as much by ideology as love and they were soon to split when Afeni fell pregnant with another man's child while out on bail. The trial collapsed when it was revealed that undercover New York cops had instigated the bomb plot. Free at last, but no longer in love, the husband and wife never spoke to each other again. It was a story that not even the most troubled deep-soul singer could have imagined.

At the time, many suspected that Tupac's father was a Black Panther called Sam Napier, a quietly authoritative man who was the circulation manager of the party's newspaper. He was murdered, shot through the back of the head, as a punishment for his loyalty to the Huey Newton faction of what had become a self-destructive organisation. However, Tupac Shakur's father was in fact a member of the Jersey City branch of the Panthers called Billy Garland. He had met Afeni Shakur at a strategy officers' meeting in New York City in 1969. When it came to registering the birth, Afeni Shakur stated that the father was dead, thus seeming to endorse the Sam Napier story. Garland contested the registration in a paternity suit after Tupac's death, when his estate was being administered, and the DNA tests confirmed he was in fact his father.

Tupac Shakur died in September 1996 after a drive-by shooting in Las Vegas on the night heavyweight boxer Mike Tyson defeated Bruce Seldon at the MGM Grand in Las Vegas. The fight was marred by controversy when Seldon lost in the first round after a series of what appeared to be 'phantom' punches from Tyson. A feeling of fix and criminal corruption was in the air when by chance two groups of warring Los Angeles gangsters clashed in a casino lobby. Tupac and the nefarious owner of Death Row Records, Suge Knight, backed by an entourage of Bloods, beat up a rival gangbanger from the Crips called Orlando 'Baby Lane' Anderson.

The Crips immediately sought revenge and a few hours later, while cruising the Las Vegas Strip in Anderson's rented white Cadillac, they spotted Suge Knight's BMW. Tupac was in the front passenger seat when Anderson took aim and shot him from the back seat of the Cadillac. The facts of the killing have been backed by witness testimony, forensics, police reports and by videotape. But for some reason numerous fanciful accounts of the night have been played out online, in supermarket magazines and in television drama that implicate the FBI, a corrupt unit of the LAPD and the East Coast rap magnate Sean 'Puff Daddy' Combs. It has become an obsession for the streaming media company Netflix, which has devoted hours to the night Tupac died. As in all good conspiracy theories, some believe he never died at all and he is variously in prison, settled down in Malaysia or, in one especially convoluted plot, his death was supposedly orchestrated by the driver on the night, the iniquitous Suge Knight. In an era prone to invention, some simply cannot accept the facts. Tupac has left mere mortality behind and joined the upper chamber of conspiracy stardom that is populated by Marilyn Monroe, Elvis Presley, John Lennon and Kurt Cobain.

In sketching-in all the details of Tupac Shakur's death, the journalist Rob Marriott, working for the hip-hop bible *Vibe*, told another unquestionable truth.

> It's become obvious to anyone paying attention that the gangsta image – for all its force and bluster – is nothing if not tragic, a myth of empowerment with the capacity to rob our generation of its potential greatness. If we as a Hip-Hop Nation can ever move beyond the directionless violence and self-destruction gangsta sometimes glorifies, then maybe we'll have 'Pac to thank for it. Perhaps, in the end, he was simply a sacrificial lamb in thug's clothing.

The 1992 election was influenced by many things, the 'Cop Killer' controversy, gangsta rap and the Sister Souljah moment among them; however, the themes of police brutality did not wane with Clinton's election. On the contrary, one of the outstanding street-rap records was released within months of his inauguration. 'Sound Of Da Police' by South Bronx rapper KRS-One hit the streets later in 1993, the second and final single from his solo album *Return Of The Boom Bap*. The song's catchphrase was not a phrase at all, but a haunting wail from the rapper emulating the sound of police sirens while samples from Sly and the Family Stone and hard-rock band Grand Funk Railroad provide the bedrock. KRS said on the track's release that it compared to the sound of 'the Beast, an evil, hellish creature that was on the hunt for black-and-brown people to lock behind bars'.

An underlying theme of the election and all that surrounded it was the triumph of family values, superficial probably, but the Clintons and the Gores had worked hard to reposition the Democrats as a party that cared about traditional values, especially law and order. In 1994, Clinton championed the Violent Crime Control and Law Enforcement Act, better known as the crime bill, which added $50 billion to build more prisons and put 100,000 more police officers on the street. Ironically, standing shoulder to shoulder with Clinton was the Delaware senator Joe Biden, who when he ran for President in 2020 had stood on a ticket that promised to reverse some of that legislation, but not all of it, reminding people the bill had also contained the landmark Violence Against Women Act and an assault weapons ban. It did, however, disproportionately incarcerate young black men who were demonised on an almost daily basis for the popular success of gangsta rap.

Clinton's inauguration on 20 January was preceded by America's Reunion on the Mall, a two-day multi-stage festival attended by one million people on the National Mall, with tents stretching from the Capitol to the Washington Monument. Metrorail recorded 440,138 trips, breaking a Sunday record for passenger travel, and it was reported to be the largest festival ever held on the Mall. On the bill were Michael Jackson, Aretha Franklin, Michael Bolton, Tony Bennett, Bob Dylan, Diana Ross and rapper LL Cool J, who had won a Grammy Award for Best Rap Solo Performance almost a year earlier. Clinton's inauguration committee took no chances, checking LL Cool J's credentials, subtly making background checks and monitoring the lyrics of his set list. It was a significant moment. If the election had proved anything, it was that rap music mattered and people cared about it as much as Clinton's teenage generation had cared about rock 'n' roll. The ceremony was also enriched by Maya Angelou reciting her specially written poem 'On the Pulse of Morning', which she delivered with all the eloquent command of a great storyteller. Although the poem itself was not universally liked, its themes of social change and moral responsibility within an America that crouched too long in 'the bruising darkness' matched the sonorous ambition of the occasion, and her delivery was enough to win a Grammy for Best Spoken Word Performance.

Although rap was seen within the Washington Beltway and by mainstream journalism as a problem of law and order, it had always been a musical form, like jazz, which had an in-built capacity to reinvent. In 1994, hip-hop enjoyed one of its most successful and imaginative years. It was the year of Nas, of Common and of Method Man, a year of unrivalled creativity. There were at least three contributing factors to what happened in 1994: a reaction against West Coast gangsta, the start of the New York City Renaissance and the official rise to prominence of southern hip-hop. It was the year that a young man from Brooklyn, Nasir bin Olu Dara Jones, known simply by his nom-de-rap as Nas, released the epic album/mixtape *Illmatic*, a remarkable tour de force that broke from the swaggering ghetto-fabulous image of gangsta rap and took on the tone of soundscape art, layered, intelligent and almost filmic. The website HHGA (Hip-Hop's Golden Age) described *Illmatic* thus:

> One of the very best Hip-Hop albums in history, period. A young and hungry, insanely talented emcee comes together with some of the finest producers in the game, who all bring their best work. No skits, no fillers – just nine 5-star tracks that combine into a seminal work that will forever be revered as one of the most important releases in Hip Hop. *Illmatic* is a monumental masterpiece.

In the album's second track, 'N. Y. State Of Mind', Nas laid out his interpretation of a world in which gun law had become entwined in contradictions and where a near-military police force had identified black teenagers as their wartime enemies. It was a premonition of the discord that would lead to the Black Lives Matter movement, and Nas, the so-called poetic sage of the Queensbridge Housing projects, was already reflecting on lost lives in deprived communities. In *Born to Use Mics*, a book entirely dedicated to unravelling the complexities of the *Illmatic* album, academic and cultural critic Sohail Daulatzai sees a hugely sophisticated response to the impending passage of Bill Clinton's Violent Crime Control and Law Enforcement Act. Emboldened by his Sister Souljah moment, Clinton maintained a conservative commitment to law and order, 'indicative of a larger pattern in which huge cutbacks in education and infrastructure were met with drastically increased funding for the formation of an urban police state and massive increases in prison building, as the organised confusion of Reaganism addressed the symptoms not the causes of urban poverty,' Daulatzai wrote. When Clinton brought his bill into law in September of 1994, he told the assembled parties, 'Today the bickering stops. . . . The era of excuses is over; the law-abiding citizens of our country have made their voices heard. Never again should Washington put politics and party above law and order.'

Those who imagined that Ice-T's career could not survive the pummelling it took over 'Cop Killer' had not accounted for hip-hop's mercurial reinvention or the way that American film and television was adapting to new urban demographics. In 1991, in the early days of the presidency of his nemesis George H. W. Bush, Ice-T signed up to appear alongside Wesley Snipes as a NYC police detective, in Mario Van Peebles' action thriller *New Jack City*. He then reappeared in the cop show franchise *Law and Order* as an undercover narcotics officer Fin Tutuola.

There was something surreal about Ice-T playing a cop but it soon became commonplace for urban musicians to cross over to other forms of media. Black music's great surge into the mainstream of American life was reflected in film and television but most powerfully in music sales. Ten years after the Los Angeles riots something seismic happened. In October 2003, for the first time ever, the top ten singles by sales were all by black artists. It was a watershed moment. 'Baby Boy' by Beyoncé – resplendent in the video in a chain-mail bikini – and featuring dancehall reggae star Sean Paul, occupied the top spot for over two months. It led the charge of emergent artists including P. Diddy, Jay-Z and Black Eyed Peas. In years to come this generation would reshape the way the music industry was managed and take decisive control over their creative lives.

The 'Cop Killer' saga bequeathed one final legacy. It brought America's chequered history of urban policing and its fatal love affair with the gun into stark relief but in doing so it cast a young black man as a national villain. Neither the artist nor the politicians who rose up against him could have foreseen the future. The countdown was on to one of the most combustible periods of American politics, when roles would be reversed and the uniformed police would be cast as villains. The era of Black Lives Matter was on the horizon.

On 2 September 2005, people gathered in downtown Detroit to protest against the Bush administration's slow response to Hurricane Katrina.

© Jim West / Alamy Stock Photo

8

HURRICANE KATRINA

Listen Up: 'Hurricane Season' by Trombone Shorty (2010)

On Monday 12 October 1998, Joseph Murray, the Principal at Marion Abramson High, the largest high school in New Orleans, brought his pupils together in the school's crammed gymnasium. It was not good news. The night before, one of the school's most popular teachers, Raymond Myles, had been murdered on the fringes of the Latin Quarter. Some wailed when the news was announced, others cuddled together in small groups and others stood stoically still, trying to make sense of the tragic news. A group of girls spontaneously began to sing a psalm, quietly at first, and then with resounding devotion. They were members of the school choir that Mr Myles had coached. This was the gymnasium where they rehearsed, and it would find its own fateful place in history when the dark waters unleashed by Hurricane Katrina swept through New Orleans seven years later.

According to the National Oceanic and Atmospheric Administration, Katrina was 'the most destructive storm to strike the mainland of the United States and the costliest storm in U.S. history'. It caused $125 billion in damage. But the financial cost was small by comparison with the chasm it opened between the citizens of New Orleans and the federal government, under the dithering leadership of George W. Bush. Hurricane Katrina and the failure of the Bush presidency to anticipate and react to the catastrophe hangs heavy over the story of New Orleans R&B and frames the untimely death of Raymond Myles. As the African American academic Michael Eric Dyson wrote in *Come Hell or High Water*, his compelling and outraged account of the hurricane's impact on the city's poorest communities: 'If Hurricane Katrina's lethal fury unleashed unforgettable images of suffering in its wake, the Bush administration answered one of the nation's worst natural disasters ever, with a political maelstrom fed by ineptitude, inexperience and ignorance.'

As Hurricane Katrina was about to hit land, the New Orleans Regional Transit Authority designated Myles's school as a place from where people could receive transportation to the Louisiana Superdome, a shelter of last resort. Many never made it to the buses.

Gary Younge, a journalist working with the *Guardian* in London, reported from the damaged streets of New Orleans. He said that a journalist with the French newspaper *Libération* was told that 1,200 people drowned at Abramson High, a figure that has been challenged and disputed ever since. It was more likely that hundreds died, but in the absence of clear governance and reliable data, rumour held sway. One of the most virulent was that high-school kids unable to get aboard buses to the Superdome had hung tight at the gymnasium only to be engulfed in putrid brown water that gushed fatally through the doors and windows. Among their number were four or possibly five members of the RAMS (the Raymond Anthony Myles Singers), Myles's hand-picked backing chorus who had supported Harry Connick Jr in New York. Many others were local children who had been hurried to the gymnasium by their parents in the vain hope of escape.

Alonzo Horton spent weeks believing he had lost two of his brothers. He was a star of Abramson High's football team. Permanently in the gym but never one to join the choir, he had won a scholarship to Auburn

University in Alabama. Horton witnessed the devastation through social media and a series of painful text messages home. He had grown up in a tiny home on 4635 Dale Street in the city's 9th Ward, which was wiped away in the first wave of floods. His first text from home told him that his aunt Hattie had drowned in her own house. She had scurried up to the attic to escape the rising waters but then the sheet-rock ceiling collapsed and dropped her to her death. Horton desperately sent messages to his mother and father but could get no reply. It transpired that his mother was safe, his brothers were still missing, and his father was unaccounted for. Then, just before midnight, his cellphone erupted into life again with messages from old school friends and neighbours; a cousin told him that Hurricane Katrina had surged into the school gymnasium, which was by then being used as an assembly point for evacuees. His younger brothers Jerry (8) and DeLorean (6) were presumed dead, caught in floods in the gymnasium while waiting to be taken by bus to the safety of the Superdome. It later transpired they had narrowly escaped and had been evacuated by bus.

The murder of music teacher Raymond Myles was a moving event in its own right, but it grew to become a sad prequel to the tragedy in the gymnasium. Myles was born into grinding poverty in New Orleans' 7th Ward, in a welfare family of ten children. It was a neighbourhood vulnerable to the breaking levees and many of his own surviving family perished. He was a much-loved teacher and one of the city's most talented gospel-soul singers, and although he was long dead when Katrina struck, the tragedy rekindled his remarkable voice and brought him a new-found attention that at times eluded him in life.

On Sunday 11 October 1998, just hours after playing the 9th Ward's Free Music Festival, Raymond Myles died of multiple gunshot wounds on the corner of Elysian Fields and Chartres Street. A passer-by discovered him lying on his back, bleeding and unresponsive. New Orleans police lieutenant Marlon Defillo told local reporters that Myles was dead when the authorities arrived and that they had neither a suspect nor a motive for the killing. A search began for Myles's sports utility vehicle, which was missing, presumed stolen, and it soon transpired that the weapon that killed him was the pistol he carried for self-defence. Almost immediately the rumour mill went into overdrive.

Myles was an openly gay man. Some assumed he had been cruising for sex, while others claimed he had been driving around looking for someone to sell him marijuana. Many suspected he knew his killer, but the majority presumed it was just the ebb and flow of New Orleans crime, an opportunistic carjacking in which the victim was killed for his money or his vehicle. Police later established that his killer had been in the vehicle, shot him and then pushed him out of his Lincoln Navigator in the Faubourg Marigny district, where Cajun bistros, sidewalk musicians and bohemian jazz bars still had the feel of old New Orleans.

In the years immediately preceding his death, he had taken on the role of a peripatetic music teacher for the public-school system and was a vocal coach to the city's outstanding local talent. Never shy when it came to enhancing his own career, he also played talent scout, and the best singers he could find joined the ranks of his backing singers, the RAMS, who toured extensively in the South and in Europe, supporting among others Al Green, Shirley Caesar, Patti LaBelle and Aretha Franklin. He was known for an energetic form of church music the recording industry had classified as 'urban gospel', the genre that also included artists like Yolanda Adams, The Winans and Kirk Franklin.

Myles had started his career as a more conventional child star, following in the footsteps of Aretha Franklin, Gladys Knight and Little David Ruffin, who were paraded around the gospel circuit as children, sometimes in ways that came close to exploitation. He toured across the southern states, opening the show for his mother, gospel singer Christine Myles. As a 5-year-old he was spotted and tutored by the great Mahalia Jackson, and when Mahalia died he performed solo at her funeral at the Rivergate auditorium in New Orleans. Myles made a record, 'Prayer From A Twelve Year Old Boy' (Kent, 1970), when he was still a child. It was a song which had a naïve but charming plea to end the Vietnam War and bring US military personnel home. A regional hit in the southern United States on a local label called Peek-A-Boo, it came with a smooth B-side – 'You Made A Man Out Of Me Baby' – which at the time was deemed to be too racy and inappropriate for such a young boy. A minor backlash among the New Orleans Christian community landed his mother in trouble with her local congregation.

Raymond Myles's debut single brought him to the heart of a New Orleans recording dynasty. It was produced by a giant of the local soul scene, the so-called Creole Beethoven, Wardell Quezergue, a composer, arranger, bandleader and producer who was a dominant force in New Orleans R&B for more than fifty years. After serving in the Korean War, Quezergue had returned home to form two bands, the Royal Dukes of Rhythm and Wardell and the Sultans, and then in 1962 he set up one of the most enduring record labels of the sixties soul epoch: Nola Records. Nola took its name from the colloquial initials of New Orleans, Louisiana, and became a relatively successful independent among the myriad of small under-capitalised labels. It was hardwired to the local talent sector and gave opportunities to Eddie Bo, Willie Tee and Smokey Johnson, before producing one of the stand-out hits of dance craze, Robert Parker's 'Barefootin'' (Nola, 1966).

Quezergue's commercial instincts were finely attuned to the soul music of the late sixties and in 1971, as the new decade drove the music in a grittier streetwise direction, he produced the supreme song of the times, Jean Knight's irrepressible double-platinum hit 'Mr. Big Stuff' for Stax Records in Memphis. The song was recorded in a low-key studio in Jackson, Mississippi, with a group of session musicians who had been ferried by bus from New Orleans. Over the following twenty years Myles and Quezergue's paths crossed and recrossed: they shared studios, recommended talent to each other, and joined forces if a record needed the authentic sound of gospel. After Myles's death, when his old producer should have been enjoying a restful retirement, Wardell Quezergue's last few years were lived out in a sad decline. A diabetic, he was almost blind by 2005, when he lost his house and his precious collection of musical memorabilia, including his entire collection of sheet music, in the aftermath of Hurricane Katrina. In the last days of his life, he was part of a band of local musicians performing benefit shows to help older R&B musicians get back to work.

After years of clinging devotedly to gospel, Raymond Myles had eventually demonstrated a willingness to cross over into the commercial field. In 1992, he starred in a phenomenally successful fifteen-night run opening for the New Orleans crooner Harry Connick Jr at Madison Square Garden. *Billboard*, the record industry bible, wrote: 'After years as New Orleans' best-kept secret, Myles seems poised for a major leap into the mainstream.' Recording offers flooded in, as well as invitations to high-end summer festivals. Hopes were soaring. 'We thought he would be one of the biggest artists in the world,' said Allen Toussaint, the legendary New Orleans songwriter. Myles signed a recording deal with NYNO Records, the label Toussaint had started with the radio entrepreneur Joshua Feigenbaum. It was a label that had history on its side and a legacy of creativity dating back to the late sixties when the Toussaint brothers were a dominant force in African American music.

In an excited feature in *Billboard*, the journalist Leo Sacks described Myles as being 'like Little Richard, Liberace, Michael Jackson, Donny Hathaway and James Cleveland, all rolled into one'. It was spot on. His mannerisms at the keyboard were remarkably like Little Richard, his camp personality resembled Liberace, but his stature was closer to the great seventies soul star Barry White, the bear-like love machine of romantic soul. His voice meanwhile was much more resounding, like a soulful Pavarotti, and capable of commanding huge public spaces, indoor or out. Myles was hot but he was also an anachronism. In an era obsessed with visuals, the body-beautiful and pop-video sexuality, he was talented enough for fame but in truth too XXL for an industry dominated by artifice more than substance. Sacks also contends that Myles's career 'was stymied by his sexuality, and that the rejection he felt led him to dangerous habits, like cruising the city streets for sex'.

A few days after Myles's killing, a suspect surrendered to the New Orleans police after learning he was wanted. Rodrick Natteel (21), discovered that police were after him when officers turned up to search his mother's home following an anonymous phone call. Natteel was subsequently charged with first-degree murder but there were many unexplained loose ends. The authorities said robbery appeared to have been the motive for the killing but, whatever the motivation, the two men were not strangers. Myles allegedly knew Natteel, but police gave no further details about their relationship other than to say they were acquaintances. In the absence of facts, there was speculation that Natteel was a drug dealer, that he was a man who preyed on single gay men. Still others wondered whether Myles knew Natteel from the music classes he taught across ghetto communities in New Orleans. Police said they were still searching for a second suspect, whom they did not name, and then claimed the other suspect was already dead, shot in a street-gang incident. This left Natteel in the courts on his own, and in the summer of 2001 the career criminal pleaded guilty to 'accessory after the fact to first-degree murder'. He was sentenced to twenty years in Louisiana's notorious Angola state prison, the brutal penitentiary portrayed in Gil Scott-Heron's 1978 song 'Angola, Louisiana'. Prison did not reform Natteel. He served twelve years and almost immediately on his release returned to crime and was arrested again, this time booked in the St Bernard Parish jail for armed robbery.

Raymond Myles had been immersed in the New Orleans scene. He was a popular fixture at funerals and every funeral director in Louisiana had his phone number. Only three weeks before he died he had sung around the clock at a visitation and tribute held at the opulent D. W. Rhodes Funeral Home for the blues, jazz and gospel singer Johnny Adams, and performed at benefits for his widow with Aaron Neville and Walter 'Wolfman' Washington. Lying in state wearing his trademark chunky eyeglasses, in life Johnny Adams had been the personification of versatility, bucking fashion and musical trends and clinging to down-home soul. His recording career began by chance in Hollygrove in New Orleans' 17th Ward, an impoverished neighbourhood of frame-houses on the city's western edge, when his upstairs neighbour Dorothy LaBostrie, who had co-written Little Richard's 'Tutti Frutti' in 1955, knocked on his door and asked if he would consider singing the demo tracks for two R&B songs she planned to pitch to Joe Ruffino's Ric and Ron Records. At the time, Adams was working as a roofer in the local construction trade and seized the chance. One of the songs was 'I Won't Cry' (Ric, 1959), which started Adams, nicknamed 'The Tan Canary', on a career that spanned five decades and graced almost every subgenre of soul music, including his soul-food funk song 'Spunky Onions' (Pacemaker, 1965), deep-soul rarity 'Best Of Luck To You' (Gamma, 1970), his reflective cover version of 'I Wish It Would Rain' (Atlantic, 1972) and his effortless modern soul song 'You're A Bad Habit Baby' (SSS International, 1974). Finally, in 1984, Adams found a record company and a producer with whom he could have a lasting and fruitful relationship. He began working with Scott Billington of Rounder Records, a collaboration that would last until his death. A traditional jazz funeral followed Adams' service and several of those congregated around the grave – members of the Musicians' Mutual Protection Union and nursing auxiliaries from Our Lady of the Lake Regional Medical Center – met their own fate when Katrina struck.

Johnny Adams spoke to one of the enduring strengths of New Orleans soul: a diversity of styles and a capacity to surf the various sounds that had grown from the first shoots of rock 'n' roll. Nothing was out of bounds. He worked with, supported or toured with some of the greatest bands to emerge from the bayous, among them Art Neville's band The Meters, who along with James Brown and his Famous Flames were one of the pioneers of the funk sound. Even today their big singles – 'Here Comes The Meter Man', 'Sophisticated Cissy', 'Cissy Strut', 'Look-Ka Py Py' and the album track 'Fire On The Bayou' – are standards at funk clubs and raided for their slap-happy breakbeats by hip-hop and house DJs. Adams was a contemporary of Allen Toussaint, who worked originally as an A&R manager for Minit Records, then after a spell in the army set up some of New Orleans' most respected independent labels, Sansu, Tou-Sea and Deesu, with his business partner Marshall Sehorn.

One of the major problems that confronted New Orleans and its music was geography. With songwriting and major labels concentrated in Manhattan, and a talent base drawn to the northern soul capitals of Detroit, Chicago and Philadelphia, New Orleans was hidden away, seemingly remote, and far south. Its cultural history and French influence gave the city a different dynamic too, often infusing its music with French, Creole, Cajun and zydeco styles. One of the clearest manifestations of this distinctive New Orleans soul came in 1976, when the four brothers of the Neville family – Art, Charles, Aaron and Cyril – came together to take part in a recording session of a Mardi Gras Indian group, The Wild Tchoupitoulas, led by the Nevilles' uncle George Landry aka 'Big Chief Jolly'.

Mardi Gras and the summer festival circuit that fanned out across the southern states provided a platform where eclectic forms of black music could co-exist. It was not uncommon for Raymond Myles and the RAMS, Johnny Adams and The Neville Brothers to find themselves on the same bill at a jazz festival, a summer jam or on a Mardi Gras stage. The global festival circuit, whether it was Glastonbury, the New Orleans Jazz and Heritage Festival, Coachella or Summerfest in

Milwaukee, meant that the best-known New Orleans bands were often on the road. It turned out to be a blessing in disguise, as many were far from home when Hurricane Katrina struck.

Aaron Neville was on tour in upstate New York with his brothers when the hurricane wrecked his home, a ranch-style brick house at the end of a cul-de-sac in Eastern New Orleans. For sixteen months, Neville stayed away, monitoring the news from afar, absorbing the horror and telling those closest to him that he was coping in exile. Rather than confront the wreckage, he bought a new home near an arboretum in the leafy town of Brentwood, Tennessee, south of the songwriting mecca of Nashville. Aaron struggled emotionally after the hurricane. He broke down in public while performing with the Nashville Symphony orchestra, his final performance before losing his wife Joel to cancer. He was said to be inconsolable during the country lament 'Why Should I Be Lonely'. Frightened of what he would find and what emotions it would unlock, he only ventured back to New Orleans to bury Joel, laying her to rest in the family's vault at Mount Olivet Cemetery.

Myles's backing singers suffered too. Disoriented by their leader's murder and drawn in different creative directions, they had performed at the New Orleans Jazz Festival only once since his death seven years earlier. Many of the singers were working-class, from desperately poor backgrounds, and were at the forefront of loss as the hurricane struck. Some scattered to safe cities beyond New Orleans to find work, some simply gave up on professional music and took regular jobs to earn a living and a few lost their lives in the hurricane.

Early on the morning of 29 August 2005, the first floodwaters crossed the doorway of Allen Toussaint's Sea-Saint Studios. One after another, the canals bordering Lake Pontchartrain failed and water spilled into Gentilly, the residential neighbourhood where Toussaint had his home and studio. Although much of the greater metropolitan area was below sea level, federal officials initially thought that New Orleans would dodge a bullet. The city had been spared a direct hit but the levee system which held back the waters of Lake Pontchartrain and Lake Borgne was completely overwhelmed by ten inches of rain. Areas east of the Industrial Canal were the first to flood and by the afternoon of 29 August some 20 per cent of the city was underwater, with the sweep of flooding encroaching on the safe zones near Abramson High School and the Superdome. Even as the storm moved out towards rural Mississippi, the lake relentlessly poured in and within eighteen hours the Sea-Saint Studios were fully submerged.

The small studio on Clematis, formerly an Exxon oil station which sold paint and building supplies, had become home to the city's famous musical diversity, hosting recordings by The Meters, LaBelle, Jean Knight, Fats Domino, Dr. John, Clifton Chenier and His Red-Hot Louisiana Band, Paul McCartney and Wings, and Joe Cocker. At least two globally famous records borrowed their Louisiana influence from Sea-Saint Studios – LaBelle's 'Lady Marmalade' (1974), the story of a French Quarter street prostitute, and Jean Knight's 'My Toot Toot' (1985), a rocking zydeco soul song which charmed dancers with its swaying beat and flagrant innuendo. What was less well known was that Sea-Saint had also provided low-cost facilities and downtime rates to emergent local artists to record demos and independent releases, among them the talented female artist Clem Easterling and a local harmony group brought to the studios by Wardell Quezergue called The Pro-Fascination, whose underground double-sider, 'Try Love Again'/'I Want to Wrap You In My Arms' (MOT, 1979), is a highly sought-after indie soul record. The record was mostly sold at wedding parties but Katrina destroyed the group's stock and so it disappeared into rare obscurity. Raymond Myles had once auditioned to join the group, but his huge bombastic gospel voice was thought to be too ostentatious to suit their tight and interwoven harmonies.

As the hurricane raged, Allen Toussaint evacuated first to Baton Rouge and then to New York City, where he stayed for the next few years. His studios were simply abandoned. Most of the equipment was wrecked, the desks floating from their moorings and the instruments kept there for freelance musicians unusable. Less than 25 per cent of Sea-Saint's total tape archive was salvaged, the rest unravelled and lost in the stagnant and filthy water. Most of what was recovered came from the studio's second storey, in the room adjacent to Toussaint's office. The salvaged tapes were bought at a junk auction years later. No one, not even Toussaint himself, can be precise about what was lost.

The politics of loss was even greater. The Federal Emergency Management Agency (FEMA) response to Hurricane Katrina was woeful and President Bush's own performance staggeringly bad. The initial evacuation in advance of the storm went relatively well. Approximately a million people left the greater New Orleans area. Then the wheels came off. Those without access to transportation out of the region found themselves stranded, among them thousands of elderly and disabled residents. It was not a time to be poor or dependent. It is now estimated that as many as 100,000 people did not have cars to escape the city. While twenty-one Louisiana nursing homes were evacuated before the storm hit, thirty-six did not evacuate until after the storm, leaving many without electricity, food or water. Some patients died while they awaited rescue. Back-up generators of some of the city's biggest hospitals flooded and left them without electricity.

The New York Times reported one horrific incident as the Memorial Medical Center was submerged:

> The hurricane knocked out power and running water and sent the temperatures inside above 100 degrees. Still, investigators were surprised at the number of bodies in the makeshift morgue and were stunned when health care workers charged that a well-regarded doctor and two respected nurses had hastened the deaths of some patients by injecting them with lethal doses of drugs. Mortuary workers eventually carried 45 corpses from Memorial, more than from any comparable-size hospital in the drowned city.

Local failures paralleled serious federal errors of judgement. New Orleans police captain Timothy P. Bayard revealed after the fact:

> We were not prepared logistically. Most importantly, we relocated evacuees to two locations where there was no food, water, or portable restrooms. We did not implement the pre-existing plan. We did not utilize buses that would have allowed us to transport mass quantities of evacuees expeditiously. We did not have food, water, or fuel for the emergency workers. We did not have a backup communication system. We had no portable radio towers or repeaters that would have enabled us to communicate.

FEMA was officially created in 1979 through an executive order by President Jimmy Carter with the aim of supporting citizens and first responders in disasters or national emergencies but it is an agency with mixed heritage, whose prestige and funding has grown and retreated depending on ideology and who is in the White House. President Clinton was a significant supporter and, in the context of major emergencies like 9/11 and the Oklahoma City bombing, terrorism in all its forms occupied FEMA priorities and led ultimately to the establishment of the Department of Homeland Security a year after the Twin Towers fell. The reorganisation of the homeland agencies had unintended consequences, further eroding FEMA's status as the federal bureaucracies merged and overlapped. With George W. Bush's election to the White House fatal mistakes were made, not least populating FEMA with cronies and old pals from Texas. Notably, a close friend of the Bush family, Michael Brown, was fast-tracked to lead FEMA despite a laughable resumé which featured several years as Commissioner of the International Arabian Horse Association. As Michael Eric Dyson noted savagely in *Come Hell or High Water*, 'Brown's mediocrity even for a crony was unmistakable.' Mayor Ray Nagin of New Orleans lobbied FEMA with a detailed list of emergency aid his city desperately needed. Most of the requested supplies and other assistance did not arrive for days.

The ineffectual Brown became the face of the botched federal response despite being praised during a presidential tour of the destruction in 2005. Bush jovially told him live on air – 'Brownie, you're doing a heck of a job.' The dead were stacked up in makeshift morgues, and the displaced living in shacks in Mississippi, the survivors clinging to hope on the roofs of their flooded homes and those with no food or water or sheltered in the Superdome disagreed. Almost everything that could go wrong did. Huge numbers of National Guardsmen from Louisiana and the surrounding states were deployed in Iraq and only depleted numbers could be marshalled as support. Eight hundred thousand people were without power, straining the communication systems, and cellphones which were useful for a time lay uncharged. There were reports of widespread looting but they were exaggerated as huge parts of the city were inaccessible and many shops already ruined. The President witnessed the chaos from the high vantage point of *Marine One* and did not visit the wreckage until five days had passed. He played guitar with the country singer Mark Wills at a naval base near San Diego – an informal moment which played terribly in the context – and in what was admittedly a truncated vacation he returned to his ranch in Crawford, Texas, unaware of how his personal conduct was playing out.

Michael Eric Dyson described the President's behaviour as 'cheerful indifference' and said that 'the image of Bush partying while his people plunged to watery grave couldn't be erased'. He wrote:

> As the ideological children of Ronald Reagan, Bush and his administration had thrived on tax cuts, downsizing, the neglect of civic infrastructure, the shredding of the safety net, the will to privatisation, the degrading of the public sector, and advocating Reagan's idea that government is the enemy of the people. The Bush administration's incompetence in Katrina was the most devastating indictment of such a philosophy.

Black music rose up in response to Hurricane Katrina. Jazz and soul sketched a solemn requiem to the tragedy and a much angrier form of blistering and socially charged hip-hop savaged the President and his tattered reputation. One of the outstanding musical memorials can be found in the work of trumpeter Terence Blanchard, who follows a long line of great New Orleans jazz giants including Louis Armstrong, Sidney Bechet, Jelly Roll Morton and the Marsalis brothers. He grew up at a time when jazz had enriched the city's tourist economy and become a mainstay of its academic reputation too. Blanchard was already an established name but he reached out beyond the city as the composer of the score to Spike Lee's Peabody Award-winning documentary *When the Levees Broke*.

The score uses the experience of numerous people confronting the tragedy, including his own mother. Wilhelmina Blanchard returned home in Pontchartrain Park and opened her front door having been forewarned to expect a floating muddy mess of destroyed possessions, lost heirlooms and drowned memories. But the warning did not prepare her for the loss. Her son recorded his mother's experiences and those of her friends and neighbours, and their stories influenced *A Tale Of God's*

Will (A Requiem For Katrina) (Blue Note, 2007), a ghost-like symphony of a city in turmoil. 'After Katrina my mother moved to Los Angeles,' Blanchard told the *Socialist Review*. 'One day we were talking about her wedding, the people at her wedding party, and she got up and said, "Let me look at the pictures," and then she stopped, and got extremely sad, and she realised the pictures were gone. They were destroyed.' These stories are brought to life on the track 'Dear Mom' and, as Blanchard reflects, 'My mom's block looks barren. It's pretty awful. It's so surreal. It still doesn't look like what it was, and it breaks my heart . . . These are the people my trumpet is crying for.' Blanchard shared compositional duties with members of his quintet, each writing songs that share their perspectives on the storm and its aftermath.

> I drew inspiration from the stories people had told me about their experiences in the aftermath of the hurricane. It wasn't so much about music for me. It was really more about what people had to endure. I just want people to reflect on what happened here and what people had to deal with, and how things can go terribly wrong in what is supposed to be the richest country in the world.

These were trying times for musicians across the city. Jazz music, the lingua franca of New Orleans, found a mood of sombre anger. The New Orleans Jazz Orchestra appeared at Christ Church Cathedral eleven weeks after the storm. More than a thousand souls crammed into the historic cathedral to listen to an orchestra that had returned from across America. A stand-out piece was the premiere of 'All The Saints', a suite by trumpeter Irvin Mayfield, whose father was still missing in the floods, presumed dead. Witnesses say that when Mayfield's horn caressed the opening bars of the tune 'Just A Closer Walk With Thee', in which he was accompanied by his old school friend Ronald Markham on piano, there was a moment of unforgettable magic, subdued, reverent and uplifting. It received a standing ovation and, fighting back the tears, Mayfield said, 'If we don't believe in our city, nobody else will.'

Irvin Mayfield Sr, a 65-year-old maintenance supervisor for the US Postal Service, was not found until three months after the hurricane, when his family finally tracked him down as an unidentified 'John Doe' in a morgue in Saint Gabriel, miles away from the family home.

In a bitter twist to the story, Mayfield and Markham each pleaded guilty to conspiracy to commit fraud stemming from their time with a charitable foundation that raised money for libraries and the jazz orchestra. Prosecutors alleged that they steered more than $1.3 million from the New Orleans Public Library Foundation to themselves largely by funnelling it through the New Orleans Jazz Orchestra.

Another astonishing concert in the aftermath of Hurricane Katrina was Bruce Springsteen and the Seeger Sessions Band at the New Orleans Jazz and Heritage Festival. Springsteen was as condemnatory of Bush as any rapper and excoriated the President's incompetent response to the storm with 'How Can A Poor Man Stand Such Times And Live?'. After visiting the city's 9th Ward, the most devastated area of the city, Springsteen said: 'I saw sights I never thought I'd see in an American city . . . The criminal ineptitude makes you furious.' Then Springsteen stunned the audience with a celebratory version of the old spiritual standard 'When The Saints Go Marching In', which shifted from the funereal to the furious as the audience responded to its sporting connotations with the local New Orleans Saints American football team. Springsteen was joined on vocals by Marc Anthony Thompson aka Chocolate Genius, a gifted blues and soul singer considered a part of the new-soul movement, who dressed as a rural fieldworker to bring a civil rights presence to the song. Terence Blanchard shared Springsteen's anger, describing the situation as 'a national tragedy' caused by federal failures to maintain the levees properly over decades. He told *Advocate* magazine:

> The thing that hurts the most, is that it wasn't a terrorist attack. It wasn't an act of violence; it was an act of negligence . . . The irony of all this stuff, of us fighting for freedom in Iraq and people suffering and dying in their homes in New Orleans, was not lost on me, and I think it's an interesting commentary on the times that we live in . . . I've been saying for a long time that the country is on the brink of disaster because we've allowed politicians to run amok and we've allowed them to lie to us with no consequence.

Such was the terrible visibility of Hurricane Katrina, played out in prime time, on 24-hour news and analysed daily in the press, it inevitably encouraged a succession of benefit concerts. One of the outstanding testimonies was *Hurricane Relief: Come Together Now*, a musical tribute to the city and its suffering. It is highly unlikely that this brilliant but painful double album found its way into George W. Bush's record collection. Some of the tracks paid homage to the city itself and its rich jazz heritage, such as Louis Armstrong's 'Do You Know What It Means To Miss New Orleans?', Sting's 'Moon Over Bourbon Street', Professor Longhair's 'Mardi Gras In New Orleans' and Dr. John's 'Goin' Back To New Orleans'. Others spoke directly to the tragedy, including Harry Connick Jr's 'City Beneath The Sea' and Clint Black's 'When The Levee Broke'. Urban music lent tracks from R. Kelly, Kanye West, Norah Jones and Wyclef Jean. A stand-out track was 'After All' by modern Detroit gospel giants The Winans (credited as 'The Winans Family'), who had frequently shared a stage with Raymond Myles over the previous two decades.

If jazz, the city's heritage, lacerated President Bush then hip-hop brutally attacked him. It showed no mercy. On 2 September 2005, the television network NBC Universal broadcast a live telecast called *A Concert for Hurricane Relief*, an hour-long show intended to raise money and relief in response to the loss of life and human suffering that resulted from Hurricane Katrina. It turned out to be highly divisive moment in the story of the presidency and black music. One of the presenters, Kanye West, deviated from the prepared script and improvised an analysis that was not only widely held within African American communities but was the dominant view within the hip-hop fraternity. West, at the time an A-list rapper, looked nervously down the camera lens as comedian Mike Myers squirmed next to him. He said:

> I hate the way they portray us in the media. You see a black family, it says, 'They're looting.' You see a white family, it says, 'They're looking for food.' And, you know, it's been five days [waiting for federal help] because most of the people are black. And even for me to complain about it, I would be a hypocrite because I've tried to turn away from the TV because it's too hard to watch. I've even been shopping before even giving a donation, so now I'm calling my business manager right now to see what is the biggest amount I can give, and just to imagine if I was

down there, and those are my people down there. So anybody out there that wants to do anything that we can help – with the way America is set up to help the poor, the black people, the less well-off, as slow as possible. I mean, the Red Cross is doing everything they can. We already realize a lot of the people that could help are at war right now, fighting another way – and they've given them permission to go down and shoot us!

He culminated his direct address to camera with an incendiary accusation, one that has resonated across the years. 'George Bush doesn't care about black people,' he said unprompted. Behind the scenes NBC executives panicked. They considered pulling the show and going to a stand-by replacement programme, or issuing an urgent on-air apology, but it was not clear who would be willing to deliver it. The Red Cross, a major recipient of the concert's donations, was supposedly furious about West's comments and worried that donors would pull their money as a result but it didn't happen and the telecast eventually raised more than $50 million.

The backstage fury finally calmed down when Harry Connick Jr, a native of New Orleans and one of the stars of the appeal, convinced them that to take a rash decision would only give greater oxygen of publicity to the criticism of the President. Connick Jr told the producers they were overreacting. He told them that West's comments wouldn't ruin the show's legacy but would ensure it had one and that for many people including a majority of African Americans, West's comments were important and correct. It proved to be true. YouTube, which had launched earlier that year, allowed users, many of them young people, to upload, watch and share the video, and draw their own conclusions. In terms of music pure and simple, Harry Connick Jr and Wynton Marsalis were among the true stars of the show, delivering an intimate rendition of 'Do You Know What It Means To Miss New Orleans', but it was a moment overshadowed by the controversy surrounding Kanye West.

West was undaunted. He appeared later in the week on *The Ellen DeGeneres Show* and said, 'People have lost their lives, lost their families. It's the least I could do to go up there and say something from my heart, to say something that's real.' NBC, increasingly rattled by the attention, issued a corporate statement designed to protect its reputation:

President George W. Bush flies over the devastation of Hurricane Katrina aboard *Marine One* on 2 September 2005, as the local authorities struggled to evacuate thousands of people. He conceded later in life that he had made mistakes: 'The photo of my hovering over the damage suggested I was detached from the suffering on the ground. That wasn't how I felt. But once the public impression was formed, I couldn't change it.'

Kanye West departed from the scripted comments that were prepared for him, and his opinions in no way represent the views of the networks. It would be most unfortunate if the efforts of the artists who participated tonight and the generosity of millions of Americans who are helping those in need are overshadowed by one person's opinion.

President Bush has since stated that hearing West's ad-libbed comments insinuating that he was a racist was the most wounding moment of his presidency. In his memoir *Decision Points* he wrote: 'I faced a lot of criticism as president. I didn't like hearing people claim that I lied about Iraq's weapons of mass destruction or cut taxes to benefit the rich. But the suggestion that I was racist because of the response to Katrina represented an all-time low.'

Kanye West is a complex man whose upbringing differed from most of the urban rappers of his generation. Born in Douglasville, a city on the fringes of Atlanta, Georgia, his father Ray West was a former Black Panther and a talented social-realist photographer who worked for the area's main daily newspaper the *Atlanta Journal-Constitution*. His mother, Dr Donda C. Williams West, was an academic in the English faculty of Clark Atlanta University. When she divorced her husband and moved with her son to Chicago, her career flourished and she eventually became Chair of the English Department of Chicago State University. During her rise up the ranks of academia, Donda travelled on an exchange programme to China and for a time Kanye studied Mandarin at primary school. Unlike most old-school rappers who had emerged from Morrisania in the Bronx, or the sprawling housing complexes of Queensbridge in Long Island, or the gun-infested streets of South Central Los Angeles, Kanye grew up in the urban village of Oak Lawn, Illinois. He attended Polaris High School, where he was exposed to books and to big ideas, and routinely guided away from the dangers of crack and guns plaguing inner-city America.

His articulate image and cultured background did not fit the gangsta archetypes that the music industry had helped construct. Few label bosses were willing to take a chance on a smartass who came over like a middle-class art-school dropout, so he hung around with friends who were trying out fashion and the media before he returned to hip-hop again. His autobiographical debut album, *The College Dropout*, has been described by hip-hop critic Paul Bowler as 'one of the most astonishing debut albums in hip-hop history. Multi-faceted, idiosyncratic, and packed with enough pop nous to conquer the charts, it brought him both critical acclaim and huge commercial success.' It was the pop nous that set him apart. As some hip-hop was determined to stay in a self-incriminating ghetto, Kanye wanted to break out to the biggest possible global audience.

Released on 10 February 2004, *The College Dropout* reached number two on the US *Billboard* 200 chart and won Best Rap Album at the 2005 Grammy Awards. One of the album's trendsetting achievements was to have R&B singers partnering the rapper and vocalising over a breakbeat. 'All Falls Down', featuring Syleena Johnson, had its own powerful pedigree. Johnson was the daughter of the Chicago soul singer Syl Johnson, who recorded for Twinight Records and for the Hi label owned by the legendary Memphis bandleader Willie Mitchell. Johnson's mother Brenda Thompson was one of the first black female police commissioners in the USA, in the Johnsons' hometown of Harvey, Illinois, and one of a new generation of professionally successful Chicago-based African Americans who became the standard-bearers of Barack Obama's audacious journey to the White House.

Despite his wealth of ideas, Kanye's career almost ended before it began. In October 2002, when he was travelling home from a recording session in a California studio, he fell asleep at the wheel of his car and was involved in a horrific head-on crash. He underwent reconstructive surgery on a shattered jaw and later recorded 'Through The Wire', a self-reflective and emotionally honest song delivered with his jaw wired shut. The accident, and the act of singing 'through the wires', helped his visibility to soar and his seductive pop hip-hop provided a commercial alternative to the gangsta scene. West self-consciously played down the harder funk breaks that had been the lifeblood of old-school hip-hop in favour of chic pop and R&B samples, notably Chaka Khan's mid-tempo 'Through The Fire'. It was not only the song title that Kanye lent on, and there was a frosty stand-off between the artists. 'The best thing I could give him was silence,' Chaka Khan said on a television talk show. Asked if she'd at least earned royalties from the sample, Khan emphatically said yes. Music copyright had been disrupted by hip-hop and in a series of high-profile legal disputes established R&B artists such as George

Clinton, James Brown and Chaka Khan exerted their rights over music now being reactivated in new and sometimes shameless ways.

Kanye's mother Donda, who tragically died in 2007 after complications from cosmetic surgery, left her role in academia to guide him through the shark-infested waters of the recording industry and together they set up a production company that bore her name. As West's success grew, his controversial comments about President Bush refused to recede. In fact, his memorable performance on television seemed to have ignited a new chapter in the irrepressible bildungsroman of hip-hop as the next generation of urban artists queued up to pulverise the President. But television was changing too.

Back in 1999, in the relatively obscure world of Dutch television, a producer called John De Mol had launched a high-concept TV show called *Big Brother*, borrowing a title and visual grammar from George Orwell's dystopian novel *Nineteen Eighty-Four*, in which the all-pervasive state apparatus 'Big Brother' watched over its citizens at play and at work. That show and other producer-controlled reality shows such as *Survivor* and *Idols* set the stage for two decades (and counting) of constructed-reality and concealed-camera shows. Among the cast of characters, contestants and attention-seekers who flocked to have their lives scrutinised were the Kardashian family, which included voluptuous sisters Kim, Kourtney and Khloé. *Keeping Up with the Kardashians* was launched by the cable network E! in 2007 and was destined to become one of the most successful family reality shows ever. As President George W. Bush's presidency wilted, the Kardashians were at the early height of their notoriety and, in what was a complicated set of relationships, Kim Kardashian married her friend and then lover Kanye West. It was a public fusion of rap and reality television which advanced both their careers.

West, the public scourge of the Bush presidency, would later weirdly befriend Bush's Republican successor. They met at Trump Tower in New York following Trump's election victory in November 2016. On a subsequent visit to the White House, in 2018, West wore a 'Make America Great Again' (MAGA) cap, an item widely despised within African American music and fashion. He hugged Trump and declared: 'I love this guy right here.' He also said without apparent irony that the hat made him feel 'like Superman'. According to subsequent press reports, they discussed North Korea, prison reform, mental health and even designs for a new hydrogen-powered plane. Like some melodramatic interchange, Kardashian and West's relationship overlapped in the Oval Office. West's love life and political leanings were frequently contrasted with the marriage of Beyoncé and Jay-Z, who were publicly associated with Barack Obama's White House. Almost as an act of retaliation, Jay-Z – the one-time Brooklyn rapper turned multimillionaire – helped launch the Reform Alliance and encouraged sports stars and business leaders to pledge $50 million to reform the US criminal justice system.

Kanye West finally ran for president himself as leader of the Birthday Party. On Independence Day 2020, he announced on Twitter: 'We must now realize the promise of America by trusting God, unifying our vision and building our future. I am running for president of the United States!' It was a shambolic and troubling campaign which suffered from missing a crucial Federal Election Commission deadline and failing to qualify for the ballot in West Virginia and Wisconsin. Worse was to come. At a rally in South Carolina, in an emotional outburst which cast doubt on his mental health, the troubled star, who had a bipolar diagnosis, said he and his wife had considered an abortion when she was pregnant with their daughter, North. Then, at a rally in Georgia, West appeared to walk on water during a Sunday Service stunt which evoked a delusionary Jesus complex.

Casting real characters in emotionally hyped formats became an obsession within Hollywood and across global television. One of the most obvious and enduring approaches to reality television was the talent show, a time-honoured form of conventional family entertainment which included, among many, *American Idol*, a derivative of the UK format *Pop Idol* which had been pioneered by the guru of reality talent shows, the British artist-manager Simon Fuller. *American Idol*'s unsophisticated concept was to discover talent amongst unsigned acts and audition them in front of industry judges. The series ran from June 2002 to April 2016, for fifteen seasons, on Fox then in its sixteenth season moved to ABC. It was on air as a top-rating show when Hurricane Katrina struck, straddled the dog days of President Bush, remained popular when Barack Obama ruled the White House, and finally came to an end as Donald Trump took office.

American Idol's stand-out success was the soul singer Jennifer Hudson, who bafflingly came only seventh in the third series. She had been a hidden talent for years until her exposure on television delivered a role in a film adaptation of the musical stage play *Dreamgirls*. Hudson was cast in the role of Effie White, a thinly veiled version of Florence Ballard, an original member of The Supremes. Hudson was an on-screen natural. Her character was fighting weight gain and bearing the burden of being marginalised by the record label. Hudson managed to hint at the emotionally damaged decline of Ballard during her estrangement from Motown. It was a performance that was noticed. Hudson won both the Oscar and a Golden Globe for Best Supporting Actress for her role.

Hudson had battled hard for her break. She grew up in Bronzeville, the one-time 'Black Metropolis' on Chicago's South Side, which in years gone by had rivalled Harlem as one of the capitals of African American culture. Hudson attended Dunbar Vocational High School, itself a legacy school which boasted Lou Rawls and sixties soul singer Barbara Acklin among its former pupils. This was the local community power base from which Senator Barack Obama embarked on the final stages of his journey to the presidency. Hudson had earned respect as a club singer in Chicago bars but none of it turned into much. She scrabbled around looking for breaks and eventually took an entertainment contract with a Disney theme cruise around the Caribbean and the Bahamas, singing nightly in the dining room and at deck-parties. It was in frustration that she applied to appear on *American Idol*, never imagining that losing on national television would change her life.

However, in 2008, a family tragedy would lend intrigue to her story. On October 24, the bodies of Hudson's mother and brother were found in the family's South Side home. Reported missing was 7-year-old Julian King, the son of Jennifer's sister Julia Hudson. Three days later the body of the missing boy was found in the back seat of an SUV parked on Chicago's West Side. He had also been shot and a .45-calibre gun found near the vehicle was linked to all three of the shootings. The stolen SUV was later confirmed to be that of Hudson's murdered brother.

Hudson's celebrity status gave the story national notoriety and the police investigation soon focused on William Balfour, Julia's estranged husband. Balfour had been thrown out of the Hudson home in the winter of 2007 after a series of threats and domestic disputes. When the case came to court much time and argument was spent on jury selection. Potential jurors in the trial were given questionnaires which asked if they were familiar with Hudson's career, if they regularly watched *American Idol*, and even if they were members of Weight Watchers, the programme for which Hudson was a celebrity spokesperson. The jury deliberated for eighteen hours before finding Balfour guilty on three counts of murder. He was sent to Stateville Correctional Center near Joliet, Illinois. 'You have the heart of an arctic night,' the judge said, in sentencing. 'Your soul is as barren as dark space.'

Parallel to Jennifer Hudson's rise from reality-TV loser to Hollywood star, two different events refracted the changing dynamics of the presidency. At the Commander-in-Chief's inaugural ball, Barack Obama paid tribute to his wife Michelle, saying, 'Some may dispute the quality of our president, no one disputes the quality of our First Lady.' Then, as the couple took to the floor for their first dance, Jennifer Hudson sang Al Green's love song, 'Let's Stay Together'. Meanwhile, as *American Idol*, *Survivor* and *Extreme Makeover* dominated the ratings, NBC had acquired the US rights to the global television franchise *The Apprentice*, a format that invited contestants, mostly young and aspirational, to compete to work with a high-flying entrepreneur. The character NBC chose to star in the show as the all-knowing boss was the New York real-estate tycoon Donald J. Trump. It was the platform Trump used to diversify his wealth portfolio and begin a populist campaign to win the Republican nomination for the presidency in May 2016.

Raymond Myles had operated at the opposite end of the talent-show spectrum. He regularly judged talent shows across New Orleans, including monthly talent showcases in the gymnasium at Abramson High School, and in part built his popularity by offering his gospel-singing services free of charge to any family bereaved by either drug deaths or gang violence. It was an offer taken up by many. Before the storm, New Orleans was reeling, with daily killings and gun-crime rates as high as they had ever been in the city's history. Controversially, a Louisiana State University criminologist, Dr Peter Scharf, later claimed that Hurricane Katrina was 'was one of the greatest crime-control tools ever deployed against a high-crime city'. Scharf projected that without the hurricane there would have been 316 killings in 2005.

In 1997, the year before his death, Myles became aware of a precocious new pupil whom he briefly but unsuccessfully tried to invite into his gospel choir. Dwayne Carter Jr was 15 and transferred into Abramson from another local high school. He was a precociously talented teenager, already an accomplished rapper. Assuming the stage name Lil Wayne at only 12 years of age he had signed a deal with the leading New Orleans hip-hop label Cash Money Records.

By the time Lil Wayne arrived at Abramson High, the school was buckling under the weight of social deprivation. Absenteeism was rife, guns were commonly waved in the corridors and a local newspaper had run a damaging feature which claimed that kids were so intimidated by the school bathrooms they used toilet facilities in a nearby Taco Bell fast-food restaurant. Carter's mother sensed the dangers and worried that her son was being drawn closer to gang violence. She withdrew him from school again and he moved to a local community college.

Lil Wayne was in Miami when Hurricane Katrina struck. He watched Kanye West attack President Bush on television and was inspired to write the rap classic 'Georgia . . . Bush', a blistering takedown of the very public federal failure to respond to the hurricane. Using a backing track of Ludacris and Field Mob's seductive social-realist song 'Georgia', Lil Wayne lacerated the president and alluded to the deaths in his old school gymnasium of a cousin and several school friends.

'Georgia . . . Bush' wrestled for hip-hop attention with another slice of political commentary, Mos Def and Immortal Technique's 'Bin Laden', a radical take on America's public enemy number one, which deftly told the story of how the CIA funded the rise of al-Qaeda. The hookline, 'Bin Laden didn't blow up the projects', intentionally sent the right-wing media into a frenzy and prompted demands that the track be withdrawn. The same voices that had screamed about gangsta rap were now enraged by these critiques of the Bush administration and the national narrative around terrorism. More followed on the polemical path that Lil Wayne and Mos Def had travelled. Juvenile's 'Get Ya Hustle On', from his album *Reality Check*, came with a powerful video shot among the debris of the hurricane that lambasted the federal government and Fox News.

Hidden beneath the chaos of Hurricane Katrina was another bleak reality. On the first day of September 2005, three days after Katrina crashed into New Orleans, Donnell Herrington, then a sturdy 32-year-old, was blasted by a shotgun. 'I just hit the ground. I didn't even know what happened,' he recalled. He slumped to the ground, life spilling from a hole in his throat, his vision blurred and distorted. Herrington was with two friends and he shouted at them to run while he turned to face his attackers, a vigilante gang led by three armed white males. According to the findings of 'Katrina's Hidden Race War', an award-winning piece of investigative journalism by the *Nation*/ProPublica reporter A. C. Thompson, the vigilantes were suspected of having shot as many as eleven African American men while law enforcement authorities turned a blind eye and may even have stoked the violence.

> Algiers Point, a largely white community, is perched on the west bank of the Mississippi River, linked to the core of New Orleans by a ferry line and twin grey steel bridges. When the hurricane hit, Algiers Point was protected by geography and the dynamics of the floods. Most homes and businesses in the area survived intact and as word spread that the area was dry, desperate people began heading towards the west bank, some trudging over bridges, others paddling by boat. The National Guard then designated the Algiers Point ferry landing an official evacuation site and more refugees arrived, with soldiers loading them onto buses to take them to the safety of Texas.
>
> Facing an influx of refugees, a group of white residents who were 'convinced that crime would arrive with the human exodus' attempted to seal off the area, setting up roadblocks by dragging lumber and downed trees into the streets. They stockpiled handguns, assault rifles, shotguns and at least one Uzi and began patrolling the streets in pickup trucks and SUVs. The newly formed militia, a loose band of about fifteen to thirty residents, most of them men, all of them white, were scouting for thieves, outlaws or, as one member put it, anyone who simply 'didn't belong'.

White supremacism and vigilantism went unseen amidst the deluge of wrecked houses, floating cars and public buildings battered beyond repair. So too did the damage to the dead as cemeteries came under siege from the floods. In New Orleans, much of which is below sea level, tombs are routinely installed above-ground because deeply dug graves become too easily submerged. Hurricane Katrina uprooted some 1,500 graves and destroyed many more memorial statues and tombstones. Death certificates traditionally tucked inside coffins were destroyed by water and labels washed away, leaving many graves unidentified and reduced to rubble.

A benefit show for Raymond Myles was arranged at Tipitina's, a New Orleans live music institution named after a song by blues maestro Professor Longhair. Myles's body lay in state at the Municipal Auditorium and seven thousand mourners passed to bid him farewell. The 'Little Richard of Gospel' was resplendent in a snakeskin suit and matching boots. The service was held at Greater St Stephen Full Gospel Baptist Church on Read Boulevard, next to one of the schools where he had taught. A convoy of limousines took relatives, friends and church and community leaders to his burial at Providence Memorial Park, a few steps away from his mentor, the legendary Mahalia Jackson. His gravestone is inscribed with the word 'Maestro'.

Until the fifties, up to 90 per cent of all public cemeteries in the USA reflected some form of racial restrictions, in what the celebrated cultural geographer Professor Wilbur Zelinsky referred to as 'the spatial segregation of the American dead'. The Hope Mausoleum in New Orleans was the traditional home of white burials while Providence was historically the resting place for African Americans.

New Orleans was a city famous for its music but beneath the joyful noise of jazz, gospel and zydeco it was a city stubbornly separated by race and imperilled by a landscape vulnerable to the extreme ravages of nature. Years after their deaths, Hurricane Katrina would rock Raymond Myles and Mahalia Jackson's graves but somehow, by the grace of God, they held firm.

Juneteenth block party, Scranton, Pennsylvania. The 19th of June was
established by President Joe Biden as a federal holiday in 2021,
the first since Martin Luther King Jr Day in 1983.

9

THE BATTLE FOR CHOCOLATE CITY

Listen Up: 'Bustin' Loose' by Chuck Brown and The Soul Searchers (1978)

Marvin Gaye was born in 1939, less than two miles from the White House at Freedmen's Hospital in Washington D.C., a historic medical centre that had been built in 1862 as the first hospital designed to aid the treatment of formerly enslaved people. By the time Richard Nixon was impeached in 1974, Marvin was universally seen as the greatest soul singer of all time. At D.C.'s Cardozo High School in Northwest, he was a gifted soprano in the choir but left education early to sing with doo-wop groups across the city. He was briefly a member of a group called the D.C. Tones, then The Rainbows, a mid-fifties harmony group that recorded for the legendary Harlem record store owner Bobby Robinson and his R&B label Red Robin. After a short spell in the US Air Force,

Gaye returned to the nascent Washington D.C. music scene to join a group called The Marquees. It was during a short residency as an opening act at the Apollo Theater in Harlem that Gaye met Harvey Fuqua, the man who was destined to become his mentor, his brother-in-law and the doorman to a phenomenal career at Motown in Detroit.

At Motown, Marvin Gaye's vocal dexterity continued. He was positioned initially as a romantic lead and aspired to replace Nat King Cole as a black crooner, but then he found huge success as a duet singer with Mary Wells, Kim Weston and ultimately Tammi Terrell. Their partnership would produce some of the most memorable records of their era, but was cut short in 1967 when Terrell was diagnosed with a brain tumour. After she died in 1970, Marvin fought depression and cocaine addiction to begin crafting his magnus opus, the era-defining concept album *What's Going On* (1971), the record that most vividly painted the social landscape of Nixon's America: the deepening crisis of Vietnam, police brutality in inner-city streets and a culture of despair about America's capacity to transform itself. The restless and unfathomable Gaye left Detroit, then Los Angeles, and spent a recuperative time fighting his demons in Ostend, Belgium, before returning to L.A. for the catastrophic final phase of his life in the family home, where he was eventually killed by his own father.

Marvin Gaye never seemed settled, musically or emotionally. The one constant was his love/hate relationship with his hometown. He once told his biographer, David Ritz: 'I hated Washington. The place filled me with a feeling of hopelessness. Nothing happened in Washington. Nothing was made or produced or sold. It was all government, papers, bureaucrats, and bullshit. Here was a city blessed with musical talent and no place to record, no real labels or promoters or distributors.' His homecoming concerts, first at the old Howard Theater and then at the Kennedy Center, were usually troubled. At one concert, almost to emphasise the point, Gaye sang his introspective track 'Inner City Blues' three times. Although he was born so close to the White House, he considered Detroit to be his home and when asked about those early days he often hid behind evasive regret, as if he wished he had been born somewhere else.

*

Washington D.C. is a unique city, and some of Marvin Gaye's regrets were founded on the curious reality that black music thrived there but was always overshadowed by politics. Although it is historically a majority African American city – unlike Chicago, Detroit, Harlem, Philadelphia and New Orleans – Washington D.C. has hidden its musical scene out of sight, masked by the Beltway politics that dominate the city and its media. But Gaye was wrong on one substantial count. As he gravitated north to Motown, a major R&B rival label was already ahead of the game, and ironically it had its origins in post-war Washington D.C. in the predominantly white community of ambassadors and senators that Marvin Gaye despised.

Atlantic Records was an anomaly. While most independent soul labels were under-capitalised and barely surviving in ghettos across America, Atlantic had emerged from a world of comparative wealth. Implausibly, Atlantic's story starts amidst the leafy prosperity of Sheridan Circle, in the well-appointed 'embassy row' along Massachusetts Avenue. In 1935, Ahmet Ertegun and Nesuhi Ertegun moved into their splendid home on 23rd Street with their father, the Turkish ambassador Mehmet Ertegun. As teenagers they were already jazz fans and D.C.'s thriving jazz scene was like a second heaven. They visited jazz clubs on U Street and record shops on 7th Street, and became regular customers at Waxie Maxie's, the music shop owned by Max Silverman, a local DJ and one-time manager of the top-selling fifties doo-wop group The Clovers. Silverman had started his business back in the 1930s with a radio repair shop and soon expanded into selling deleted records and old stock. He gradually transformed the store into a leading music retail and distribution chain that virtually controlled the soul-music market in Maryland and Virginia. In the nascent days of R&B, crowds gathered to watch local disc jockeys from radio station WOOK-AM broadcast nightly from a glass booth in the front window of the record store on 7th and T Streets NW. It was common for the top sixties soul singers to appear live at the old Howard Theater and travel by taxi to Waxie Maxie's to promote their latest releases.

The brothers began organising jazz concerts at home but, unable to charge entrance fees and sell liquor, and persistently fending off complaints from white neighbours, they eventually broke from these constraints and launched the first desegregated shows in the capital at the Jewish Community Center at 16th and Q Street. Historian Maurice Jackson told *The Washington Post*, 'Two Muslim brothers bringing Black music to the center belonging to our Jewish brothers and sisters. This is historic.' It was their first tentative steps in music promotion.

When their father died in 1944, President Roosevelt and his wife Eleanor, a long-time champion of the arts, sent their condolences, as did the Secretary of State Cordell Hull. The formal messages gave a subtle hint at the ambassador's unique and welcoming demeanour. A White House statement read:

> The death of Mehmet Münir Ertegün has filled us with a sincere and deep sorrow, a sorrow which we share with his hundreds of friends in this country. His kindly and noble spirit and his great ability have given him a beloved position both in and out of Government circles. His loss will not be forgotten. For more than ten years he has represented Turkish interests in the United States with skill and honesty and all of us in the Department of State will miss his many high qualities.

With no settled home and no great need to remain in Washington D.C., the Ertegun brothers began to collaborate with another student, Herb Abramson, who was studying dentistry at NYU. Gradually, they left Washington D.C. and moved north to New York, where they set up makeshift offices in the Ritz Hotel before opening the first Atlantic offices on West 54th Street. In the early fifties, under the conditions of his student grant, Abramson was required to join the US Army dentistry squad and sent to Germany. On his return, his role had been taken by one of the major figures in the popularisation of R&B, Jerry Wexler, an outstanding salesman and producer who would later describe Atlantic as 'the West Point of R&B' as it showcased LaVern Baker, Ray Charles, The Drifters, Otis Redding, Wilson Pickett, Aretha Franklin and Donny Hathaway.

Ruth Brown was the label's first major signing and that too was in odd circumstances. She was scheduled to debut at the Apollo in Harlem when she was seriously injured in a car crash near Philadelphia and rushed to hospital with both legs broken. Ruth Brown signed for Atlantic on 12 January 1949 while in her hospital bed in Chester Hospital, Pennsylvania. She stood on crutches to record her first session for Atlantic, and one of the songs – the blues-inspired ballad

'So Long' – became a hit. Atlantic pushed her to try more upbeat songs and in the next few years she became the best-selling black female performer of the early fifties. The car crash that threatened to end her career turned out to be a tiny moment in the journey towards soul music. Ruth took to wearing voluminous ball gowns on stage, initially to conceal her crippled leg and disguise the orthopaedic cast she was forced to wear, but it became her trademark style, lending glittering sophistication to the rawness of R&B.

With Atlantic now firmly based in Manhattan, Washington D.C.'s next tilt at becoming a centre of black music production was left to two incomers, Raynoma Gordy and her boyfriend the writer-producer Eddie Singleton. Raynoma 'Miss Ray' Gordy was the ex-wife of the Motown Corporation owner Berry Gordy. She had met Singleton when she headed up Motown's writer-development office in New York. Incandescent with the poor divorce settlement she had been offered by her former husband, Raynoma made the ill-advised decision to bootleg several Motown hits, including Mary Wells' 'My Guy', and consequently was arrested by the FBI and spent a night in jail. With the cash from the divorce settlement, and keen to build a roster of new artists, Raynoma and Singleton fixed on Marvin Gaye's theory that Washington D.C. was territory ripe for exploitation. They even tried to talk Marvin into moving home, but it was never on.

During the first half of the twentieth century when Washington D.C. was strictly segregated, the U Street Corridor was the economic, cultural and jazz headquarters. Duke Ellington had been born and raised there and the now-historic Bohemian Caverns jazz club, which hosted Charles Mingus, Miles Davis and Nina Simone, dominated the intersection of 11th and U Street NW. It was there that Ramsey Lewis recorded his ground-breaking modernist track 'The In Crowd', featuring Eldee Young and Isaac Holt of Young-Holt Unlimited.

Gordy and Singleton set up Shrine Records, now widely eulogised within the obsessive community of collectors and crate diggers as the world's most sought-after record label. Shrine began recording in the emotional aftermath of the assassination of President Kennedy and chose as its label insignia a shrine based on Kennedy's resting place at Arlington Cemetery. In 1964, Gordy and Singleton signed a lease on an office building within a townhouse at 3 Thomas Circle NW,

Washington D.C. A grand house with three storeys, nineteen rooms and a basement which doubled as a rehearsal space. Singleton was armed with a catalogue of songs he himself had written, and Raynoma Gordy, a gifted singer with perfect pitch and a classical background, began to scour D.C. for singers and R&B acts they could attract to the new label. Cautious about over-committing to studio time, their preference was for one-take experienced singers and so Singleton chose to record the Beltway vocalist Leroy Taylor and two other established talents, Ray Pollard and J. D. Bryant. The latter's song 'I Won't Be Coming Back' (Shrine, 1966) has since become one of the holy grails of the Shrine catalogue.

Night after night the Shrine producers trekked around the city's major R&B venues: the Lion's Den, the Colt Lounge, the Flamingo Room, Turner's Arena and Ed Murphy's Supper Club on Georgia Avenue, which hosted shows by Stevie Wonder, Redd Foxx, Oscar Brown Jr, Gil Scott-Heron and Roberta Flack. A sign at the door of Ed Murphy's club said, 'Gentlemen are expected to wear neckties, turtlenecks, ascots or dashikis.' Tall and articulate, Murphy was the kind of local entrepreneur that Richard Nixon tried to attract to his 'black capitalist' crusade. He sported a platinum watch, drove a grey Cadillac with the licence plate 'Murph' and published *Black Dollar*, a magazine for the black business community. His heart and soul were faithful to civil rights, however. He was respected for his social work, volunteering at shelters for the homeless and helping to cook Thanksgiving dinners at the House of Imagine, a women's refuge in Northwest Washington.

By 1965 black pop music was emboldened by the international success of The Supremes, and Shrine joined the long queue of small independent labels desperate to unearth an all-girl group who could capture the soul zeitgeist. They signed The Cautions, a male harmony group in the style of The Temptations, who formed as teenagers in the playground of Stuart Junior High School in the Stanton Park neighbourhood in Northeast Washington, and two groups that sounded like the famous Motown girl groups: Les Chansonettes, from Baltimore, and The DC Blossoms, who took their name from the spectacular cherry trees gifted to the city by the Mayor of Tokyo as a gesture of friendship back in 1912. By the mid-sixties, the annual Cherry Blossom Festival had reached out to the African American community and was staging summer soul music events in inner-city parks. There were several barriers that stood between The DC Blossoms and success, regrettably. One was body image. The group's lead singers, Jacqui Burton and her sister Vicky, were both overweight and unsuited to the shimmering modernist style that The Supremes had adopted while performing in fashionable venues such as the Copacabana and the casino hotels on the Las Vegas Strip. Diana Ross had set standards of sophistication and physical allure that had broken with the R&B of the past. Ironically, the rich soaring voices of The DC Blossoms – redolent of traditional gospel choirs or the bar-room chanters of the Chitlin' Circuit – would become desirable again at the height of disco, when similarly styled singers such as Two Tons o' Fun aka The Weather Girls used their weight as a humorous calling card. When Aretha Franklin played a gospel-inspired diner waitress in *The Blues Brothers*, she used her bulk to reinforce her commanding image.

The biggest barrier was not calories, however, it was the financial state of Shrine Records itself. In the vinyl trade distribution was king and Shrine struggled to get records into shops beyond the Beltway. The label was over-dependent on a small chain of record stores on the East Coast and even their most successful releases only barely dented the national charts. Still bitter about the collapse of her marriage, Raynoma subsequently claimed that Motown's formidable sales force had maliciously blocked Shrine's route to market. It was a plausible but exaggerated factor in the demise of Shrine Records. By 1966, the label was struggling to pay its bills, and like many small companies before and since it became a victim of under-capitalisation. The fatal blow was struck on one of D.C.'s darkest nights, when in April 1968 word of the assassination of Martin Luther King hit the prime-time news bulletins.

The Washington Post reflected on a night that came to shape the streets around the White House for years to come.

The day had been warm and breezy, with a high near 70. But the teeming intersection of 14th and U streets was tense. There had been an ugly fight there two days before. Objects had been thrown at police, and two arrests had been made. As the sun set, this cultural and financial centre of black Washington was still volatile.

It was hoped protest would be short-lived but the Peoples Drug Store on the corner of 14th and U streets became the epicentre of intense rioting. Store windows were shattered, and bystanders became opportunistic looters, dashing inside to grab what they could: TVs, clothing, food, beer, hats, shoes. One man bled to death when he slashed his neck and chest on a broken store window. The destruction was unprecedented, so close to the White House. More than 900 businesses were damaged, including half of the city's 383 liquor stores. Nearly 700 dwellings were destroyed, and police arrested 7,600 adults and juveniles on riot-related charges. Once-bustling blocks were reduced to rubble. In four days of upheaval, thirteen people were killed. The skeleton of one victim was found in the rubble three years later, and two others were never identified.

As Washington burned and the flames became visible from the White House President Johnson contacted his security to assess whether he could visit the most troubled area. It was deemed so unsafe that the most cautious advised the President to stay put. LBJ rightly believed that would be interpreted either as uncaring or the sign of a terrified President. A compromise was struck, and General Westmoreland's helicopter was called into service. According to Clint Hill, the Secret Service special agent in charge of presidential protection, Johnson flew across the city to assess the riot damage. From the air, through the haze of burning smoke, the city looked like a battlefield. The President immediately ordered troops to reclaim the streets. A convoy of soldiers from Fort Myer in Virginia crossed Memorial Bridge into the city, and more came in from Fort Meade in Maryland, until eventually 13,000 troops were on the streets of Washington D.C. – the most to occupy an American city since the Civil War. Like Detroit and Los Angeles, Washington would come to witness a middle-class exodus from certain districts that was known by the ungainly term 'white flight'. Roderick Harrison, a sociology and anthropology professor at Howard University, claimed that 'people thought of them as areas you don't go into at all, much less live in, unless you were essentially looking for trouble.'

Shrine Records, already collapsing into bankruptcy, were victims of the fires too. After releasing nearly two dozen singles, 'Do What I Want' (Shrine, 1967) by the Cavaliers finally brought the shutters down. Like many other Shrine releases, the label's final record disappeared and was only played a few times on local radio. What remained of its stock was stored in a branch of Waxie Maxie's on 14th Street, one of the first buildings to be burned to the ground in the riots. The destruction of Shrine's stock only added to the label's rarity and so its many enduring myths.

Known colloquially as 'The Mecca', Howard University's influence on the development of soul music is immense. Situated in Northwest Washington, close to the troubled streets that were burned to the ground following King's assassination, Howard has a track record of attracting the best black students from across America. By the sixties, half of America's black doctors and a quarter of its black lawyers were Howard graduates. The university was often called 'the black Harvard' and because of its proximity to the White House was frequently the place where presidents would choose to address students, and so the nation. Bill Clinton gave an emotional speech at the university's graduation ceremony in the immediate aftermath of the Asian tsunami, and his wife, Hillary Rodham Clinton, was honoured there in 2018. Two years previously, at the university's Commencement Convocation event, Barack Obama was given an honorary degree. 'Just two years after the civil war,' he intoned, 'they created this university with a vision – a vision of uplift; a vision for an America where our fates would be determined not by our race, gender, religion or creed, but where we would be free – in every sense – to pursue our individual and collective dreams.'

In one of many resentful retaliations against the Obama administration, President Donald Trump later claimed that while Obama had spoken fine words it was in fact he who had secured the university's future at a time of financial crisis, a typical exaggeration based on the fact that Congress had approved STEM funding, a portion of which filtered down to historically black universities, Howard among them. Among Howard University's alumni are giants of African American politics, including Thurgood Marshall, the first black judge on the Supreme Court; Andrew Young, who rose from the civil rights movement to become Jimmy Carter's Ambassador to the UN and the Mayor of Atlanta; David Dinkins, the 106th Mayor of New York; and Vice President Kamala Harris.

For all its governmental connections, however, it was in the realm of music and radical community politics that Howard set itself apart. Although Washington failed to produce a long-standing black-music record label, it had a university that was in every respect an academy of soul and jazz. Howard was the campus that educated Jessye Norman, Carla Thomas, Donny Hathaway, Roberta Flack, Leroy Hutson, The Clark Sisters, Donald Byrd, The Blackbyrds, local go-go band Trouble Funk and ultimately one of the superstars of rap music Sean 'Puff Daddy' Combs.

One of black music's hugely transformative soul songs, Donny Hathaway's 'The Ghetto' (Atlantic, 1969), was conceived near the Howard campus in the immediate aftermath of the riots. Hathaway, a nervy, impetuous and brilliant musician, had a near-neurotic interest in the future direction of black music and wanted to bring the improvisational genius of jazz back into the soul mainstream. He and fellow-student Leroy Hutson sketched out an early version of the song while sharing an apartment next to the campus. Hutson remembers the day 'The Ghetto' first flickered into life. It was during a late summer thunderstorm, the sun burning through dark ominous clouds when the heavens opened. Rain fell like a drum solo. 'There was thunder, rain and sunshine all at once,' Hutson reminisced, 'and the two of us knelt at the windows of the apartment and looked out, and it was like the traffic was synchronised to the movement of the song. It was all so magical and a very wonderful occasion.'

To fully understand their epiphany, you have to understand the streets outside. Inner-city Washington was still smouldering, buildings charred into rubble, the white middle-classes and particularly the political establishment already fleeing. Standing proud amongst the ghetto's many social problems, the university campus stretched from decaying streets around 14th and up the vertiginous acres of Rock Creek Park. Hathaway and Hutson's apartment was near the corner of 14th and T Street, one of the intersections where the riot bit hardest.

The apartment where 'The Ghetto' was conceived was a hive of improvisation. Their classmate Roberta Flack, who had been the youngest student ever to enrol at the university when she won a piano scholarship at 15, provided guest vocals and soon became Hathaway's recording partner in a series of stunning love duets, including the quiet-storm classics 'Where Is The Love' (1972) and 'The Closer I Get To You' (1978). A sister record to 'The Ghetto', the powerful 'Trying Times', had the same depth and social anger. It too was co-written with Leroy Hutson and given to Roberta Flack for her debut album on Atlantic in 1969. At Howard, Donny Hathaway also met his future wife Eulaulah, the mother of modern soul star Lalah Hathaway, at choir practice.

In the late sixties, Howard University was in the process of establishing what was to become a world-class jazz-studies curriculum, to be led by Professor Donald Byrd. Herbie Hancock was already studying there and Byrd's new intake of students became the successful funk group The Blackbyrds. Among their batch of hits was the jazz-funk club hit 'Walking In Rhythm' (1974) and an up-tempo homage to the university's outdoor playground 'Rock Creek Park' (1975). By the time The Blackbyrds were on campus, Donny Hathaway had drifted. For a while he returned home to Chicago, where he became an A&R producer for Curtis Mayfield's Curtom label and recorded a top-drawer duet 'I Thank You' with June Conquest (1972). Hathaway stayed at Curtom long enough to sign his friend Leroy Hutson as a vocalist and produced studio sessions for local singers Garland Green and Syl Johnson. In a furious twelve months of activity, Hathaway also contracted another progressive group from Howard, The Winstons, of 'Amen Break' fame.

As students Hathaway and Hutson witnessed a social decay around the Howard campus which was the prequel to a militant phase in the university's history. In March 1968 about 1,000 students took over the administration building, leading to the shutdown of the school for a week. Among the leaders of the campus uprisings were Tony Gittens, at the time of writing the director of the Washington D.C. International Film Festival, and Stokely Carmichael, the Trinidadian student who was a prominent figure in the Student Nonviolent Coordinating Committee (SNCC) and Honorary Prime Minister of the Black Panther Party. The sit-ins were to protest the Vietnam War and the lack of a black studies curriculum. The protesters improvised a chant with passing motorists – 'Beep Beep Bang Bang Ungawa Black Power'. Although the term 'Black Power' is commonly credited to Carmichael, he concedes that it was first used by a now long-forgotten Howard University student, and that he simply amplified it.

Black Power challenged orthodox electoral politics and sent a charge of electric energy through music. The Diplomats, formed by Sam Culley, a precociously talented young man from North Brentwood across the District line in Maryland, and another group called The Young Senators stand out. Their backing band, 7th & T, took their name from a busy intersection on the southern edges of Howard University which has since been christened Chuck Brown Way, in honour of the go-go legend. But it was the transformation of The Diplomats into the mysterious Skull Snaps that speaks volumes about the changes that surged through black American music in the dark days of the Nixon administration.

The Skull Snaps recorded a stellar LP that featured a montage of skulls on a front sleeve that looked more like a Satanic thrash-metal album and a back cover that carried an image of a female skeleton wearing a fancy Victorian hat. 'At that particular time, in '73, black bands weren't getting a lot of play or getting signed,' Sam Culley told attendees of the Red Bull Music Academy. 'So [we decided] to take our pictures off and went with the three skulls on the album cover. And one day I was in the store and the records on the shelf, and I said, "Damn, that looks like a rock album."' It was a marketing distraction that became a legend.

In early 1973, The Diplomats travelled to Venture Sound Studios in the small township of Hillsborough, New Jersey, to record an album that became an underground classic as inspirational to the soul avant garde as The Temptations' *Psychedelic Shack* had been to the mainstream. They had a promise of financial backing from GSF Records, who behind the scenes were struggling to stay afloat.

When the key members of The Diplomats – Ervan Waters, Sam Culley and George 'Buzzy' Bragg – checked into Venture Sound it was nearing the height of its success. The studio was owned by musical arranger Tony Camillo, who was enjoying a creative purple patch. He had just recorded Gladys Knight & The Pips' globally successful torch song 'Midnight Train To Georgia' and Millie Jackson's exquisite deep-soul version of Phillip Mitchell's 'Hurts So Good' (1973). The studio was bursting at the seams and so The Diplomats were matched up with local in-house producer, George Kerr, who was at the time also using his mobile studio to record inside Rahway State Prison.

Kerr and his friend, the prolific arranger Bert Keyes, encouraged The Diplomats to follow their instincts and abandon the final remnants of sixties soul. The Skull Snaps were born, and in one hectic studio session they recorded an album that in time would enrapture musical subcultures across decades, including northern soul, rare groove and ultimately hip-hop. Among the stand-out tracks were the prophetic 'It's A New Day', the pounding 'My Hang Up Is You' and a blaxploitation cult sound, 'I'm Your Pimp', which sounded like it had fallen from the heavenly out-takes of *Super Fly*. 'It's A New Day', a Black Power rallying call, was sampled and re-versioned in hip-hop tracks by The Pharcyde, Eric B. & Rakim and Common, then finally into songs by chart outfits such as The Prodigy and even Alanis Morissette. It is the kind of cult album that urban hipsters never tire of raiding.

For all its political suaveness, Washington D.C. housed raw and uncut funk. In the sixties and seventies, just miles from the White House, was a grassroots sound that declared war on gentility. Among its remarkable array of street bands were Harmon Bethea's band The Maskman and the Agents, Zeke and the Soul Setters, The Sounds of Shea, The Skull Snaps, The Dynamic Superiors, Curtis Pope and The Midnight Movers, The Brute Band, Chuck Brown and The Soul Searchers, Oneness of JuJu and the El Corols, a hired backing band for Stevie Wonder, Curtis Mayfield and The Temptations, who released 'Chick Chick' (Rouser, 1968), another northern-soul funk treasure. For a brief and bright spell in the mid seventies Washington D.C. had its own funk indie label, Black Fire Records, which profiled drum-heavy Afrocentric music. Every day, deep funk would blast out on the airwaves on WHUR-FM courtesy of jazz student Jimmy Gray, who used the moniker Black Fire. In these years, the civil rights and Black Power movements appeared poised to usher in a new era of progressive black governance. The city had just achieved a form of 'home rule' in 1973 and for the first time since Reconstruction its large black population were able to elect their own leaders. 'Culture generally imitates life,' Charles Stephenson, the manager of the band Experience Unlimited, said reflectively, 'and at that point in time the Black consciousness movement was in full stride.'

Such was the reputation of Washington D.C.'s funk underground that, in April 1975, the eccentric agitator George Clinton released

Chocolate City, a nine-track album paying homage to the city and its drum-and-bass credentials. The title track satirised the capital as a chocolate city with vanilla suburbs and praised the demographics that were changing inner-city America. The album cover featured the Lincoln Memorial and the Capitol Building dripping with molten chocolate. What was less visible to the mainstream was the collective of artists that Clinton had gather around him – the master bass guitarist Bootsy Collins, vocalists Clarence 'Fuzzy' Haskins and keyboardist Bernie Worrell. It was, in the words of rock criticism, a 'supergroup' but in the story of soul music it nodded backwards to the great sixties showbands such as James Brown and his Famous Flames, Motown's Funk Brothers, and Stax band The Bar-Kays. But a new generation of multi-artist bands had emerged in the seventies, among them War, Rufus featuring Chaka Khan, The Brothers Johnson, Graham Central Station, Con Funk Shun, The Fatback Band, Kool and the Gang, Change, Cameo and The S.O.S. Band.

The act that best exemplified this showband style was one of the most famous groups ever to emerge from Washington D.C. – Chuck Brown and The Soul Searchers. Brown, a former D.C. street kid who served a sentence for murder in Virginia's Lorton Correctional Complex, traded cigarettes for a guitar and became a self-taught lead guitarist. On release from prison, he toured as a back-up musician with Chicago soul singer Jerry Butler and then joined a Hispanic band called Los Latinos, picking up skill in Latin percussion. His first hit was 'We The People' (1972), a phrase borrowed from the introduction to the US Constitution and subsumed into black politics. Later hits include 'We Need Some Money' (1984), a blistering attack on Reaganomics, and the evergreen 'Bustin' Loose' (1978), an anthem played to this day as a rallying song for the Washington Nationals baseball team.

It was Chuck Brown who paved the way for go-go, a genre of music virtually unique to Washington. For years it was a shadow-sound to New York hip-hop and was based on a hypnotically danceable groove produced by banks of live musicians rather than a DJ. Brown had a residency at the Maverick Room at 4th Street and Rhode Island, where regulars would play a call-and-response game with him and his musicians beneath the shrapnel lights of the old revolving mirror ball. According to go-go historian Natalie Hopkinson, 'Go-Go can feel a lot like a Pentecostal church service. Both are run for extended hours, and you never know when they will end. Neither erects a huge barrier between who is performing and who is watching.' Brown was helped along the way by the speculative Maxx Kidd, a local entrepreneur and go-go label owner who had been a singer with the Shrine group The Enjoyables but stayed put in Washington after Shrine's demise. Go-go took its name from the live nightclubs along 14th Street, where the 1968 riots had originated, and with Chuck Brown leading the charge numerous local bands sprang up over the coming decade, among them Experience Unlimited, The East Coast Connection, Rare Essence, Trouble Funk, Little Benny & The Masters, Redds and the Boys, and the Petworth Band.

Go-go was the closest black-music movement to the White House geographically but it might as well have been from another planet. At the scene's height in the eighties none of the major bands were invited to play for President Reagan, no doubt because go-go was an underground phenomenon popular in public-housing projects such as the Southwest's James Creek, the Northeast's Trinidad neighbourhood or Southeast's Barry Farm. It rose as a subculture at a time when deprived areas of Chocolate City were ravaged by drug crime. Angel dust had become intrinsically associated with the nation's capital and after steady year-on-year increases the annual rate of homicide had risen above 400. The comedian Jay Leno seized the opportunity to mock the image of the 'murder capital', telling late-night audiences in a reference to the basketball team, 'The Washington Bullets are changing their name. They don't want their name associated with crime. From now on they'll just be known as The Bullets.' In a bungled press conference, the Mayor of Washington, Marion Barry, told journalists, 'If you take out the killings, Washington actually has a very very low crime rate.' There was logic in there somewhere, but Barry was not fit to explain it. A few years later he was arrested on charges of possession of crack cocaine at the downtown Vista International Hotel after an undercover sting by the FBI and D.C. police.

Possibly Trouble Funk's global album *Go-Go Crankin': Paint the White House Black* helped entrench the stand-off between underground funk and mainstream politics but it was not until Black Music Month in 2001, when President George W. Bush invited Queen Latifah, Boyz II

Men, Lionel Hampton and Chuck Brown to assemble at the White House to sign a proclamation honouring the contribution of black music to American society, that go-go breached the perimeters of the big house.

Some of the most prominent go-go artists were students from the Howard campus but many more had learnt to play in the city's remarkable network of high-school marching bands, enabled in part by enlightened local education policies that allowed kids from often the most deprived neighbourhoods to take brass and percussion instruments home at night. One obvious reason that the bands were supported was the services they provided to the White House and the federal buildings along Pennsylvania Avenue. Almost every major state occasion and commemorative event hosted by embassies across Washington D.C. featured a marching band with mostly African American teenagers colourfully dressed in their band uniforms. One of the most successful, the Cardozo High School Marching Band, under the leadership of musical director Robert Gill, became the first band from the District of Columbia to march in the famous Rose Bowl parade in Pasadena, California, performing for approximately 1.5 million spectators. What the go-go funk bands and the high school marching bands shared was a pounding in-step beat and an improvisational cleverness that allowed them to imitate various styles and move effortlessly from 'Marching Through Georgia' to the theme from *Star Wars*. One outstanding early go-go record, 'Summer In The Parks' (New Directions, 1974) by The East Coast Connection, audaciously merged imitations of performances by Chuck Brown, James Brown, Earth Wind and Fire and Kool and the Gang without dropping a note. A stomping masterclass in clever and improvisational live funk.

The Ellipse is a fifty-two-acre park just south of the White House. During the Civil War it was used as a corral for horses and mules, then it became a makeshift baseball ground and in 1923, when President Calvin Coolidge lit the first National Christmas Tree, it became the site of one of Washington's enduring presidential rituals. Each year the serving president lights the tree, situated on the northeast quadrant of the Ellipse. The walkway to the tree is called the Pathway of Peace and traditionally the ceremony is used as an opportunity to reiterate

A street flyer for Washington D.C. go-go bands Trouble Funk and Hot, Cold Sweat. The hardcore go-go rock band Craig Rosen's Static Disruptors are the openers. Rosen sold his precious Marvel comic collection to pay for their 1982 single, 'D.C. Groove'.

America's commitment to global peace. Nothing has been allowed to disrupt the event: not the Vietnam War, not the invasion of Cambodia, not the Iran–Contra affair, wars in Afghanistan and Iraq, nor al-Qaeda's destruction of the Twin Towers. But the Ellipse has another purpose: it is a gathering place for marches, demonstrations, sit-down strikes and rallies against the federal government. And the government doesn't have a monopoly on Christmas trees either. By the Christmas of 2020, as division in America deepened, the Washington D.C. chapter of the racial justice movement Black Lives Matter Black erected trees across the city, adorned with the names of victims of police violence.

The story of America's unfolding democracy can be told through the major marches or demonstrations that the seat of government has attracted. Martin Luther King's historic 'I Have a Dream' speech was delivered on 28 August 1963 during the March on Washington for Jobs and Freedom. On Saturday 15 October 1969, more than a quarter of a million people attended the First Moratorium to End the War in Vietnam, and on Saturday 15 November the Second Moratorium attracted more than 500,000 demonstrators. The latter was preceded by the March Against Death, which began on the Thursday evening and continued throughout that night and the following day. More than 40,000 people gathered at the Ellipse to parade silently down Pennsylvania Avenue to the White House. Hour after hour, they walked silently in single file, each bearing a placard with the name of a dead American soldier or a destroyed Vietnamese village. It was a dignified theatre which spoke eloquently of America's growing disenchantment with both President Nixon and the war.

Almost every major public issue since has found expression through marches on Washington. On 9 July 1978, the March for the Equal Rights Amendment brought 100,000 women to D.C.; two days later, the Longest Walk saw thousands of Native Americans finish their 3,200-mile-long walk from San Francisco, rallying at the National Mall to advocate for rights and religious freedoms. On 14 October 1979, Washington drew between 75,000 and 125,000 gay men and lesbians to demand equal civil rights. On 16 October 1995, the Million Man March gathered to oppose negative stereotypes of black men, to highlight urban poverty and to increase voter registration within African American communities. In a stand-off familiar in marches across the globe, the organisers estimated an attendance of somewhere between 1.5 and 2 million whereas the United States Park Police estimated no more than 120,000. It was a disagreement that led to an almighty uproar. One of the march organisers, the Nation of Islam leader Louis Farrakhan, threatened to sue the police and consequently it was decided not to publish police estimates in future. Whatever the statistics, the Million Man March was unanimously seen to be one of the largest civil rights demonstrations in history, with men flooding into Washington from every state in the union to listen to speeches by Stevie Wonder, Maya Angelou and the dowager of civil rights, Rosa Parks.

At the time of the march the economy was strong and yet still the black jobless rate was 9.9 per cent, more than double that of whites. Race relations were improving, but the acquittal of O. J. Simpson in the trial of the century had divided opinion and the death of an unarmed black motorist, Jonny Gammage, the cousin of NFL footballer Ray Seals, prompted outrage among many African Americans. Gammage was stopped by police while driving his cousin's Jaguar in a suburb of Pittsburgh and died of asphyxiation at the hands of serving police officers. It was a macabre precursor of police killings yet to come and of how Washington D.C. would become an ideological battle ground for the histrionic turmoil of the Trump presidency.

Rappers such as Ice Cube and Chuck D spoke out in support of the Million Man March and encouraged young people to get to Washington by any means necessary. Shaggy, Method Man and Coolio were riding high in the R&B charts, only marginally overshadowed by the superstar generation of Whitney Houston, Mariah Carey and Michael Jackson. An album commemorating the March – *One Million Strong* – featuring Snoop Dogg, Chuck D and RZA of Wu-Tang Clan was released a month after the march. It is totemic in rap circles, featuring one of the only collaborations on vinyl of the great tragedians of hip-hop, Tupac Shakur and Biggie Smalls, a prescient urban anthem called 'Runnin' From Tha Police'. In 1996, filmmaker Spike Lee directed a film titled *Get on the Bus*, featuring music by Michael Jackson and Curtis Mayfield, which follows a group of unconnected black men from quite different backgrounds who take a bus trip from Los Angeles to Washington to join the march.

One of the overriding messages that the Million Man March advocated was that African American men should stand up and take responsibility for their lives, their community and their families, to challenge the myth of errant and fitful fatherhood that had stigmatised them for decades. Many brought their young children with them, as a statement of proud parenthood. A village of tents sprung up on the Ellipse, populated by families who had given their mothers time off. It was a throwback to Resurrection City, the tented city that Martin Luther King's movement had built in the summer of 1968 to bring the hurt of poverty to the seat of power.

Although women were not excluded from the Million Man March, community groups argued that they should not attend, and so leave the demonstration to assert the role of men in family life. It was a warm day in every respect. *Washington Post* reporter Michael A. Fletcher wrote that it was the perfect day to 'bathe in the soothing warmth of brotherhood'. Also present was an unknown young lawyer called Barack Obama, who told the *Chicago Reader* on his return home: 'What I saw was a powerful demonstration of an impulse and need for African American men to come together to recognize each other and affirm our rightful place in the society.' Despite fears of violence, there was little sign of drinking, drugs or disruption. When it was all over, teams of clean-up men scoured the site collecting rubbish, denying any opportunity for negative media. The Mall was left pristine, as if the gathering had never occurred. Billy Paul's Philadelphia anthem 'Bring The Family Back' was revitalised for the march, its mainstream family values turned into a statement of racial justice.

In October 2002, Washington was gripped by two simultaneous dramas: the political escalation that would lead to the invasion of Iraq and a series of frightening sniper attacks on otherwise unconnected citizens going about their daily lives at gas stations, fried chicken outlets and parking lots. Ten people were killed and three others seriously wounded in a series of shootings in the Beltway area. One of the victims, Lori Anne Rivers, was shot while cleaning her car. She resided in Silver Springs, Maryland, in a house near Jose Williams' D&B Sound Studios, which since the seventies had been one of the spiritual homes of DC soul, where The Summits, Clifton Dyson, Eddie Drennon and the harmony group Promise had all recorded. The murder of Lori Anne Rivers sent shockwaves through the northern Beltway suburbs and panic spread as the killings continued down into the heart of D.C. itself. Another victim was Metro bus driver Conrad Johnson, a regular face on the local go-go circuit at clubs like The Ice Box and Byrne Manor in Oxon Hill where he befriended Anwan 'Big G' Glover, the lead talker of The Backyard Band, who broke out from the local go-go circuit and became nationally known as an actor, playing Slim Charles in HBO's *The Wire*.

The mastermind behind the sniper killings was John Allen Muhammad, a singularly complex character in America's dark catalogue of serial killers. An army veteran of Desert Storm during the first Gulf War, he left the military as a decorated sergeant and then joined the Nation of Islam, where among his list of duties was acting as a steward at the Million Man March. As the marchers reflected on positive fatherhood his life was about to fall apart, shattered by a bitter divorce and an intense custody battle in which he lost access to his children. Muhammad informally adopted a homeless Jamaican teenager, Lee Boyd Malvo, who he raised and mentored. Their relationship was both disturbing and touching, and together they embarked on a bizarre killing spree, involving sniper fire from the converted back trunk of a Blue 1990 Chevrolet Caprice. The two killers were eventually caught sleeping in the car that had become their home, parked in a rest stop on Interstate 70, near Myersville, Maryland. Speaking in a weekly radio address at the time, President George W. Bush spoke of the continuing threat of terrorism, but many in the Metro area saw it as a coded reference to the sniper attacks at home. 'Last week the national terrorist threat level was raised to "high",' he said. 'This is primarily a signal to federal, state and local law enforcement to take additional precautions and increase security measures against potential terrorist attacks.'

The marches on Washington did not let up during the sniper attacks. On 15 February 2003, less than four months after the capture of Muhammad, up to 11 million people turned out in 650 cities around the world to protest the US push to invade Iraq. Washington D.C. was awash with placards and protesters once again as part of what was the largest one-day global protest the world has ever seen. Barack Obama, by then an Illinois state senator, had spoken at an anti-war rally in Chicago the day that the resolution authorising the use of military force in Iraq was introduced in Congress. The Senate voted and passed the resolution for war by a 72–23 vote, and it was subsequently signed into law by President George W. Bush five days later.

With no clear UN mandate, the US and its 'Coalition of the Willing' began a 'shock and awe' bombing campaign and invaded Iraq. In a special report, the *New York Times*' Chicago bureau chief Monica Davey wrote:

> If rock 'n' roll, the sounds of Jimi Hendrix, Jefferson Airplane and Creedence Clearwater Revival, was the music of American service members in Vietnam, rap may become the defining pulse for the war in Iraq. It has emerged as a rare realm where soldiers and marines, hardly known for talking about their feelings, are voicing the full range of their emotions and reactions to war. They rap about their resentment of the military hierarchy. But they also rap about their pride, their invincibility, their fallen brothers, their disdain for the enemy and their determination to succeed.

Echoing James Brown's tour of military encampments during the Vietnam War, the USO, the organisation that provides entertainment to the military, responded by sending Nappy Roots, Bubba Sparks, 50 Cent and G-Unit to perform for soldiers in Iraq. Then, southern rapper Ludacris appeared at a giant welcome home at Fort Hood, Texas, for the soldiers of the 4th Infantry, the division that had captured Saddam Hussein. Hip-hop's prevalence was now global, and the protests were not confined to western cities. Iraq's three top rap stars – Saket, Hamid and Anhar – had all been born in the nineties and lived through wars and political crises, and in different ways spoke to the brutal realities of the American invasion on their own doorstep.

By the time Obama entered the White House, the invasion of Iraq was already in the rear-view mirror but two of the most combustible issues in American politics converged yet again. Gun law and race relations ignited primal emotions and a rush to defend the Second Amendment. But another factor emerged in Obama's first term in office, one that is now rarely talked about. In his book *What Were We Thinking*, Carlos Lozada gnaws away at the differences and the divisions that ultimately drove a wedge between Obama and the unpredictable Donald Trump. It was not about race alone; it was also about the deep-seated insecurities of Trump's core supporters. The Obamas' children went to Sidwell Friends School, the Quaker school in Bethesda where Tricia Nixon, Chelsea Clinton and Joe Biden's grandchildren had also studied. What Lozada saw was not just the first black president but a man with an elite education at Harvard and 'a wholesome family' living a glamorous lifestyle in Washington, which made him seem alien to many poorer whites.

Donald Trump worked assiduously to cultivate a hatred for Obama and his policies 'for reasons that are nothing to do with the colour of his skin'. With a transition team in place, the Obama family arrived in the White House and the cobwebs of the past were swept aside. The children coached their father on how to build Spotify playlists and to abandon his sentimental attachment to records and CDs. Michelle's mother, Marian Robinson, joined them as a grandmother-nanny, leaving her small brick bungalow in Chicago's South Side where she had grown up in the era of Sam Cooke, Curtis Mayfield and the brutalised youngster Emmet Till. Like all grandmothers, she shook her head in disbelief at her granddaughters' music, the infernal beat of R&B and the risqué lyrics of urban hip-hop. Malia Obama, Sasha Obama and their pet dog Bo, named after the R&B guitarist Bo Diddley, soon became fixtures in the soap opera of the White House. Barack Obama kept a dossier of quotes and comments from former presidents and one that loomed large was Harry S. Truman saying, 'If you want a friend in Washington, get a dog.' In 2009, he wrote his daughters an open letter, published in *Parade* magazine, advising them 'to grow up in a world with no limits on your dreams and no achievements beyond your reach, and to grow into compassionate, committed women who will help build that world'. It was affirmative, uplifting and chicken soup for the soul – but for the white lower-working-class, left behind by globalisation, it was hard gruel to swallow. In her book *White Trash*, historian Nancy Isenberg wrote: 'For all the country's self-styled egalitarianism, America has always had a class system, with the white working class hanging on in the lower rungs . . . We can no longer ignore the stagnant, expendable bottom layers of society in explaining the national identity.'

On 26 January 2013, the Ellipse was once again buzzing with marchers drawn from across America. The March on Washington for Gun Control came in the immediate aftermath of the Sandy Hook Elementary School massacre, which took the lives of twenty school-children and six adults. It had been a distressing landmark in Barack Obama's first term in office and prompted him to strengthen his campaign for tighter gun laws. Taking their lead from the Million Man

March, gun-control lobbyists launched One Million Moms for Gun Control and staged protests in about a dozen cities, including San Francisco and Austin, Texas. According to a Reuters report, Education Secretary Arne Duncan, one of Obama's networks of Chicago colleagues, said that one student had died because of guns every two weeks while he was chief executive of Chicago's public schools. He denied that gun control was about limiting firearm rights guaranteed by the US Constitution. 'This is about gun responsibility. This is about gun safety. This is about fewer dead Americans, fewer dead children, fewer children living in fear,' Duncan told a rally in D.C.

The statistics were damning. About 11,100 Americans died in gun-related killings in 2011, and there were nearly 20,000 suicides by firearms. The One Million Moms for Gun Control organisers backed Obama's call for a ban on military-style assault weapons and high-capacity ammunition magazines, and for background checks for all gun sales. But the President's proposals faced an uphill battle in Congress and were opposed by gun advocates such as the well-funded NRA.

With goodwill on his side, Obama reached out to supporters in the world of urban music and encouraged R&B and hip-hop artists not to glorify guns and not to undermine social change by fetishising weapons in pop videos or in their lyrics. It was a far from simple exercise. Some responded. Nicki Minaj's next song 'Favorite' (2014) had an anti-gun message, as did Kanye West's earlier collaboration with Jay-Z, 'Murder To Excellence'. But the gun was so deeply embedded in the mythology of rap, disentangling it was far from easy. Since the days of urban decay in the eighties, prominent rap groups had defended the constitutional rights of African Americans to bear arms. Public Enemy's 'Miuzi Weighs A Ton' (1987), Boogie Down Productions' '9mm Goes Bang' (1986) and Ice Cube 'Man's Best Friend' (1991) all glorified gun ownership and challenged the presumption that guns were the sole preserve of white southerners or small-town militias. As the 'Cop Killer' controversy that permeated the Bush and Clinton administrations had shown, it was easy to spark a moral panic for newspaper editors to draw upon and for the growing army of right-wing radio hosts who had emerged in the wake of Rush Limbaugh to exaggerate. America had an imaginary new villain in its midst: he was male, African American, wearing a hoodie and presumed to be carrying a gun.

The killing of Trayvon Martin was the first full page in a story that would once again tear America asunder. Trayvon was an African American high-school student from Miami Gardens, Florida, who was visiting his father in a gated community in Sanford when he was approached by a neighbourhood watch captain named George Michael Zimmerman. Neighbours report hearing gunfire, and Zimmerman subsequently acknowledged that he shot the boy, claiming it was self-defence. Much hinged on what Trayvon Martin was carrying or wearing when he died. His clothing included a black hooded top with a badge pinned to it showing a picture of his dead cousin. There was also his cell phone, on which he had been talking to his girlfriend. In his pockets were a cigarette lighter, some earphones, a can of Arizona watermelon juice, just over $40 in cash, a bag of Skittles he'd just bought from a nearby 7-Eleven, and no weapon of any kind. The packet of Skittles became an icon that seemed to encapsulate an everyday act of an ordinary boy caught up in random circumstances, one of many small glimpses into a society that seemed to harbour a racist pathology.

In a way that would have daunted previous presidents, Barack Obama took to the podium in the James S. Brady Press Briefing Room in the West Wing of the White House and spoke from the heart.

You know, when Trayvon Martin was first shot, I said that this could have been my son. Another way of saying that is Trayvon Martin could have been me 35 years ago. And when you think about why, in the African American community at least, there's a lot of pain around what happened here, I think it's important to recognize that the African American community is looking at this issue through a set of experiences and a history that doesn't go away . . .

There are very few African American men in this country who haven't had the experience of being followed when they were shopping in a department store. That includes me. There are very few African American men who haven't had the experience of walking across the street and hearing the locks click on the doors of cars. That happens to me – at least before I was a senator. There are very few African Americans who haven't had the experience of getting on an elevator and a woman clutching her purse nervously and holding her breath until she had a chance to get off. That happens often.

It was a theme picked up by Ta-Nahisi Coates who went to great lengths to track the widely circulated myths about Trayvon Martin. A photograph shared on social media claiming to be of the 16-year-old victim was actually a 32-year-old rapper with facial tattoos. Coates exposed the fact that imagery of Trayvon Martin had been used for target practice by law enforcement officers and the existence of iPhone games in which he was the target in crude shooter videos. He even unearthed a theory put out to the press by George Zimmerman's family that Martin was a gunrunner and drug-dealer. Neither was even remotely true.

The cultural discrimination that surrounded Trayvon Martin's death did not go unnoticed. In 2013, following Zimmerman's acquittal, three female black organisers – Alicia Garza, the daughter of a single mother from Oakland, California; Patrisse Cullors, an artist and activist from Los Angeles; and Opal Tometi, a Nigerian American from Phoenix, Arizona, with a history of campaigning for immigrant rights – created a political movement called Black Lives Matter. It began as a coalition of like-minded young women and grew virally with the global reach of the internet to become the largest mass movement for racial justice ever. One of its principal motivations channelled the female civil rights leader Fannie Lou Hamer: 'We are sick and tired of being sick and tired.' In Washington D.C. core organiser Nee Nee Taylor built a coalition of groups across the city to give Black Lives Matter high visibility in the most visible square mile in America. The principle was always to act local.

Alicia Garza had also started the Black Futures Lab and the Black to the Future Action Fund, trying to get people to take their protests to the polls. Although there was a long-standing tendency for R&B musicians to support the Democrats, in August 2020 rapper Ice Cube laid down a challenge to both presidential campaigns via a pamphlet called 'Contract with Black America'. Ice Cube never met Trump face to face, but he travelled to a Washington hotel to meet the President's campaign team, who responded with the 'Platinum Plan', a list of vague policy goals and action items which included more affordable healthcare at the very moment that Trump was demonising Obamacare, his predecessor's health plan. Also on the 'Platinum Plan' was improved voter registration, an issue that had been an open sore within black communities dating back to slavery and the brutal repression of the Ku Klux Klan. With time, it became one of the ace cards of the civil rights movement and slowly began to shape electoral change, delivering the first modern-day black mayors in the major urban centres, among them Richard Hatcher in Gary, Indiana, Carl Stokes in Cleveland, Ohio, and Walter Washington in the nation's capital. They were all elected in 1967.

In those pioneering days black musicians largely played the role of fundraisers, appearing at rallies and concerts and periodically releasing records that carried the message of change: Sam Cooke, Nina Simone and the Chicago group the Impressions were prominent among them. More recently, with the facility of the internet, web forums and social media, R&B artists have come to play a much more visible role as influencers directly engaged with their global fan bases. The singer John Legend, a high-profile advocate of criminal justice reform, led a celebrity campaign to restore the voting rights of former criminals. As a child Legend had been a voracious reader and over-achiever at high school in Springfield, Ohio, reading political biographies and the slave narratives of the Underground Railroad. Others prominent in campaigns to increase voter registration among the poorest communities were soul singers Stephanie Mills, Chaka Khan and Lalah Hathaway. One of the stand-out tracks from the civil rights movie *Selma* featured John Legend. 'Glory', co-credited to Chicago-born rapper Lonnie Lynn, better known by his stage name Common, blends piano-led soul and sonorous speechifying rap to commemorate the titanic Selma–Montgomery march in 1965, when 50,000 gathered at the state capital of Alabama to demand passage of the Voting Rights Act. 'Glory' is a track that speaks as much to the story of black American music as to the emotional rage about the accumulating deaths on America's streets. When the civil rights campaign was at its height music was sold primarily on vinyl, which was in many respects poorly promoted, limited in its radio coverage and restricted to local markets within black neighbourhoods. By the time *Selma* was released in 2014, with the Black Lives Matter movement in its infancy, music was digital, international and easily shared on the web. Even the most obscure urban track or mixtapes could find a following unrestrained by old distribution methods. The building blocks were in place for a truly global mass movement.

Black Lives Matter emerged in an era of hashtag activism, mobilising online as much as in the real world, but it was a cumulative series of deaths in cities across America that gave urgent momentum to the movement. On 17 July 2014, Eric Garner, a horticulturist from the Tompkinsville neighbourhood of Staten Island in New York, was pursued by police who suspected him of selling single cigarettes from packs without tax stamps, a low-level crime he had been charged with many times before. He was held down by a group of officers, restrained in an illegal chokehold and pronounced dead an hour later at a local hospital. Garner's suffocation was captured on video by Ramsey Orta, a local member of the activist group Copwatch, who record and document police activity using mobile phone cameras. Orta was later arrested, accused of carrying a concealed weapon and incarcerated in Rikers Island penitentiary. During his time in jail, Orta was allegedly poisoned by guards when rat poison pellets were found in his food.

Not even a month after Garner died, the fatal shooting of Michael Brown on 9 August by police officer Darren Wilson in Ferguson, Missouri, further fuelled online campaigns against police brutality. Again, Brown's death began in relatively trivial circumstances. He had reputedly taken a packet of cigarillos from a convenience store without paying. In the Garner case, police officer Daniel Pantaleo was eventually sacked by the NYPD. Garner's dying words – 'I can't breathe' – became a rallying cry for Black Lives Matter and a foreshadowing of the death of George Floyd in Minneapolis six years later.

Black Lives Matter was founded with a mission 'to eradicate white supremacy and build local power to intervene in violence inflicted on Black communities by the state and vigilantes', and it was a white supremacist and vigilante, Dylann Roof, who perpetrated the next major racial atrocity, the slaughter of nine people at the Emanuel African Methodist Episcopal Church in Charleston, South Carolina, on 17 June 2015. For many it was an act of domestic terrorism that evoked memories of the spate of Ku Klux Klan attacks on black churches at the height of the civil rights movement.

The historic resonances and biblical connotations of the slaughter of the innocents led President Obama to give the eulogy. But it was the remarkable musical polymath Rhiannon Giddens who most convincingly honoured the event. Her specially composed song, 'Cry No

More', featured a church choir and Giddens' haunting frame-drum. It is gospel, blues and soul in a starkly original form, created in the days after the killings by one of the very few artists who can combine R&B with opera and Celtic rhythms. Giddens told NPR: 'The massacre at AME church in Charleston is just the latest in a string of racially charged events that have broken my heart . . . No matter what levels of privilege you have, when the system is broken, everybody loses.'

The 2016 presidential election became a bitter and unedifying battle between real-estate magnate turned reality TV star Donald Trump and the Secretary of State Hillary Clinton. No love was lost between the two, and the campaign took on a surreal dimension when Clinton's campaign chairman's private emails were leaked and conspiracy theorists on the deranged fringes of Trump's campaign claimed that when the term 'cheese pizza' was used in an email it was in fact code for child pornography. The crackpot theory centred on a pizza restaurant in Washington D.C. and tipped into terrifying reality after the election when Edgar Maddison Welch, a 28-year-old fantasist from North Carolina, entered the restaurant carrying an assault rifle. Threatening staff, he made his way to the door that he believed led to a debauched chamber of child abuse only to find the café's cleaning equipment, mops and buckets. A police operation swept the neighbourhood and Welch was arrested at gunpoint.

Although the pizzagate conspiracy was arrant rubbish, it morphed into a wilder subculture that believed Trump was fighting a noble war against the deep state. This became known by the sinister name QAnon, after an anonymous poster called Q on the 4chan web forum. A new battle for the soul of America was taking shape and it inevitably found a key battlefield in Chocolate City. The growing forces of Black Lives Matter, racial justice campaigners and anti-fascist activists were warring online and eventually on the streets with alt-right groups and hardcore Trump supporters who were organising themselves into militias, among them the Proud Boys, the Three Percenters and the Oath Keepers.

Although Trump's support was strongest in small towns, in chunks of the Rust Belt his 'Make America Great Again' slogan played well to older voters and to those who imagined America had lost its way through deindustrialisation and the surrender of some of its global power. But racial justice campaigners were winning elsewhere, in the big urban centres, on the campuses, in liberal strongholds and most visibly of all in popular music. Trump struggled to attract any musicians of note to his campaign, and some even pursued him legally. Neil Young, Leonard Cohen and, inevitably, Bruce Springsteen all publicly opposed Trump's attempts to use their music. Adele refused him the right to use 'Rolling In The Deep', Prince's estate refused use of 'Purple Rain', and on behalf of The Beatles, George Harrison's estate refused the use of 'Here Comes The Sun'. Mick Jagger and Keith Richards opposed Trump's use of the song 'You Can't Always Get What You Want', sending a cease-and-desist order in 2016 and again in June 2020. Michael Stipe of R.E.M. was among the most vociferous. When Trump and Texas senator Ted Cruz used 'It's The End Of The World As We Know It (And I Feel Fine)' at a rally, Stipe let rip. 'Go fuck yourselves, the lot of you – you sad attention-grabbing, power-hungry little men,' he railed. 'Do not use our music or my voice for your moronic charade of a campaign.'

One of the biggest disputes centred on Pharrell Williams' 'Happy', a song that had been a feelgood feature of Obama's presidency and in the early street protests of Black Lives Matter. In October 2018, Trump played the song at his Future Farmers of America rally in Indiana just hours after eleven people were murdered at a Pittsburgh synagogue in an anti-Semitic mass shooting. Williams responded by having his lawyer send Trump an impassioned cease-and-desist letter.

> On the day of the mass murder of 11 human beings at the hands of a deranged 'nationalist,' you played . . . 'Happy' to a crowd at a political event in Indiana. There was nothing 'happy' about the tragedy inflicted upon our country on Saturday and no permission was granted for your use of this song for this purpose.'

For the avoidance of doubt, his management underlined their stand.

> Pharrell has not, and will not, grant you permission to publicly perform or otherwise broadcast or disseminate any of his music (and) any future use of the song will commit copyright and trademark infringement.

Trump had a smattering of musical supporters, but they were few and far between and often unpopular within the industry. Mike Love, a dyspeptic survivor of The Beach Boys, frequently posed with Trump but Erik Hedegaard, a reporter with *Rolling Stone*, damned even that relationship with relish.

> Love is considered one of the biggest assholes in the history of rock & roll. That's been the popular opinion of him for several decades. He just can't seem to shake it. He's been called a clown, the Devil, an evil, egotistical prick, a greedy bully, sarcastic and mean-spirited.

Even when he tried something different, Trump's dalliances with music were ill-fated. Al Wilson could have been a contender. He was born in Meridian, Mississippi, the same railway town as the famous Ruffin brothers – David Ruffin, the gifted lead singer of The Temptations, and Jimmy Ruffin, the Motown vocalist. Wilson's biggest hits were 'Show And Tell' (1973) and the mid-tempo Vietnam song 'LaLa Peace Song' (1974). But it was a song he had recorded back in 1968, on the California indie Soul City Records, that caused the fuss. 'The Snake', written by Atlantic Records recording artist Oscar Brown Jr, told the story of an untrustworthy lover trying to wriggle his way into the heart of a young woman. Although it failed to register on its release, it achieved anthemic status on Britain's northern soul scene, and there was disbelief when Trump quoted the song, changing its lyrics' intentions entirely and framing it as a warning about Syrian immigrants sneaking into the USA. Trump, however, wrongly credited the words of the song to Al Wilson, which at least gave some comfort to the daughters of the late lyricist, who had died in 2005. Maggie Brown, a talented soul and jazz singer in her own right, told news outlets that she was disgusted by the way the song had been hijacked but was relieved that her father had not been named or directly implicated in Trump's racist rhetoric. Oscar Brown Jr, a lifelong political activist, had hosted *Jazz Scene U.S.A.*, a television show that introduced jazz to a nationwide audience. 'I want people to be hip,' he told viewers, 'I want "hip" to stand for human improvement potential because every human has some potential within them.' He had also been a collaborator with Max Roach in what is now seen as one of the outstanding records of its time, *We Insist! Max Roach's Freedom Now Suite*.

Collaboration was at the heart of Black Lives Matter too. From 2012 onwards it was commonplace for artists to work together on mixtapes and videos, for rappers to feature on R&B and soul tracks, and vice versa. The year before his death Prince recorded a song called 'Baltimore' for his 2015 album *Hit N Run Phase Two*. It featured Chicago R&B singer Eryn Allen Kane and was a prototype of many tracks yet to come which deployed urban music and deep lyrics to protest deaths in police custody. The official video began with imagery of protesters taking to the streets of Baltimore protesting the police's role in the death of Freddie Gray. The song's hookline – 'If there ain't no justice then there ain't no peace' – was fast becoming another Black Lives Matter motto.

Freddie Gray died on 19 April 2015. He had been arrested on 12 April in a street near Baltimore's Gilmor Homes housing project, suspected of carrying a knife. Beaten and restrained in the back of a police wagon, his handcuffs tethered to a seat belt, the wagon then went on a circuitous trip round Baltimore attending other incidents as Gray was tossed around in the back. He died of spinal injuries a week after his arrest.

The Baltimore that Freddie Gray grew up in was fighting a long battle with social problems and industrial decline. The city had already been controversially eulogised in song. In 1977, the L.A.-born Randy Newman released 'Baltimore'. It was not universally loved by its citizens, who saw a portrait of hookers and drunks, its docklands and padlocked warehouses rotting by the sea, and viewed it as a slight on an honest city caught in a cycle of post-industrial decline. Nina Simone covered the song a year later, turning it into a virtuoso reggae-funk anthem which eventually blared from loudspeakers as marchers supported Freddie Gray and his family. By the time Prince staged his benefit concert Rally 4 Peace in May 2015, at Baltimore's Royal Farms Arena, to mark the end of the curfews, the city had long been synonymous with the HBO drama series *The Wire*, which had lent weight to Baltimore's image as a city ravaged by drugs and crime but also showed the city being transformed by the prospect of post-industrial consumerism. Prince asked people to come to the rally dressed in grey, in a tribute to 'all those recently lost in the violence', and nervous police were not sure if it was a wake, a celebration or the prelude to another night of disturbances. The Rally 4 Peace was in many respects a triumph not only of community engagement but of the power of the internet. For those who could not get to Baltimore it was aired via Jay-Z's streaming service Tidal, which removed its paywall for the event, and Prince posted the full audio of the gig free on Soundcloud. Beyoncé, Alicia Keys, Jay-Z, Miguel, Estelle, Raheem DeVaughn and Questlove were all in attendance, speaking to fans on behalf of Gray and the family of Michael Brown. In one of his last public statements before his death Prince effectively handed the baton to Black Lives Matter and the next generation of urban musicians. 'The system is broken,' he said. 'It's going to take the young people to fix it this time. We need new ideas, new life . . .'

Young people were in the ascendancy and black music had found new and inspired heights of creativity. Beyonce's magnus opus, the visual album *Lemonade*, was released a year later in April 2016, nearly twelve months after the AME church massacre, and was supported by a 65-minute film simultaneously shown on HBO. The album, which has been interpreted as a public therapy session and a feminist masterpiece, features vocals by James Blake, Jack White and the ubiquitous Kendrick Lamar. It digs deep into the tragic history of female blues singers such as Bessie Smith. A stand-out track titled 'Freedom', which samples works by the great folk-musicologist Alan Lomax, is a mesmerising essay on emancipation and racial justice. In the black-and-white filmed interlude that followed the song the mothers of Trayvon Martin, Eric Garner and Michael Brown held up portraits of their dead sons.

Drawing upon the same themes, Jay-Z's 'Spiritual' was partly inspired by Michael Brown's death in Ferguson, Missouri. By 2020, Jay-Z's achievements were manifold. He was head of his own music and sports agency Roc Nation, having led the hip-hop indie Roc-a-Fella, and secured the complete rights including master tapes to his entire back catalogue. Jay-Z was the entrepreneur the US magazine *Black Enterprise* had long dreamt of. When Jimmy Carter went on his presidential walkabout in the burnt-out blocks of the South Bronx, no one could have predicted how influential and economically commanding hip-hop would become. In 2021, twenty-five years after Jay-Z's debut album *Reasonable Doubt* was released, the entrepreneur announced a global deal to sell his luxury champagne brand, Armand de Brignac, and, along with Kanye West and Diddy, was the highest-grossing hip-hop star of the year.

Black music had travelled a long way from the pioneering days in the late fifties and early sixties, when Motown was hatched around the kitchen table of the Gordy family in Detroit, and Sam Cooke and his partner J. W. Alexander registered their own wholly owned independent label SAR Records.

In early March 2022, Snoop Dogg revealed in an interview with *Tidal* that Jay-Z had been prepared to sever his business relationship with the NFL if they objected to aspects of the Super Bowl LVI half-time performance that featured Snoop, Dr. Dre, Mary J. Blige, Eminem, Kendrick Lamar and 50 Cent. Rumours had emerged that NFL executives were concerned about portrayals of Snoop's gang affiliation, Jay-Z's lyrics about 'not loving the police' in Dr. Dre's song 'Still Dre Day' and Eminem kneeling in tribute to NFL quarterback Colin Kaepernick, who has knelt to highlight police brutality and inequality.

Snoop Dogg described their feelings after the performance: 'It was as if we won a championship . . . He's the one on the East. I'm the one from the West. We love each other . . . for him to bat for us and tell the NFL, "Fuck that. They perform or I quit," that was the most gangster shit out of everything.'

The epic show remained unchanged and made history, with estimated viewing figures of over 112 million.

In the past few years, music that speaks to the cause of racial justice has found renewed urgency. Lauryn Hill's 'Black Rage' (2014) came out in response to the killing of Michael Brown. Daye Jack's 'Hands Up' (2015), featuring Killer Mike of Run the Jewels, received attention in the wake of the death of the former Houston old-school rapper George Floyd. Another collaboration from the same year was 'Chains' by vocalist Usher, featuring hip-hop wonderkid Nas and the German-American singer Bibi Bourelly. The video was a powerful checklist in black and white of the lives lost at the hands of the police. Z-Ro featuring Mike Dean recorded 'No Justice No Peace' in 2016. Miguel's 'How Many' (2016), which sampled the soothing jazz guitar of George Benson's understudy O'Donel Levy, was released in the aftermath of the police shootings of Alton Sterling in Baton Rouge and Philando Castile outside the Twin Cities, Minnesota. The song's stark subject matter bursts through the gentle guitar sounds, describing human lives being turned into hashtags and prayer hands.

Nobody deserves to die in a police raid, least of all an Emergency Room nurse relaxing in her apartment. In March 2020, Breonna Taylor was shot multiple times by Louisville Metro Police Department officers trying to track down her former partner after they entered her home with a 'no-knock' warrant, which allowed the police to enter without warning or without identifying themselves as law enforcement. Again, the R&B community were quick to offer support. Rhianna and Beyoncé both spoke out about her death. Los Angeles singer Doja Cat donated $100,000 to a fund set up to honour Taylor's life and rapper Cardi B took a swipe at some of her male colleagues, saying they were not doing enough to profile the injustices in the killing of Breonna Taylor. 'She looked like she was listening to your music. She looked like she was your fan. You should stick up for her,' she protested.

One elderly man decided to stand up for Breonna Taylor and to fight the ramifications of the COVID-19 pandemic in his own unique way. Afro-funk legend James 'Plunky' Branch, one of Washington D.C.'s great seventies generation, had returned home to Virginia because he was unable to perform in his usual local nightclub. He made the decision to coincide with the nightly Black Lives Matter protests in front of the White House and gave socially distanced concerts every night at 7 p.m. from his porch on Richmond's Rosewood Avenue. His belief in the power of music to unite communities had not wavered since his first success as a funk musician. Talking to journalists, he said:

> Black music, our music, has always been about telling our story and inspiring us to keep on keeping on. Our beats, words, and melodies can produce instantaneous pleasure and a profound vision of future possibilities. While the business of music has become a very complex enterprise, for me, it's still about presenting rhythms, energy, improvisations, and songs in service to our community. Our music fuels our mythology and magic, and it impacts the whole world.

But the deaths kept coming, and they were made more visible by mobile phone footage. It was the killing of George Floyd, on 25 May 2020, in Minneapolis – suspected of proffering a fake $20 bill, he was suffocated in a 'choke-hold' for almost ten minutes while uttering the now tragically familiar words 'I can't breathe' – that ignited a global response. As many as 26 million people in more than 500 locations participated in Black Lives Matter protests in the weeks after his death, making it one of the largest movements in US history. Many of the protests were highly localised, attacking the civic legacy of the slave trade and the structural funding of police operations. The George Floyd protests in Washington D.C. continued into June, drawing thousands to the area around the White House where the US under President Donald Trump confronted its biggest collective reckoning on racism since the civil rights era. One of the defining songs of the movement was inspired by Floyd's last words. Gabriella Wilson's recording under the pseudonym H.E.R. won a Grammy for 'I Can't Breathe', a multi-layered poem of resistance that lent a whole set of slogans and demands to a movement already laden with urgent music. On receiving her award, she told the socially distanced audience in a marquee outside the Los Angeles Convention Center: 'Remember, we are the change that we wish to see, and you know that fight that we had in us the summer of 2020, keep that same energy. Thank you.'

The urban magazine *Pitchfork* paid tribute to George Floyd's own roots as a well-known rapper on the Houston hip-hop scene, journalist Brandon Caldwell reporting:

> By the time he reached his twenties, George Floyd was already a legend on the streets of Third Ward, a historically Black and culturally rich enclave on the south side of Houston, Texas. A two-sport athlete at Jack Yates High School, he was the generous giant of a tight end who helped lead his team to a state championship game in 1992. At six and a half feet tall, Floyd was unmistakable and easily earned the nickname of 'Big Floyd.' In the Cuney Homes, a dormitory-style housing project where Floyd grew up, everyone knew him.

Long before his gruesome death at the hands of the police, George Floyd was a close friend of Houston rap-artist DJ Screw, and a member of the influential rap collective Screwed Up Click. Before he moved north to Minneapolis, he had appeared on six DJ Screw mixtapes between 1996 and 1998. On his birthday in 1997, Floyd and Screw released the mixtape 'Chapter 007: Ballin In Da Mall', now a piece of hip-hop history given relevance by Floyd's death. At a hometown protest in his honour 60,000 people took to the streets of downtown Houston. The mayor of Houston, Sylvester Turner, spoke from the steps at City Hall and then again at

Floyd's funeral. Thousands of signs mentioned Floyd's name, and his music with the Screwed Up Click streamed out of portable speakers. 'He meant a lot, he was the OG to the community,' Junebug, a Third Ward native, told *Pitchfork*. 'He was gonna stay on you to make sure you're staying positive.'

America was under perilous strain and a war of ideas and attitudes was boiling over. The Trump presidency had brought many of America's unresolved conflicts to the surface. In her landmark book *No Is Not Enough*, the cultural commentator Naomi Klein predicted the characteristics that would come to dominate the Trump presidency and rip America apart. Reaching back to his chequered history in real estate, she described him as 'Trump the luxury lifestyle brand. Trump the neoliberal standard-bearer for the entitled rich. Trump the disaster-capitalist. Trump the climate change denier.' Klein reasoned that Trump personified values that had lurked in the darker corners of America's soul for decades.

> Trump is not a rupture at all, but rather the culmination – the logical end point of a great many dangerous stories our culture has been telling for a very long time. That greed is good. That markets rule. That money is what matters in life. That white men are better than the rest. That the natural world is there for us to pillage. That the vulnerable deserve their fate and the one percent deserve their golden towers.

Klein argued that Trump's brand is synonymous with winning at all costs, always fighting, whether against immigration, China, the news media, the Democrats, the Never Trump Republicans, street demonstrators or his own staff. She could have added to that list opponents of the Black Lives Matter movement, the vast majority of popular musicians and, as the COVID-19 pandemic gripped the world, prestigious scientists, epidemiologists, and even mask-wearers.

In June 2020, at the emotional height of protest about the killing of George Floyd, Trump improvised a bold but ultimately self-defeating gesture. He insisted that police break up the crowds of peaceful demonstrators gathered around the White House, including a contingent of Howard University students who had taken up camp there for weeks, tying Black Lives Matter posters to the peripheral fence. According to the *Guardian*, the crowd gathered in Lafayette Square were 'assaulted by national guardsmen and federal officers: gassed, shot with rubber bullets, [and] forcefully cleared from the president's path'. Trump staged a photo-op, holding the Bible, outside Washington's St John's Episcopal Church, the so-called Church of the Presidents. With a small group of aides, his daughter Ivanka among them, Trump walked through the aftermath of what had been a fierce dispersal. His antics disgusted senior church figures, with the Bishop of the Episcopal Diocese of Washington, the Right Reverend Mariann Edgar Budde, telling journalists that 'the presidents are welcome as citizens of this country to pray alongside fellow citizens, to kneel before God in humility and to rededicate themselves to the task to which they've been elected', but she stressed that Trump 'is not entitled to use the spiritual symbolism of our sacred spaces and our sacred texts to promote or to justify . . . an entirely different message'.

The inner-city geography of Washington D.C. and specifically the few square miles around the White House had become a key battleground in a ferocious war for control of the streets of Chocolate City and the wider social conscience of America. Bill Clinton voiced outrage at what was unfolding: 'At a time like this, the Oval Office should be a Command Center. Instead, it's a Storm Center. There's only chaos. Just one thing never changes – his determination to deny responsibility and shift the blame. The buck never stops there.' He added that Trump's tactics consisted of 'denying, distracting and demeaning'.

Outside the Oval Office, a relentless shuttle of protesters ensured that Black Lives Matter slogans like 'I Can't Breathe' and 'No Justice No Peace' were once again attached to the railings of the White House and that a vigil of candle flames never went out. In a wave of events that touched even the mainstream of American politics Utah's Republican Senator Mitt Romney, the GOP presidential nominee in 2012, joined a march on the White House. Romney told his fellow protesters, 'We need a voice against racism. We need many voices against racism and against brutality. And we need to stand up and say Black Lives Matter.'

The city of Washington capped nearly a week of demonstrations by hiring local artists to paint the words Black Lives Matter in enormous bright yellow letters spanning two blocks on 16th Street NW leading to the White House. The African American Mayor, Muriel Bowser, said the painting was 'intended to send a message of support and solidarity to Americans outraged over the killing of George Floyd by police in Minneapolis'. She also pushed through a local mandate to rename part of 16th Street NW as 'Black Lives Matter Plaza'.

The 2020 presidential election brought urban black music screeching to the fore. It was a battle of values and personalities, pitting Trump's showmanship against Joe Biden's political pragmatism. For the first time ever, black music played a role as a factory of ideas and as a street-level soundtrack. Ice Cube's 'Contract with Black America' was prefaced by Darrick Hamilton, of the Kirwan Institute for the Study of Race and Ethnicity at Ohio State University, who wrote: 'It is abundantly clear that the racial wealth gap has nothing to do with Black behaviour and everything to do with White privilege.' Ice Cube went on the road to radio stations, college campuses and community halls, calling for a 'second reconstruction' to combat economic injustice. The contract's list of demands and daring policy ideas were always more likely to align with Biden's campaign, but Ice Cube made overtures to President Trump and argued that black people should not simply vote Democrat out of habit or, worse still, stay away from the polls altogether out of disenchantment with the democratic system.

Ice Cube was not alone. The anthem to end all anti-Trump anthems had already been released via mixtape by the Compton rapper YG, featuring the Crenshaw-based community activist Nipsey Hussle. It was a rap song that did not shy away from opinion and came with the abbreviated title 'FDT' – 'Fuck Donald Trump'. Okayplayer, the rap website, described 'FDT' as full-on vitriol against the 45th President or, as he became known on social media, #45:

A reminder that we as a nation will never stop fighting against ignorance, injustice and immorality – together. Preaching the gospel of loving your brother, loving your sister, and never, ever stop waving your middle finger toward #45 until he is removed from the White House and placed where he belongs – a dingy, dank, dark jail cell.

It didn't quite pan out like that, but it could have done.

Beyoncé and her younger sister Solange were also high-profile supporters of a campaign directed at Senate Majority Leader Mitch

McConnell urging the Senate to pass the Heroes Act, legislation that would provide $3 trillion for those most affected by COVID-19, which had a disproportionate impact on black, Hispanic and Asian communities. An open letter had been written by Beyoncé's mother, Tina. 'We are concerned Black women,' she wrote. 'Many of us are mothers of Black sons and daughters – some of whom have lost our children – and we have a vision for a new America.' Among the other signatories were Sybrina Fulton, the mother of Trayvon Martin; Gwen Carr, the mother of Eric Garner; and the elegant R&B singer Janelle Monáe, the daughter of a hotel maid and truck driver, who hailed from Kansas. In the great tradition of the start-up singer, she had sold her debut mixtape 'The Audition' from the back of her Mitsubishi Galant car. Monáe became one of the first female singers to set up her own label – Wondaland. The Atlanta warehouses where the label was based became a centre of black culture in Georgia, and the cast and crew from the 2018 movie *Black Panther* hung out there during filming. It is rumoured that the now-deceased actor Chadwick Boseman, yet another graduate of Howard University, played drums on Wondaland sessions. In March 2021, Beyoncé would set a record at the Grammy Awards, with her 28th win, for *Black Parade* – a celebration of black power and achievement – becoming the most-awarded woman in the history of the awards, overtaking bluegrass singer Alison Krauss.

As the divisive political climate worsened, the streets around the White House became a microcosm of a gathering civil war. Undaunted, Black Lives Matter supporters returned to Lafayette Square, to the Ellipse and to the symbolic fences around the White House. Their numbers swelled with students from the Howard campus and teenagers from the Black Swan Academy, a D.C. group demanding 'police-free schools'. The Washington chapter of Black Lives Matter periodically came face to face with the Proud Boys, who had taken up residency in the city's oldest operating hotel, the Harrington, located five blocks from the White House and one of the most affordable hotels in the heart of the District of Columbia, significantly cheaper than the nearby Trump Hotel. Meanwhile in the nearby Willard Hotel, in a set of rooms and suites known as the Command Center, some of President Trump's most loyal lieutenants were working day and night with one goal in mind: overturning the results of the 2020 election.

The Washington chapter of Black Lives Matter had come to realise that city-centre hotels were attracting armies of people loyal to Trump and they appealed to local politicians to respect public health COVID-19 guidelines and close the city to visiting Trump supporters.

Trump's defeat in the presidential election had tripped a switch. On 12 December 2020, confrontations broke out across Washington D.C. when Proud Boys wearing their signature black and gold colours congregated by the outdoor patio of Harry's Bar by the side of the Harrington. They stalked the streets in packs, chanting and trying to provoke fights. The chairman of the Proud Boys, Enrique Tarrio of Florida, was arrested after torching a Black Lives Matter banner he stole from the Asbury United Methodist Church, a landmark African American church. On the night the banner was set alight, Mayor Bowser tweeted that the District's 'faith-based organizations are at the very heart of our community and an attack on them is an attack on all of us'. According to church elders, 'The conduct of the Proud Boys . . . amounted to a new and dangerous chapter in the long and terrible history of white supremacist violence targeting Black houses of worship.' The Proud Boys made several attempts to invade and occupy the area renamed as Black Lives Matter Plaza and running battles erupted. Filmmaker Ken Burns, who has spent his career documenting American history, saw the coming together of a toxic infection. 'We're beset by three viruses, are we not?' he said at the time. There's 'a year-old COVID-19 virus, but also a 402-year-old virus of white supremacy, of racial injustice . . . And we've got an age-old human virus of misinformation, of paranoia, of conspiracies.'

As winter bit, Washington D.C.'s freezing-cold dry air chapped lips and chilled hands. The Metropolitan Police hoped for snow to fall to force protesters back indoors. It didn't happen and rival groups prowled the streets in puffer jackets, hoodies and COVID facemasks, only the peaks of red baseball caps signifying the MAGA militias or shades of black signifying the local antifa battalions. Skirmishes escalated. One of the worst flared in a downtown street when four people were stabbed, one critically, during a scrum near the Proud Boys' hangout at Harry's Bar. A man remonstrated with the mob, who closed in, pulled off his black facemask and began to punch and kick him until he was trapped in a doorway. The doorway in question, at 930 F Street, was the original site of Washington D. C.'s legendary post-punk nightclub 9:30. According to the club's own official history, 'the 9:30 Club first opened its doors in a section of Washington, D.C. that was scarred with boarded-up buildings from the '68 riots. The block was rife with drugs and peppered with peep shows. It was as notorious for its rats and distinctive stench as it was for breaking acts like Nirvana, Red Hot Chilli Peppers, Public Enemy, Fugazi, Bad Brains, R.E.M. and Black Flag.'

Still refusing to accept defeat, Donald Trump whipped up a frenzy of opposition to the result of the 2020 election. Using ominous speeches and a poisonous Twitter account, Trump fanned the flames of political insurrection. Right-wing militia groups and disenchanted oddballs began to gather on social media as Trump engendered a big day in Chocolate City which culminated in the shocking assault on the Capitol Building. Five people died, four of them Trump supporters. The other was Brian Sicknick, who joined the Capitol Police in 2008 and died the day after he was overpowered and beaten by rioters.

The German American novelist and comic book artist Oliver Markus Malloy described the situation in stark terms: 'When the rest of the world watches the news from America, they see a third world dumpster fire. A failed state.'

To portray Donald Trump as someone who was universally despised by black musicians would be a convenient endpoint, but it is only partly true. He had befriended Kanye West, Lil Wayne and Jeezy. From its earliest days on the streets of the South Bronx and the pioneering vinyl sold by ghetto indies such as Enjoy and Sugar Hill hip-hop had valorised boasting, self-aggrandisement and flashy wealth. Trump pushed all those buttons and when he became a network reality TV star his fame grew and his appeal broadened. Bakari Kitwana, Executive Director of Rap Sessions, the hip-hop business network, told ABC News: 'He was an American icon that stood for success and wealth, and that was something that was valued, particularly among a community of folks that were coming from lower-class backgrounds and people who were locked out of the mainstream American economy.'

In 2018, Kanye West pronounced on Twitter: 'You don't have to agree with Trump but the mob can't make me not love him. We are both dragon energy. He is my brother. I love everyone. I don't agree

Kanye West, sporting a Make America Great Again cap, came face to face
with President Donald Trump in the Oval Office, on 11 October 2018.
He discussed stop-and-frisk policing and the imprisonment of gangster Larry
Hoover, and asserted that his bipolar diagnosis was wrong. Afterwards
Trump remarked, 'That was quite something,' to which West replied,
'It was from the soul. I just channelled it.' West then hugged the President,
saying, 'I love this guy right here.'

with everything anyone does. That's what makes us individuals. And we
have the right to independent thought.' Chance the Rapper initially
came to West's defence. 'Black people don't have to be democrats,' he
tweeted. Days before the presidential election, Lil Wayne joined fellow
rappers such as 50 Cent and Lil Pump in expressing his support for
Trump's policies and posing for a photo opportunity with the Republican
candidate. On his final night as President, Trump granted a swathe of
pardons, one of which was for Lil Wayne. He had pleaded guilty to
possessing a loaded, gold-plated handgun when his chartered jet landed
in Miami in December 2019. He was pardoned along with seventy-two
others, including Steve Bannon, Trump's former chief strategist, who
was charged with defrauding donors of more than a million dollars to
support the building of the US–Mexico border wall.

It was Bryson Gray, a rapper from Greensboro, North Carolina, who became hip-hop's most visible Trump supporter. He stood out not only for his right-leaning opinions but for his ancestry – his grandmother was a former Black Panther and his father a liberal schoolteacher. Bryson became prominent when he responded to a challenge that Trump had set online, namely, to write lyrics that 'make liberals cry'. Bryson's father, however, despised his son's lyrics and told the *New Yorker* magazine: 'The Devil done blessed his tongue.'

As much as Donald Trump lived a life of superlatives, the one he was left with was the 'most often impeached president in history'. During his impeachment hearings, US House of Representatives delegate Stacey Plaskett referenced songs by cult hip-hop acts. Plaskett, a Democrat from the US Virgin Islands, quoted lines from Run the Jewels' 'Early' – 'truth's truth when denied or not' – and followed that with words from GZA's 'Breaker, Breaker' – 'the truth is usually seen and rarely heard'. The ultimate proof that hip-hop had reached the highest echelons of the land, the journey from the public high schools of the South Bronx to Capitol Hill complete.

But Trump was not done yet. He claimed he had been cheated by the election result and broke with historic protocol and refused to attend Joe Biden's inauguration, leaving the White House on *Marine One* to his final presidential address at Andrews Air Force Base. Under cease-and-desist orders from countless internationally known rock, pop and R&B artists, he landed to the strains of the song 'Gloria' by Laura Branigan and descended from the helicopter to the sound of 'Don't Stop Believin'' by Journey, both of which had become standards at his political rallies. Within minutes of the television news coverage going out, Laura Branigan's legacy management instructed Trump to stop using her song too.

Due to the pandemic, Joe Biden's inauguration was quiet. International travel was abandoned, few had flown in from other US cities and Washington D.C. was still reflecting on one of the worst days of American democracy, the attack on the Capitol Building on 6 January which aimed to disrupt Congress and overturn Biden's victory. Amanda Gorman, a young spoken-word performer, recited her poem 'The Hill We Climb'. It signified hope in the aftermath of chaos and the hill of racial justice that had yet to be climbed. It was hopeful, aspirational, and captured the spirit of a new dawn. Back out on the street, brashly confident as they strode down Black Lives Matter Plaza, was Howard University's Showtime Marching Band, featuring the Ooh La La! Dancers and the Flashy Flag Squad. They had performed at inaugurations before but this time they were out to support one of their own, Kamala Harris, who took the oath of office to become the first woman and the first woman of colour to occupy the office of Vice President. The Showtime Band was drawn from a department of music that had fed soul music over fifty years – Carla Thomas, Donny Hathaway, Roberta Flack, Leroy Hutson, Twinkie Clark, The Blackbyrds, Trouble Funk, Angela Winbush, Sean 'Puff Daddy' Combs, Meshell Ndegeocello and Sadat X – a defiant legacy expressed in words and music that ultimately no militia could rival.

President Joe Biden came to the dais and spoke haltingly at first, then with increasing confidence in his vision.

> Few periods in our nation's history have been more challenging or difficult than the one we're in now. A once-in-a-century virus silently stalks the country. It's taken as many lives in one year as America lost in all of World War II. Millions of jobs have been lost. Hundreds of thousands of businesses closed. A cry for racial justice some 400 years in the making moves us. The dream of justice for all will be deferred no longer.

Up on V Street, Freedmen's, the old hospital built to care for formerly enslaved people, was now a radio station. Marvin Gaye, the hospital's most famous birth, was near forty years dead, shot by his own father, a Pentecostal minister who preached by the banks of the Anacostia River but never reconciled his son's fame with the Scriptures.

God works in mysterious ways.

R.I.P. Keith Barrow (1954–1983)

HEY AMERICA! PLAYLISTS

Black Music and the White House

'Impeach The President' by The Honey Drippers (Alaga, 1973)
Roy C. Hammond's high-school funk band savage Richard Nixon and gift great breakbeats for hip-hop mixtapes in the years to come.

'Money's Too Tight (To Mention)' by The Valentine Brothers (Bridge, 1982)
The greatest protest song of the era of Reaganomics. Beware of imitations.

'Lord, What's Happening To Your People' by Kenny Smith (Goldspot, 1972)
Opening with a great sermonising intro, this gospel-soul record was recorded during the 1972 presidential election, which Richard Nixon won with a landslide.

'It's All In The Game' by Four Tops (Motown, 1970)
Levi Stubbs rocks the VP. The original backing track, 'Melody In A Major', was composed by Charles G. Dawes, later Vice President under Calvin Coolidge.

'(Your Love Keeps Lifting Me) Higher And Higher' by Jackie Wilson (Brunswick, 1967)
Barack Obama's signature song, it was played at his triumphant victory rally at Grant Park, Chicago.

'Hey Boy' by The D.C. Blossoms (Shrine, 1966)
Storming northern soul on Shrine Records, whose offices were a taxi ride from the White House. The local girl group were named after Washington's famous cherry trees.

'You Can Have Watergate, Just Gimme Some Bucks And I'll Be Straight' by Fred Wesley & The J.B.s (People, 1973)
Great slab of street-funk by James Brown's virtuoso trombonist Fred Wesley.

'Impeach Me Baby' by Arlene Brown and Lee 'Shot' Williams (Dynamite Records, 1974)
Emotionally pleading duet – an errant woman accepts she's the Richard Nixon of love.

'Funky President (People It's Bad)' by James Brown (Polydor, 1974)
James Brown – describing himself as the Minister of New New Super Heavy Funk on the single – claimed this was dedicated to Gerald Ford's short presidency.

'Reaganomics' by Johnnie Taylor (Beverly Glen, 1981)
The B-side of 'What About My Love', this is one of soul music's all-time giants turning on Reagan's economic policies.

Beltway Soul
Rare Vinyl from Just Beyond the White House

'I'll Always Love You' by Sam Moultrie (Warren Records, 1967)
Extraordinary northern soul from the heart of D.C. before the riots.

'Broadway Sissy' by Roscoe and Friends (Tec Records, 1965)
Relentless street funk from the father of one of D.C.'s great jazz musicians, Michael Bowie.

'Five Minutes' by The Differences, (Mon'ca Records 1971)
Great vocal soul led by one of D.C.'s truly great singers Clifton Dyson.

'Chick, Chick' by El Corols Band & Show (Tiny, 1968)
Pioneering go-go funk band party hard.

'Every Way But Loose' by Plunky & the Oneness of Juju (Black Fire, 1980)
Effortless afro-funk from one of D.C.'s unsung heroes.

'I Won't Be Coming Back' by J.D. Bryant (Shrine, 1966)
Super-rare soul dancer from the legendary Shrine catalogue.

'Summer In The Parks (Pt. 1)' by The East Coast Connection (New Directions, 1974)
Multitalented band pay homage to Kool and the Gang, Earth, Wind and Fire and D.C.'s own Soul Searchers.

'Don't Let Him Hurt You' by Les Chansonettes (Shrine, 1966)
Another Shrine classic which could have been from Detroit's Motown's hit factory.

'I Wonder (Am I Still On Your Mind)' by Promise (New Directions, 1975)
Unknown and uncredited female vocalist rescues this local D.C. release.

'Before I Let You Go' by Expression feat. Paul Bumbry (Swollen Records, 1996)
Jazz-funk boogie voiced by Washington D.C'.s answer to Frankie Beverly & Maze.

BIBLIOGRAPHY

Primary Sources

Jean Blackwell Hutson Research and Reference Division, Schomburg
　　Center for Research in Black Culture, New York

Amsterdam News, Special Collections, Columbia University Library,
　　New York

Blues & Soul magazine 1968–1975, author's own collection

COINTELPRO Papers, The FBI Education Center, Pennsylvania
　　Avenue, Washington D.C.

The FBI Vaults – released and in part redacted files of FBI
　　investigations on Cassius Marcellus Clay, Charles 'Sonny' Liston,
　　Malcolm X and the Nation of Islam

The Source: The Magazine of Hip Hop Music, Culture & Politics

The Archives of Obama's White House

The Clinton Digital Library

Home Select Committee on Assassination (1976–1979), Library of
　　Congress, Washington D.C.

New York Post 1963–76, New York Public Library, New York

The New York Times 1963–76, Columbia University Library, New
　　York

The Papers and Correspondence of the Reverend Dr Martin Luther
　　King Jr, 'The King Center', Atlanta, GA

Wax Poetics magazine 2007–20

Secondary Sources

Baradaran, Mehrsa, *The Color of Money: Black Banks and the Racial Wealth Gap*, Cambridge, MA: Harvard University Press, 2017

Bingham, Clara, *Witness to the Revolution: Radicals, Resisters, Vets, Hippies, and the Year America Lost Its Mind and Found Its Soul*, New York: Penguin Random House, 2016

Blackstock, Nelson, *COINTELPRO: The FBI's Secret War on Political Freedom*, 3rd edition, New York: Pathfinder Press, 1988

Bowman, Rob, *Soulsville U.S.A.: The Story of Stax Records*, New York: Schirmer Trade Books, 2003

Branch, Taylor, At Canaan's Edge: America in the King Years 1965–68, New York: Simon & Schuster, 2006

Brown, Robert J., *You Can't Go Wrong Doing Right: How a Child of Poverty Rose to the White House and Helped Change the World*, New York: Convergent Books, 2019

Carpenter, Bil, *Uncloudy Days: The Gospel Music Encyclopedia*, San Francisco: Backbeat Books, 2005

Clinton, Bill, *My Life*, London: Arrow Books, 2004

Cosgrove, Stuart, *Detroit 67: The Year That Changed Soul*, Edinburgh: Polygon, 2016

Cosgrove, Stuart, *Memphis 68: The Tragedy of Southern Soul*, Edinburgh: Polygon 2017

Cosgrove, Stuart, *Harlem 69: The Future of Soul*, Edinburgh: Polygon 2019

Cripps, Thomas, *Black Film as Genre*, Bloomington: Indiana University Press, 1978

Dalzell, Tom, *The Battle for People's Park, Berkeley 1969*, Berkeley, CA: Heyday Books, 2019

Deppe, Martin L., *Operation Breadbasket: An Untold Story of Civil Rights in Chicago, 1966–1971*, Athens, GA: University of Georgia Press, 2017

Donner, Frank J., *The Age of Surveillance: The Aims and Methods of America's Political Intelligence System*, New York: Alfred A. Knopf, 1980

English, T.J., *The Savage City: Race, Murder, and a Generation on the Edge*, New York: HarperCollins, 2011

Felber, Garrett A., "'Those Who Say Don't Know and Those Who

Know Don't Say": The Nation of Islam and the Politics of Black Nationalism, 1930–1975', PhD thesis, University of Michigan

Freeman, Scott, *Otis: The Otis Redding Story*, New York: St Martin's Press, 2001

Gamson, Joshua, *The Fabulous Sylvester: The Legend, the Music, the Seventies in San Francisco*, New York: Picador, 2005

Gentry, Curt, *J. Edgar Hoover: The Man and the Secrets*, New York: W.W. Norton & Co., 1991

George, Nelson, *Where Did Our Love Go?: The Rise and Fall of the Motown Sound*, London: Omnibus Press, 1985

George, Nelson, *The Death of Rhythm and Blues*, London: Penguin, 1988

Gordy, Berry, *To Be Loved: The Music, the Magic, the Memories of Motown – An Autobiography*, New York: Warner Books, 1994

Gordon, Robert, *Respect Yourself: Stax Records and the Soul Explosion*, New York: Bloomsbury, 2013

Haas, Jeffrey, *The Assassination of Fred Hampton: How the FBI and the Chicago Police Murdered a Black Panther*, updated edition, Chicago: Lawrence Hill Books, 2019

Hamilton, Marybeth, *In Search of the Blues: Black Voices, White Visions*, London: Jonathan Cape, 2007

Hopkinson, Natalie, *Go-Go Live: The Musical Life and Death of a Chocolate City*, Durham, NC: Duke University Press, 2012

Howard, Josiah, *Blaxploitation Cinema: The Essential Reference Guide*, Fab Press Limited: Godalming, 2008

Isenberg, Nancy, *White Trash: The 400-Year Untold History of Class in America*, New York: Viking, 2016

Jones, Thom, *Sonny Liston Was a Friend of Mine*, London: Faber, 1999

Kahn, Ashley, *The House That Trane Built: The Story of Impulse Records*, New York: W. W. Norton & Co., 2006

Kindred, Dave, *Sound and Fury: Two Powerful Lives, One Fateful Friendship*, New York: Free Press, 2006

Kitt, Eartha, *I'm Still Here: Confessions of a Sex Kitten*, New York: Barricade Books, 1993

Klein, Naomi, *No Is Not Enough: Resisting Trump's Shock Politics and Winning the World We Need*, New York: Haymarket Books, 2017

Kot, Greg, *I'll Take You There: Mavis Staples, The Staple Singers, and the March Up Freedom's Highway*, New York: Scribner, 2014.

Kotz, Mick, *Judgment Days: Lyndon Baines Johnson, Martin Luther King Jr., and the Laws That Changed America*, Boston: Mariner Books, 2006

Lozada, Carlos, *What Were We Thinking: A Brief Intellectual History of the Trump Era*, New York: Simon & Schuster, 2020

Malcolm X, *The Autobiography of Malcolm X*, as told to Alex Haley, London: Penguin, 2007

Marable, Manning, *Malcolm X: A Life of Reinvention*, London: Allen Lane, 2011

Mayfield, Todd, *Travelling Soul, The Life of Curtis Mayfield*, Chicago: Chicago Review Press, 2017

O'Reilly, Kenneth, *Racial Matters: The FBI's Secret File on Black America, 1960–1972*, New York: Free Press, 1991

Pepper, William F., *An Act of State: The Execution of Martin Luther King*, New York: Verso, 2003

Posner, Gerald, *Motown: Music, Money, Sex, and Power*, New York: Random House, 2005

Pruter, Robert, *Chicago Soul*, Urbana and Chicago: University of Illinois Press, 1992

Quinn, Eithne, '"Tryin' To Get Over": *Super Fly*, Black Politics, and Post-Civil Rights Film Enterprise', *Cinema Journal*, Vol. 49, No. 2 (2010): 86–105

Quinn, Eithne, *Nuthin' But a 'G' Thang: The Culture and Commerce of Gangsta Rap*, New York, Columbia University Press, 2004

Ritz, David, *Divided Soul: The Life of Marvin Gaye*, New York: McGraw-Hill, 1985

Salvatore, Nick, *Singing in a Strange Land: C. L. Franklin, The Back Church, and the Transformation of America*, New York: Little Brown and Co., 2005

Smith, R. J., *The One: The Life and Music of James Brown*, New York: Gotham Books, 2012

Smith, Suzanne, E., *Dancing in the Street: Motown and the Cultural Politics of Detroit*, Cambridge MA: Harvard University Press, 1999

Staff and editors of *Newsday*, *The Heroin Trail*, London: Souvenir Press, 1974

Sugrue, Thomas J., *The Origins of the Urban Crisis: Race and Inequality in Postwar Detroit*, Princeton, NJ: Princeton University Press, 2005

Thomas, Evan, *Being Nixon: A Man Divided*, New York: Random House, 2015

Toop, David, *The Rap Attack: African Jive to New York Hip Hop*, London: Pluto Press, 1984

Ward, Brian, *Just My Soul Responding: Rhythm and Blues, Black Consciousness and Race Relations*, London: UCL Press, 1998

Warner, Jay, *Just Walkin' in the Rain*, Los Angeles: Renaissance Books, 2001

Wesley, Fred Jr., *Hit Me, Fred: Recollections of a Sideman*, Durham, NC: Duke University Press, 2002

Wexler, Jerry, *Rhythm and the Blues: A Life in American Music*, New York: Knopf, 1993

Wilson, Robert A. (ed.), *Character Above All: Ten Presidents from FDR to George Bush*, New York: Simon & Schuster 1996

Wolff, Daniel, *You Send Me: The Life and Times of Sam Cooke*, New York: William Morrow, 1995

INDEX